future -

Leonard Sbrocci

chiville, 10/12/'76

THE COMEDIES OF
ARIOSTO

THE COMEDIES OF
ARIOSTO

Translated and Edited by
EDMOND M. BEAME
and
LEONARD G. SBROCCHI

The University of Chicago Press/Chicago & London

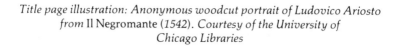
Title page illustration: Anonymous woodcut portrait of Ludovico Ariosto from Il Negromante *(1542). Courtesy of the University of Chicago Libraries*

EDMOND M. BEAME is Associate Professor of History, McMaster University

LEONARD G. SBROCCHI is Assistant Professor of Italian, The University of Virginia

The University of Chicago Press, Chicago 60637
The University of Chicago Press, Ltd., London

INTERNATIONAL STANDARD BOOK NUMBER: 0-226-02649-3
LIBRARY OF CONGRESS CATALOG CARD NUMBER: 74-5739

Contents

Preface

THE PRESENT PROJECT AROSE OUT OF A CHANCE CONVERSATION in which the translators discovered their mutual interest in Ariosto the playwright. Originally the translation was to embody only a single dramatic work, the *Suppositi*; but the intriguing nature of Ariosto's plays and a growing conviction that the lack of a complete translation represented a serious loss to the English stage led us to expand the project to encompass all the comedies.

It is difficult in a cooperative venture such as this to identify any portion of the work with either of the translators. However, there was some division of labor; E. M. Beame was mostly responsible for the texts of the translations and L. G. Sbrocchi for their accuracy and interpretation. The procedure was for Sbrocchi to produce a preliminary draft that Beame used as a guideline for a second translation. This was then jointly examined, corrected, and given final form. The introductory essay was written by Beame with the assistance of Sbrocchi after both did independent research.

The list of those who have helped in various ways to make this book a reality is too long to itemize. We, nevertheless, would like to express our appreciation to Professors Beatrice M. Corrigan and Antonio C. Alessio for their continual encouragement and advice; to Professors Julius A. Molinaro and James W. Daly who read portions of the introduction and provided helpful suggestions; and especially to Professor Michael Ukas whose painstaking critique of the introduction was invaluable.

HAD LUDOVICO ARIOSTO NEVER WRITTEN THE *ORLANDO Furioso* he would still deserve a chapter, although a brief one, in the history of Italian literature. Indeed, the immense popularity and fame of his epic masterpiece may well have obscured the full scope of the genius and personality of the Ferrarese poet. Ariosto, like many of his contemporaries, was true to the Renaissance type of the *uomo universale*, combining his life as a poet with an active career in the service of the Este family. Courtier, diplomat on embassies to popes, princes, and emperor, soldier and horseman of no mean accomplishments, valet and personal secretary to Cardinal Ippolito d'Este, governor of the unruly Garfagnana province, as well as paterfamilias to eight younger brothers and sisters—he managed to intersperse his literary activities between the mundane and often arduous duties of these roles. Despite the burdens of his career, despite five years spent studying law, Ariosto produced a remarkable literary output in Latin and Italian poetry that included, apart from the *Orlando*, odes, elegies, epithalamiums, sonnets, *canzoni*, epigrams, *capitoli*, satires, and comedies.

Of these so-called minor writings the comedies stand high above the others, with the possible exception of the satires, as works of distinction and innovation. His earliest comedies, *La Cassaria* (1508) and *I Suppositi* (1509), written first in prose (later versified) well before the publication of the *Orlando* (1516), have gained for Ariosto the reputation as the initiator of Italian "erudite" or vernacular comedy (*commedia erudita*) and perhaps of the modern European stage.[1] Later he was to produce three other comedies in verse—*Il Negromante* (two versions, 1520 and 1528), *La Lena* (1528), and the unfinished *I Studenti*—each of which pointed the way toward the development of a distinctly Italian theater.

Yet Ariosto the playwright has not fared especially well. Outside of Italy his comedies have been neglected, with interest in them limited to the sixteenth century; and the closest that English-speaking audiences have come in nearly half a millennium to viewing his plays was in George Gascoigne's *Supposes* (1566), a paraphrase of the *Suppositi*. Italian literary critics, moreover, have been anything but enthusiastic about them. Not only have they suffered from the inevitable comparison with the *Orlando*, but they have shared with the whole of sixteenth-century erudite comedy the accusation of being monotonous, unimaginative, and slavishly imitative of Roman comedy. De Sanctis, whose work influenced at least two generations of literary scholars, criticized erudite comedy for its artificiality and applied the terms "conventional" and "superficial" to Ariosto's plays; only for Machiavelli's *Mandragola* did he reserve praise. Croce found scarcely any literary merit in the comedies and virtually ignored them in his study of Ariosto; even Sanesi and Toffanin, whose assessments of Ariosto's dramatic talents are somewhat more favorable, praise mainly the technical and not the aritistic quality of his plays.[2]

The stigma of being imitative and artifical placed on Renaissance comedy by these eminent critics has been difficult to eradicate and slow to disappear, even though it derives to some extent from distortions and preconceived notions about the nature and purposes of drama. Sanesi's obsession with artistic originality led him to overlook many of the aesthetic virtues of erudite comedy; while De Sanctis exaggerated its sterility when he failed to see in it his vision of the vital Italian Renaissance spirit. He tended to ignore the fact that classical imitation when pursued without academic reverence did not necessarily stifle creativity. Literary tastes, however, are subject to change, and scholars have now come to focus on the positive achievements of sixteenth-century comedy, on its intrinsic value as a mirror of Italian life. This approach was signaled a century ago by Agresti and it has been followed by such modern students of the theater as Grabher and Pandolfi.[3] Their studies point to the need for historical perspective and call for an evaluation of erudite comedy as a formative phase in the evolution of Italian comic drama; to assess it outside this context is to misunderstand and underestimate it. If this be so, then an appreciation of Ariosto's merits as a dramatist and his contribution to the theater can only come if his plays are considered in their historical setting, at the root of modern comic drama.

ITALIAN COMIC THEATER BEFORE ARIOSTO

Italian vernacular comedy of the early sixteenth century was neither original nor especially profound. Like much of Renaissance culture and intellectual life, it was eclectic and derivative, drawing heavily upon both medieval and classical precedents. The revival of Latin drama was the major impetus behind the prolific output of Italian comedy during the cinquecento, the principal sources of inspiration being the plays of Plautus (254-184 B.C.) and Terence (185-159 B.C.), which in turn had been modeled upon those of the Greek comic playwrights such as Philemon, Menander, and Apollodorus. Several dramatic forms, which developed on the Italian peninsula after the mid-thirteenth century, also exerted a strong influence on the erudite comedy of Ariosto and his contemporaries.

Among them were the sacred dramas (*sacre rappresentazioni*), vernacular rustic plays (*maggi* and *contrasti*), and comedies along classical lines written in Latin by humanists. In addition, the cinquecento playwrights had at their disposal a well-defined tradition of native folktales, the *novelle*, which were brought together so conveniently in Boccaccio's *Decameron*.

Although Italian comic theater in the formal sense did not exist prior to the fifteenth century, comic elements were present in medieval drama where they mingled with its more serious components in the mystery play. Sacred drama developed comparatively late in Italy and never flourished there as vigorously as in England and France; but the same factors that were operative elsewhere—the emphasis on Christian pageantry and ceremonial, the concern for a visible expression of faith, and the desire to instruct the faithful more vividly—gave rise in the thirteenth century to an Italian version of the mystery play. Like its northern counterpart, it began as a dramatization of the liturgy in which priests served as actors, the congregation as an audience, and the chancel as a stage. In time the subject was expanded to include various gospel themes—the Annunciation, the Nativity, the Crucifixion, the Resurrection—and extrabiblical stories drawn from the lives of the saints. Eventually the mystery play outgrew its liturgical mold and emerged from the church as a mature theatrical form in the *sacra rappresentazione*, an urban drama that originated in Florence and flourished there in the fifteenth century.[4]

While the *sacre rappresentazioni* were essentially devout and moral plays, their religious character was considerably modified by the introduction of vulgar and comic elements designed to amuse the larger audiences who now viewed them in the public piazzas. The humor was often coarse. At times the use of grotesque names or droll or irrelevant words served for comic diversion, as in the *Santo Grisante e Doria;* or laughter might be evoked, as in Castellani's *Figliuol Prodigo,* by a verbal duel or an actual brawl. Satire figured prominently in the *rappresentazioni*, originally for didactic purposes and moralizing, but often merely to burlesque typical comic types. Such vices as hypocrisy, luxury, dishonesty, idleness and gluttony in the monasteries, and greed and corruption in high places were commonly ridiculed on stage, a practice that was carried on by the dramatists of the sixteenth century. Castellani's mockery of astrology in *Santa Orsola*, for example, prefigured Ariosto's treatment of the magical arts in the *Negromante*. In fact, caricatures of the avaricious merchant, the pompous and pedantic doctor, the uncouth peasant, and the hypocritical friar were seen in sacred dramas well before they appeared on stage in learned comedies.

In the course of the fifteenth century these comic characteristics increased as the secular features of the sacred drama tended to displace the spiritual. Some of the later *rappresentazioni* contained little that was sacred. Instead of biblical incidents and miracles of the saints, they used chivalric romances, profane legends, and novellistic subjects as their themes;[5] and whatever remained of the pious atmosphere surrounding the drama was tainted by the proliferation of between-the-scenes interludes or *intermezzi*. At first their function was to explain the mystery, but later they were transformed into purely worldly entertainments—dramatic recitations, pantomimes, songs, and dances—extraneous to the play itself. Such modifications help explain the demise of the *sacra rappresentazione*, for not only did its mixture of the sacred and the profane come to be frowned upon by the Church, but it also failed to satisfy the demands of the Italian Renaissance for a modern secular drama.[6]

Paralleling the development of the *sacra rappresentazione* was a rustic drama prevalent in Tuscany, which varied with locality and was known by different names. Among them were the *maggi* (May plays) and the *contrasti* (debates). Essentially these were only embryonic dramas and consisted of little more than a dialogue on moral subjects recited by two or three people; but they were rather free in form and, like the mystery play, usually combined religious and secular elements. Despite their crudeness, the pastoral dramas were extremely popular, undoubtedly because of the improvisations of the actors, which gave a burlesque quality to the performance; and this comic matter, like that of the sacred drama, was to find its way into sixteenth-century comedies and farces.

The more immediate antecedents of the vernacular comedy, however, are to be found in the humanistic theater. For more than a century before Ariosto's *Cassaria* appeared, humanists had been writing Latin comedies, both in verse and in prose. Although humanistic comedy was not solely an Italian phenomenon, the list of literati who composed Latin plays contains a preponderance of Italian names, including such leading Renaissance figures as Petrarch, Pier Paolo Vergerio, Leonardo Bruni, Aeneas Sylvius, and Leon Battista Alberti.[7] The reverence of these humanists for Latin literature made it inevitable for them to look to classical models and seek to make their own works replicas of Roman comedies. But their knowledge of ancient comedy was incomplete, and the plays that they produced cannot accurately be termed classical drama. Plautus and Terence may have provided the inspiration for some of the character types and dramatic material, but much of the content of their comedies was Italian, deriving from folktales, *novelle*, and contemporary life. The result was a hybrid that does not resemble closely either of its component strains.

A significant feature of the humanistic comedies was their strictly secular and almost obscene nature. The world that they depict is a pagan world in which religion is not present or exists only incidentally. If monks or priests appear it is merely to be mocked and derided as hypocrites. Many of the plays reflect contemporary student life in the Italian universities, with its hedonism and licentiousness.[8] In fact, the relationship between humanistic theater and the university was very close, for not only did university life provide material for the plays, but frequently student groups were responsible for staging them. The richness of the university scene did not escape later authors of erudite comedy, among them Ariosto, who used the university as a backdrop for his *Studenti.*

Apart from student life, the recurrent subjects of the humanist comedies center around various aspects of worldly and sensual pleasures, with such themes as lust, homosexuality, adultery, and other forms of illicit love. The *Conquestio Uxoris Cavechioli,* a reworked version of the final tale on the fifth day of the *Decameron,* consists of an obscene dialogue between a homosexual husband and a neglected wife. In the *Cauteraria* a sexually starved wife is punished for an adulterous act with a priest by having her offending parts branded; while both Bruni's *Polescina* and Ugolino Pisani's *Philogenia* involve schemes to seduce a young girl, who in the case of Philogenia eventually succumbs to complete promiscuity. The variations on this hedonistic theme were infinite, and if the subject is not carnal pleasure it is likely to be gastronomical delights. This is not to say that these humanists reveled in depicting the profane, for the sensuousness is frequently neutralized by moral and didactic passages and by the occasional display of pathos; but their expression of the new and freer ethics of the Renaissance is clear and unmistakable.

The Italian humanist playwrights were not markedly innovative and left no notable comic masterpieces. They were too busy trying to recreate Roman comedy to develop a new dramatic form; and at most they succeeded in introducing a number of classical motifs into Renaissance settings. Even then, their conformity with the principles of Roman drama was limited, for their comedies remained loosely structured and only occasionally adhered to the rigid five-act pattern of Plautus and Terence. Yet the work of the humanist playwrights was important to the evolution of Italian comedy. Their attention to literary style and their fusion of the classical, the novellistic, and the contemporary was a necessary preparation for the writers of learned comedy who succeeded them. Ironically, when in the early years of the following century Ariosto, Nardi, Machiavelli, Bibbiena, and others produced a modern Italian comic drama, they did so by going to the very same sources as their humanist predecessors, but they handled them more maturely and substituted the vernacular for Latin. This development was preceded, however, by a careful study of classical drama and by the experience of producing Roman comedies on the Italian stage.

No single event did more to awaken an interest in classical drama and in the theater as a whole than Nicolas of Cusa's discovery in 1429 of twelve lost plays of Plautus. Excitement among humanists everywhere ran high as they vied with each other for an opportunity to examine the manuscript. Scholars scrutinized the text, filled in the gaps, and before long the Latin comedies were being presented to Italian audiences as they had been in ancient Rome. Interest in Terence was stimulated when in 1433 Giovanni Aurispa came upon a manuscript of Donatus's commentary on the Terentian comedies. By the 1470s printed editions of the works of both playwrights circulated widely, and vernacular translations soon followed.

Their study and assimilation of Latin drama and, most important, their reading of Donatus's analysis of the Terentian plays drew the attention of Italian dramatists to the structure and techniques of classical comedy, which they proceeded to imitate more closely.[9] Two classical principles, in particular, came to be regarded as inviolable rules for dramatic composition—the five-act form and the unities of place, time, and action: the setting of the play, usually a street or a public square, had to remain the same throughout; the action had to be limited to a single day; and there had to be economy of plot with few characters and subplots. According to Donatus, comedy should have a tripartite thematic structure: after the prologue, the dramatic action begins with the *protasis* or statement (Acts I and II) in which the predicament is described and a clever solution is offered; there follows the *epitasis* (Acts III and IV), the introduction of complicating incidents, in which the original plan is thwarted and a new scheme is improvised; leading to a *catastrophe* or resolution (Act V).

The bondage of Renaissance dramatists to Roman theater went beyond rules of structure and composition. Much of the dramatic material that they poured into the classical mold was itself copied from Latin originals. Hackneyed comic effects and theatrical devices were reproduced with little modification: substitutions or exchanges of identity, unexpected arrivals, frequent asides and soliloquies directed to the audience, and simultaneous speeches by characters who are unaware of each other's presence. Similarly, the stock characters and types so familiar to Roman audiences now reappeared on the Italian stage: crafty slaves and servants who dupe their old masters, spendthrift sons competing with miserly fathers, lost children suddenly retrieved, greedy procurers, obsequious parasites, braggart soldiers, and enticing courtesans. Even the very dialogue often followed patterns prescribed for various characters and plot situations. Classical comedy, however, provided little in the way of character development and psychological insight. It was a theater of stereotypes and surfaces and hence artificial and anachronistic for the late fifteenth and sixteenth centuries.

Anachronistic as the classical theater was, the revival of Plautus and Terence was nevertheless indispensable to the advent of erudite comedy. This new dramatic form is distinguished from its predecessors, the sacred drama and the Latin humanistic comedy, largely by its strict adherence to classical structure. It originates in imitation, in first the resurrection and then the emulation of a pure form of Roman theater. Imitation, however, gives way to adaptation and innovation. Originality begins with modifications in the translations and variations in the staging of Latin comedies. Then modern authors go on to appropriate the plots of classical comedies, altering them to fit their own requirements. Playwrights such as Ariosto adopted the practice of combining elements from a number of ancient dramas in a single play; and they filled strict classical forms with themes from the *novelle* or contemporary life. The shift to the vernacular, the introduction of dialect and even jargon, meant that the flavor of the plays would be more Italian than classical. Latin characters, situations, and plots, of course, continued to be utilized, but they were modified in accordance with the Italian scene. The Latin slave became the servant of a wealthy burgher; the *miles gloriosus* had a modern counterpart in the mercenary captain; the parasite often reappeared as a poor courtier; the Latin *puer* became the Italian *ragazzo*. And new comic types appear—the pedant, the necromancer, the hypocritical friar. The result was a distinctly Italian comedy that, in spite of its classical exterior, was more than an adaptation of the Roman theater. Erudite comedy, which makes its debut during the first decade of the sixteenth century in the plays of Ariosto, has been disparagingly described as merely Plautus and Terence "brought up to date."[10] Nevertheless, it was a dramatic type entirely in keeping with the age, reflecting the social conditions, the moral standards, and the customs and life of Italians of the late Renaissance, presenting them in the highly stylized manner typical of the period. As such it fulfilled Cicero's requirement, so familiar to contemporary scholars, that comedy be "the imitation of life, the mirror of custom, the image of truth."

THE THEATER IN FERRARA

The renewed interest in Plautus and Terence was accompanied by increasing attention to the presentation of their plays on stage. Toward the end of the fifteenth century there were frequent performances of Latin comedies at schools, academies, and in princely courts throughout Italy. Florentine students produced them not only in their schools, but in the Palace of the Signoria and the Medici house where Terence's *Andria* was performed in 1476.[11] At the Palace of Cardinals in Rome a group of pupils and friends of Pomponius Laetus introduced the local populace to Roman comedy; in 1484 they produced the *Aulalaria* and two years later the *Epidicus*. The principal center of this renaissance of dramatic activity, however, was Ferrara, where the performance of classical comedy became an integral part of courtly spectacles, banquets, and other celebrations.

The development of a flourishing theater in Ferrara must be attributed to the princes of the House of Este who sponsored productions of classical comedy as part of their determination to make the city a center of culture. The Marquis Leonello d'Este (d. 1450), a poet himself, initiated an intellectual transformation in Ferrara when he brought Guarino of Verona to the university. Guarino had been one of the first to study the recently discovered Plautine plays, and his presence introduced students to the finer points of Latin drama; not long after Guarino's arrival the first humanistic play, Francesco Ariosti's *Isis* (1444), was performed at court.[12] Under Leonello's successor, Borso, however, there was only limited interest in the theater, and a full-fledged dramatic renaissance had to wait until the reign of Duke Ercole I (1471–1505), who promoted the theater as a matter of public policy.

Although his own knowledge of the classics was limited, Ercole had a deep interest in Plautus and Terence, and he directed his patronage to both the restoration of Latin comedy and its adaptation to modern conditions. For this purpose he surrounded himself with eminent poets—Battista Panetti, Niccolò da Correggio, Pandolfo Collenuccio, Girolamo Berardo, Battista Guarino (the younger), and others—who prepared the texts, made translations and even wrote their own imitations in Italian. Ercole preferred the plays in translation principally because it was his express desire to have the townspeople share in the dramatic events.[13] Like many Renaissance despots, the Este princes mitigated their absolutism with a form of social democracy, and comedy became an integral part of the lavish entertatinment designed to divert the populace and demonstrate the ruler's munificence.

The first recorded performance of a classical comedy in Ferrara took place on 25 January 1486, when an Italian version of Plautus's *Menaechmi* was presented before an immense throng in the palace courtyard. Bernardino Zambotto noted in his chronicle that as many as ten thousand, among them the marquis of Mantua and his fiancée, Isabella d'Este, looked on attentively at the elaborate production. A large wooden platform supporting battlements was built for the occasion, and a high point in the play came when a boat carrying one of the twins and his entourage was pulled across the stage; the performance ended with a spectacular display of fireworks. The following year there was an equally extravagant presentation of the *Amphitryon* that featured a Mount Olympus with stars and little children dressed in white representing the planets; however, the performance was interrupted by rain and had to be postponed.[14] This may have been the reason why the scene of subsequent presentations of the *Menaechmi* in 1490 and 1491 was transferred indoors to the great hall of the palace. The Milanese ambassadors, who were present at the latter showing, have left a detailed account of the performance, and their description makes especial note of the improvisations of the actors and the supplementary entertainments.[15]

Rarely were the Roman comedies presented without some form of accompanying entertainment. Since the plays were usually staged as part of other festivities—a wedding, a banquet, or a carnival celebration—it was customary to enliven them with numerous *intermezzi* consisting of music, dancing, pantomimes, and tableaus. Plautus and Terence may have held a fascination for Italian scholars; however, it is probable that the larger audiences attending these spectacles greeted their comedies with much less enthusiasm than they did the incidental entertainments. So it was with Jano Pencaro, Isabella d'Este's informant in Ferrara, who witnessed performances of the *Eunuchus*, the *Trinummus*, and the *Poenulus* at the carnival of 1499. In his reports to the marchioness he barely mentions the comedies, but discourses at length on each of the *intermezzi*; and when Isabella came to Ferrara from Mantua for a private showing a few weeks later her greatest delight was reserved for the accompaniments.[16]

Classical theater was a thriving concern in Ferrara through the end of the century and beyond, save for the years 1494 to 1498 when dramatic activity was suspended due to the preoccupation of the duke with the French invasions. Duke Ercole, however, was not the only patron of the theater in Ferrara. Tito Vespasiano was given to producing comic spectacles at the Strozzi Palace where on 10 May 1493, before a large gathering, a play by Ercole Strozzi was performed "with certain morris-dances in the middle, which was really most delightful."[17] A few days later the Strozzi play was repeated in the garden of the ducal palace to an audience that included Ludovico Il Moro and his Ferrarese bride, Beatrice d'Este, and this was followed by a performance of the *Menaechmi*. Il Moro was evidently impressed with what he saw, for he requested the Ferrarese to recite the comedies in his duchy of Milan. That same August Duke Ercole himself, accompanied by Don Alfonso, set out for Pavia by way of Mantua with a troupe of twenty players, including young Ludovico Ariosto.

The zenith of classical theater in Ferrara was reached during the first few years of the sixteenth century when there was an increase not only in the number but in the splendor of the productions. Italians had always manifested a love of display, and the performances of these ancient comedies tended to become occasions for staging magnificent spectacles. Prominent local artists—Mantegna in Mantua, Nicoletto Segna and Fino and Bernardino Marsigli in Ferrara—were recruited at considerable expense to design and paint ornate scenery, while sumptuous and colorful costumes contributed to the picturesque brilliance of the *intermezzi*. So frequent and lengthy did these *intermezzi* become that sometimes performances lasted as long as six hours.[18]

Few dramatic presentations were accompanied by such scenic splendor as that surrounding the theatrical festivities in Ferrara for the marriage of Alfonso d'Este and Lucrezia Borgia in 1502. Five Plautine comedies were staged, and the details of the production are recounted by Isabella d'Este in letters to her husband. The great hall, which served as the theater, was prepared to hold five thousand spectators, with seats arranged along one side in tiers and aisles separating the men from the women. On the opposite side of the hall a parapet was constructed in the form of a city wall on top of which were six houses from which the players issued just as in the sacred dramas. Before the first performance, Duke Ercole showed his guests the one hundred and ten costumes that had been prepared for the occasion, none of which would have to be used twice in any of the plays. The marchioness, however, showed little enthusiasm for the comedies, which she apparently found a bore; only when it came to the *intermezzi*, of which there were five during the *Epidicus*, does her interest awaken. How, after all, could Plautus compete with morris dances in which soldiers in ancient dress and fighting armor beat time with maces, battle-axes, swords, and daggers, or with Moors running about the stage holding torches or with lighted candles in their mouths?[19]

Such extravagant displays understandably dulled the taste for classical comedy. The carnival atmosphere at the performances was distracting, for whatever mood was set by the plays tended to be destroyed by the extraneous amusements; and at times, as Zambotto's chronicle reveals, the plays themselves were transformed into spectacles in what was undoubtedly an attempt to compromise with popular taste. At best what appeared on stage were distorted versions of Plautus and Terence. One explanation for this, according to Sanesi, is the poor Italian translations. Translators like Guarino and Collenuccio were inclined to paraphrase and refashion the Latin texts, taking liberties that frequently altered the spirit of the plays. Instead of the crisp, succinct dialogue of Plautus, Italian audiences were treated to elongated lines of monotonous tercets that weakened the humor of the original. Little wonder then that Isabella found the *Bacchides* "so long and wearisome."[20] Yet the waning interest in classical comedy may not have been the result of inaccurate translation or the distractions of the *intermezzi*, but rather the want of a drama more in keeping with contemporary life; by now the Latin comedies had already outlived their usefulness in stimulating an interest in the theater, and Italians were ready for a more relevant type of comedy.

This does not mean that Latin comedies disappeared from the Italian stage. They continued to be performed with some frequency in Ferrara at least until the middle of the century, and Ariosto was deeply involved in their production right up to his death; but they ceased to be the principal dramatic attraction at the princely courts, a role now assumed by erudite comedy. The four Roman plays produced in 1503 represent the termination of the main phase in the revival of classical theater in Ferrara. No plays were performed in 1504 due to the death of Pope Alexander VI, and with the passing of Duke Ercole the following year local drama lost its Maecenas. While Alfonso I (1505–1534) showed some of his father's interest in drama, he was more at home on the battlefield than in the theater; and the continuance of dramatic activity in Ferrara was due largely to the patronage of the duke's brother, Cardinal Ippolito d'Este, who among other things encouraged the playwriting of a young man in his entourage, Ludovico Ariosto.

ARIOSTO AND THE THEATER

Ariosto and the theater were inseparable. The theater was his first love, and from his youth until his final years he always consecrated a portion of his energies to the stage. This zest for theatrical endeavors no doubt was stimulated by the atmosphere of the Ferrarese court; but it also arose out of his own literary experience: his passion for classical poetry; his love for the satirical; his desire to restore comic theater to its former dignity. It was Ariosto's good fortune to be able to study the Latin poets under Gregorio da Spoleto, whom Ercole I brought to Ferrara in 1494 as a tutor for the young Este princes; and there is little question that he derived a deeper appreciation of Plautus and Terence from his mentor.

Ariosto's earliest acquaintance with the theater coincides with the beginnings of the revival of classical comedy in Ferrara. Young Ludovico must have been very impressed when, as a boy of eleven, his father took him and his brother Gabriele to the initial performance of the *Menaechmi* in 1486.[21] This delightful spectacle apparently fired the boy's imagination, for soon after this he was staging dramatic performances of his own. On the ground floor of the house of Niccolò Ariosto on the Via Giuoco del Pallone there is a room, commonly known as the "little theater of Ariosto," where it is believed that the youthful poet directed his brothers and sisters in reciting parts that he had prepared for them. It was for this group of budding thespians that Ludovico composed his first dramatic work, the *Tragedia di Tisbe*, a play in five acts in verse, based on material taken from Ovid's *Metamorphoses*. Unfortunately, the manuscript of the *Tisbe* has been lost, and there is no record of similar plays that the child prodigy may have written at this time. A few years later we find Ariosto entering the mainstream of Ferrarese theatrical life when, as a law student, he participated in the Latin comedies that were being promoted by the duke. It is more than likely that Ariosto was one of the actors when his friend Ercole Strozzi's play was presented before Ludovico Sforza in 1493; and he almost certainly took part in the production of the *Menaechmi* that followed. We know from the notes of his son Virginio that Ludovico was among the twenty youths who later that year "were taken by Duke Ercole to Pavia for the purpose of playing comedies."[22] As preparation for the tour the troupe spent some time practicing at Reggio under the direction of Matteo Boiardo, and this may have been the first close encounter between the two epic poets.

It has been suggested that Ariosto was commissioned by Ercole I at this time to translate Latin comedies; in particular he is supposed to have produced a translation of Terence's *Phormio* with a prologue of his own in tercets.[23] But there is no contemporary evidence to substantiate this, and it seems highly unlikely that the duke would have had recourse to an untried youth when he had so many able poets at court. Later on in his career Ariosto did have occasion to translate Latin plays as part of his task of supervising court productions. The first of these was written early in 1529 at the behest of Alfonso I who wished to welcome his bride, Renée, to Ferrara with a French performance of the *Menaechmi*. As no available Frenchman was sufficiently versed in the language of Plautus, the poet was called upon to produce an Italian version as a guide. "Not only did Ariosto translate it," writes an early biographer, "but he composed a summary of each act of the play in a few Italian verses, which were recited before each act after some graceful and witty lines of his own."[24] Subsequent translations were made of the *Aulalaria* and of Terence's *Eunuchus* and *Andria*, all of which were staged at various times.

But translating Latin comedy was only an incidental activity of Ariosto in his long theatrical career; and his role in the modernization of ancient comedy was a more important one than that of translator. Sometime during 1507 he turned to composing vernacular comedy in classical form, briefly putting aside work on the *Orlando*, which he had begun a few years earlier. What other than his general interest in Roman drama led him to this undertaking can only be conjectured. Toward the end of 1503 Ariosto had entered into the service of Cardinal Ippolito d'Este in the capacity of an attendant gentleman, a position whose duties he found increasingly burdensome; but the *famigliare* found in his patron someone who shared his own enthusiasm for the theater. It was probably at the instigation of Ippolito, who was seeking some new dramatic entertainment for the carnival of 1508, that Ariosto undertook the composition of his first comedy.[25]

The *Cassaria*, which in its prose form was presented before the court on the evening of 5 March 1508 at the command of Cardinal Ippolito, captivated its aristocratic audience. Bernardino Prosperi, chancellor of the ducal court, in a letter to the Marchioness Isabella, had the highest praise for the play

which from beginning to end was as elegant and as delightful as any other that I have ever seen performed and was greatly lauded by everyone. The subject was a most beautiful one of two enamoured youths and two harlots brought to Taranto [Mytilene] by a procurer and the play contained so much artifice and deceit, so many new incidents and such excellent morality and a variety of things half of which are not in those of Terence; and it was embellished with honourable and good actors, all from without, with most beautiful costumes and sweet melodies for interludes, and with a morris-dance of cooks heated with wine, with pots tied in front of them, who beat time with their wooden sticks to the sound of the Cardinal's music.[26]

Prosperi was particularly taken with the scenery, which had been painted by Peregrino da Udine for use throughout the carnival: represented in perspective was a section of a town with its houses, churches, belfries, and gardens "such that one could never tire of looking at it."

In the prologue, written in rhymed tercets, Ariosto declares his objective of providing a viable Italian counterpart to Plautus and Terence, a novel type of vernacular drama worthy of comparison with the achievements of the Roman comic writers. "I bring you a new comedy," he begins, "filled with various witticisms that neither Greek nor Latin tongue has ever recited on the stage." Ariosto was perfectly aware that he was creating something different. But what was it that was distinctive about the new comedy? Surely it was not the fact that he united a classical, secular theme with a vernacular text. Poliziano had done this nearly thirty years before in his *Favola di Orfeo* (1480), a pastoral melodrama based on Greek mythology; and in Ferrara Boiardo had earlier refashioned a subject from Lucian in Italian tercets in his *Timone*. Yet the form of the *Orfeo* and the manner of presentation of both plays was still that of the *sacra rappresentazione*; their originality lies in the substitution of a pagan for a Christian fable. What Ariosto did in the *Cassaria* was to move the vernacular play closer to the Roman drama in form and subject matter. His originality comes not from breaking with the classical tradition but, paradoxically, from associating with it through what he himself termed "poetic imitation."[27]

While the play is far from a slavish copy of Plautus and Terence, imitation does permeate its entire fabric. This is evident in the title, *Cassaria* (coffer), which conforms to Plautine usage (*Aulalaria, Asinaria, Mostellaria*, etc.); in the scene of the action, which is a piazza or a street in front of Crisobolo's and Lucrano's house; in the characters, the traditional young lovers, the strict father, the greedy procurer, and the servants, some crafty, others drunk; in the dialogue, with its profusion of monologues; and in the plot. Here Ariosto is close to reproducing the spirit and form of the Latin comedy. Even the setting of the play, Mytilene, reinforces the atmosphere of antiquity, although the circumstances are those of the modern city under Turkish rule.[28] The novelty of the play to which Ariosto alludes in the prologue consists of contemporary references and his own inventions that fill out the classical framework.

The argument of the *Cassaria* owes much to several Latin

comedies from which Ariosto borrowed liberally. Basic thematic material was drawn from the *Andria* and the *Heautontimorumenos* of Terence as well as from Plautus's *Mostellaria* and *Phormio*, while the *Pseudolus, Adelphi, Poenulus,* and *Aetheria* supplied lesser ideas for particular passages and characters.[29] This is not to say that the play is a mere pastiche. Ariosto modified or elaborated upon the classical material and wove it into an original and rather involved plot, one more complicated than any conceived by Plautus or Terence. And in spite of the heavy reliance upon Roman comedy, it has been argued that the spirit of the play is as much Boccaccian as it is classical. The influence of the *Decameron* is more subtle. It appears at times in the language, in a particular turn of phrase or figure of speech, in certain character traits found in the servants, Volpino, Trappola, and Fulcio, in the deceptions and cunning tricks perpetrated on Lucrano, and more specifically in Fulcio's soliloquy (V, 3) satirizing the inordinate concern of women with their toilette, a speech indebted not only to the *Decameron* but to the more antifeminist *Corbaccio*.[30]

While the Roman comic writers and Boccaccio provided essential ingredients for the *Cassaria*, Ariosto was able to remove his gaze from these sources sufficiently long to create something new. Much of that novelty results from applying sixteenth-century touches to traditional materials, but occasionally something quite different is introduced. Such is the underworld jargon used by Lucrano and Furba (I, 7; III, 7). This obscure language not only serves to complete the character description of Lucrano and to inject a dash of earthy, contemporary life, but it is also a technical device to further the action of the play. Ariosto's use of servants was equally innovative. One can readily trace the character types of Volpino, Fulcio, and even Nebbia to the slaves of Latin comedies, but so numerous a contingent of servants, as in scenes three and four of the fifth act of the *Cassaria*, is not found in Roman drama. The staccato dialogue of these half-inebriated servants, which culminates in the snatching of Eulalia from Trappola, adds what Grabher terms a "choral" tone to the comedy and provides the liveliest action at the center of the play.[31]

A number of the characters bear the mark of Ariosto's individuality, even though they follow classical prototypes. The glimpses that we get of the ill-treated girls, Eulalia and Corisca, reveal graceful feminine types, not the usual female slaves of antiquity. They appear as rather sympathetic creatures, an effect heightened by Lucrano's complaints about them and Eulalia's tears when led away by Trappola. In Lucrano Ariosto added a new dimension to the unsavory Plautine character of the procurer. One side of his personality almost evokes pathos, as in the lamentations about his economic plight (I, 7), or his difficulties in disciplining the girls, or in his humiliation as reported by Fulcio (V, 1); the other displays a sardonic aloofness and is ingeniously brought out in his patter with Trappola (III, 3), one of the most humorous scenes of the play. It is through the figure of the astute servant, Volpino, however, with his vivacious manner, his witty remarks and parries, that Ariosto develops his own style of humor, and it is Volpino who gives real life to the comedy. Nowhere is this illustrated better than in his conversation with Crisobolo in which he attempts to implicate Nebbia in the loss of the coffer (IV, 2).

These sparks of originality, considered individually, would hardly seem to substantiate the author's pretension of having created a "new comedy"; but collectively they give a very different flavor to the play, one that was extremely pleasing to sixteenth-century audiences. The *Cassaria* was admired, applauded, and restaged during Ariosto's lifetime more than any of his subsequent comedies.[32] Ferrarese must have laughed at the satires of contemporary customs with which the play abounds. Ariosto directs his darts at the predatory Spanish soldiers, at scoundrels at the court of Rome, at corrupt magistrates and customs officials, and at parsimonious young noblemen and vain women. Occasionally his prologues become the vehicles for these satirical barbs, and here he diverges considerably from the practice of his Roman predecessors. Whereas Plautus and Terence employed their prologues either to announce the argument or as an apologia, Ariosto's prologues provide occasions for the author to give vent to his feelings, to make a witty observation, or to taunt his audience. This is notably the case in the second version of the *Cassaria*.

In 1529 Ariosto took up the *Cassaria* again and rewrote it entirely in verse, ostensibly because the original text had been distorted by the printers. It was first presented in its verse form on 19 February 1531 in the new theater in the ducal palace that the author had designed.[33] In the second *Cassaria* Ariosto completely reformulated and expanded the original and did not merely modify it. The changes range from minor alterations—shifting the scene from Mytilene to Sibaris and modifications in the spellings of character names—to substantial dramatic revisions: four scenes were added and a number transposed; several servants were eliminated; and a new character is introduced, Lucramo's maid, Stamma, whose complaint highlights the cruelty of the procurer. Lucramo, in fact, is made to appear as a more loathsome character than in the first version; and the minor figure of Brusco is expanded into that of a simple though irascible peasant with a singular interest in livestock, instead of a mere underling of Trappola.

The most conspicuous change in the verse recasting was Ari-

osto's greater use of satire, particularly in the extended monologues. A satirical tone is set immediately in the prologue. Here the
author compares his refashioning of the play to the labors of men
and women to make themselves appear younger. In so doing he
makes light of their numerous artificialities—their wigs, their
make-up, their perfumes—and prepares the audience for Fulcio's
caricature in Act V, Scene 3, of women at their toilette. Vignettes of
women adorning themselves can be found in the *Mostellaria* and
in earlier humanistic comedies, but Ariosto's description is far more
pointed. He goes on, moreover, to criticize the effeminate youths
who emulate vain women:

> But what will we say about our young men who should be
> known and honoured for their manliness [*virtù*]? Instead of
> devoting their time to acquiring it, they too waste time in
> beautifying themselves and in putting on grease paint and
> rouge. They copy the women in all things: ... They're ex-
> perts in making up, not heroic or elegaic verses, but with
> moss, amber, and civet.

Satire, however, at times hinders the dramatic flow as with
Lucramo's speech (I, 5) deploring the stinginess and pretentiousness
of Sibaris—that is, Ferrarese—society, a speech nearly four times
as long as in the prose version. Throughout the second *Cassaria*, in
fact, Ariosto tended to be prolix, lengthening lines from the
original until they frequently lose their incisiveness; so it is not
surprising that the initial performance lasted some four hours. The
result is a comedy that lacks the lively and spontaneous quality of
the prose version, with its simple development of the action, but
surpasses it in sophistication, in subtlety, and in literary style.

The enthusiastic reception of the *Cassaria* in 1508 was followed
immediately by Ariosto's composition of a second prose comedy, *I
Suppositi*, which he also later recast in verse. The new comedy
received its premiere on 6 February 1509 at the ducal palace, and
Prosperi, who was again present, found it "a truly modern play,
totally delightful and full of morality and words and actions to
arouse laughter with triple deception or substitution."[34] The author
himself recited the prologue, and he must have titillated the
audience with his salacious play on the verb *supponere*;[35] but
judging from the fact that Prosperi found the comedy "full of
morality" it was not offensive. Ariosto went on to confess his
indebtedness to the Roman playwrights whom he had imitated just
as they in turn had imitated the Greeks: "He has taken part of his
plot ... from Terence's *Eunuchus* and part from Plautus's *Captivi*,
but so little, indeed, that if either Terence or Plautus knew, they

wouldn't be offended and would call it poetic imitation rather than plagiarism."

This acknowledgment by no means accounts for the full extent of his obligation to Plautus and Terence, for the *Eunuchus* and the *Captivi* are not the only Latin plays from which he borrowed. Nor is he indebted only for his plot. Some of the character-types can be found in the Roman comedies, although the similarities are not nearly as marked as in the *Cassaria*. Pasifilo is modeled upon the classical parasite, whose gluttony is a distinguishing trait; Ariosto's character is a close approximation of Ergosilus in the *Captivi* and Gnatho in the *Eunuchus*. Caprino has his antecedent in the Plautine *puer*, while Filogono, the loving, indulgent father, is a Terentian type. The characters in the *Suppositi*, however, are more true to life than their classical counterparts. This is especially so in the case of Caprino, the mischievous tease whose antics are the subject of Dalio's complaint (III, 1) and whose rude gesture (*taruò*) identifies him as a typical street urchin. The parasite, moreover, was a type not entirely unknown to Italian literature.[36]

While the *Suppositi* follows the Roman structure, maintaining the traditional three unities, on the whole there is less imitation of the ancients than in the *Cassaria*; and with each subsequent play Ariosto became more and more independent. Instead of a setting in a Greek city, the action now shifts to Ferrara sometime between 1490 and 1500, to a period when the young poet was just getting to know his city. Instead of the standard classical story in which youths carry off slave girls, the plot turns on the novellistic theme of a rich and noble youth posing as a servant in order to possess his beloved (*Decameron*, VII, 7). Instead of quick-witted servants with shrewd schemes and cunning tricks, it is the student, the doctor of laws, the parasite, a merchant from Catania, and a gentleman from Siena who occupy the stage. The cunning and artifice that dominate the *Cassaria* have only a limited importance in the *Suppositi*. Dulippo's far-fetched tale to the Sienese gentleman only serves to add an element of absurdity to the play and to introduce a doltish comic character; in the final analysis the old gentleman's masquerade as Filogono is not essential to the outcome of the story. But it does enable Ariosto to initiate a novel type of substitution to which he alludes in the prologue to the verse version.

The influence of Boccaccio is evident not only in the plot, but also in the characters of Damone and Cleandro. Several tales in the *Decameron* have as their theme the offended father out to avenge his daughter's dishonor. Ariosto, however, adds a touch of pathos to the character of Damone by having him blame himself for his daughter's predicament. The figure of Cleandro, the pedantic doctor of laws, may well have been modeled on that of Riccardo di Chinzica, the Pisan judge (*Decameron*, II, 10) who seeks to convince his kidnapped wife to return home. Both men are rich, both are learned in the law, both believe that wealth and intelligence are sufficient to hold a woman, and both are made to appear ridiculous. Similar types also appear in a number of Plautine comedies. Cleandro, nevertheless, is a new and fully developed dramatic figure, and to Ariosto goes credit for introducing the character of the pedant on the Italian stage.[37] The "old doctor with the long cap" who spouts pedantic Latin is shown as an extreme egotist and a gullible object of flattery, and there are hints of homosexuality, a vice commonly associated with pedants. Variants of this comic character can be found in numerous erudite comedies, especially those of Bibbiena, Aretino, and Dolce; and the pretentious pedant was to appear among the dramatis personae of the *commedia dell'arte* stereotyped as *Il pedante*.

Satire plays a lesser role in the *Suppositi* than in the *Cassaria*, although Ariosto directs salvos at two of his favorite targets—customs officials and lawyers—and there is a pun about the "rare faith" (*fé rara*) of the Ferrarese. Contemporary life, nevertheless, comes into the play through references to various Ferrarese landmarks, to the family ties between Naples and Ferrara (II, 1), and to the Turkish occupation of Otranto in 1480.[38] This incursion of the Turks onto Italian soil is given more than a passing reference; Ariosto makes the historical event a pivot on which the outcome turns and thereby gives a political and social relevance to his play.

What the *Suppositi* lacks in satire it makes up for in sentiment, as the author portrays deeper human feelings than he did in the *Cassaria*. Erostrato's love is a case in point: it is of a higher order than that of Erofilo and Caridoro whose object is merely to possess their women. He already enjoys Polinesta's favors; yet after two years his love pangs have only intensified and his fear of losing his beloved points to marriage as the only recourse. Love sentiments of a different nature are revealed in Filogono's longing to be with Erostrato and his concern for his son's health and safety, while the pity that Psiteria displays for her distraught mistress is quite poignant. Even Cleandro becomes somewhat emotional when he talks about his lost son and later when he discovers him to be Dulippo. Such displays of emotion give to the *Suppositi* a realism that is not apparent in Ariosto's earlier comedy; nevertheless, in its organization, in its plot, which relies upon chance for its resolution, the *Suppositi* is distinctly inferior to the *Cassaria*. The verse redaction does nothing to correct its defects, for it diverges little from the original; only the prologue, in which the author makes further insinuations about the indelicate meanings of the verb *supponere*, shows evidence of reworking.

For ten years after the *Suppositi* we hear virtually nothing about Ariosto's theatrical activity. The poet was preoccupied during this period with, among other things, extensive diplomatic and military missions, with attempts to secure papal patronage and with seeing the first edition of the *Orlando* through the press. In the meantime the concept of the *commedia erudita* had been further developed with Nardi's *I Due Felici Rivali* (1513), Bibbiena's *Calandria* (1513), and Machiavelli's *Mandragola*.[39] On 6 March 1519 Ariosto's *Suppositi* in prose was again presented, this time at Rome in the presence of Leo X. Alfonso Paolucci, the Ferrarese chancellor, has left a vivid description of this memorable performance, which took place in the apartments of Ariosto's friend, Cardinal Cibo, the pope's nephew: The scenery for the play, which was painted by Raphael himself, was that of a city in perspective, representing Ferrara. Above the city the sky was illumined by candelabras, each with five torches, and formed into letters to read: "Leo X. Pon. Maximus." The evening's entertainment included the usual musical interludes with the last a morris dance symbolizing the Fable of Gorgon. Ariosto composed a new prologue for the occasion; and it was reported that the pope "laughed very heartily" at the obscene allusions to the "substitutions." Some Frenchmen present, however, were "scandalized," and others thought that such highly spiced words should not be said in the presence of His Holiness.[40]

Leo X evidently did not agree, for when the next carnival drew near he requested that the poet send along another play. Soon after the successful debut of the *Suppositi* Ariosto had actually begun working on his third comedy, but, displeased with his efforts, he had put it aside; he "now finished in two or three days what ... he could not complete in ten years" and had it ready for the carnival of 1520.[41] The play referred to is the *Negromante* for which the author chose a new form—the *verso sdrucciolo*, unrhymed hendeca-syllabic verse that comes close to being prose. The controversy as to the relative merits of verse and prose as media for the theater was carried on by literary critics later in the century. Although the Roman comedians had written in iambic trimeter, many Italian playwrights looked to the prose form of the *Decameron* as their model; Duke Federigo Gonzaga was to refuse to stage Ariosto's plays in Mantua merely because he did "not like to have them recited in verse."[42] Modern critics have condemned the *sdrucciolo* form, with its dactylic endings, as unnatural to the Italian language; De Sanctis, for one, considers it an "awkward form which attempts to be poetry and fails to be prose."[43] Whatever the defects of *sdrucciolo* meter, its use by Ariosto represented an attempt to give to Italian poetry a comic verse form comparable to that of Plautus and Terence. He himself referred to the verses as *"jambi volgari."*

The *Negromante* evidently failed to please the pontiff, and it was not performed at Rome.[44] Whether Leo X was offended by the author's remarks in the prologue about absolution and a plenary indulgence we cannot tell; needless to say, though, they were ill-chosen, coming at a time when the Lutheran disturbance in Germany was about to reach a climax; and the soothing words that follow extolling the pope's virtues would not seem to mitigate this indiscretion. When the *Negromante* was finally presented to the public in Ferrara during the carnival of 1529, it was a version that had been considerably augmented and improved.

The prologue to the *Negromante* reveals a more confident Ariosto. No longer does he find it necessary to justify himself vis-à-vis the Roman playwrights or to make claims to originality. The audience is introduced directly to the setting and subject of the play and is prepared for miraculous happenings: he tells us that Cremona's presence on stage is a miracle no less credible than the miracles of Orpheus, Apollo, and Amphion, and we are led to believe that the necromancer is responsible for it. In the revised prologue the author deleted the objectionable mention of ecclesiastical abuses and replaced it with an awkward satire aimed at gossips who frequent the piazza. Also omitted was a reference to the language question. Machiavelli, who wanted to see the pure Tuscan of Dante and Petrarch as the literary language of Italy, had criticized the poet for mixing Tuscan with Ferrarese in the *Suppositi*.[45] Ariosto jocosely apologizes in the first prologue for having failed to rid himself of his Lombard accent.

In the *Negromante* we see a refinement of Ariosto's talents as a comic playwright. His first two plays, despite their elements of originality, still retain much of the superficiality that characterized Latin comedy. The clever tricks of the *Cassaria*, the interchanges of the *Suppositi*, focus attention on the farcical quality of these plays. Occasionally the author's view of human nature is revealed, and we get a glimpse of human sentiments and foibles, but the highly contrived plots do not permit him to dwell very long upon these. With the *Negromante* there is a change. It was not a matter of Ariosto's emancipation from classical influence—his use of the *sdrucciolo* form indicates a continued proclivity toward imitation. Rather it is the prominence he gives realism, a realism that is brought out through the medium of human folly.

Structurally the *Negromante* consists of two parallel elements, which are developed almost independently; one is an intricate plot, largely of classical origin, built upon the predicament of Cintio's bigamy; the other—and more important—is a comic study of character that centers upon the figure of the necromancer.[46] The plot situations are derived to a large extent from the comedies of Terence: the *Hecyra* provided Ariosto with the theme of a marriage unconsummated because of the husband's love for another woman; in the *Phormio* there is a clandestine marriage necessitated by a girl's refusal to give herself except by honorable means; and Camillo's longing for Cintio's wife is similar to the love of Charinus for the betrothed Pomphilus in the *Andria*. In both the *Phormio* and the *Andria*, moreover, the resolution involves the recovery of a lost child. Little of the structure of the play is derived from the *novelle*, although the device of hiding Camillo in a box may have been suggested by any of several tales in the *Decameron*.

The plot may not be very original but it does allow Ariosto to develop the main theme of the play—human foolishness—a theme he explores through the central figure of the comedy, the magician, Jachelino. Jachelino is an archimposter who uses his self-created reputation for magical skills to prey upon the gullible. He "professes to be a philosopher, an alchemist, a doctor, an astrologer, a magician, and even a conjurer of spirits"; but "he knows as much about these and other sciences as a donkey or an ox knows about playing the organ" (II, 1). His sole object is to swindle people and to profit from unhappy domestic situations. The character of the necromancer was not a creation of Ariosto; it comes right out of contemporary life and has its precedent in literature in the *Decameron*. Magic and demonology, in fact, were important features of the supernatural world of the Middle Ages and Renaissance, and Italians were familiar with the practices of witchcraft and sorcery. Ariosto's necromancer comes from this source as does Ruffo, the magician in Bibbiena's *Calandria*. In Italy, however, superstition was exploited for its practical effects, and the sorcerer and magician were frequently regarded as imposters out to fleece anyone who could be taken.[47] It was just such a type that Ariosto made into a stage character in Jachelino, the necromancer, a character-type that was to be more fully developed by Ben Jonson in his *Alchemist*.

Ariosto was not so much concerned with magic itself in the *Negromante* as with the credibility of the magical art, and his satire is directed less at the fraud of the necromancer than at the stupidity of those who believe in his powers. It is only "with the help of folly, which abounds in the world," that Jachelino is able to fleece his victims. Massimo's anxiety to have his son's marriage consummated makes him a willing prey; while Cintio, convinced that the necromancer "performs wonders," is ready to offer him Fazio's money to be rid of Emilia forever. Of all those duped, however, Camillo Pocosale ("little wit"), the impulsive youth who becomes ecstatic at the very mention of his beloved's name, is the biggest fool. His belief that Emilia's aloofness has been turned by the magician's art into passion for him, his extravagant address to what he believes is Emilia's letter, his willingness to hide inside a box at the magician's behest combine with his own egotism to create a ridiculous character quite unlike Charinus in the *Andria* and in keeping with the buffoonery of the farces and the *novelle*. The only characters not taken in by the necromancer are his servant, Nibbio, who knows him for what he is, and Temolo. Temolo interjects some down-to-earth good sense when he disparages the faith of Cintio and Fazio in the magician in a scene marked by ironic humor (I, 3); and it is he who completes the necromancer's defeat by stealing his cloak.

In the second version of the *Negromante* Ariosto refined the play in language, style, and, above all, in theatrical effect.[48] By adding three scenes to the end he gave the play a logical development and a completeness that it had lacked, for the absence of so important a character as the necromancer after the third act had deprived it of a proper denouement. Ariosto rectified this by having him reappear in confrontations with the very individuals who had been aware of his guile, Temolo and Nibbio. Other revisions include several transpositions and combinations of scenes, the substitution of Fazio for Cambio, and a prolongation of the action that tends to dilute the freshness and spontaneity of the original. Such is the case with Act III, Scene 3, which is expanded so that Camillo can read Emilia's letter aloud, an expansion that adds humor, but, nevertheless, is superfluous and banal.

The presentation of the *Negromante* in 1529 was part of a renascence of theater in Ferrara. After the performance of the *Suppositi* in 1509 there had been a hiatus in dramatic activity lasting nearly twenty years as the Este state was being threatened from without; but beginning in 1528 interest in the theater again picked up and Ariosto became the guiding spirit of this revival. Not only were his own comedies featured; he was also in charge of all court productions, directing plays as well as acting in them. And it was under his supervision that a permanent theater was erected in the Sala Grande of the Corte Vecchia. Instead of dismantling the stage after each carnival, as had been the practice, a fixed stage was constructed with permanent sets on which were painted elaborate scenery designed by the poet, scenery that was equally useful for classical or erudite comedies. Indeed, the completion of the new theater in 1531 was celebrated with successive performances of Plautus's *Captivi* and the *Cassaria* in verse. The magnificent theater, however, lasted but two seasons; fire gutted the Sala Grande the very night that Ariosto contracted what was to be a fatal illness. "The burning of that scene," wrote Giovanni Pigna, "was a sign in anticipation of his death, even as a comet or a thunderbolt presages the death of princes."[49]

The Ferrarese theatrical revival of 1528 was ushered in with the production of Ariosto's last complete comedy, the *Lena*. It was presented at the carnival of that year, was possibly staged again soon after the arrival of Duchess Renée, and was repeated at the carnival of 1529 after being lengthened by two scenes and given a new prologue. The *Lena*, written in *sdrucciolo* verse, is generally regarded by critics as the best and most original of Ariosto's comedies. Grabher believes that it "signals the point of arrival" of Ariosto as a dramatist, for in it he developed further that independent spirit he had displayed in the *Negromante*.[50] That the poet was aware of the originality of his play is clear from the revised prologue in which he introduces Lena as a stylish woman and disparages people "who always disapprove of all modern fashions and only praise those that date from ancient times." Corbolo echoes this emphasis on innovation when he announces (III,1) that he is not a Davus or a Sosia and that Ilario is not the credulous old man of Latin comedy.

Corbolo's assessment is accurate, for, while both he and Ilario bear a certain resemblance to Roman types, they are not mere copies, and the outcome of the story is determined by *fortuna*, not by a servant's wiles or a father's gullibility. Nor is Lena the typical Latin bawd or Fazio the typical *senex*; they are new and authentic creations that Ariosto developed independently of classical models. Classical elements, in fact, are not very conspicuous in the *Lena*; they are easily eclipsed by its contemporary features. Not only do the figures of Lena, Pacifico, and Fazio come from the contemporary world, but so do the minor characters—Menica, Torbido, the policemen, and the duke's footmen; and Ariosto gives the play a distinctively modern setting by repeated allusions to familiar landmarks and institutions: notorious Ferrarese drunkards; the Gorgadello Tavern; prominent local financial establishments; the Paradiso Palace; Gambaro Street with its bawdy houses; the statue of Duke Borso in the piazza; the vendors in front of the ducal palace; and Ariosto's own district of Mirasol. All these, and in addition frequent references to particular hours of the day—to the *Predica* and *Ave Maria*—provide a realism beyond that found in any of Ariosto's other comedies.

In the *Negromante* Ariosto had treated the theme of folly; now he turns in the *Lena* to that of corruption. Corruption in all its facets is woven into the very fabric of the play as Ariosto examines the complicated ways in which it intrudes into human affairs. This comes through in the frequent satires, which in the *Lena* are skilfully integrated into the plot; but it is most evident in the character portrayals. All of the deadly sins except gluttony are personified in Lena, Pacifico, and Fazio, while specific examples of lust, greed, and covetousness are found in Flavio's amorous objectives and in the activities of the policemen and the footmen.[51]

At the center of this picture of depravity is Lena, whose various relationships enable Ariosto to explore his main theme. Lena, however, is by no means totally corrupt, as her foul life is not entirely of her own doing. She has been led into evil ways by "that good-for-nothing Pacifico," and she pursues her profession out of an instinct for self-preservation and with a fatalistic resignation rather than for sensual pleasure or calculated gain. Her decision to prostitute Licinia is, of course, reprehensible, and for this she is taken to task by Pacifico; but it is due less to greed than to anger and her determination to repay Fazio in kind. In the end she is happy that the affair leads to marriage, even though she is out twenty-five florins.

Sloth is at the root of Pacifico's corruption. He is quite ready to live off his wife; in fact, he encourages her in her profession, and only when she is unsuccessful in her enterprise does he berate her for attempting to corrupt "honest men's daughters" (V, 11). Yet Pacifico, whose very name ("the peaceful one") alludes to the nature of his chief vice, is a rather pathetic figure who is not really pleased living the role of a cuckold. Fazio, on the other hand, is an example of unmitigated evil; he has no redeeming qualities. In him Ariosto has combined lust with a calculated wickedness. It is not enough that he has corrupted Lena and Pacifico with his promises; he cynically proceeds to manipulate them, withholding all but a minimum of benefits and deriving pleasure from their misery. He taunts Lena by pretending to sell the modest house she occupies; and when he hears that she has been found with Flavio he becomes enraged at her betrayal, a betrayal that disturbs him more than the violation of his own daughter. If at the end he is ready to become reconciled with Lena, it is under the same degrading conditions as before.

Apart from Flavio's marriage to Licinia, in fact, the comedy ends where it began, with all the major figures resuming their original positions and relationships. Ariosto neither allows for character development nor does he penetrate into the psychology of evil; he is content merely to paint a realistic picture without subtlety or symbolism. There is some moralizing, most of it in the penultimate scene between Lena and Pacifico—a scene that was added to the original play—in which we see the fruits of a dissolute life in the recriminations of husband and wife; but the author's criticisms are not obtrusive and for the most part he maintains an attitude of detachment. However, the fact that the *Lena,* like the *Suppositi* and the *Negromante,* concludes with a marriage is evidence that harmony and order have been restored.

Ariosto began a fifth comedy, *I Studenti,* which he never finished. The three acts and more than three scenes that he completed were written in verse probably during 1518 and 1519, which would place the play chronologically between the first draft of the *Negromante* and the *Lena.* After the poet's death two versions of the ending and two prologues were written, one by his son, Virginio, and the other by his brother, Gabriele, the latter of whom published the entire play in 1547 under the title *La Scolastica.*[52] Despite its incompleteness, the *Studenti* is not a mere fragment or the outline of a comedy; it is a polished segment, one that takes the plot well into the *epitasis,* and as such it represents a stage in Ariosto's dramatic development.

The title of the play is somewhat misleading. One might expect to find in the *Studenti* a portrayal of sixteenth-century university life in the tradition of the *Paulus* and the *Janus Sacerdos* of the preceding century; however, the namesakes of the drama are hardly student types and the closest we get to the University of Pavia is Claudio's account of events at his boarding house. As a matter of fact the *Studenti* is little more than an updating of the standard classical story of two enamored youths; in its plot, in the way events unfold, and in its theatrical devices it displays more Roman influences than either the *Negromante* or the *Lena.* The changes of identity, the unexpected arrivals, the reliance on ruses and schemes, and the final recognition are typical elements of Latin comedy; and the main stratagem of the play, Accursio's attempt to pass off Ippolita and the Veronese woman as the daughter and wife of Master Lazaro, is reminiscent of an identical situation in the *Heautontimorumenos.*

By the time he wrote the *Studenti,* however, Ariosto had passed the point where he needed Latin comedy as a crutch; and the characters of the plays are almost all taken from real life rather than from classical prototypes. Accursio, in any case, is over-shadowed as a fomenter of love schemes by the more sensitive Bonifazio. The placing of an old man in such a role is a departure that Bonifazio himself defends: "In truth, helping a poor lover doesn't seem to me to be a servile task, but one that requires a gentle soul" (IV, 1). Ariosto also delineates a different kind of character in Claudio. If he is not a student type, neither is he true to the model of the classical lover. His melancholia, his agitation, his almost pathological jealousy are echoes of Orlando's mad distraction in the *Furioso*, and he reaches a level of emotionalism that is matched by no other Ariostian character. Another noteworthy figure is the hypocritical friar whose origins are found in both the *novelle* and humanistic drama and whom Ariosto and Machiavelli simultaneously introduced into erudite comedy. The friar of the *Studenti*, though, is only a peripheral character, a mere shadow of Fra Timoteo of the *Mandragola* with his sophisticated cynicism.

Unlike the *Negromante* and the *Lena*, the *Studenti* does not explore an aspect of man's moral weakness. Whatever significance it has for Ariosto's dramatic development lies instead in his outline of new characters and his elaboration of a contemporary Italian setting; in these respects the *Studenti* is a precursor of the *Lena*. The frequent mention of university cities, local towns, and villages and of traveling on the Po helps to build a geographical environment for the play; while references to the fighting around Pavia and to Ludovico Sforza's loss of his duchy—an event also alluded to in the *Negromante*—place it within the framework of contemporary politics. Despite its modern orientation, the play contains a minimum of satire, although Ariosto could not refrain from taking a passing thrust at the luxury of the Roman court (II, 4).

Because of its unfinished state it is difficult to evaluate the *Studenti* as a dramatic entity. Still, Ariosto delineated enough of the plot for Gabriele to fit his *Scolastica* and Virginio his *Imperfetta* within the context of the original three-and-one-half acts, by utilizing ideas from his other comedies; Virginio, however, found it necessary to add three minor characters to complete his version. Gabriele's prologue has a certain charm, even though it does become rather involved; otherwise the continuations tend to be ponderous and monotonous, lacking genuine literary merit. Both authors at least were aware of their limitations, and Gabriele warns the audience in his prologue not to "be surprised if the style of the last part seems somewhat different, for the dead are not like the living."

Ariosto left an invaluable legacy to Italian cinquecento theater. His comedies, coming as they did at a time when the reawakened interest in Roman drama was losing its momentum, were a vital link in the evolution of a new dramatic form. Of all the early authors of learned comedy, Ariosto had the longest career as a playwright and the distinction of being the most prolific. He was not the first to write a vernacular comedy along classical lines, and in none of his plays did he attain the high level of artistic naturalism that Machiavelli achieved in the *Mandragola*; yet the progress of the *commedia erudita* during the first quarter of the sixteenth century is virtually a reflection of his development as a dramatist. From his first attempt at a "new comedy" in the *Cassaria*, Ariosto proceeded almost lineally to emancipate himself from a slavish imitation of Latin comedy; with each subsequent play he became more daring and more original, introducing comic characters that never had appeared on the Roman stage, dealing with nonclassical themes, exploring human foibles, and placing his comedies in a contemporary Italian setting. It is true that he continued to adhere to the Roman unities and five-act form and to utilize classical plot situations; but by the time his career ended Ariosto had created a genuine Italian comedy. The *Lena*, which represents the maturation of his dramatic talents, is indicative of the emergence of a new genre.

The importance of Ariosto's comedies for the history of the theater does not end here. Their influence upon later generations of Italian playwrights was proportional to the viability of erudite comedy itself. Succeeding dramatists by no means ignored classical and novellistic traditions; but they also drew many of their comic situations and characters from earlier vernacular comedies, among which those of Ariosto were prominent. They were particularly attracted to his portrayal of the pedant and the necromancer. This is true not only of the writers of formal comedy, but also of the popular *commedia dell'arte*, which frequently based its plots, its characters, and even its speeches on the *commedia erudita*. [53]

In the second half of the sixteenth century Italian comic theater spread across the Alps where it introduced European authors to classical dramatic techniques and satirical comedy. The interest of northern playwrights in comedies of intrigue naturally led them to the plays of Ariosto, which they utilized much as he had used those of Plautus and Terence. Spanish dramatists found material for their comedies in the *Lena* and the *Negromante* while the *Suppositi* was a favorite in France and England. Twice before midcentury it was translated into French; and through Gascoigne's *Supposes* it passed to the Elizabethan scene where it may have been the source of the deception in Shakespeare's *Taming of the Shrew*. [54] The extent of this influence, of course, should not be exaggerated, for the various national theaters developed their own indigenous styles; nevertheless, Italian erudite comedy by virtue of its priority was able to provide both characters and thematic material, and the comedies of Ariosto yielded more than their share.

ARIOSTO'S COMEDIES AND RENAISSANCE THEMES

The familiar Aristotelian adage that "art imitates nature," echoed in the closing lines of the *Negromante*, can be considered as a guiding principle of Ariosto's dramatic art and, indeed, of erudite comedy in general. If there is anything distinctive about early Italian vernacular comedy it is its ability to mirror faithfully the realities of contemporary life, and for Ariosto reality was the humanistic world of the early cinquecento. His comedies are an ample source for details of Ferrarese society and present an accurate picture of Italian customs of the time; and they reveal as well the attitudes and state of mind of the artist and intellectual near the close of the Renaissance.

Ariosto was a symbol of his age, exhibiting most of its cultural and intellectual tendencies. The world that he represents was not the mobile society of the early quattrocento with its dynamism and its spirit of enterprise; it was a highly mannered, sophisticated environment that he knew, one in keeping with the aspirations of a bourgeoisie that had attained aristocratic status and was bent upon preserving its power and its comfortable position. It was a society whose center was the urban court with its conventionality and chivalric ideals, ideals that found expression in the *Orlando*. This was also the world of the comedies, for in spite of the fact that most of the characters are drawn from the middle or lower classes, courtly spectators would have had no difficulty in recognizing themselves as the objects of satire. It is this world that Ariosto parodies, but it is also the one in which he feels most at home.

Ariosto's satire of Ferrarese high society is not acerbic, and it is with a mixture of seriousness and levity that he lays open the artificiality and immorality of courtly life. This is most evident in the *Cassaria* where he has Lucramo mock the pretensions of Ferrarese gentlemen, those "lords without dominions," who would aspire to noble status: "Apart from their titles, their boasting and their vanity, their ostentation and their fables, I found little that's splendid about them." Whereas Castiglione describes the courtiers at Urbino as models of morality, refinement, and grace, Ariosto saw those in Ferrara as ne'er-do-wells, hangers-on, and social climbers: "These people consider all employment as lower-class and they'll only call someone noble who lives in idleness and doesn't work" (verse version, I, 5). The vices of the nobility—their effeminacy, their adulteries, their simony—are the subject of quips in virtually all of the comedies; but these aspersions do not seem to have antagonized Ariosto's aristocratic audiences. Perhaps they took the poet at his word when he stated that his object was merely to amuse, or perhaps his own identification with Este court society made his sarcasms tolerable. In any case we know that they were greatly amused at what Machiavelli would regard as the mirror of their own decadence.

If the weakness of late Renaissance society is revealed in Ariosto's portrayal of courtly life, then its vigor is indicated by his treatment of *fortuna*. One philosophic manifestation of the Renaissance "discovery of man" was a new dimension given to the timeless problem of the relationship between freedom and necessity. Man, according to the medieval world view, was a helpless creature subject to impartial, deterministic cosmological forces that struggle to control his life. These forces were personified as Fortune, that fickle lady whom Dante pictured as producing constant mutation among persons and empires through the turn of her wheel.[55] During the Renaissance this concept of Fortune was altered to give man greater freedom. Determinism did not disappear; Ariosto reveals its continued presence when he has Filogono say in the *Suppositi*: "There isn't a single leaf that falls unless moved by the Divine Will" (V, 8). But *fortuna* is now balanced by another force, *virtù*, man's strength, his valor, his mind. The old image of man being whirled about on the rim of Fortune's wheel, sometimes raised high, sometimes dragged low, gives way to that of a sailboat with man at the helm. To Machiavelli, Fortune yields not to those who oppose her, but to those who shift with her winds, who are agile and act boldly. "A man should take her for his star and, as much as possible, should every hour adjust to her variation."[56] The Neoplatonic emphasis on human dignity and creative power has replaced the stoic fatalism of the late Middle Ages.

Ariosto's comedies are a manifestation of this new philosophical outlook, for in all but the *Studenti*, Fortune, dressed in Renaissance garb, becomes a silent character. Her presence is most evident in the *Cassaria* where Volpino recognizes her as the persistent obstacle to human felicity: "Oh evil Fortune, you're always ready to oppose our plans!" (IV, 1). And the traditional image of Fortune's wheel comes through in Fulcio's lament: "How fickle Fortune has turned everything upside down! She had been so favorable to us for a while and would have remained so had she not been interrupted by the short memory of this fool" (IV, 8). But Fortune reigns supreme over only half of human affairs, leaving man free to steer safely through her tempests. "You're seated at the helm of this boat," Volpino reminds himself (IV, 1). "Will you be the first to let himself be dismayed by such a small storm?" Volpino, however, lacks the necessary cunning and boldness to carry his scheme through successfully, and in the end it is Fulcio's "army of lies" that overcomes the inimical cosmic forces. Fulcio recognizes the necessity of Fortune's favor, and to obtain it he vows a three-day drunken spree in her honor; yet he attributes the successful outcome solely to his own "talents and abilities [*virtù*]" (V, 4).

The treatment of *fortuna* in the *Suppositi* is more medieval. *Virtù* is lacking, and Chance plays the dominant role. Erostrato uses the analogy of a game of dice to describe the intervention of Fortune in the love-battle for Polinesta's hand. She has taken him up and down and has now left him in a state between hope and despair (III, 1). Dulippo details how cruel Fortune has heaped misery upon him by timing Filogono's arrival to coincide with the discovery of Erostrato's love-scheme; and Damone rails against "outrageous Fortune" for having sent the false Dulippo to destroy his honor (III, 1). Yet, none of them can do anything but utter curses against Fortune; they are powerless to divert her, and the outcome is a happy one only because she once again turns in their favor. In the *Negromante* Temolo alone has *virtù*, but it is the necromancer, himself the victim of his own faulty schemes, who philosophizes on the subject: "When Fortune begins to smile at you things begin to improve for a while, and whoever doesn't take advantage of this has only himself and not her to blame" (V, 5). Corbolo puts this more positively in the *Lena* when he asserts that Fortune "smiles on the daring" (III, 1); and while his plan is far from a brilliant success, it does contribute to the resolution of the plot. Only in the *Studenti* do we get an expression of the futility of man's actions. Accursio compares the plight of his companions to that of birds caught in a net: "The more they struggle to escape, the more entangled they become," and without a miracle their efforts will not save them (IV, 3). But even in his despair he does not blame the vagaries of Fortune; he sees the cause of failure primarily in the lack of *virtù*.

The exaltation of man's dignity through the concept of *virtù* is indicative of a marked shift in the attitude toward religion discernible among the Italian upper and middle classes during the Renaissance. Ethics replaced pietism and dogmatic Christianity as the avenue to salvation, and while there was adherence to outward ecclesiastical forms, the role of Christ as mediator between man and God diminished. Indifference, worldliness, faith in human freedom tempered by skepticism were prominent features of this changed religious outlook, an outlook that Ariosto shared with many of his contemporaries. In none of his writings did he reveal his inner thoughts and convictions, and the comedies are particularly silent on matters of faith, a fact that is hardly surprising considering the medium. Where he does touch upon religion, however, he shows little more than a formal acceptance of the Catholic Christianity of his day. Ariosto's belief in man's sinfulness and corruption is clear from his character portrayals and comes through most forcefully in the *Lena*; yet nowhere does he suggest a Christian remedy for the human predicament. Instead there is a pervasive cynicism, a pessimistic attitude toward man's moral regeneration, whose tone is evident in the necromancer's advice to Cintio: "Don't hesitate to hurt someone else, Cintio, if it's to your advantage. We live in an age when it's rare to find those who don't, when they have the opportunity" (III, 1). Shades of Machiavelli and a natural consequence of a secular ethic! This cynicism is again evident when Ariosto comes to satirize church corruption. He displays neither the vehemence of the Lutheran denunciator nor the sympathetic concern of the Catholic reformer; and his ridicule of the fraud, malice, slander, and luxury of the Roman Curia is accomplished with the flippancy of a disinterested humorist. Only in the *Studenti* where he has the friar chaff at the penitential system of the Church does he come close to being a serious critic.

Lighthearted as his comments are, Ariosto established himself in his comedies as a noteworthy critic of his society, censuring its artificiality, its folly, and its corruption. What northerners like Erasmus and Sebastian Brant derided in their formal satires, he ridiculed from the stage. Although their targets are not necessarily the same, there is a decided similarity in the nature of their criticism: they contrast simplicity with formalism and ceremony, honesty with hypocrisy and peculation, and common sense with oversophistication. Ariosto's scrutiny does not approach the profundity of some other humanist critics; not only did the requirements of Italian comic theater preclude this, but his own inclination was to describe rather than to analyze. He preferred to remain the dispassionate spectator occasionally throwing a dart at a vulnerable target while hiding behind his characters. Yet Ariosto's analytical abilities were no less acute, and whether he is dealing with abuses of officialdom, the legal and judicial system, and the Church, or the affectations of social customs and courtly life, he usually manages, even in a passing remark, to touch a sensitive spot. He may have lacked the temperament of a reformer, but that in itself suited him for the role of a keen observer of Italian life; and we would agree with J. S. Kennard that in many respects he was "the best interpreter of his age."

> Free from passion and serious thought, lacking enthusiasm, with rare analytic powers and an acute insight into human nature, accepting the world as he found it, without hate, scorn, indignation, or revolt, he represented the weakness of

the sixteenth century of Italy. But he also embodied its strength, especially that sustained pursuit of beauty in form, that width of intellectual sympathy, that urbanity of tone and delicacy of perception, which rendered Italy the mistress of the arts, the propagator of culture for the rest of Europe.[57]

A NOTE ON THE TRANSLATION

The lack of a translation of Ariosto's comedies for so many centuries has deprived English audiences of some delightful moments. But now that there is discernible a growing interest in Renaissance drama, both as an historical phenomenon and an aesthetic experience, the time has come to introduce the author of the *Orlando* to the modern English stage. We have undertaken this task with the object of providing a text that would be suitable for production as well as useful for the student of the theater; hence we have attempted to make our translation as contemporary as we could without straying far from the language of Ariosto.

Wherever feasible, names of persons and institutions have been left in their Italian form. Ariosto's reference to a wide variety of coinages made it difficult to maintain consistency. The *denarius*, which he used primarily to denote a small value, we have rendered as "penny," and where the *picciolo* and the *aspro* have been so used, we have done the same; otherwise the Italian has been kept. Another problem arose in translating the jargon at the end of the first and third acts of the prose *Cassaria*. Only by employing modern slang were we able to leave the meaning of Lucrano's and Furba's lines as obscure as the author intended.

Ariosto's text included no stage directions, and we have tried to hold ours to a minimum, using punctuation as a substitute where needed: Asides are enclosed in parentheses; a redirection of address within a speech is indicated by a dash at the end of a sentence; and where two conversations take place on stage simultaneously the one farthest from the center of the action is set off by dashes.

Limitations of space made it impossible to include all of Ariosto's dramatic writings. However, the principal omission, that of the verse redaction of the *Suppositi*, is not a serious loss, for the author changed little other than the form in rewriting it; and the few significant variations along with the entire second prologue have been included in the notes. We have also omitted all but the prologue of Virginio Ariosto's *Imperfetta*; its interest is largely antiquarian. The same could be said of Gabriele's *Scolastica*; but of the two continuations of the *Studenti* it is more in keeping with the structure begun by Ariosto. A compromise was made in the case of the *Negromante* where it was not possible to print both versions in full. While the basic translation is that of the second version, it is possible to reconstruct the first by following the symbols in the text and the supplementary notes.

There was no difficulty in selecting an Italian text. Catalano's standard edition of the comedies, constructed for the most part from surviving manuscripts, provided the basis for our translation. We also found the editions of Borlenghi and Segre particularly useful, and our reliance upon their explanatory notes is obvious. Besides these we consulted a number of printed editions of individual plays published during Ariosto's lifetime. The following is a list of these textual sources:

Commedie. A cura di Aldo Borlenghi. Milan, Rizzoli, 1962.
Le Commedie, con VIII tavole fuori testo, a cura di Michele Catalano. 2 vols., Bologna, N. Zanichelli, 1933.
Opere Minori. A cura di Cesare Segre. Milan, R. Ricciardi, 1954.
Comedia nuoua titolata Chassaria compota per Lodouico Ariosto nobile ferrarese. [Florence, Bernardo Zucchetta, 1509 or 1510.]
Comedia di Lodovico Ariosto intitolata Cassaria. Venice, Nicolo di Aristotile detto Zoppino, 1525.
Commedia nuoua [gli Soppositi] composta per Lodouico Ariosto nobile ferrarese. [Florence, Bernardo Zucchetta, 1509 or 1510.]
Comedia di Lodovico Ariosto intitolata gli Soppositi. Venice, Nicolo di Aristotile detto Zoppino, 1525.
La Lena Comedia di messer Lodovico Ariosto. [Venice, Marchio Sessa, 1533 or 1536.]
Il Negromante. Commedia di messer Lodovico Ariosto. [Venice, Francesco Bindone and Mapheo Pasini, 1535.]
Scolastica comedia di M. Lodovico Ariosto. Novellamente posta in luce. Venice, [G. Griffio], 1547.

1. Publio Filippo Mantovano's *Formicone* (1503) actually has the distinction of being the first "erudite" comedy to be performed, while Jacopo Nardi's *Comedia di Amicitia* may well have been written even earlier.

2. Francesco De Sanctis, *Storia della Letteratura Italiana*, 7th ed. (Bari, 1962), 2:5–9; Benedetto Croce, *Ludovico Ariosto*, 5th ed. (Bari, 1963), pp. 25–26; Ireneo Sanesi, *La Commedia*, 2d ed. (Milan, 1954), 1:221–45; and Giuseppe Toffanin, *Il Cinquecento* in *Storia Letteraria d'Italia*, 7th ed. (Milan, copyright 1965), pp. 157–62.

3. Alberto Agresti, *Studii sulla Commedia Italiana del Secolo XVI* (Naples, 1871), esp. pp. 143–44; Carlo Grabher, *Sul Teatro dell'Ariosto* (Rome, 1946), esp. pp. 205–13; and Vito Pandolfi, *Storia Universale del Teatro Drammatico* (Turin, 1964), 1:235–99. See also Pandolfi's introductions to *Teatro Goliardico dell'Umanesimo*, ed. by Ermina Artese and Vito Pandolfi, and Achille Mango, *La Commedia in Lingua nel Cinquecento* (Milan, 1966). A recent study in English to adopt such an approach is Douglas Radcliff-Umstead, *The Birth of Modern Comedy in Renaissance Italy* (Chicago, 1969).

4. Spectacular performances of *sacre rappresentazioni* were staged in Florence under the patronage of Lorenzo the Magnificent (1478–92), who, along with a number of leading court poets—from Feo Belcari to Antonia Pulci—wrote some of the better-known sacred dramas.

5. The *Santa Guglielma*, the *Santa Uliva*, and the *Stella*, for example. The most comprehensive collection of religious plays is Alessandro D'Ancona, *Sacre Rappresentazioni dei Secoli XIV, XV, e XVI* (3 vols., Florence, 1872).

6. Although they lost favor during the sixteenth century, sacred dramas continued to be performed in convents and Jesuit schools and occasionally were presented at carnival time in Florence. There, versatile playwrights like Cecchi and Grazzini composed religious plays in addition to more popular learned comedies.

7. Italian playwrights, moreover, led the way, for with one or two exceptions it is not until late in the fifteenth century that we find German and other transalpine scholars writing neo-Latin comedies. See Antonio Stäuble's admirable treatment of the subject in his *Commedia Umanistica del Quattrocento* (Florence, 1968), esp. pp. 236–49.

8. This is the theme of Vergerio's *Paulus*, the only extant fourteenth-century humanistic comedy, of Alberti's *Philodoxus* (ca. 1426), and of the *Janus Sacerdos* (probably written by Pisani).

9. Horace's *Ars Poetica* and Aristotle's *Poetics* (which was translated into Latin in 1498) were also considered by contemporary dramatic commentators as essential guides to understanding the principles of classical comedy. However, the importance of Aristotle's contribution to Renaissance comic theory has been seriously questioned by Marvin T. Herrick in *Comic Theory in the Sixteenth Century* (Urbana, Illinois, 1964), pp. 1–5, 61–70, 144–47.

10. K. M. Lea, *Italian Popular Comedy: A Study in the Commedia dell'Arte, 1560-1620 with Special Reference to the English Stage* (New York, 1962), p. 174.

11. A discussion of Florentine productions can be found in Sanesi, *La Commedia*, 1:184–85.

12. Francesco Ariosti was a distant relative of Ludovico.

13. The extent of Ercole's knowledge of Latin is uncertain. In any case, he gave careful attention to the work of translation and even admonished the scholarly Guarino for departing from literal meanings in rendering the *Asinaria* of Plautus. See Guarino's letters of 18 and 26 February 1479 to Duke Ercole, reproduced in A. Luzio and R. Renier, "Commedie Classiche in Ferrara nel 1499," *Giornale Storico della Letteratura Italiana* 2 (1888): 177–78.

14. *Silva Chronicarum Bernardini Zambotti*, fols. 173r°, 181v°. Those portions of Zambotto's chronicle that refer to the theater in Ferrara have been reproduced by Giuseppe Pardi in "Il Teatro Classico a Ferrara," *Atti e Memorie della Deputazione Ferrarese di Storia Patria* 15 (1904): 1–27.

15. "Nozze e Commedie alla Corte di Ferrara nel Febbraio 1491," in *Archivio Storico Lombardo* 2d ser. 1 (1884): 751–53. See also Anna Maria Coppo, "Spettacoli alla Corte di Ercole I," in *Contributi dell'Istituto di Filologia Moderna* (Milan, 1968), pp. 30–59.

16. Pencaro to Isabella d'Este, 9, 10, 11, and 13 February 1499, reproduced in Luzio and Renier, "Commedie Classiche in Ferrara," pp. 182–89. On the other hand, Pietro Bembo, who was also present at the performances, evinces a humanist's interest in the dramatic events and does not even allude to the *intermezzi* in a letter to Angelo Gabrieli. *Epistolarum Familiarum*, lib. I, no. 18, in *Opere del Cardinale Pietro Bembo....* (Venice, 1729, facs. ed. Ridgewood, New Jersey, 1965), 4:159–60.

17. Isabella d'Este to her husband, Francesco Gonzaga, 10 May 1493, quoted in Michele Catalano, *Vita di Ludovico Ariosto Ricostruita su Nuovi Documenti* (Geneva, 1931) 1:122. See Bernardino Prosperi to Isabella, 24 May 1493, in Luzio and Renier, "Commedie Classiche in Ferrara," p. 179n.

18. Zambotto, *Silva Chronicarum*, fol. 182v°, in Pardi, "Teatro Classico," p. 12.

19. Letters of 29 January and 3 February 1502, quoted in Sanesi, *La Commedia*, 1:188. Formal comedy, of course, has never been able to compete successfully for public attention with popular amusements. Even Terence had the humiliation of seeing his audience leave the theater en masse to watch acrobats and gladiators in a circus.

20. Ibid., pp. 189–93. See also Radcliff-Umstead, *The Birth of Modern Comedy*, p. 61.

21. Ludovico's father, Niccolò, had moved his family from Reggio to Ferrara in 1485 where the elder Ariosto was made Judge of the Twelve Sages.

22. *Diario Ferrarese*, quoted in Catalano, *Vita di Ariosto*, 1:123.

23. This is the view of Sanesi (*La Commedia*, 1:221–22). Catalano, however, doubts the possibility (*Vita di Ariosto*, 1:124–25).

24. Girolamo Garofolo, *Vita di M. Lodovico Ariosto* (Venice, 1584), quoted in Edmund G. Gardner, *The King of Court Poets: A Study of the Life and Times of Lodovico Ariosto* (London, 1906), p. 205.

25. There is some uncertainty about when the *Cassaria* was written. Giovan Pigna relates an incident that occurred in 1492 that might indicate an earlier date of composition. Niccolò Ariosto, on learning that Ludovico had been associating with men of questionable character, delivered a long lecture to his son accusing him of fast becoming one of the most dissolute young men in Ferrara. Ludovico afterward confessed to his brother, Gabriele, that he hoped to incorporate this scene into a comedy he was writing, and this could have been the inspiration for the second scene of Act Five.

See Gardner, *King of Court Poets*, pp. 24–25. Sanesi (*La Commedia*, 1:222–25) contends that there may have been an earlier version of the play than that first published in 1509, one written entirely in tercets. He bases his conclusion on Prosperi's letter (see below) referring to the setting as Taranto rather than Mytilene and stating that the play was "traducta in forma de barzeleta o sia frotola" and on the fact that the prologue of the published edition is in tercets. However, there is nothing in Ariosto's letters or other writings to substantiate this. The similarity between Act V, Scene 2, of the *Cassaria* and Act V, Scene 8, of Terence's *Andria* throws some doubt on the validity of Pigna's story, and it could be that certain inaccuracies entered into Prosperi's description due to the excitement of the evening's entertainment. See also Catalano, *Vita di Ariosto* 1:302–4.

26. Letter of 8 March 1508 in G. Campori, *Notizie per la Vita di Lodovico Ariosto* (Florence, 1896), pp. 48–49.

27. With the prologue to the *Cassaria* Ariosto entered the debate that was raging among humanists over the question of *imitatio*: how far could modern writers diverge from classical models without violating the standards of eloquence? Latin purists, led by Paolo Cortese, considered Cicero the only source of *bonae litterae* and insisted on close imitation of his style; but more venturesome humanists such as Poliziano and Ermolao Barbaro would not be limited in this way and attempted to develop a style of their own.

As Cicero provided no model for dialogue, it was to Plautus and Terence that the Latinists looked with reverence for their standards of dramatic form and style. Ariosto, in his notion of "poetic imitation" and his apologies for novelty, showed his high regard for these classical models; but he also refused to be slavishly imitative, and as a consequence he helped to evolve an Italian form of comic drama. This ambivalence toward imitation of the classics was characteristic of writers of erudite comedy. Only later in the century do we find playwrights like Grazzini calling for complete independence. In the prologue to *La Strega* he wrote: "Aristotle and Horace saw their own times; but our times are different. We have different manners, a different religion, and a different way of life. Therefore comedies should be written in another way. In Florence we do not live as they once did in Athens or Rome."

28. Caridoro's father is referred to as *Bassa* or Pasha.

29. The similarities between the *Cassaria* and the *Andria* are more than casual: in both there are two young lovers aided by servants or slaves in obtaining their hearts' desires; there is the contrast between one slave loyal to the father and another loyal to the son; there is the plan that backfires only to be reformulated; and in both there is a touching scene in which a father reprimands his son. From the *Heautontimorumenos* Ariosto may have taken material for the first scene of Act II in which Volpino becomes increasingly annoyed at Erofilo's reluctance to follow his schemes. The idea of a father unexpectedly returning to interrupt the plans of a profligate son probably comes from the *Mostellaria*, while Lucrano's soliloquy (Act III, Sc. 7) in which the procurer compares himself to a fowler was most likely inspired by a similar passage in the *Asinaria*.

30. Grabher, *Sul Teatro dell'Ariosto*, pp. 43, 53–57. Grabher is determined to prove the originality of the *commedia erudita* and to minimize its debt to classical theater; hence he emphasizes Ariosto's use of novellistic sources. Admittedly, though, these Boccaccian features can also be found in classical comedy. Yet it is also conceivable that Ariosto may have

derived his ideas from no other source than his own experience and his observation of the life and customs of his time.

31. Ibid., pp. 46–47.

32. Giraldi Cinthio, a contemporary critic, considered it Ariosto's best effort, although his opinion is far from universal. *Discorsi di M. Giovambattista Giraldi Cinthio, . . . Intorno al Comporre dei Romanzi, delle Comedie e delle Tragedie e di Altre Maniere di Poesie* (Venice, 1554), pp. 213–14.

33. See pp. xxix–xxx. Cristoforo Messibugo, the chief entertainer at court, refers to a performance of the *Cassaria* on 24 January 1529, but this was probably the prose version. The first mention of a new *Cassaria* appears in a letter of Girolamo da Sestula to Isabella d'Este (20 February 1531) reproduced in Catalano, *Vita di Ariosto,* 2:302, 310.

34. Letter to Isabella d'Este, 8 February 1509, in Campori, *Notizie,* p. 50.

35. See n. 3 of the *Pretenders.*

36. A discussion of the history of the parasite is found in Vincenzo De Amicis, *L'Imitazione Latina nella Commedia Italiana del XVI Secolo* (Florence, 1897), pp. 142–43.

37. Grabher, *Sul Teatro dell'Ariosto,* pp. 68–69.

38. See n. 6 of the *Pretenders.*

39. The date of the composition of the *Mandragola* has been the subject of much controversy. For the latest view see Sergio Bertelli, "When Did Machiavelli Write *Mandragola*?", *Renaissance Quarterly* 24 (Autumn, 1971): 317–26.

40. Alfonso Paolucci to the Duke of Ferrara, 8 March 1519, in *Lettere di Lodovico Ariosto con Prefazione Storico-Critica Documenti e Note,* ed. by Antonio Cappelli (Milan, 1887), pp. clxxvi–clxxxii.

41. Ariosto to Pope Leo X, 16 January 1520, in ibid., p. 35.

42. Letter to Ludovico Ariosto, 25 March 1532, in Catalano, *Vita di Ariosto* 2:323–24.

43. *Storia della Letteratura Italiana* 2:6.

44. This was not the first disappointment that Ariosto experienced from Leo X, for his expectation of papal patronage at the accession of Giovanni de' Medici had been dashed in 1513.

45. *Discorso o Dialogo Intorno alla Nostra Lingua,* in *Opere Letterarie,* ed. by Aldo Borlenghi (Naples, 1969), p. 438. Ariosto, under the influence of his friend, Pietro Bembo, came to agree with Machiavelli on the *questione della lingua,* and in the final edition of the *Orlando* he defers to the language of Petrarch and Boccaccio.

46. This is the view of G. Marpillero in "Il Negromante," *Giornale Storico della Letteratura Italiana* 33 (1899): 303 ff.

47. An excellent discussion of magic as it pertains to sixteenth-century drama is found in R. Warwick Bond, *Early Plays from the Italian* (Oxford, 1911), pp. xxxi–xxxvii.

48. A comparison of the two versions is found in Grabher, *Sul Teatro dell'Ariosto,* pp. 95–108.

49. Quoted in Gardner, *King of Court Poets,* p. 259.

50. *Sul Teatro dell'Ariosto,* p. 129.

51. The relationship between Ariosto's ethics and the personification of sins in the *Orlando* is discussed in Julius A. Molinaro, "Ariosto and the Seven Deadly Sins," *Forum Italicum* 3 (June, 1969): 252–69.

52. See preliminary note on the *Students.*

53. Although historians of the theater are in disagreement about the origins and sources of the *commedia dell'arte*, most are ready to admit that this improvised comic form was closely connected with the erudite comedy of the sixteenth century. For a discussion of the relationship between the two see Winifred Smith, *The Commedia dell'Arte* (New York, 1964), pp. 67–102. Sanesi (*La Commedia*, 1:515) contends that the *commedia dell'arte* was "the popular expression or travesty of the learned comedy."

54. The influence of Ariosto's comedies upon the European theater was extensive, though often indirect and obscure. There are, for example, possible Ariostian influences in Shakespeare's *Love's Labour's Lost*, *Twelfth Night*, and *The Tempest*, but these may have come indirectly through the *commedia dell'arte*; and one can trace Ben Jonson's *Alchemist* back to the *Negromante*, even though the two plays are developed differently. Similarly, it is possible to discern character-types such as the pedant, the necromancer, and the friar in the *Autos* of the sixteenth-century Portuguese writer, Gil Vicente. A more direct appropriation occurred in France and Spain: the *Suppositi* was imitated by several French writers during the sixteenth century, among them Jean Godard (*Les Desguisez*, 1594), and Molière made good use of it in *L'Avare* (1668); while the Spanish playwright, Juan de Timoneda, drew upon the *Lena* for his *Farsa Trapacera* and upon the *Negromante* for his *Comedia Ilamada Cornelia*. For details of these influences see Antero Meozzi, *La Drammatica della Rinascita Italiana in Europa Sec. XVI-XVII* (Pisa, 1940), esp. pp. 37–41; Maurice Mignon, *Etudes sur le Théâtre Français et Italien de la Renaissance* (Paris, 1923); and Sijbrand Keyser, *Contribution à l'Etude de la Fortune Littéraire de l'Arioste en France* (Paris, 1933).

55. *Inferno* canto 7, ll. 61–97.

56. *Di Fortuna*, in *Opere Letterarie*, p. 148.

57. Joseph S. Kennard, *The Italian Theatre from Its Beginning to the Close of the Seventeenth Century* (New York, 1932), p. 113.

THE COFFER
La Cassaria

A Prose Comedy

CHARACTERS

EROFILO	*Young man*
NEBBIA ⎱ GIANDA ⎰	*Crisobolo's servants*
EULALIA ⎱ CORISCA ⎰	*Young ladies*
CARIDORO	*Young man*
LUCRANO	*A procurer*
FURBA	*His servant*
VOLPINO	*Crisobolo's servant*
FULCIO	*Caridoro's servant*
TRAPPOLA	*A cheat*
BRUSCO	*His helper*
CORBACCHIO ⎫ NEGRO ⎬ MORIONE ⎭	*Crisobolo's servants*
CRISOBOLO	*Erofilo's father, a merchant*
GALLO	*Crisobolo's servant*
CRITONE	*A merchant*
ARISTIPPO	*His brother*
MARSO ⎫ ROSSO (silent) ⎬ MAROCHIO (silent) ⎭	*Crisobolo's servants*

The action takes place in Mytilene

I BRING YOU A NEW COMEDY FILLED WITH VARIOUS WITTICISMS that neither Greek nor Latin tongues ever recited on the stage. I notice that most of you are inclined to disapprove of it merely because I said that it was new, without listening to the first half or staying to the end; you think that such an undertaking is not an appropriate subject for modern writers and you only consider what the ancients have said to be perfect. It's true that neither our vulgar prose nor our verse can be compared to those of the ancients; nor does our eloquence match theirs. But today's talents are not so different from those of the past, for they were created by the same Supreme Artist who created them in former times. Granted that our vernacular, which is mixed with Latin, is barbarous and uncultured; however, with a few witticisms one can make a story less dreary. Those capable of doing this are not to be found everywhere; and this author is not so audacious as to place himself among these few. I have said these things only so that you'll be patient while his play is presented to you; and let no one say that he dislikes it until it is finished.

In order to begin right away, and so that I don't omit anything, I want you to know that the story the author is going to present is rightly called the *Coffer*; and also that he would have it take place in a city called Mytilene.[1] The plot, which remains to be heard, he has entrusted to a servant called Nebbia. Now, on behalf of the one who serves the feast, I beg those of you who watch to be silent.

ACT ONE
SCENE ONE
EROFILO, *a young man*; NEBBIA, *a servant*

ERO: [*To his father's servants*] Now, as I told you, you're to go find Filostrato and do everything that he orders; and make sure that I don't hear any bad reports about you. Where is my instructor, my teacher, my wise custodian? Does he expect you to wait at his pleasure until evening? Is he still not coming? By God, if I go back...! All of you, go and drag him out by his hair. Words mean nothing to that ass; he never obeys except by dint of a cane. [*To Nebbia*] See, I got you out.

NEB: Go to the devil! The feast cannot be finished without me. I know how much you want me to leave; but I can't take it any more.

ERO: [*To his father's servants*] Go away, and don't any of you dare come back here until you have been given permission. Do you hear me?

Scene Two

GIANDA, NEBBIA, *servants*

GIAN: It's sheer madness, Nebbia, that of all us servants you alone are always ready to oppose Erofilo. You certainly ought to realize how nice he has been to you until now. Obey him, for God's sake, regardless of whether he orders you to do right or wrong. After all, he's the son of our master, and considering his age, he'll be around to command us much longer than the old man. Why do you insist on staying at home when he wants you to go out?

NEB: If you were in my place you would do the same and even worse.

GIAN: Perhaps. But I don't think so, for I don't see how this can really help you.

NEB: I musn't do otherwise.

GIAN: And why not?

NEB: If you listen, I'll tell you.

GIAN: I'm listening; go on.

NEB: Do you know the pimp who moved into the neighborhood about a month ago?

GIAN: Yes, I know him.

NEB: I'm sure you've seen a couple of gorgeous girls in his house.

GIAN: I've seen them.

NEB: Well, Erofilo is so taken with one of them that he would sell himself in order to buy her; and the pimp, aware of his great desire for her and knowing that he's the son of the richest man in Mytilene, is asking him ten times as much for her as he would anyone else.

GIAN: How much is he asking?

NEB: I don't know exactly, but I do know that the price is high; in fact it is so high that even if Erofilo borrowed from all his friends he wouldn't be able to come up with half of it.

GIAN: What can he do then?

NEB: What can he do? He can do a great deal of harm to his father as well as to himself. I think he has his eye on plundering the wheat that the old man has accumulated over the past two or three years; or on looting the silk, the wool, or other things of which, as you know, the house is full. His

4

adviser and guide is that thief, Volpino. They've waited a long time for the occasion when the old man would leave, as he has today, to go to Negropont.[2] They want me out of the house so that no one will witness their scheme. Now they're sending me to find Filostrato in order to keep me busy. He won't let me return until they've accomplished their purpose.

GIAN: Why the devil should you care so much, even if they emptied the house? After all, he'll be heir to what remains, not you, stupid.

NEB: It's you who are stupid, Gianda; you have no more sense than an ox. If Crisobolo returns, what will happen to me? Don't you know that when he left this morning he entrusted me with all the keys to the house? He warned me, if I valued my life, not to give them to anyone, and especially not to his son; and no matter what happened, never to set foot out of that door. Now you see how I obeyed him. I believe that no sooner had he left than Erofilo asked for the keys, saying that he wanted to look for a hunting horn that he had lost; and so, in spite of me, he got them. Perhaps you were there.

GIAN: No, I wasn't there, but from where I was I could easily hear the sound of heavy blows, and you received more than ten before you gave them up.

NEB: If I hadn't given them to him I think he would have killed me. What should I have done?

GIAN: What should you have done? You should have given them to him the first time he asked for them; and you should also have left the house with us the moment he ordered it. Couldn't you always justify yourself to the master and explain to him exactly how it happened? Won't he be aware of the fact that you, at your age and in your condition, are no match for an ardent young man such as Erofilo?

NEB: Won't Erofilo be able to throw the whole blame on me? And will he lack witnesses in his favor? After all, he's the master; and I know that all of you in the house despise me, not because I deserve it, but because I stand up for the old man and I don't allow him to be robbed.

GIAN: Also because it's your misfortune that you're not able to make friends.

NEB: Do you know anyone in any household who has my job and isn't also hated?

GIAN: Because those like you are wicked and have horrible dispositions. Masters, in choosing someone to supervise their servants, always select the worst man they have in the house so that they can more readily shift the blame to him for any hardships that are suffered. But let's change the subject. Tell me something: who is that young man who just entered the house, the one whom Erofilo honors as if he were his superior?

NEB: He's the son of the governor³ of this island.

GIAN: What's his name?

NEB: Caridoro. He's in love with the other pretty girl in the procurer's house; but I don't think that he has any better chance than Erofilo of buying her, unless he, too, tries to rob his father. But look, look, that girl near the door of the pimp's house is the one whom Erofilo loves; the other one, the one further out in the street, is Caridoro's girl friend. What do you think of them?

GIAN: I think that if their lovers see things as I do, the pimp would become very wealthy. But let's go, for if Erofilo comes out we'll get it.

SCENE THREE

EULALIA, CORISCA, *young ladies*

EUL: Corisca, don't go too far from the door; if Lucrano catches us he'll be angry.

COR: Don't worry, Eulalia, we have better eyesight than he has, and we would see him first. So, let's take this small pleasure now that he's away from the house.

EUL: What pleasure would compensate for a thousandth part of our misfortune? How miserable we are! We're slaves, a condition that could be tolerable if we belonged to someone who was humane and reasonable. But among all the procurers in the world none could be found who is more greedy, more cruel, more furious, and more beastly than the one to whom the cruelest fate has entrusted us.

COR: Let us hope, Eulalia. You have Erofilo and I have Caridoro, and both have promised us many times and have sworn a thousand oaths to free us soon.

EUL: The many times that they have promised it and have not kept that promise is a sure sign that they don't intend to. If they had denied it a thousand times and then promised only once, I would hold out great hope; but, as it is, I have very little. If they intend to do so, why are they delaying? They want to have their fun while they keep us dangling with smooth talk. And they do us great harm, for others might have come to free us—with fewer words and more deeds—but out of regard for these two they've held off. What's more, they've angered Lucrano, who has seen the whole affair dragged out with vain

6

promises. Yesterday he told me—perhaps you were there—that he couldn't afford the expenses here any longer and that if someone doesn't come to buy our freedom within ten days he would have us, whether willingly or not, earn our bread; and, as he couldn't sell us as a whole, he would sell us a little at a time, for four or six quattrini⁴ or for whatever he could get. Oh, poor us!

COR: Let him do it. What in heaven's name can happen? Yet, I'd like to think and be sure that our lovers won't allow us to come to such misery.

EUL: Perhaps we had better go inside, for it would be unfortunate if Lucrano caught us out here.

COR: Ah! I see our sweethearts coming this way. Let's not go so soon; wait and see what they have in store for us today.

Scene Four

EROFILO, CARIDORO, *young men*; EULALIA; CORISCA

ERO: Oh, what a happy meeting this is, Caridoro! One could have wished for nothing better in the whole world.

CARI: Here are the serene and shining stars whose lovely appearance can calm the storms of our troubled thoughts.

EUL: You could speak more truthfully about us, for you would be our blessing and salvation if you really loved us as much as you try to show with words. You make great promises when you're with us: "Give me your hand, Eulalia. Give me your hand, Corisca. Today or tomorrow, without fail, we'll free you; if not, may we be ..." Listen to them. As soon as you turn your backs on us, you laugh at our troubles.⁵

ERO: You're wrong in saying this, Eulalia.

EUL: Even though you're gentlemen, even though you're rich and are citizens here, you shouldn't scoff at us and make fun of us: we come from good families, although misfortune has brought us to this condition.

ERO: Alas, Eulalia, don't make my love more sorrowful than it is with your tears and recriminations. I would be the most ungrateful, the rudest villain in the world if by tomorrow ...

EUL: Please! I can hardly believe you any more.

ERO: Let me finish: I cannot tell you everything, but rest assured that by tomorrow at the latest you'll be free from this wholly corrupt procurer. This situation has been allowed to go on longer than it need have or than I believed it would; but I couldn't do anything more about it. Don't think that because I dress well and because I'm the only son of Crisobolo, who is considered the richest merchant in Mytilene, I can dispose of his wealth as I please. And what I say about myself is true of him also; for our old men are no less rich than greedy, and our desire to spend is no stronger than their diligence in watching our spending. But now that my father has sailed to Negropont and will not have his eyes constantly on my hands, you'll see the clearest evidence of my love for you, and soon.

EUL: May God move your heart to do so. If you love me and care for my well-being, do your duty, for since the moment we met I have always held you dearer than my own eyes and my own heart.

CARI: Corisca, I want you to have the same faith and understanding; very little remains to be done to reach a successful conclusion.

EUL: Enough now; we don't want Lucrano to catch us here.

ERO: Two days won't pass before you'll be safe in my arms.

EUL: I'll live in the hope of it.

COR: And me, too, right?

CARI: We'll not provide for the well-being of one without looking after the other. Keep up your spirits. Good-bye.

COR: Good-bye.

ERO: Farewell, root of my heart.

EUL: Farewell, my life.

SCENE FIVE
EROFILO; CARIDORO

ERO: Should I not show her how much I love her? Can I allow her to remain in servitude any longer? This scheme must not be prolonged further. If Volpino doesn't come up with a good solution today, I'll no longer listen to his false promises, promises with which, from morning until night, day after day, for more than a month, he has led me on. First he promises to extract the money to buy her from my father's hand; and now he promises to set a snare for this Albanian thief from which he'll never escape unless he lets me have the girl. Should I continue to listen to him? By God, I won't. If I cannot accomplish my objective secretly, I'll do it openly; no keys or nails can keep something closed to me that I know is necessary for my purpose. I would be worse off than Tantalus if I let myself die of thirst in the midst of water. In the house there are all sorts of cloth— silks, woolens, gold and silver draperies—wine and wheat which in an hour I could convert into as much cash as I want. Am I to be so timid and cowardly that for once I would not satisfy my desires?

8

CARI: If only I were in your situation, with my father away, by God, I'd find my own means to satisfy myself and I wouldn't look elsewhere! If he would only leave Mytilene for two days they would suffice me for a hundred: I'd cleanse the granary so well and clean out all merchandise from the rooms and halls that it would seem as if the Spaniards had lodged there for a year.⁶ But here he comes.

ERO: Who? Yes, yes, Lucrano. I wish he were being carried here [in a coffin]. Let's go inside and do what Volpino told us to, so that when he returns he cannot excuse himself on account of our negligence.

CARI: Let's go.

Scene Six
LUCRANO, *a procurer, alone*

LUCR: When you hear a woman's beauty, a lord's liberality, his riches, his knowledge, or similar things being lauded and praised to the skies, you would not be mistaken if you believed little of it; because, when it comes to the proof, you'll find that they are not as great as their reputation would have them. Nor would you be wrong if, upon hearing a miser, a cheat, a thief, or other such corrupt persons being condemned, you believed more than what you heard; for when you come to know them, you'll always find their vices greater than they first appeared.

I cannot explain why this is so, but I know the results because of the considerable contact I have daily with both types; right now I'm experiencing one type more than the other. I was told that the young men of this city were wealthier, more liberal, and spent more on women than in any other place in Greece. But I discovered the opposite to be true, for, in everything except their dress, I find them extremely stingy. They are such spendthrifts that I understand that most of them, like the turtle, carry all they possess on their backs.

Every day one or another of them comes and tells me that he wants to buy this woman or that one; and, when it's time to pay they try to satisfy me with promissory notes, with promises or idle words. In other places when you sell something you see money; here—I don't know by what miracle—the spending is done invisibly. Not mine, however, for if I want bread or wine or other essentials of life I have to make the money appear. If I could provide myself with such things by means of words, then I would be happy to sell what I have for words. It won't do for me to accept the kind of money that I cannot spend for my needs.

If one could change the past at will, then I would wish I had never come here. By staying here much longer without profiting more than I have until now, I'll use up what little I brought with me from Constantinople, where my trade served me well; I fear that I may reach the point where I'll die of hunger.

There's only one hope left for me, and that lies in my neighbor, Erofilo, who loves my Eulalia. If he desires her as much as he seems to, I know that he has the means with which to pay me well; but he behaves with so much malice toward me. He realizes that by staying here I incur considerable expense and gain little profit and that very few, apart from him, are about to buy any of my women from me. He also thinks that I don't have the means to leave here and that as the days go on I'll have even less. So he's waiting until, forced by necessity, I'm reduced to the position of begging him to take the girl for whatever it pleases him to give me; and, if I don't take care and act with equal cunning toward him, he'll easily succeed in his plan.

I've considered pretending to leave; and to suit this purpose a ship has arrived that will be sailing for Syria either tomorrow or the next day. I spoke to the owner about passage for myself, my household, and my belongings, and I've made this fact known to some whom I think may have already reported it to Erofilo. I'll get the idea out of his head that I'm constrained to stay here because I don't have the means to leave. And here, just in time, is my Furba, who will be a great help in this matter.

Scene Seven
LUCRANO; FURBA, *a servant*

LUCR: You returned when you couldn't delay any longer. Whenever you're given a task you need no less than a whole day to do it, you good-for-nothing ass. Run to the port, may the devil take you; run, I say, and come back quickly. Hey, where are you going? Aren't you going to wait to hear what I want? Look for the master of the ship from Beirut, the one with whom we spoke this morning, and find out from him for certain if he intends to leave tonight or how long he's going to stay. If he confirms what he told you this morning—that he intends to sail tonight—return immediately and bring two carts and three or four porters with you, for before this day is over I want to have the entire house cleared out and all my things loaded, so that nothing can prevent us from going with him. Perhaps we can make this voyage more profitable than the one that brought us here to live—to a place where foreigners are hated more than truth in the courtrooms. Well, what are you looking at? Why haven't you gone? Hurry off and don't slow down in that place so that we can palm off the bird on the mark.

FURBA: I'll respond with counterpoint.[7]

LUCR: (I sang loudly enough so that if Erofilo is in the house he certainly heard me.)

ACT TWO
Scene One

EROFILO, CARIDORO, *young men;* VOLPINO, FULCIO, *servants*

ERO: I can't imagine why Volpino is so late in returning.

CARI: If Fulcio doesn't find him at least he ought to come back.

ERO: I think that all the fates have conspired against us.

CARI: My goodness, here they come.

VOLP: ——Could one possibly devise a more remarkable scheme than this, Fulcio, in order to save two lovers and destroy such a greedy pimp?

FUL: Volpino, despite all the self-confidence I have, this plot reminds me of a fertile but poorly cultivated field that is no less full of weeds than it is of lovely plants.

VOLP: Even if it doesn't succeed at least we can take comfort in the fact that we won't be punished for some small thing. What more can we get than a beating?

FUL: I'm sure you won't have to ask for stronger shoulders than the ones you have; they're quite sufficient to tire anyone's good arm.——

CARI: It seems that they're laughing as they come.

VOLP: ——If I had to find yet stronger ones, I'd take yours.——

ERO: What do you suppose? Maybe they got hold of some good wine, which was the reason for their delay, and it must be this that accounts for their laughter.

VOLP: ——Let's walk faster. Don't you see that our masters are waiting for us?——

CARI: Let's go meet them, for their gaiety gives me high hopes.

ERO: They probably don't know that Lucrano is planning to leave, otherwise they wouldn't be walking so sprightly.

VOLP: May God give you long life.

ERO: Yes, but in a happier state than we're in now.

VOLP: As long as there's life there's hope; let only the dead despair.

ERO: Volpino, don't you know that Lucrano expects to leave tomorrow or perhaps even tonight?

VOLP: May he leave in a storm. But I don't believe him; that's a ruse he's using to frighten you.

ERO: Be still. If you had heard what he just told Furba—not realizing that we could hear him—you wouldn't call it a ruse. Ask him.

CARI: That's the truth.

ERO: Alas! How will I be able to live if he takes my only love away with him? Wherever Eulalia goes my heart will go with her.

VOLP: If your heart is going to leave tonight let me know about it early enough so that I can get a bill of lading before the customs house closes.

FUL: And so that we can make a gown or something else to cover it.

VOLP: Why a gown?

FUL: So that birds of prey, who frequent lands beyond the sea, won't peck at it on finding it naked.

ERO: See, Caridoro, how these rascals make fun of us! Ah, how unhappy is he who is the servant of love!

VOLP: And unhappier still is the servant of the servant of love. Erofilo, I didn't think you were so fainthearted that, knowing Volpino is around, you would let a trifle such as this discourage you.

ERO: Is this a trifle? Nothing could matter more to me.

VOLP: Listen to me carefully. You said that the procurer is leaving, right? Now, provided that you don't fail me through cowardice, both of you will have your women in your arms before an hour of darkness has passed—even though there is scarcely any daylight left; as for Lucrano, that arrogant fellow, I'll shear him like a sheep.

ERO: Now, there's a worthy man!

CARI: Oh, my good Volpino!

VOLP: But tell me, did you prepare the shears with which to clip him, as I asked?

ERO: What shears did you tell me about?

VOLP: Didn't I ask you to get the keys to your father's room from Nebbia?

ERO: I did that.

VOLP: And to remove the coffer that I showed you?

ERO: I did so.

VOLP: And to send all the servants out of the house?

ERO: I've done that.

VOLP: And above all Nebbia?

ERO: I've done everything you asked me to.

VOLP: Fine. These are the shears that I asked for. Now listen to what I want done: I came across an old friend of mine, a servant of one of the sultan's Mamelukes who is in Mytilene

on his master's business; he has never been here before, and
I don't think anyone here knows him. I had many dealings with
him in Cairo where I went with your father last year and spent
more than two months. Well, tomorrow at dawn he has to leave.

ERO: What are we to make of this friendship?

VOLP: Listen and I'll tell you: I'll have him dress up as a merchant
using some of your father's clothes. He makes a good appearance, and besides this I'll dress him in such a way that no one
on seeing him would ever imagine that he isn't a great merchant.

ERO: Go on.

VOLP: Disguised in this way, he'll go to see the procurer; he'll
bring along the coffer that you've taken and leave it with
him as security.

ERO: As security?

VOLP: And he'll get him to give up the woman.

ERO: With whom do you want the security left?

VOLP: With the procurer.

ERO: The procurer?

VOLP: Until he brings him payment for your Eulalia.

ERO: What the devil! What is he to leave with the procurer?

VOLP: I said the coffer. He'll get the woman and take her to you.

ERO: I understand all right; but I don't like it.

VOLP: Then, we'll go immediately. . . .

ERO: Think of something else. Do you expect me to place such
valuable goods in the hands of a fleeing pimp?

VOLP: Let me take care of it: listen.

ERO: There's nothing to listen to; it's too risky.

VOLP: No it isn't. If you listen, we could easily . . .

ERO: What do you mean, easily?

VOLP: If you'll be quiet, I'll tell you. It's necessary for anyone
who wants . . .

ERO: What stories are you about to tell me?

VOLP: It's your hard luck if you won't listen. I must be mad.

CARI: Let him speak.

ERO: Go ahead.

VOLP: May I die if I ever . . .

CARI: Don't go away Volpino; he'll listen to you.——
Listen to him; let him explain.

ERO: Well then, what do you want to say?

VOLP: What? What do I want to say? All day long you beg me,
you urge me, and you pester me to find a way for you to get
your woman. I've found a hundred ways, but you don't like
any of them. One seems difficult to you, the other perilous;
this one is too long, that one too obvious. Who can figure you

out? You want it and don't want it; you desire something but you don't know what! Oh, Erofilo, believe me, you cannot do something memorable without some risk and effort. Do you think that the procurer will relent and give her to you because of prayers and lamentations?

ERO: It would seem rather foolish to place a thing so valuable in such obvious danger. Don't you realize, as I do, that this coffer is full of gold brocade you could scarcely buy for two thousand ducats? And furthermore, that it belongs to Aristandro for whom my father is keeping it on deposit? It seems to me that these are shears to clip us rather than the sheep you were telling me about.

VOL: Do you think that I have so little intelligence as to try to lose something so precious without first thinking about how to get it back at once? Leave it to me, Erofilo. If the plan doesn't succeed I'm in more danger than you are; of this I'm sure. You would only hear shouts; I would feel the master's cane, or I'd be placed in irons, jailed, or sent to the galleys.

ERO: How could we get it back unless we bring him money? And money is just what we lack most of all. What if, in the meantime, my father returns or Lucrano secretly steals away? Where would we find ourselves then?

VOLP: If you'll have enough patience to listen to me you'll see that my plan is good, that there is no danger, and that, without any loss, we would get back our merchandise immediately.

ERO: I'm listening; go on.

VOLP: As soon as Lucrano receives the coffer and our merchant has brought you the woman, we'll go to the governor—to Caridoro's father—and complain to him that this coffer has been taken from your house and that you suspect that a procurer, a neighbor of yours, has removed it.

ERO: I see; such a thing is plausible.

VOLP: You'll ask to have a policeman go with you to search his house. Caridoro will so influence his father that he may even send the chief-of-police[8] for this purpose.

CARI: That will be easy to do, and if necessary, I'll go myself.

VOLP: We'll work so fast that he won't have time to transfer the coffer elsewhere, and we'll find it right there in his house. He'll say that a merchant left it as a guarantee of payment for one of his women. But who will believe that someone would leave goods worth more than a thousand ducats for something worth scarcely fifty? Having been found guilty of theft, he'll be dragged off to prison and perhaps hanged; he may even be drawn and quartered. What will we care about him?

14

ERO: By God, the plan could work.

VOLP: As soon as the procurer is taken, you, Caridoro, can accomplish your purpose by yourself. While your servants are taking Lucrano to prison, you'll do what you please with your Corisca. The procurer will be only too happy to give her to you as a present, provided that you offer to use your influence with your father in his favor, so that at least his life may be spared.

CARI: Oh, Volpino, you deserve a crown.

FUL: Rather a miter and a standard.⁹

VOLP: Not everybody can attain such honors as yours, Fulcio.

ERO: Where is this fellow whom you're going to dress up as a merchant?

VOLP: I'm surprised he's not already here; but he'll be here shortly.

ERO: Do you expect him to carry the coffer himself?

VOLP: No. He has a fellow servant with him for that purpose. Now go inside the house and, so as not to waste any time, select one of your father's gowns, one that seems appropriate to you.

CARI: Is there anything for me to do here?

ERO: You can go home; I'll let you know the results. Good-bye.

CARI: Good-bye.

FUL: If you don't need me any longer, I'll go with my master.

ERO: As you please.

SCENE TWO
VOLPINO, TRAPPOLA, BRUSCO, *servants*

VOLP: (I should have remembered that Trappola rarely tells the truth. I was a fool to let him out of my sight before bringing him here. If he has deceived me—though I doubt it—then I won't be able to carry out any of my plans. But, thank God, here he is; my luck was better than my foresight.)

TRAP: Isn't it great, Brusco, that you can never do a favor for anyone without expecting something in return.

BRUS: It's even greater, Trappola, that your business and that of your master never give you enough to do, so that you have to meddle in the affairs of strangers, affairs that don't concern you at all.

TRAP: I don't consider Volpino a stranger and I always consider it my business to seek out new friendships, especially those of young men, such as I understand his master, Erofilo, to be.

BRUS: If you want new friends you ought to acquire them by your own work, without troubling me or others who don't have such desires.

TRAP: What else have we got to do today?

BRUS: We have to provide bread and wine and other things for

15

our use aboard ship; if we're going to sail at daybreak we won't have enough time.

VOLP: (They're walking so nonchalantly that, indeed, they look like princes.) Trappola, I thought you had deceived me.

TRAP: I'm sorry that you thought so.

VOLP: You were walking with great deliberation.

TRAP: Isn't it right for a servant who is going to become an austere man to learn how to walk with gravity?

VOLP: Who should know how better than you, you who spent most of your life with irons on your legs?

TRAP: There isn't an animal with so forceful a trot that it wouldn't slow down to an amble if its rider made it tote heavy loads with such kindness as your master loads you with shackles.

VOLP: Let's go; there's no reason to delay.

ACT THREE
SCENE ONE
VOLPINO; TRAPPOLA; EROFILO

VOLP: Before you leave, listen carefully so that you'll be able to find your way to where I told you to bring the woman. Remember that after you pass the portico down the street, it's the third house on the right-hand side.

TRAP: I'll remember.

ERO: Wouldn't it be better, in order to avoid any mistakes, for him to bring her here first and for us to take her there?

VOLP: Not at all, for a neighbor might see her, and the snares that we're laying for the procurer would be discovered.

ERO: What you say is true.

VOLP: It's a small door that has recently been built.

TRAP: You've already told me that.

VOLP: The owner of the house is called Lena.

TRAP: I remember.

VOLP: There's a wooden shed across the way.

TRAP: Don't worry about it; I'll be able to find my way there as surely as I can get to a tavern.

VOLP: We'll go there and wait for you; and, in the meantime, we'll have supper ready.

TRAP: Make sure that there's plenty to drink, because this long gown has already made me thirsty.

VOLP: You'll have enough. Now be careful, so that the procurer, who's as cunning as the devil, doesn't become suspicious.

TRAP: Hah, hah, hah! Look who's trying to teach me how to tell lies. Why I had lies in my mouth before you had paps in yours!

VOLP: Go now, and may the plan work out well.

SCENE TWO
BRUSCO; TRAPPOLA

BRUS: Hurry up. What else is there for us to do this evening?

TRAP: We have to sup and be merry.

BRUS: May I break my neck if I wait around for you another minute after I've put this chest down.

TRAP: Then do as you please; but be quiet, for I hear that door being opened. This must be our pimp, if I'm not mistaken.

SCENE THREE
LUCRANO; TRAPPOLA

LUCR: I'd better leave the house before those chatterboxes deafen me. They're splitting my head, they're killing me with their prattling. [*To the girls inside*] You'll do what I say as long as I'm your master, no matter what.

TRAP: (Others have the signs of their trade on their chests; this fellow has it on his face!)

LUCR: How arrogant, how insolent all these devilish whores are! They're always searching for ways, they're always attempting to do the opposite of what you want. They have their hearts set on nothing but stealing from you, defrauding you, bringing you to ruin.

TRAP: (I never heard anyone praise the merchandise he wants to sell so highly!)

LUCR: I think that if someone was guilty of every possible sin and he kept women for sale, as I do, and put up with their ways without screaming and cursing heaven and earth a thousand times a day, he would acquire more merit from his patience alone than from all the abstinences, all the vigils, all the sackcloth and the means of penance that there are in the world.

TRAP: (I know very well that keeping them in your house is a purgatory for you; but for the poor things being kept it's a gloomy hell. However, let's proceed.)

LUCR: That man coming this way must have just disembarked, for a porter with a heavy load is accompanying him.

TRAP: ——It can't be very far. Here's the big house across from which I was told that he lives.——

LUCR: It sounds to me as if he cannot find lodging.

TRAP: ——Ah, there's someone just at the right moment who perhaps can direct me, for I'm not very familiar with this place.——

Tell me, my good man . . .

LUCR: You certainly show that you're not very familiar, for you called me by a name that has never been applied to me, to my father, or to any of my relatives.

TRAP: Forgive me; I hadn't gotten a good look at you. I'll correct myself. Tell me, my wicked man, from a long line of wicked men ... But, by God, perhaps you're just the person I'm looking for, or maybe his brother or his cousin, or at least one of his relatives.

LUCR: That's possible; and whom are you looking for?

TRAP: A cheat, a perjurer, a murderer.

LUCR: Slow down, for you're about to find him. What is his name?

TRAP: His name..., his name..., I just had it on the tip of my tongue. I don't know what I've done with it.

LUCR: You either swallowed it or spit it out.

TRAP: I may have spit it out, but I didn't swallow it, for I couldn't have fed my stomach such rotten food without immediately vomiting it up.

LUCR: Well, then, gather it out of the dust.

TRAP: I can describe him in so many ways that there'll be no need to search for his name. He's a curser and a liar.

LUCR: These are precisely the attributes of my profession.

TRAP: A thief, a forger, and a cutpurse.

LUCR: Is it so evil to know how to profit by manipulating one's hands?

TRAP: He's a pimp.

LUCR: That's the mainstay of my trade.

TRAP: He's an informer, a slanderer, a sower of discord, and a scandalmonger.

LUCR: If we were at the Court of Rome one might wonder whom you were looking for; but in Mytilene you could only be looking for me. And to remind you of my proper name, I'm called Lucrano.

TRAP: Lucrano. Yes, yes. Lucrano with the pox.

LUCR: May God give it to you. I'm just the person you're looking for. What do you want from me?

TRAP: Are you really the one?

LUCR: The very one. Tell me, what do you want?

TRAP: First let him place his load in your house, and then I'll tell you why I'm here.

LUCR: Go inside and put it where you like. Hey, you, help him unload.

TRAP: The admiral, who is a close friend and can order me about like a master, has been staying at Alexandria as of late. He knew that I would be coming to this city shortly and he asked me when I did come to buy from you, on his behalf, one of your girls by the name of Eulalia, whose beauty has been praised by more than one person who has seen her in your house. As soon as I've bought her, I'm to have her taken to him by his servant whom he has sent with me for this purpose. A boat is leaving tonight for Alexandria; and, since I want to serve him readily and well, I've come to see you to make a quick bargain so that I can get her at once and send her to him. Now tell me, how much are you asking?

LUCR: The truth is that I had already agreed upon a price with a wealthy man from this city who is supposed to come tomorrow with the money and take the girl; however, when . . .

TRAP: Don't you mean, "However, if I give you more . . ."?

LUCR: You get the idea. My duty is always to serve whomever gives me more.

TRAP: But let's go into the house. I'm sure we'll come to a fair agreement.

LUCR: Very well put; let's go inside.

Scene Four

CORBACCHIO, NEGRO, GIANDA, NEBBIA, MORIONE, *servants*

CORB: Filostrato is truly a kind and liberal young man.

NEGRO: Men like him are the ones to serve, for they give you little work and plenty of drink.

CORB: And what a snack he prepared for us!

MOR: What about the wine, which certainly has touched my heart.

CORB: I don't think there's better wine in this land.

MOR: Did you ever see any that was clearer, more beautiful, than this?

CORB: Have you ever tasted any that was more fragrant, that was sweeter, than this?

GIAN: And what power! It's worth every penny.

CORB: I wish I had a pitcher of it at my bedside tonight.

GIAN: I'd prefer to have the whole barrel to myself.

MOR: I only wish that our master would decide to send us to work for Filostrato every day, as he has done today.

GIAN: Yes, provided that he would provide such enjoyment every day.

CORB: I don't know how you feel; as for me, I'm so happy I can hardly contain myself.

GIAN: I think we're all in the same condition.

NEB: I only wish that it were so when the old man returns! While drinking and eating we have all been companions; but when he returns I alone will have to pay for the wine and suffer.

GIAN: Don't worry about trouble that hasn't yet arisen, stupid; don't kick back before you've been stung. How do you know what the future has in store?

NEB: I may not be a prophet or an astrologer, but you'll see. As soon as we get home everything that I predicted today will happen.

GIAN: I told you this morning, and now I tell you again, that you should try to become friendly with Erofilo and you'll see that all will go well for you. If you persist in making him hate you by obeying the old man, then you'll always have him on you, either with fists or a cane on your face or head; one day he'll maim you or kill you, and you'll be the one to suffer. But, if, in order to please the youth, you don't obey the old man in every instance, you'll find that the old man, who's wiser and more moderate, will always be easier to pacify. He'll understand how difficult it is for someone like you to oppose such a strongheaded youth like his son. I tell you this as a friend.

NEB: I certainly know that what you say is true, and I'm always willing to change my mind. But wait a moment.

GIAN: What is it?

NEB: Who is that coming out of the pimp's house and taking one of the girls with him? He must have bought her.

GIAN: It looks like our master's girl friend.

NEB: It's her without a doubt.

CORB: Indeed it is.

GIAN: Wait, hold it. Let's stay back here and see where he takes her so that we can then tell Erofilo. Shhshh.

Scene Five

TRAPPOLA; GIANDA; CORBACCHIO; MORIONE; NEBBIA; NEGRO

TRAP: ——Brusco has gone. Oh, what a stupid ass, to leave me here alone at night with this burden on my hands!——

GIAN: From what I can see he's taking Eulalia away.

CORB: Oh, poor Erofilo!

GIAN: Oh what sorrow, oh what melancholy he'll experience as soon as he learns of this!

TRAP: ——Don't cry, my beautiful girl.——

GIAN: Should we do it?

NEB: Do what?

GIAN: Take her from him and bring her to Erofilo.

TRAP: ——Are you really sorry to leave Mytilene?——

GIAN: As soon as he goes a little further let's take her away from him.

MOR: How will we do that?

GIAN: What do you mean how? With punches and kicks. We are five, and he's alone.

TRAP: ——Don't cry, because of that. . . . ——

NEGRO: The plague to him who hesitates.

TRAP: ——For I assure you, I won't take you far away.——

NEB: What if he shouts; won't the whole neighborhood come to his aid?

GIAN: Oh yes, of course, they'll come right out!

TRAP: ——Why don't you answer?——

CORB: Who, on hearing someone scream at night, would come running into the street?

TRAP: ——Please! Don't stain such beautiful cheeks with your tears.——

GIAN: Here's your chance, Nebbia—that is, if you help us in this— to make Erofilo a friend forever by doing him a great favor.

NEB: Fine; but let's not bring her into the house, for we'll be recognized. It would be a mistake to do so.

GIAN: Where will we take her, then?

NEB: How should I know?

NEGRO: Let's not stop because of this. We can take her to the house of Chiroro de' Nobili, who's a close friend of Erofilo and one of the finest men in the city.

GIAN: You couldn't name a better place.

TRAP: ——I'm worried about walking all alone at such a late hour. I didn't think that that ass would leave me.——

MOR: You keep him busy with kicks and punches; Corbacchio and I will take the girl away.

GIAN: Let's go then, and no more talk.

TRAP: ——Good grief! What's this mob following me?——

GIAN: Hold it, merchant.

TRAP: What do you want?

GIAN: What merchandise is this?

TRAP: You seem strangely interested in it. Am I to pay you a customs duty?

GIAN: You probably didn't declare it at the customs office. Where's your certificate?

TRAP: What certificate? This isn't dutiable merchandise.

GIAN: Duty has to be paid on all merchandise.

TRAP: You pay duty on merchandise by which you profit, not on merchandise on which you lose.

GIAN: Which you lose. Well said, for you have lost it. We caught you smuggling; let go of her.

CORB: Eulalia, let's go find your Erofilo.

GIAN: Let go or else I'll . . .

TRAP: Is this how you murder foreigners?

GIAN: If you don't shut up I'll scratch your eyes out.

TRAP: Rascals, do you think that by this? . . . Help, Help!

GIAN: Break his head; tear out his tongue.

TRAP: Is this how you take my woman away from me, you traitors?

GIAN: Let's go away and let him croak.

TRAP: Woe is me; what shall I do? I'll follow them to see where they take her, even if I have to die.

GIAN: If you don't go away I'll break that fat head of yours into more pieces than if it were made of glass. If you want to demand your rights, show up at the customs office tomorrow.

TRAP: ——I'm in bad shape: they've taken the woman from me; they've thrown me in the mud; they've torn my gown; and they've battered my face.——

Scene Six
EROFILO; VOLPINO; TRAPPOLA

ERO: That fellow certainly delays enough in bringing her here.

VOLP: Don't come out any further, for you'll ruin all our plans.

TRAP: (How will I dare face Erofilo?)

ERO: I think I see him there.

TRAP: (How can I ever explain this; I hope he doesn't think . . .)

VOLP: By God, it's him.

TRAP: (That I willingly let them take Eulalia and that they didn't take her by force.)

ERO: But he doesn't have the girl with him.

VOLP: Nor the coffer, which is even worse.

TRAP: (Ah, woe is me! I don't know what to do.)

ERO: Trappola, what happened? Didn't you get my Eulalia?

VOLP: Where did you put the coffer?

TRAP: I got Eulalia.

ERO: Eulalia?

TRAP: I had almost brought her here.

ERO: Good grief!

TRAP: And then I was attacked by more than twenty men who took her away from me.

ERO: They took her away from you?

TRAP: They beat me up and left me on the ground for dead.

ERO: They took my Eulalia from you?

TRAP: Yes, they took your Eulalia! And they're not far away.

ERO: Which way did they take her?

VOLP: Where did you put the coffer?

ERO: Let him answer me; this is more important.

VOLP: The coffer is much more important.

TRAP: The ones who beat me up went that way.

VOLP: Where's the coffer?

ERO: Why am I waiting to go after them?

TRAP: It's in the procurer's house.

22

VOLP: Where are you going? What are you thinking of doing?

ERO: I'll either get my woman or I'll die.

VOLP: Wait a moment. Remember that the coffer is in jeopardy; take care of that first, and then . . .

ERO: What should I take care of first, if not my heart, my soul?

VOL: Don't go, for God's sake! Do you know with whom you have to deal?

ERO: If you're afraid, then stay here. After losing my Eulalia I don't care about anything. She's my life.

VOLP: He's gone, and I'd better follow him anyway to see that he doesn't lose the coffer. You, wait for me here in my master's house so that in addition to the other damages you won't lose the gown as well. Hurry up and knock, for I see the procurer coming out. Hurry, so that he doesn't see you with me. And don't leave here until I return.

SCENE SEVEN
LUCRANO; FURBA

LUCR: There never was a fowler more fortunate than I am; for, having prepared a snare today for two paltry little birds who hung around and sang all day, by chance a big fat partridge came along and got caught in it. By a partridge I mean a certain merchant, because it seems to me that he's more partial to loss than to gain. He came to buy one of my women, and with two words he closed the deal. I asked for one hundred saraffi[10] and he agreed to give me one hundred saraffi; and, as he didn't have the money on hand, he left me as security a chest full of gold brocade that I believe is worth more than fifteen times as much. He opened it in front of me, then he closed it and sealed it; he took the key and told me to keep the chest until he brings me the amount agreed upon.

This is an opportunity that rarely comes, and if I'm such a fool as to let it go, I'll never come across a similar one. If I take this chest with me someplace else, I'll never be poor for the rest of my life; and I've decided to do just that. So, the pretense of leaving this city, which I made this morning, was actually a forecast, because as things stand now I'm going to leave at dawn. This merchant, moreover, cannot claim that he was deceived by me, for before I let him come into my house I informed him that I was a cheat, a swindler, a thief, and a man with every vice. If he still was willing to trust me, let him suffer the consequences. Ah, there is Furba just on time. Is the ship leaving tonight? If not, when?

FURBA: Haven't you finished your little game with him?

LUCR: Hurry off to the master of the ship and sing a song about sailing tonight, for I have the flower in my hand and I want to buy the whole bouquet.[11]

ACT FOUR
Scene One
VOLPINO, *alone*

VOLP: Ah, poor Volpino. You're assailed on all sides by so many adversities, by so many misfortunes, that if you're able to defend yourself against them you could boast of being the foremost swordsman of our day. Oh, evil Fortune, you're always ready to oppose our plans! Who could have imagined that, having got Eulalia out of the procurer's house, we would lose her so soon and so foolishly? This turn of events is not so much contrary to Erofilo's love as it is perilous to our chances of ever retrieving the coffer.

I thought that, as soon as Eulalia was in our hands, Erofilo would go and complain to the governor of the island and follow the course we had set this morning; but I have been mistaken in my trust, for he's intent only on finding the girl who has been taken away and is running here and there all over the city. Neither my arguments and my pleas, nor the actual danger of losing the coffer, which is worth so much, can induce him to do that which, if he fails to do, will bring about, not only the undoing and ruin of his father and himself, but a continual war in the house; and for me it will lead to torments, life imprisonment, and maybe even death. Perhaps I could stave off this misfortune, serious as it is, if I had enough time to think about it somewhat, or even if I had a little time to breathe! But I'm troubled, on the one hand by the thought that the procurer may flee tonight with the coffer, and on the other by the sudden fear that my old master will return and will seize and hold me so that I won't even have time to buy a rope with which to hang myself. I don't know where to run and break this miserable head of mine.

I just met a servant from Calibassa[12] who told me that my old man never left port, because just as he was about to set sail a boat arrived from Negropont bringing letters informing him about the very matters for which he was going, thus making the trip unnecessary; he was surprised that he wasn't home yet and that I hadn't seen him. If I were really convinced that this were true I would run immediately, without a moment's hesitation, as fast as my legs could carry me, and drown myself in the sea. But what is that light coming from over there? Oh, my God, could it be the old man? Alas! It's the master all right. You're a dead man, Volpino! What will you do, poor fellow? Where can you hide? Where can you rush off and fling yourself to escape from all the torments that are being prepared for you?

CRISOBOLO, *an old master;* VOLPINO, GALLO, *servants*

CRIS: I stayed so long in the magistrate's[13] house that I didn't realize it was getting dark; actually, I didn't waste any time, for I settled some accounts with him, and I attended to something that I had wanted to finish for some time.

VOLP: (Ah, cowardly and fainthearted Volpino! What has become of your boldness? Where is your usual ingenuity? You're seated at the helm of this boat. Will you be the first to let himself be dismayed by such a small storm? Cast all fear aside and show your true colors in the face of danger. Find your old cunning and put it to work, for you're in need of it now more than in any previous undertaking.)

CRIS: It really is much later than I thought.

VOLP: (On the contrary, it's much earlier than it need be for me. But let him come; let him come as he will, for I have already prepared the neatest bag of tricks and the finest sleight of hand that any juggler has ever devised.)

CRIS: Oh, how lucky for me that I didn't have to leave Mytilene at the present time!

VOLP: (And how unlucky for us.)

CRIS: For I didn't feel very assured leaving my affairs and my goods at the discretion of a prodigal young man, such as my Erofilo, and of faithless servants.

VOLP: (You weren't mistaken.)

CRIS: But I've returned so quickly that not only didn't he have time to do any damage, he didn't even have time to think about doing it.

VOLP: (You'll find out. If you had run faster than a leopard you couldn't have arrived soon enough. But why am I waiting to begin my little trick?) Oh, how unfortunate we are. What are we to do? We're finished, we're ruined.

CRIS: Isn't that Volpino shouting over there?

GALLO: I think so.

VOLP: Oh, this wicked city, full of scoundrels!

CRIS: There must have been some mishap that I don't know about.

VOLP: Oh, Crisobolo, how will you take it when you find out?

CRIS: Oh, Volpino.

VOLP: But whoever trusts a drunken slave more than his own son deserves this and even worse.

CRIS: I tremble and sweat with fear that some great misfortune has come upon me.

VOLP: He entrusts his room, filled with so many things, to a senseless idiot who always leaves it open and never stays at home.

CRIS: Why don't I call to him? Oh, Volpino.

VOLP: If we don't get it back tonight, it will be lost forever.

CRIS: Volpino, don't you hear me? Volpino, whom am I talking to?

VOLP: Who's calling me? Oh, it's the master; what do you know, it's my master!

CRIS: Come here.

VOLP: Oh, Master, could it be that God . . .

CRIS: What's wrong?

VOLP: . . . has brought you here now?

CRIS: What's the matter with you?

VOLP: I was desperate and I didn't know to whom to turn.

CRIS: What has happened?

VOLP: But now that I see you, Oh Master . . .

CRIS: Tell me, what is it?

VOLP: . . . I can begin to breathe.

CRIS: Tell me, hurry up.

VOLP: I was dead, alas! But now . . .

CRIS: What has happened?

VOLP: . . . I'm revived.

CRIS: Briefly, tell me, what is it?

VOLP: Your Nebbia . . .

CRIS: What has he done?

VOLP: That thief, that drunkard . . .

CRIS: What is it he's done?

VOLP: I've been running up and down so much all day long that I can hardly catch my breath.

CRIS: Tell me, in a word, what has he done?

VOLP: He's ruined you through his stupidity.

CRIS: Finish me off; don't hold me in suspense.

VOLP: He allowed someone to steal . . .

CRIS: What?

VOLP: . . . from your room, the very one in which you sleep . . .

CRIS: What?

VOLP: . . .the one whose keys you gave to him alone, and you warned him so much about them. . .

CRIS: What did he allow to be stolen?

VOLP: That coffer that you. . .

CRIS: What coffer that I. . .?

VOLP: The one that, because of the lawsuit between Aristandro and ——what's his name?

26

CRIS: The coffer that I have in trust?

VOLP: You don't have it. I tell you it was stolen.

CRIS: Ah, unhappy and wretched Crisobolo! To leave your house in the care of these rascals, of these poltroons, of these gallows-birds! I could have just as well left it with so many donkeys.

VOLP: Master, if you find the kitchen in a mess, punish me and make me suffer the torments, because I'm responsible for it. But what have I got to do with your room?

CRIS: Is this how Erofilo uses his discretion? Is this the duty of a good son? Is this the care and concern that he has for my things and his?

VOLP: To tell you the truth, you shouldn't be angry with him. How the devil could he be at fault? If you would allow him to manage and take care of your house, as other fathers allow their sons, he would do his duty. He would take charge, and perhaps things would go better for you. But if you trust a drunkard, a runaway servant, more than your own flesh and blood, you can rightly blame no one but yourself if things go wrong.

CRIS: I don't know what to do; I'm the most ruined and most broken man in the world.

VOLP: Master, now that you're here, I have hopes that the coffer will not be lost and that God has brought you back in the nick of time.

CRIS: What do you mean? Have you some clue by which we may be able to find it?

VOLP: I searched for it all day, and I went around like a blood-hound, first here and then there, and now I think I can point out where your goods are.

CRIS: If you know it why didn't you tell me?

VOLP: I'm not saying that I know it, but I think I do.

CRIS: Where do you suspect it may be?

VOLP: Come a little closer to me, still closer, and I'll tell you. Come even closer.

CRIS: Whom are you afraid will hear?

VOLP: The one whom I think stole it.

CRIS: Does he live nearby, then?

VOLP: He lives in this house.

CRIS: What? Do you think that the procurer who lives here has stolen it?

VOLP: I think so; in fact, I'm certain of it.

CRIS: What proof do you have?

VOLP: I said I'm certain of it; but for God's sake, let's not waste time by asking me to relate how, by what means, and with what skill I became sure of it, because delay is very dangerous. I can tell you that he's preparing to flee at dawn, the little thief.

CRIS: What do you think I should do? Suddenly I find myself so overwhelmed that I don't know where to turn.

VOLP: I think that we ought to go immediately to the governor and inform him that a procurer, a neighbor of yours, has stolen your coffer and is preparing to flee with it. Ask him to have justice done and to send some of his men along with you to search for your goods, because you suspect that the procurer still has them in his house.

CRIS: What evidence, what proof can I give him to convince him that this is so?

VOLP: Isn't it proof enough that, being a pimp, he's also a thief? And if you say it, wouldn't you be believed more than ten other witnesses?

CRIS: If we have nothing better than this, we're finished. Nowadays whom do the authorities give more credence and more favor to than pimps, and whom do they scoff at more than law-abiding and virtuous men? Whom are they out to get if not men like me who have the reputation of being rich and moneyed?

VOLP: If I come along with you I'll present the governor with so many indications and conjectures, so much proof, that even if he didn't want to he couldn't help but believe you. I'm not telling them to you in order not to waste any more time. Let's hurry, let's quicken our pace so that the procurer won't make fools of us while we waste time talking.

CRIS: Let's go, for ... Hey, wait a minute; a better idea came to my mind.

VOLP: What can you do that's better than this?

CRIS: Rosso, run to Critone's house and ask him for me to come here immediately and to bring his brother or any of his servants with him. Run, I say; I'll wait for you here, run.

VOLP: What do you want them for?

CRIS: I want to get into the procurer's house unexpectedly. Can't I remove my goods from wherever I find them, provided that I have one or two good witnesses with me? If we go now and speak to the governor, it would be in vain: we'll either find him having supper, playing cards or dice, or wanting to rest, weary of the day's work. Don't I know the habits of those who govern us? The more they're alone and scratch their bellies, the more they try to show how busy they are. They place a servant at the door who lets in gamblers, pimps, and perverts and sends away honest citizens and virtuous men.

VOLP: If you made him realize the importance of this matter he wouldn't deny you an audience.

CRIS: And how would you get him to listen? Don't you know how doorkeepers and porters usually reply—"You cannot speak to him." "Tell him it's me." "He's ordered me not to give him any messages"—Once they've said this there's no other reply. But I'll do it my way, which will be better and much safer, provided that the coffer is there.

VOLP: It's there for sure; so go in with confidence. Your idea is excellent.

CRIS: While we're waiting for Critone, tell me something: how and when did you realize that the coffer had been stolen, and how did you come to know that this procurer had it?

VOLP: It would be a long story, and we don't have time. Let's find the coffer first, and then I'll tell you the whole thing.

CRIS: There's enough time and, if you cannot tell me the whole story, at least tell me part of it.

VOLP: I'll begin, but I know that I won't be able to tell you half of it; there won't be enough time.

CRIS: You could have already told me part of it; now go on.

VOLP: Since you want me to tell you, I'll do so. Now listen. Today, shortly after we had eaten lunch, and your son—who ate elsewhere—had returned home, Nebbia came to see Erofilo and gave him the key to your room, without anyone asking him for it.

CRIS: This was a fine way to begin obeying me! That's exactly what I had ordered him to do!

VOLP: He said: "I want to go to the piazza on some business of my own; keep this key until I return." Erofilo, without giving it any thought, took it; and Nebbia left the house and never returned.

CRIS: In this he also obeyed me very well; as if I hadn't expressly ordered him never to leave the house!

VOLP: You see! We stayed a while chatting about one thing and another; then, in the course of the conversation, we began talking about going hunting one day. At this point Erofilo remembered a horn he used to have that he hadn't seen for some time. He decided to look for it in your room; so he took the key, opened the door, and I followed him in. On entering, it was your son who first noticed that the coffer was missing. He turned to me and said: "Volpino, do you know whether my father has returned Aristandro's coffer that he has held so long in trust?" I looked around and was dumbfounded; and I said that you hadn't. I remembered for certain that when you left I had seen it at the head of the bed where it used to be. Immediately I realized the stupid ploy of Nebbia who, as soon as he had seen that the coffer was missing, brought the key to your room to

Erofilo in order to make him share the blame, although he alone
is guilty. Do you see what I mean?

CRIS: I understand. Ah, that rascal! If I live . . .

VOLP: He plays dumb, but he has more malice than the devil himself; you don't know him very well.

CRIS: Go on.

VOLP: Now, as I was saying, my dear Master, Erofilo and I, upon
noticing this, considered the situation and discussed who could
have taken it. I asked Erofilo his opinion and he asked mine:
what were we to do; how were we to go about finding evidence
—we debated and argued for a while, but we didn't know where
to turn or what to do. Oh, my kind Master, never in my life
was I more uneasy or more troubled. I found myself so downcast, so desperate today that, in short, I wished I were dead; in
fact, I wished I had never been born. But here's Critone with
his brother, Aristippo; I'll tell you the rest when we have
more time.

CRIS: With all your chattering you haven't come up with a single
proof that it's the procurer rather than anyone else who has
my coffer; nor do I know what hope I can have of finding it when
I enter his house.

VOLP: Enter with assurance, and if you don't find it, then hang me
with my permission. If I weren't more than certain of it, I
wouldn't tell you to go in.

SCENE THREE
CRITONE, CRISOBOLO, *merchants;* VOLPINO

CRIT: There are thieves everywhere, but there are more of them in
this city than in any other place in the world. How can we merchants have the courage to go about when we're not even secure
in our own houses? Oh, Crisobolo, may God preserve you;
we're here to help you if we can.

CRIS: I'm sorry to bother you at this hour; you can impose upon
me some other time.

CRIT: You don't have to say that to us; we would willingly do
anything for you.

CRIS: Please come with me into this house and be witnesses to what
I'm about to do.

CRIT: You can call upon me for this and even greater favors.

CRIS: Enough said; come on.

CRIT: Let's go.

VOLP: Line up along the wall and hide the light. I'll knock, and
when they open, everyone go in. I'll stand guard so that while
you're searching in one place the procurer won't take the coffer

out of another and send it elsewhere.

CRIS: Knock and do what you think best.

SCENE FOUR

FULCIO; VOLPINO

FUL: There are some braggarts who try to hoodwink you by boasting that they can do certain things; but, when put to the test, they don't dare to attempt them. Among these is that drunkard, Volpino, who boasted today that, with the help of one of his friends, he would play the most cunning and best conceived trick in the world on the procurer in order to get one of his girls; and that he would afterward let us know about its success, so that we could complete those parts that he couldn't manage. Caridoro and I have been waiting all evening long and we still haven't heard any news. I am going to find out whether he's changed his plans or whether he's encountered some obstacle.

VOLP: (I hear someone coming this way; it seems that he's going to knock on our door.) Hey there, what are you looking for? Whom do you want?

FUL: Oh, Volpino, I seek no one, I want no one, but you.

VOLP: I didn't recognize you, Fulcio. What do you want?

FUL: What are we to do? Have you changed your mind? Or don't you remember what we agreed on today?

VOLP: Oh, Fulcio, the devil must not only have put his tail in, as they say, but his head and his horns as well, in order to destroy all our plans.

FUL: What has gone wrong?

VOLP: I'll tell you, but ... be quiet, shh, shh.

FUL: What mob is this coming out of the procurer's house with so much noise and such an uproar?

SCENE FIVE

LUCRANO; CRISOBOLO; VOLPINO; CRITONE

LUCR: My good man, is this the way to treat foreigners?

CRIS: Is this the way to treat citizens, you thief?

LUCR: It won't end the way you think; I'll cry to high heaven.

CRIS: I won't take my complaints to such high places, but rather to a place where your wickedness will be punished.

LUCR: Don't be so sure that because I'm procurer I won't be listened to ...

CRIS: Do you still have the audacity to speak?

LUCR: ... and that I don't have a tongue with which to express my rights.

CRIS: A rope around your neck will make it hang nine inches out of your mouth. How indignant would he have been if he had found his merchandise in our house?

LUCR: I'll undergo torture and I'll have all in my household do the same; and I'll prove to any judge that the chest was given to me as security by a merchant in payment for one of my women, as I told you.

CRIS: Do you still have your mouth open, you notorious thief?

LUCR: Who is more notorious than you, you who come here to steal and bring witnesses with you?

CRIS: If you don't speak courteously, you swindler, I'll . . .

CRIT: Don't argue with this chatterbox; it's not fitting for someone like you. Let's go.——If you claim that he's done you an injustice, show up in the courthouse tomorrow.——Let us go.

LUCR: You'll see me there; be certain of that. Perhaps this won't end the way you think; by God, it won't. (Right now they are too many and I'm alone; but we'll soon meet in a place where they won't have such a great advantage.)

CRIS: Have you ever seen a more bold and presumptuous thief than this?

CRIT: Not really. You've had great luck, Crisobolo, and this pleases me.

CRIS: The greatest in the world.

CRIT: Is there anything else you want from us?

CRIS: Only that you call on me when I can help. Volpino, take that light and accompany them home.

SCENE SIX
FULCIO; VOLPINO; CRITONE; ARISTIPPO

FUL: Shall I wait for you, Volpino?

VOLP: Yes, I want to speak to you a moment.

FUL: Come back soon.

VOLP: I'll return immediately; but it would be better if you came with me.

FUL: Do you have far to go?

VOLP: I'm just going around the corner to the first house.

FUL: I'll come, then.

VOLP: Come, and we'll talk as we walk back. Oh, damn it!

FUL: May you break your neck. What's the matter?

VOLP: I'm ruined; I've had it.

FUL: What's the matter now?

VOLP: Here, take this light and accompany these gentlemen to their house. Damn my short memory!

FUL: You hold it and light your own way; I want to find out what just happened to this madman.

32

CRIT: Both of you certainly are good servants and courteous young men!

ARIST: We'll have to be like the knights of Naples who, it is said, accompany one another.[14]

FUL: What's the matter with you, you idiot? What happened to you just now?

VOLP: Alas! I left Trappola in the house with my master's clothes on and I forgot to rush and have him undress and give him back his own gown, which is locked in my room, before my master gets home.

FUL: Ah, you scatterbrain! Run quickly and have him hide so that at least Crisobolo won't see him.

VOLP: I think I'll be too late; in fact, I am too late, for I hear a loud noise and uproar.

SCENE SEVEN
CRISOBOLO; VOLPINO; TRAPPOLA

CRIS: Where do you think you're going? Don't move, you false-faced thief. How did you come to steal this gown of mine?

VOLP: (What will you do now, wretched Volpino?)

CRIS: You must be the fine fellow who also stole my coffer.

VOLP: (Oh, if I could only get a little closer to his ear!)

CRIS: Why don't you answer, you cheat? To whom am I talking? Help me so that he won't flee. You won't speak, eh? This fellow is either a mute or he pretends to be.

VOLP: (One couldn't have found a better remedy for this unfortunate turn of events. Now is the time to help him.) Master, what are you doing with that mute?

CRIS: I found him in the kitchen dressed the way you see him.

VOLP: Who the devil brought this mute into the kitchen?

CRIS: I can't make him answer at all.

VOLP: How do you expect him to reply if he's dumb.

CRIS: Is he a mute?

VOLP: What? Don't you know him?

CRIS: I never saw him before.

VOLP: Don't you know him? Don't you know the mute who hangs around the Monkey's Tavern?

CRIS: What mute? What monkey do you expect me to know? According to you it would seem that I frequent taverns, you scoundrel.

VOLP: I think he's wearing your gown; yes, of course, I recognize it.

CRIS: Why do you think I'm so angry?

VOLP: Isn't he also wearing your hat?

CRIS: I think that everything he's wearing is mine, down to his shoes.

VOLP: So it is, by God. This is the strangest thing in the world. Did you ask him who dressed him in your clothes?

CRIS: How do you expect me to ask him if he doesn't know how to reply and if he's dumb?

VOLP: Speak to him by means of signs. Let me ask him, for I understand him no less than I understand you.

CRIS: Well, ask him.

VOLP: Who gave you my master's gown? This thing, this thing, where did you get it?

CRIS: (Whereas others talk with their tongues, this lunatic talks with his hands.) Do you know what he's saying?

VOLP: He clearly indicates that someone from this house took his clothes and left him with these until he returns; that's why he was waiting here.

CRIS: Someone from this house? Then ask him, if you can, to indicate which one in my household it was.

VOLP: I will. Hey!

CRIS: (I could watch his hands for a hundred years and I still wouldn't be able to make any sense out of it.) What does he mean when he raises his hand or when he touches his head or face?

VOLP: He indicates that it was someone tall and thin, who has a large nose and white hair and who speaks hurriedly.

CRIS: I think that he means Nebbia, for no one else in the house is built like that. But how does he know that he speaks hurriedly? Can he hear, then?

VOLP: I didn't say that he speaks hurriedly, but that he left hurriedly. There's no mistaking it; he means Nebbia. You understood it sooner than I did.

CRIS: What did the fool hope to accomplish by taking the mute's clothes?

VOLP: Now I realize why. He must have fled when he noticed that the coffer was missing, and, in order not to be recognized, he changed his clothes.

CRIS: Why didn't he leave this fellow his own clothes instead of mine?

VOLP: How the devil should I know? Don't you know how crazy he is?

CRIS: Take him into the house and give him some old cloak so that he won't soil my gown.

VOLP: Leave it to me.

CRIS: (It could be quite otherwise; yes, indeed, it could be. One mustn't believe everything Volpino says; he isn't an evangelist.) Don't go yet, Volpino; wait a moment. Didn't the procurer say that a merchant had given him the coffer? And didn't he describe him, if I remember correctly, as being dressed precisely in this manner?

VOLP: Would you rely on the stories of that thief?

CRIS: You aren't any better, and I've relied on you. But now I'll do otherwise. Rosso, Gallo, Marochio, seize him and tie him up.

VOLP: Why are you doing this?

CRIS: I'm going to send him to the lieutenant-governor to see whether he can cure his speechlessness by means of a rope.

VOLP: Don't I know whether he's a mute? Yet, if you think that he's pretending, I'll take him to the procurer; and if he's the merchant whom you suspect, I'll know it right away.

CRIS: I don't want to delay this any longer. Hurry up and, if you cannot find any, take the rope from the well. Tie his hands behind his back; but, damn you, first take my gown off him.

TRAP: Forgive me, Volpino. As long as it was only a matter of words, I was willing to serve you . . .

VOLP: (Oh, God!)

TRAP: . . . but I won't be crippled or killed because of you.

CRIS: Oh, blessed rope, nay miraculous rope, which heals the dumb so quickly! If someone put it around your neck, Volpino, do you think that it would cure you of your villainy? Now answer me: who gave you my clothes?

TRAP: Your son and this fellow dressed me like this today.

CRIS: For what purpose?

TRAP: To send me to pick up a woman from the procurer's house.

CRIS: Were you the one who took my coffer there?

TRAP: They sent me with a chest that I was to leave there in trust, and I did so.

CRIS: So, Volpino, you had the audacity to place my goods in the hands of a fleeing pimp and in such danger; and this is how you give such good advice to my son, whom I asked you to look after. And this is how you mock me and cheat me as if I were the biggest fool in the world. You'll not boast of it, by God.——Let that one alone and tie up this traitor.

VOLP: Oh Master, your son forced me to do this; and you left me as his servant, not as his guardian or teacher.

CRIS: If I don't drop dead tonight, I'll make an example of you to these others so that they'll never again defraud me.

VOLP: Oh Master! . . .

CRIS: I'll teach you, you villain.——You, come inside now, for I want to hear the whole story.

Scene Eight
FULCIO, *alone*

FUL: Things are going badly for all of us, but especially for Volpino. How fickle Fortune has turned everything upside down! She had been so favorable to us for a while and would have remained so had she not been interrupted by the short memory of this fool. I don't know what else to do but to persuade Caridoro to abandon this project, for, if I cannot see to it that his amorous desires are satisfied, perhaps I'll be able to convince him that this would be best for his honor and peace of mind.

But alas, what will I accomplish by this? What good will my speaking to him do? No good, by God. If the unhappy Caridoro were to be diverted too abruptly from this badly managed scheme of Volpino, it would sooner lead him into dangerous despair than bring him to reason! Besides, if he doesn't succeed through my help in satisfying his desires, won't I incur great and eternal infamy? It will seem that I'm not able to hatch a plot unless I always have Volpino at my side to instruct me; and, despite the schemes that I've brought off successfully in the past, if I fail here, now that I'm alone, all the glory will go to Volpino. May God prevent me from being known as his disciple and may He save me from having such an ugly blemish mar my face! What shall I do then? I'll ... How will I do it? I'll ... No, it's no good. I'll be found out. What if I go about it in a different way?... But which way?... This way ... It would be the same. Let's try this other way; perhaps it's better. No, it isn't. Yet, it's not bad; it might suffice. But who could carry out such a scheme?... Maybe it will be good; it certainly will be. It will be excellent; it will be perfect. I've found it; I figured it out. This is how I'll do it, and it will work perfectly. I'll show them that I'm not a disciple, but the master of masters. Well, then, I'm advancing with an army of lies to inflict the first defeat upon this avaricious pimp. So favor me, Fortune, and if my plan succeeds I vow to you that I'll stay drunk for three whole days. Behold, she's answering my prayers, for she sends my enemy to me disarmed.

Scene Nine
LUCRANO; FULCIO

LUCR: (The more I delay in complaining, the more I weaken my case. I waited for Furba so that he could come with me; but, since he hasn't appeared, I'll go alone.)

FUL: Oh, God, I hope I find Lucrano at home ...

LUCR: (He mentioned my name.)

FUL: ... so that I can inform him of the ruin descending upon him ...

LUCR: (What is he talking about?)

FUL: ... so that at least he may save his life....

LUCR: (Oh dear!)

FUL: However, unless he receives some stroke of luck I think he's finished.

LUCR: Don't bother to knock, Fulcio; here I am if you're looking for me.

FUL: Oh unhappy, oh unfortunate Lucrano, what are you doing here? Why don't you run away?

LUCR: Why should I run away?

FUL: Why aren't you hiding? Why don't you disappear? Flee, you poor beggar.

LUCR: Why do you want me to flee?

FUL: You'll be hanged at once, right away, immediately, if they find you.

LUCR: Who would have me hanged?

FUL: My master, the governor. Run away, I tell you. Are you still here? Flee, you poor soul.

LUCR: What have I done that merits the gallows?

FUL: You've stolen from your neighbor, Crisobolo.

LUCR: That's not true.

FUL: He found the stolen goods in your house in the presence of witnesses. You're still hanging around? Run quickly, run. What are you doing?

LUCR: Maybe the governor will listen to my part of the story....

FUL: Don't waste time with idle talk, poor man. Run like the devil, run; the chief-of-police isn't twenty yards away. He has a warrant to hang you on the spot and he's bringing the hangman with him. Flee; disappear fast.

LUCR: Ah, Fulcio, please help me. I've always liked you ever since I first met you, and I've tried to please you whenever I could.

FUL: And this is why I came to warn you.

LUCR: I thank you for it.

FUL: If my master knew about it, he'd hang me along with you; so run, and don't croak any more.

LUCR: Woe is me! My house and my possessions!

FUL: What house? What possessions? Run like hell.

LUCR: Where should I go?

FUL: How do I know? I've done my duty; if you're hanged it's your own fault. I don't want to be hanged along with you.

LUCR: Ah, Fulcio, Fulcio!

FUL: Don't mention my name, may you be drawn and quartered!

Let no one hear you and report to my master that I warned you.

LUCR: Please don't leave me; I plead with you.

FUL: I plead with you to go to the gallows. I wouldn't, for anything in the world, want the governor to be told that I had spoken to you.

LUCR: Oh, for God's sake, listen a moment!

FUL: I can't wait a minute longer, for I think I hear something and I'm sure it's the chief-of-police.

LUCR: I'll come with you.

FUL: Don't come; run some place else.

LUCR: I'm coming anyway.

ACT FIVE
SCENE ONE
FULCIO; EROFILO; FURBA

FUL: With these and with other words and gestures, which worked with great success, I so frightened the fool that he came running after me all over the city. At every little sound he heard he shook like a leaf, as if he had the chief-of-police and the entire police force constantly on his trail.

ERO: I'm amazed that, knowing himself to be innocent of such charges, as in truth he is, he didn't have the courage to show up [at the courthouse].

FUL: How could he have the courage to show up, if I had convinced him that the chief-of-police had the strictest orders to hang him as soon as he found him, without examination or trial?

ERO: I don't see how he believed you so readily.

FUL: Don't think it strange, because my master has played similar tricks on others like him in the past, so much does he hate the name of procurer! Lucrano is well aware of this, just as he is aware of my master's short temper, for he's known him elsewhere.

ERO: Yet, knowing his innocence . . .

FUL: What? Even if he is innocent of this, in how many other crimes do you think he's implicated, the smallest of which merits a thousand hangings? He knows that he's a scoundrel, and it would be madness to go to jail and perhaps undergo torture. And, even if he were to acquit himself of one false accusation, he would run the risk of uncovering other real crimes that would easily get him condemned to death.

ERO: How come he risked going to Caridoro's room?

FUL: I gave him to understand that the governor, who had decided to have him hanged no matter what, had ordered that, if he were not found in the course of the night, no boat would be allowed to leave the island until by means of a thorough investigation and ban every house was searched until he was found. With this story and an infinite number of other lies, I brought him to such a state of desperation that I know of no tower so high that he wouldn't have leaped from it in order to be able to flee from here. Then, pretending that I wanted to save him, I suggested that he take refuge with Caridoro, whom I knew to be his friend; I told him that if he could not get help or advice from him, he could not hope to get it from anyone else.

ERO: And so you brought him there?

FUL: I jabbered so much that I finally got him there. I wish you could have seen him—pale, tearful, and trembling, asking, entreating, imploring Caridoro to have pity on him, embracing his knees, kissing his feet, and offering him, not only the girl, but all his worldly goods.

ERO: Hah, hah, hah, hah, hah!

FUL: You should have seen Caridoro, on his part, pretending to have pity on him, but feigning fear of incurring his father's wrath and begging Lucrano to get out of the house and not cause him to fall into disfavor with the very person whom he should revere and obey above all others.

ERO: Hah, hah, hah, hah!

FUL: If only you had seen me between the two, pleading for the poor fellow and proposing to Caridoro ways to help him out.

ERO: Hah, hah, hah! It would have been impossible for me to refrain from laughing.

FUL: Finally, I advised Lucrano to send for Corisca, whose presence would better dispose the young man to help him. He agreed to the suggestion; and he wrote this note and gave me this ring as a token. So now I'm going to get the woman, whose arrival I'm sure will settle everything.

ERO: Then the procurer is waiting for you in Caridoro's room?

FUL: Oh, I didn't tell you the best part. So that he wouldn't be seen by others in the household and those who come and go, we had him hide under the bed, where he remains, frightened out of his wits; he doesn't even dare breathe lest he be heard.

ERO: The fact that Caridoro has had such fine success in his love affair doubles my happiness in having found my Eulalia. Finding her now, after the many worries and fears that I had lost her forever, has given me more pleasure than if our merchant had brought her to me when I first waited for her; for in the course of waiting I had already dissipated a great part of my joy and had almost gotten over it.

FUL: So it is that the more unexpected a good thing is, the more pleasing it is when it comes.

ERO: In the same way an unexpected misfortune is more upsetting than one anticipated. I have proof of this right now with the horrible news you brought me that my father has returned, that he knows about our whole scheme, and that our adviser, Volpino, is in prison.

FUL: You can easily find a remedy for all these misfortunes. With a few good words to your father he'll be happy to forgive you and do what you wish, provided that you show him obedience and respect. Once peace is established between you, you'll be able to free Volpino from the danger in which he finds himself. It's up to you to save him, Erofilo.

ERO: I'll do what I can.

FUL: There's one other thing, no less important, that we still have to do.

ERO: What's that?

FUL: We must see to it that the procurer leaves tomorrow at dawn.

ERO: Let him go. Who's preventing him from leaving?

FUL: He doesn't have a penny[15] to his name—I can assure you— to pay for his departure with his servants and belongings and with which to live on during the trip.

ERO: Speak to anyone but me about this, for I have no money to give him.

FUL: Borrow it from someone; it won't impoverish you.

ERO: From whom?

FUL: From the Jew if no one else will help you out.

ERO: And what can I give him as security?

FUL: If you give me twenty-five or thirty saraffi that would be sufficient.

ERO: It's no use speaking to me; I don't have it and I don't know whom I can get it from.

FUL: Caridoro will then find enough to make fifty.

ERO: If I knew where to get it, you wouldn't have had to ask me.

FUL: What shall we do then?

ERO: You think of something.

FUL: I'm thinking; couldn't you give me some of it?

ERO: I couldn't give you any; you're wasting your breath. If you put your mind to it you'll find a way to do without it.

FUL: By no means can we do without it.

ERO: Well, then, you find it.

FUL: I'm thinking about where to find it.

ERO: Think harder.

FUL: I'm still thinking; perhaps, perhaps I'll find it.

ERO: I have such confidence in your ingenuity that even if none existed in the world you would create it out of nothing.

FUL: All right, then, leave it to me, for I hope to find it tonight. First I'll hurry and take the girl to Caridoro; then I'll concentrate on finding the money.——Hey, you going in there ; stop whoever you are. I want to talk to you a moment.

FURBA: Even if you owned me you shouldn't have commanded me with such arrogance; if you need me, then follow me.

FUL: This fellow clearly shows whose servant he is, so well does he imitate his master's haughty manners.

Scene Two
EROFILO; CRISOBOLO

ERO: (I'll go into the house and try to appease my father; if it weren't a matter of helping Volpino I wouldn't dare face him for ten days. But who's opening the door? Heavens, it's him! I feel my heart pounding.)

CRIS: How late the others are in returning! I still don't see them coming from any direction. Where could these rascals be at this hour? If this is what I find when I'm gone for half a day, what would happen if I were to stay away for three or four months! The next time that villain tries to deceive me, I'll surely forgive him. What a fool I was to listen to his stories!

ERO: (I'm still not sure whether I ought to show my face or stay away.)

CRIS: If, with his cunning, he's able to slip out of the shackles in which I placed him, I'll let him put me in his place.

ERO: (I must finally take courage; otherwise Volpino will be in for it.)

CRIS: Are you here, you good-for-nothing?

ERO: Oh Father, didn't you leave? When did you return?

CRIS: How do you dare face me, you rascal, you brazen young man?

ERO: Father, I regret from the bottom of my heart having upset you.

CRIS: If you're really telling the truth, you would behave better than you do. Oh, well, I'll punish you some other time when you think I've forgotten about it.

ERO: Next time I'll be better advised, and I'll never give you cause to complain about me.

CRIS: I don't want you to promise me with words what you continually try to take away from me with deeds. I didn't think, Erofilo, that the well-behaved child whom I brought up with such care would turn out to be one of the wickedest and most licentious young men in this city. I expected you to be a cane to support me in my old age; but, instead, you turn out to be a cane with which to beat me, to shatter me, and to make me die before my time.

ERO: Oh, Father!

CRIS: You call me "Father"; but then you show with your deeds that you're my worst mortal enemy.

ERO: Forgive me, father.

CRIS: If it weren't for your mother's honor, I would deny that you were my son. I don't see any resemblance to me in your manners, and I would much rather you resembled me in your good deeds than in your looks.

ERO: Blame it on my youth.

CRIS: Don't you think that I, too, was young once? At your age I was always at your grandfather's side, and with hard work and sweat I helped him increase our patrimony and property, which you, prodigal and foolish as you are, try to diminish and waste away with your lasciviousness. In my youth it was always my objective to gain the esteem of upright men; I conversed with them and attempted to imitate them as best I could. You, on the contrary, frequent pimps, cheaters, drunkards, and other such riffraff. If you were truly my son you would be ashamed to be seen in their company.

ERO: I've erred, Father; forgive me. You can be assured that this will be the last time my misbehavior will make you angry with me.

CRIS: I swear to God, Erofilo, that if you don't mend your ways you'll know my anger to your great displeasure. If sometimes I pretend not to see you, don't think that because of this I'm blind. If you won't do your duty, I'll do mine. There's less harm in being without a son than in having a wicked one.

ERO: In the future, Father, I'll try to be more obedient.

CRIS: If you try to lead a good life, you'll be doing something that not only pleases me very much and is becoming to you but will be for your own benefit; you can be certain of this.

SCENE THREE
FULCIO, MARSO, *servants*

FUL: [*To Furba inside*] Must I wait here all night, as if I didn't have anything else to do? You take care of things until I return; I'm just going nearby.——These females certainly spend enough time making themselves up. They never finish: they change their hairdo ten different times before they're satisfied. And then what do they do? First they take the cosmetics—and with what patience!—the white, then the red; they put it on; they take it off; they adjust it; they wipe it off, and then they begin again, returning to the mirror a thousand times to look at themselves and contemplate. Oh, how much care is taken, oh how much time is wasted in plucking their eyebrows, in lifting their breasts, in emphasizing their hips, in washing themselves, in oiling their hands, in cutting their nails, in rubbing themselves, and in brushing their teeth! Oh, how many little boxes, phials, jars, how many knickknacks they put to use! It would take less time to arm a galley completely.

In the meantime, I can carry on the battle that I vowed against Crisobolo with greater ease. As I already have conquered the largest fortress, before the enemy is able to set up its artillery, I want to overcome the last pocket of resistance, which is the purse of that most tenacious old man. If everything works out as I hope, I'll have broken, vanquished, and exterminated all enemies; and I alone will have the glory. Now, by knocking on this door I'll assault the guards unawares.

MARSO: Who's there?

FUL: Inform Crisobolo that a courier from his lordship the governor has a message for him.

MARSO: Why don't you come inside?

FUL: Tell him that there are good reasons why he should come outside and that I'm here about something very important concerning him.

SCENE FOUR
CRISOBOLO; FULCIO

CRIS: Who wants me at this ungodly hour?

FUL: Don't be surprised, and forgive me for having called you outside; but I have something highly secret to tell you and I was afraid that being inside we might be heard by those who would then report what I say. Out here I can easily look around and be sure that I'm not overheard by someone whom I cannot see. But let's go further out into the street; and tell your servants to stay inside.

CRIS: You, wait for me inside the house.——Now, tell me what you want.

FUL: First of all, I must greet you in the name of Caridoro, the son of the governor of Mytilene, who, because of his friendship with your son, esteems you and loves you as a father; and for this reason, when he sees that he can do something useful for you and to your honor and can help you avoid censure and injury, he will never fail to do so.

CRIS: I thank him and I'll always be obliged to him.

FUL: Now listen. As he was leaving the house to take a stroll, as young men are accustomed to do—and I was with him—we came upon a certain procurer, as your luck would have it, in front of the palace, and he claimed to be a neighbor of yours....

CRIS: Well, then!

FUL: He was shouting angrily. There were two people with him, whose identity I don't know, to whom he was complaining a great deal about you and your son.

CRIS: What was he saying?

FUL: If Caridoro hadn't stopped him he was going to go straight to the governor to complain about a fraud committed against him by your son; and, really, if he's telling the truth, it's a very serious charge.

CRIS: (Now see what trouble is in prospect for me because of the foolishness of my son!)

FUL: He said that a certain cheat, dressed as a merchant . . .

CRIS: (Ah, you see that!...)

FUL: . . . had been sent to him with a certain deposit in exchange for taking one of his women. I didn't hear all the details, for Caridoro sent me running to warn you in such a great hurry.

CRIS: He's done the duty of a good friend.

FUL: And the two persons who I told you are with the procurer seem ready to testify on his behalf and accuse you.

CRIS: Of what?

FUL: They claim that the cheat who committed the fraud is in your house and that the whole thing was done with your approval.

CRIS: With my approval?

FUL: So he says; and I also seem to have heard that you went in person to the procurer's house to seize a strongbox or a coffer.

CRIS: Ah, how the frivolity of a young man, urged on by the prodding of a rascal, can be the cause of so much evil!

FUL: I cannot relate all the details. As I was in a hurry to let you know, I was able to understand them only vaguely. Caridoro sent me to tell you that he'll prevent the procurer from speaking to the governor as long as possible. In the meantime you should find a remedy in order to avoid not only the damage, which would be considerable, but the public disgrace that you and your son would receive.

CRIS: What remedy can I find? See how misfortunes always follow me!

FUL: Have the girl returned to him or give him some money[16] to keep him quiet.

CRIS: I would gladly give him back the girl; but it seems that through their stupidity [my servants] allowed her to be taken away, they don't know by whom.

FUL: Then Erofilo doesn't have the girl with him?

CRIS: No, I tell you, and he doesn't know what's become of her.

FUL: This is even worse. What can be done, then?

CRIS: How should I know? I'm the most unfortunate and most miserable man in the world.

FUL: The simplest and best thing to do is to pay him what he would have got for the girl had he sold her to someone else, and that will keep him quiet.

CRIS: It seems strange to me to have to spend my money on something by which I won't profit.

FUL: One cannot always profit, Crisobolo; however, it's more than a small gain to invest a little money in order to avoid considerable injury and the public disgrace that it might bring. If such a complaint reaches the ears of the governor what will your situation be? Will it not be necessary to undergo a lawsuit? to have your son called to the dock? and to have your name shouted about? Besides this, think of it, you have the reputation of being the richest man in this city; while many others might get away with paying hundreds in compensation, you couldn't even get by with paying thousands. You see what I mean.

CRIS: What do you think I should do?

FUL: This procurer is poor and timid, like others in his trade. If the girl were paid for we would keep him quiet. Caridoro has already given him to understand that if he persists in taking you to court it wouldn't do him much good, for you have enough money to keep the suit going a whole lifetime; and that you also have friends and relatives who will one day make him regret having bothered you.

CRIS: Do you know how much he wants for the girl, or what he could have gotten for her?

FUL: I was told that a Wallachian soldier had offered him a hundred saraffi, and he refused; he wouldn't let her go for less than a hundred and twenty.

CRIS: One could buy a herd of cows for less. That's far too much; I won't have anything to do with it. Let him complain and do the worst he can.

FUL: It seems strange that you value such a small amount....

CRIS: A small amount?

FUL: ...more than your son, than yourself, than your honor. I'll tell Caridoro, then, that you don't intend to do anything.

CRIS: Couldn't we keep this procurer quiet for less?

FUL: One could slit his throat and that would cost less.

CRIS: I don't mean that. One hundred and twenty saraffi is a high price.

FUL: Maybe you can keep him quiet for a hundred; this is the same price that he could have got from others.

CRIS: And not with less?

FUL: How do I know? I wish, for your sake, that I could keep him quiet for nothing. If I were Crisobolo, though, I would send Erofilo at once with some money to see Caridoro; with all of us opposing the procurer we would arrange matters with the least possible expense to you.

CRIS: It's better if I go myself.

FUL: For heaven's sake, no! If the procurer sees that you're interested in this matter he'll think that your son cheated him with your consent; and he'll hesitate and be as stubborn as possible, hoping to get you to pay more. On the contrary, I think it best for Erofilo to go alone and to pretend that he's seeking this accord without your knowledge and that he managed to get the money from friends or from moneylenders.

CRIS: Erofilo go alone? Naturally, by God, for he's so cautious! He would immediately be taken in and led by his nose like a buffalo.

FUL: Don't you have any servants who are shrewd and experienced whom you could send with him? What about your Volpino? He's capable and quick-witted, and he's as good as one could ask for.

CRIS:That little thief was the cause, the director, and the chief instigator of all this knavery. I have him in irons and I'll treat him as he deserves.

FUL: Don't let your anger get the better of you, Crisobolo. Send him with Erofilo; you couldn't do any better.

CRIS: By any standard he's the worst rascal alive. However, as there is no one else in my household who knows how to put two words together, I have no alternative but to have recourse to him. I regret having to do so, though.

FUL: Forget it for now; you'll be able to punish him some other time.

CRIS: God only knows how hard it is for me to chew this bone. But let it be. Don't go away; I'll send both of them with you right now.

FUL: I'll wait for them.——Now comes the triumph that I deserve, for I've routed and totally defeated my enemies without any bloodshed, without any injury to my forces. I've razed their strongholds and all their fortresses and I've made them all in different ways tributaries of my treasury, and this I hadn't even hoped for at the beginning.

Nothing remains to be done now except to fulfill the vow that I made to you, Fortune, to stay drunk for three full days. I'll willingly fulfill it and I'll begin as soon as I have the time. But here are my soldiers coming out of Crisobolo's house, laden with booty and spoils of the enemy; and they can attribute their good fortune only to my talents and my abilities.

Scene Five

VOLPINO; EROFILO; FULCIO

VOLP: I'll try to keep him quiet with as little expense as possible. I'll do more than if you were there in person and I know that you'll be pleased with me.

ERO: Oh, Fulcio, how can I ever thank you for the great favors you've done for me? If I gave you everything that I have in the world, I don't think I could discharge my obligation to you.

FUL: It's enough for me that you regard me kindly.

ERO: But where is my only hope, my refuge, my true salvation?

VOLP: Fulcio, you've delivered this life of mine from immense tribulation, great fear, and the cruelest of torments; whenever you wish I'm ready to sacrifice it for you.

FUL: These are favors that we do for one another, Volpino. Erofilo, do you think I was able to get enough money?

ERO: Much more than we thought necessary.

FUL: I wanted to have enough so that, apart from paying the procurer, you would be able to support the girl, and there would be some for her expenses and other things that she may need.

ERO: Here, take all of it and do what you want with it.

FUL: Keep it yourself and bring it with you; as soon as I've taken Corisca to Caridoro, I'll meet you at the Moor's Inn.[17]——

You in the audience may as well go home, for the girl whom I'm going to take doesn't want to be seen coming out; and, as the procurer has to flee, it would not be proper for there to be too many witnesses. And give us a sign of your enjoyment.

The play was written in 1507 and first performed in the ducal theater in Ferrara on 5 March 1508. A second performance did not take place in Ferrara until 24 January 1529, by which time Ariosto had completed three other plays and had started a fourth. Soon after the second performance, Ariosto, apparently annoyed by errors and omissions in a number of editions, completely rewrote the play in verse, lengthening it and making stylistic and dramatic changes, but keeping the plot essentially unchanged.

1. The principal city on the island of Lesbos, a place whose reputation for immorality makes it an appropriate setting for the play. See Lucrano's soliloquy in Act One, Scene Six. The island itself, at one time, was called Mytilene.

2. Another name for the island of Eubea, the largest of the Aegean Islands.

3. The text has *Bassa*—that is, Pasha, a Turkish governor.

4. The *quattrino* was a small copper coin used in various Italian states from the twelfth to the nineteenth century. The name derives from its value in Florence, which was four *denarii*.

5. There is some discrepancy here between the earliest editions of the play and the standard modern texts of Catalano, Borlenghi, and Segre. In the Zucchetta edition of 1510 as well as in the Venetian printing of 1525 it is Erofilo who says: "Give me your hand, Eulalia; give me your hand, Corisca. Today or tomorrow, without fail, we'll free you; if not may we be . . . ," to which Eulalia replies: "Listen to them. As soon as you turn your backs on us, you laugh at our troubles." We have followed the modern texts.

6. Here is one of the earliest references to the reputation of the Spanish for plundering.

7. The last sentence of Lucrano's speech, along with Furba's reply, were written in obscure underworld jargon of the period. Lucrano orders his servant: *Spuleggia de non calarte in solfa per questa marca, che al cordoan si mochi la schioffia;* to which Furba replies: *Ciffo ribaco il contrapunto.* Ariosto uses jargon, which commonly appears in popular writings of the day, as a device by which Lucrano, while shouting loudly enough for Erofilo to hear, can let Furba know that his going to the port is only a ruse to trick Erofilo into buying Eulalia, and that he need not go. Furba's reply indicates that he understands his master. On Ariosto's use of contemporary jargon see R. Renier, "Cenni sull'uso dell'antico gergo furbesco nella letteratura italiana," in *Miscellanea di studi critici in onore di Arturo Graf* (1903), pp. 123 ff.

8. *Bargello*: the name given to the officer in charge of public security in a number of Italian states, and, in particular, in Florence. The famous Bargello Palace in Florence was so named because it was the residence of the chief of police.

9. There is a double meaning intended here. While the "miter" and "standard" are the traditional signs of office of cardinals and bishops, Ariosto uses the words to refer to something less honorable. The hat that was placed derisively on a condemned man was called a "miter"; and the "standard" was a placard he carried revealing his crime.

10. The *saraffi* or *seraph* or *ashrafi* was a gold coin of Persian origin then in wide use in Egypt and other Arabic lands; it was comparable in value to the Venetian *ducat*.

11. The last two speeches of Act Three, like the closing lines of Act One, are in jargon and cannot be translated literally. In order to convey the sense of the dialogue, it has been necessary to alter the original text in which Lucrano's final speech is omitted and his lines become a continuation of Furba's. The decision to divide the last speech between Furba and Lucrano is in accord with the Segre text (Catalano follows the original) and finds support in the verse edition (see the last two speeches of Act Three). Thus, Furba, thinking that Lucrano's question as to whether the ship is leaving is still part of the ruse, asks his master (*Non gli selasti col furbido in berta?*) whether he has not finished with his little joke. Lucrano replies, likewise in jargon (*Trucca de bella al mazo de la lissa, e cantagli se vol calarsi de Brunoro, c'ho il fiore in pugno, e comperar vo' il mazo*), to indicate that now he really wants Furba to see about leaving that night, for he has the goods in hand and wants to flee.

12. Calibassa may refer to the lower portion of the city or the port area (*calle:* road; *bassa:* low); it could also be a textual error, the original being *da casa il Bassa* (from the governor's house).

13. The text has *Plutero*, indicating perhaps the name of an official.

14. The allusion here is to the legendary gentlemen who, when left without servants, continued to accompany each other home until dawn so that neither would have to return home by himself in the dark.

15. The text has *aspro* (asper)—a silver coin of small value.

16. See n. 15.

17. The Moor's Inn was a famous tavern in Ferrara. See Ariosto, *Satira* 2, l. 67.

THE PRETENDERS

I Suppositi

A Prose Comedy

Characters

NURSE	
POLINESTA	*Young lady, Damone's daughter*
CLEANDRO	*Doctor of Law*
PASIFILO	*Parasite*
EROSTRATO	*Scholar*
DULIPPO	*His servant*
CAPRINO	*Boy, Erostrato's servant*
SIENESE	*Traveler from Siena*
SERVANT	*His servant*
CARIONE	*Cleandro's servant*
DALIO	*Cook in Erostrato's household*
DAMONE	*Polinesta's father*
NEBBIA	*Damone's servant*
PSITERIA	*Damone's housemaid*
FILOGONO	*Erostrato's father*
FERRARAN	
LICO	*Filogono's servant*
ROSSO (silent)	} *Damone's servants*
MORO (silent)	

The action takes place in Ferrara

PROLOGUE[1]

W E ARE ABOUT TO HAVE YOU WITNESS A NEW COMEDY BY the same author who presented the *Coffer*[2] to you last year. It is called the *Pretenders* because it is full of substitution and pretense.[3] As you know, children have been substituted for one another in the past, and sometimes are today. You have seen this in plays, and you have also read about it in history books. Perhaps there is someone in the audience who may have either experienced it personally or at least have heard about it. But, to have young men substituted for old men must certainly seem new and strange to you; and, yet, this has occasionally been done, as you will see very clearly in our new story. Don't take these substitutions in a bad sense, my good audience, for they are not like the substitutions illustrated in the lascivious books of Elephantis,[4] or those others imagined by Sophists in their contentious dialectics.

In this play, among other things, the servant is substituted for the master and the master for the servant. The author confesses that in this he has followed both Plautus and Terence, the one who substituted Cherea for Dorus, the other Philocrates for Tindarus and vice versa, one in the *Eunuchus*, and the other in the *Captivi*. He has done so because he wants to imitate the celebrated classical poets as much as possible, not only in the form of their plays, but also in the content. And just as they in their Latin plays followed Menander, Apollodorus, and other Greek writers, so he, too, in his vernacular plays is not averse to imitating the methods and procedure of the Latin writers.

And so, as I told you, he has taken part of the plot for his *Pretenders* from Terence's *Eunuchus* and part from Plautus's *Captivi*, but so little, indeed, that if either Terence or Plautus knew, they would not be offended and would call it poetic imitation rather than plagiarism. Whether or not the author should be condemned for this he leaves to your discretion; but he asks you not to pass judgment before you have heard the new story in its entirety, a story that unfolds part by part. And, if you deign to give this play the same kind attention that you gave to his previous one, he's sure that you will not be less satisfied. So be it.

ACT ONE
SCENE ONE
NURSE and POLINESTA, *a young lady*

NURSE: No one is about. Come outside, Polinesta, where we're not confined and where we can be sure that no one will hear us;

I believe that in the house the beds, the cupboards, and even the doors have ears.

POLI: The vases and pots and pans have ears also.

NURSE: You jest, but for heaven's sake, you would be better advised to be more cautious than you have been. I warned you a thousand times to take care lest you be seen talking to Dulippo.

POLI: Why shouldn't I speak to him as I do to others?

NURSE: I've told you "why" many times, but you don't listen to me, and this will bring ruin upon yourself, Dulippo, and me.

POLI: Oh, yes, the danger is so great!

NURSE: You'll see. Isn't it enough that through my help you and Dulippo spend the night together, even though I arranged this rather unwillingly. How I wish you were inclined toward a more respectable love than the one in which you're involved. What a shame that you've rejected so many noble youths who would have loved you and taken you as a wife. Instead you've chosen as a lover one of your father's servants from whom you can expect nothing but disgrace.

POLI: Who was the cause of it all but you, Nurse? It was you who didn't cease to endear him to me—now praising his beauty, now his fine manners, convincing me that he loved me exceedingly—until I became fond of him, and finally fell in love with him.

NURSE: It's true that from the beginning I recommended him to you because of my compassion for him and his continual pleading.

POLI: You mean because of the compensation and the payment you were getting.

NURSE: You can believe what you will; still, you can be certain that if I had thought then that you would progress this far, neither pity nor compensation, penny nor paternoster, would have brought me to speak his cause.

POLI: Who brought him into my bed the first night, if not you? Who other than you? Be quiet, for God's sake, or you'll make me say something foolish.

NURSE: Now, it's I who am the cause of all your misfortune!

POLI: Rather of all my good fortune. I'll have you know, Nurse, that it is not Dulippo whom I love, nor a servant, for I've given my heart more worthily than you think; but I'll say no more now.

NURSE: I'm glad that you've changed your mind.

POLI: On the contrary, I haven't changed it at all, nor do I intend to.

NURSE: What are you talking about then?

POLI: I don't love Dulippo, or a servant, and I haven't changed nor will I change my mind.

NURSE: Either this doesn't make sense or I don't understand. Please speak clearly.

POLI: I won't say anything more, for I promised not to tell.

NURSE: Do you hesitate to tell me for fear that I'll reveal it? You trust me in matters of honor and life and now you're afraid to tell me something that I'm sure is of little consequence compared to the secrets I already know.

POLI: This matter is more important than you think; yet I would willingly tell it to you if you promise not only to be silent, but also to refrain from giving any sign by which you might be suspected of knowing it.

NURSE: I give you my word; so speak freely.

POLI: I want you to know that the young man known as Dulippo is really a Sicilian nobleman. His true name is Erostrato, and he's the son of Filogono, one of the richest men in that country.

NURSE: What? Erostrato? Isn't Erostrato, the son of Filogono, that neighbor of ours, who . . .

POLI: Be quiet if you will and listen to me. The person whom you take for Dulippo, I told you, is Erostrato. He came to this city to pursue his studies. No sooner had he landed when he met me on the Via Grande; he immediately fell in love with me, and his love was so vehement that he suddenly changed his mind and cast aside his books and his long gown and determined that I alone would be the subject of his study. And in order to see me and talk with me more readily, he exchanged clothes, name, and status with Dulippo, the only servant whom he took with him from Sicily. So, that very day, Erostrato, master and scholar, became Dulippo, a servant, and dressed as you saw him, a student of love dealings. He plotted in such a way that before long he managed to become one of my father's servants.

NURSE: Are you sure about this?

POLI: Absolutely. For his part, Dulippo adopted the name of Erostrato, along with the clothes of his master, his books, and other things relating to studies; and, posing as the son of Filogono, he began to take up literary studies from which he has profited and gained much credit.

NURSE: Are there no other Sicilians here or are there none who have passed through who might have recognized them?

POLI: Hardly anyone who turns up here settles down, and very few pass through.

NURSE: This has been fortunate indeed. But how is it that the student, whom you claim to be Dulippo and not Erostrato, has asked your father for your hand in marriage?

POLI: This is a pretense that he uses to confound that nasty old doctor with the long cap who insists on seeking me as his wife. Alas! Is that not him coming? What a beautiful prospect for a husband! I would rather be a nun than his wife.

NURSE: You're so right. Look how he comes to show off! Oh God, there's nothing so foolish as an old man in love!

SCENE TWO

CLEANDRO, *a doctor of law*; PASIFILO, *a parasite*

CLE: Weren't some people just here in front of that door, Pasifilo?

PAS: Yes, my most learned Cleandro, didn't you see your Polinesta?

CLE: Was it my Polinesta? By God, I didn't recognize her!

PAS: I'm not surprised; the air is dense today, somewhat foggy, and I recognized her more by her clothes than by her face.

CLE: I thank God that at my age I have very good eyesight. I feel I've changed very little since I was twenty-five or thirty years old.

PAS: And why not? Are you so very old?

CLE: I'm fifty-six.

PAS: (That's ten less than he is!)

CLE: What did you say—ten less?

PAS: I said that I thought you to be ten years less; why you don't seem more than thirty-six or thirty-eight at the most.

CLE: I'm nonetheless the age I told you.

PAS: You're at a fine age, and with your good habits you'll live to be a hundred. Let me see your hand.

CLE: Are you a chiromancer?

PAS: Who makes more of a profession of it than I do? Please, show me your hand. Oh, what a beautiful and distinct line. I've never seen one quite that long. You'll live longer than Melchizedek.

CLE: You mean Methuselah.

PAS: I thought they were one and the same.

CLE: You're not very learned in the Bible.

PAS: On the contrary, I'm most learned, but in the contents of a bottle. Oh, what a nice Mount of Venus![5] We're not in a convenient place. I'd like to read it another day when we have more time, and then I'll tell you some things that will please you.

CLE: It will be a great pleasure. But tell me: whom do you think Polinesta would rather have as a husband—Erostrato or me?

PAS: Why, you, without doubt. She's a noble-minded young lady and takes more account of the reputation that she'll acquire by being your wife than that which she could hope to gain as the wife of a scholar whose status in Sicily God only knows!

CLE: Yet he acts very grand in this city.

PAS: Yes, he does so where there's no one to call his bluff. But let him be—your good qualities are worth more than all of Sicily.

CLE: It's not right for me to praise myself; yet I tell you truly, that my knowledge, when I've needed it, has been of more value than all the goods I could have had. I left Otranto, my native city, when it was taken by the Turks,[6] with only the coat on my back. I came first to Padua and then to this city, where as a reader, lawyer, and councillor I amassed, in the space of twenty years, a fortune of fifteen thousand ducats or more.

PAS: These are true virtues. What's philosophy? What's poetry? All other knowledge compared to law is mere nonsense.

CLE: Nonsense! Well said, *unde versus: Opes dat sanctio Justiniana; Ex aliis paleas, ex istis collige grana.*[7]

PAS: Excellent verse! Who wrote it? Vergil?

CLE: What Vergil? It's one of our very best glosses.

PAS: It certainly is an excellent moral, worthy to be set in letters of gold. By now you must have gained more than you had left in Otranto.

CLE: I've made triple that amount; yet the fact is I lost a five-year-old son there, a child who was dearer to me than all the possessions in the world.

PAS: Ah, truly, this was too great a loss!

CLE: I don't know whether he died or whether he still lives in captivity.

PAS: I'm crying out of compassion. But cheer up, for you'll have other children by Polinesta.

CLE: What do you think about Damone's delay?

PAS: He's a father who wishes to have his daughter well placed; before he makes up his mind he wants to think about it and then think again, but I have no doubt that in the end he'll decide in your favor.

CLE: Did you let him know that I'll give him two thousand gold ducats as a wedding gift?[8]

PAS: I told him that a long time ago.

CLE: What was his reply?

PAS: Nothing other than that Erostrato offered the same.

CLE: How can Erostrato commit himself to this without his father's consent?

PAS: Do you think that I neglected to remind him of this? Don't worry, your rival will never have her except, perhaps, in his dreams.

CLE: If you really want to help me, then go, my Pasifilo, and find Damone. Tell him that I ask for nothing but his daughter. I don't want a dowry; I'll endow her myself, and if two thousand ducats aren't enough, I'll add five hundred more, even a thousand and whatever else he wishes. Go, and do the things I know you can do. I don't want anything to make me lose this suit. Don't wait any longer; go now.

PAS: Where will I find you then?

CLE: At my house.

PAS: At what time?

CLE: Whenever you wish. I would invite you to dine with me, but today I'm fasting since it is the vigil of Saint Nicholas, whom I hold in devotion.

PAS: (Fast until you die of hunger.)

CLE: Listen.

PAS: (Speak to the dead, who also fast.)

CLE: Don't you hear me?

PAS: (And don't you understand!)

CLE: Are you hurt because I didn't invite you to dine with me? Still, you can come; you'll eat whatever I do.

PAS: Do you think I lack a place to eat?

CLE: Oh course I don't think so, my dear Pasifilo.

PAS: Be assured that there are some who beg me [to dine with them].

CLE: I'm very certain of it. But I do know that in no other place are you as welcome as in my house. I'll be expecting you.

PAS: Well then, I'll come, since you insist.

CLE: Be sure to bring me good news.

PAS: And you be sure that I find a good meal.

CLE: You'll be pleased.

PAS: And you'll see my work.——What a miserable and avaricious man! He finds an excuse to fast because he doesn't want me to dine with him, as if I had to eat with his mouth and as if he were preparing sumptuous feasts so that I would be obliged to him for an invitation. Not only does he prepare his table parsimoniously, but there is always a very great difference between his food and mine. I never taste the same wine that he drinks, nor the same bread that he eats, and there are the other little attentions that he gets from me since we share the same table. He thinks that because he occasionally has me over for dinner or supper with him, this compensates for the dirty work that I'm always doing for him. There may be some who believe that he has liberally rewarded me in some other way; but I can truly say that never, in the six or seven years that I've been involved in his affairs, has he given me as much as a shoelace-worth. He thinks that I feed on his favor because he sometimes forces himself to say a good word on my behalf.

Oh, if I weren't able to gain a living some other way, I would really be in a fix! But I'm like the beaver or the otter who lives either in water or on land depending upon where the pickings are better. I'm no less a servant of Erostrato than I am of the doctor, friendlier now to one, now to the other, depending upon which one prepares a better meal. I know so well how to stand between the two of them that even though one of them sees or hears that I'm with the other he doesn't lose faith in me, for I lead him to believe that I hang around his rival merely to pry into his secrets. And so whatever I can learn from both of them I report to one or to the other. It doesn't matter to me how this affair turns out. I shall be rewarded whichever of them is the victor.

Ah, here is Dulippo, Damone's servant. I'll find out from him whether his master is at home.

Scene Three
PASIFILO *and the false* DULIPPO

PAS: Where are you going, my gallant Dulippo?

DUL: I'm looking for someone to dine with my master, who is alone.

PAS: Don't trouble yourself any further; you won't find anyone more suitable than me.

DUL: I don't have permission to bring so many.

PAS: What do you mean, "so many?" I'll come alone.

DUL: How can you come alone when there are ten wolves in your stomach?

PAS: Such is the custom of you servants; you hate all your master's friends.

DUL: Do you know why?

PAS: Because they have teeth.

DUL: No, because they have tongues.

PAS: Tongues! And what displeasure did my tongue ever give you?

DUL: I'm joking with you, Pasifilo. Go into the house or you'll be too late, for my master is about to sit down at the table.

PAS: Does he dine so early?

DUL: He who rises early dines early.

PAS: I would willingly live with this man. I'll follow your advice.

DUL: You would be wise to.——It was a sad and unfortunate thing when as a suitable remedy for my desires I decided to exchange my name and dress with my servant and pose as a servant in this house. I had hoped that, just as hunger is relieved by food, thirst by water, cold by fire, and a thousand other such sufferings are alleviated by appropriate remedies, so by continually seeing Polinesta, by frequently talking with her, by furtive embraces, and by being with her almost every night my loving desire would be fulfilled.

Alas, of all human conditions, love alone is insatiable! It is now two years that in the guise of Damone's servant I've been a servant of Cupid, and thanks to him I've obtained as many benefits as any enamored heart could desire, and more of these than other fortunate lovers. But just when I should feel rich among such abundance and find myself satiated, I feel poorer and more desirous than ever. Alas! What will become of me if now she's taken away by Cleandro, who by means of this annoying parasite seeks to procure her as his wife? Then not only would I be deprived of the enjoyment of nocturnal love-making, but even of speaking to her. He would immediately become so jealous that he wouldn't even allow the birds to see her. I had hoped to thwart all the old man's plans by means of my servant who, pretending to be me, with my name, my clothes, and my credit, has offered himself as a rival and competitor for her hand; but every day this crafty doctor devises new schemes to incline Damone to his will. My servant has told me that he intends to set a trap in which this cunning fox would be caught; what he has concocted I don't know, nor have I seen him this morning. Now as I go to take care of the things that my master has ordered, I'll try to find him, at home or wherever he may be, so that in my love's labor I may get from him, if not help, at least hope.

Ah, here is his lackey coming outside just in time.

Scene Four
The false DULIPPO and CAPRINO, a boy

DUL: Oh, Caprino, what of Erostrato?

CAPR: Of Erostrato? Of Erostrato there are books, clothes, money, and many other things that he has in the house.

DUL: Ah, gluttonous one! I ask you to tell me about Erostrato.

CAPR: In prose or in verse?

DUL: If I grab you by your hair that will make you answer to the purpose.

CAPR: Pffft!

DUL: Wait a moment.

CAPR: I haven't the time.

DUL: By God, we'll see which of us can run faster!

CAPR: You should have given me a head start, for your legs are longer than mine.

DUL: Now tell me, Caprino, what about Erostrato?

CAPR: He left the house early this morning and didn't return. I saw him later in the piazza, and he told me to go get this basket and return there, where Dalio is waiting for me. So I'm returning.

DUL: Go then, and if you see him, tell him that I absolutely must speak to him. As a matter of fact, it would be better if I went to the piazza; perhaps I'll find him there.

ACT TWO
Scene One
The false DULIPPO *and the false* EROSTRATO

DUL: If I had a hundred eyes[9] they wouldn't suffice to look for him. I looked in the piazza, in the courtyard,[10] and there isn't a scholar or a doctor in Ferrara whom I haven't met, except for him. Perhaps he went back to the house. Ah, here he is, finally.

ERO: At last, Master, I've found you.

DUL: For God's sake, call me Dulippo; I want you to keep up the reputation that you acquired when you began to use my name.

ERO: It doesn't matter, for there's no one around to hear.

DUL: If you get into the habit you could easily slip where it will be noticed; so be careful. Now, what news do you bring me?

ERO: Good news.

DUL: Good news?

ERO: The very best; we've won the contest.

DUL: Lucky me, if it were true.

ERO: You'll see.

DUL: How?

ERO: Last night I met the parasite and without too much prodding he came with me to supper. There, with a good reception and with better things that followed, we became great friends, so much so that he revealed to me all the plans of Cleandro as well as the wishes of Damone. And he promised from now on to work for my benefit in this matter.

DUL: Don't trust him; he couldn't be more deceptive or a greater liar if he had been born in Crete or Africa.[11]

ERO: I know him for what he is, but I also found that what he told me is the absolute truth.

DUL: Well then, what did he tell you?

ERO: That Damone intends to give his daughter to the doctor, because he offered him two thousand ducats as a wedding settlement.

DUL: And this is the good news, yea, the very best news that you bring me? You say that we've won the contest?

ERO: Don't jump to conclusions before you hear the rest of the story.

DUL: Then continue.

ERO: To this I replied that I was prepared to give as large a wedding gift as Cleandro.

DUL: It was a good reply.

ERO: Wait, though, until you hear where the difficulty lies.

DUL: The difficulty? Is there worse to come?

ERO: How can I, posing as the son of Filogono, undertake such an obligation without his authority and consent?

DUL: You've studied more than I have.

ERO: You haven't wasted your time either, but the exercise book that you have before you doesn't treat of these matters.

DUL: Stop this nonsense and come to the point.

ERO: I told him that I had received word from my father and that I expected him to arrive in this city any day. I asked him that, for my sake, he plead with Damone to put off a decision about the marriage for fifteen days, because I hoped—rather I held for certain—that Filogono would confirm and approve my commitment.

DUL: At least this scheme is useful, in that it prolongs my life another fifteen days. But what will happen then? My father won't come and, even if he does, it may not be in our best interests. Alas! Wretched me! Cursed be ...

ERO: Calm down; don't despair. Do you think that I sleep when there's something to be done for your benefit?

DUL: Ah, my dear friend, revive me! Ever since this whole business began I've continually been in a state worse than death.

ERO: Well, then, listen.

DUL: Out with it.

ERO: This morning I got on my horse and rode out through the Lion's Gate intending to go toward the Polesine to attend to the business you know about; but something better came up that made me change my mind. I had ridden about two miles beyond the Po when I met an elderly gentleman of good appearance who approached in the company of three men on horseback. I greeted him, and he responded graciously. When I asked him whence he came and where he was going he replied that he had come from Venice and was returning to his native city of Siena. Immediately, with an expression full of amazement, I said to him: "You are a Sienese and you come to Ferrara?" And he replied: "And why shouldn't I come here?" I answered: "Good heavens, aren't you aware of the peril that awaits you if you're recognized as a Sienese?" With great astonishment and no less fright he stopped and asked me courteously to explain precisely what I meant.

DUL: I don't see the meaning of this deception.

ERO: I thought you wouldn't; but hear more.

DUL: Continue.

ERO: I then answered him: "My dear Sir, at one time I was a student in your city and I was so courteously and well received there that I feel most affectionately indebted to all Sienese; and thus if injury or disgrace threatens any of you I cannot tolerate it at all. I marvel that you're not aware of the insult that your countrymen gave to the ambassadors of the duke of Ferrara who were passing through Siena on their way back from the king of Naples."[12]

DUL: What story is this you're telling me? How does this nonsense concern my affairs?

ERO: It's not a story I tell you, and it concerns you very much. So listen.

DUL: Go on.

ERO: Then I continued: "The ambassadors had with them several colts, some wagons full of saddles and very beautiful harnesses, sumach, perfumes, and many other fine and luxurious things, all of which King Ferrante was sending to the duke.[13] When they arrived in Siena they were held up by the customs officials; and, despite the license that they had and the witnesses who testified that the goods belonged to the duke, they didn't release them until they paid a duty on every little thing without the remission of a penny, just as if these had been the goods of the most humble merchant in the world."

DUL: It could be that this concerns me; but I still don't make head or tail of it.

ERO: Oh, how impatient you are! But let me continue.

DUL: Go on; I'll listen as long as I can.

ERO: I proceeded to tell him: "As soon as the duke learned of this, he complained to the Sienese Senate both through letters and through an envoy whom he sent there for this purpose; but he received the most insolent and discourteous reply you ever heard. Because of this he was inflamed with such scorn and hatred against all Sienese that he ordered that any who turn up in his territories be stripped to their shirt and driven away with the utmost disgrace."

DUL: How did you invent such a big lie on the spur of the moment, and for what purpose?

ERO: You'll see; and for our purpose a better lie couldn't be found.

DUL: Well, then, I'm awaiting the conclusion.

ERO: You should have heard the expressions I used and have seen the gestures I made in order to persuade him.

DUL: I can imagine, for I know you well.

ERO: I also informed him that the duke ordered all innkeepers in Ferrara, under penalty of death, to notify the officials of any Sienese who lodge with them.

DUL: This also!

ERO: Having heard this, the man of whom I speak—and I realized at once that he wasn't the shrewdest man in the world—started to turn his horse around and retrace his steps.

DUL: No doubt in believing your story he showed little sense. How could he not know what had taken place in his own city?

ERO: It's simple. As he had left Siena more than a month ago, it well could be that he didn't know what had occurred there within the past six days.

DUL: I still say he has little sense.

ERO: I believe he hasn't the slightest bit, and I think it was our good fortune that such a man was sent to us. Now, listen.

DUL: Finish the story.

ERO: As I told you, when he heard these things, he was about to turn back. Then I pretended to think seriously about his predicament, and after a short interval I said to him: "Don't worry my good man, I know an excellent way to save you, and because I love your city I've decided to do anything necessary to prevent you from being recognized in Ferrara as a Sienese. I want you to pretend to be my father, and thus you'll come and lodge with me. I'm a Sicilian from a place called Catania, the son of a merchant named Filogono. Hence you'll say to anyone who asks you that you're Filogono, a Catanese, and that I, who am called Erostrato, am your son, and I'll honor you as my father."

DUL: Ah, what a fool I've been! Now I see your scheme.

ERO: Well, how do you like it?

DUL: Very much. But I have one reservation; one thing bothers me.

ERO: What reservation?

DUL: It seems impossible to me that after being in Ferrara a while and talking to others, he won't soon perceive that you've tricked him.

ERO: How is that?

DUL: It would be easy for him by acting once more as a Sienese to discover that everything you told him is a lie.

ERO: Certainly this could happen had I stopped here without making further provision. But I've already entertained him well and will entertain him even better. I'll honor him so that I'll be able to confide in him without fear and tell him the truth. He won't be so ungrateful then as to refuse to help me in this matter in which all that is required is a few words from him.

DUL: What do you expect him to do then?

ERO: What Filogono would do if he were here and were happy with the marriage. I believe that it won't be too difficult for me to induce him to complete in the name of Filogono any documents, contracts, and other obligations that I'll ask of him. What trouble would it be for him to pledge someone else's name, since he wouldn't suffer the least harm from this?

DUL: Provided that the plan succeeds.

ERO: At least we cannot have any regrets, for we've done everything possible to help ourselves.

DUL: Now, then, where have you left him?

ERO: I had him dismount outside the city at the Crown's Inn; as you know, we have neither hay, straw, nor stalls to accommodate horses at our house.

DUL: Why haven't you brought him with you?

ERO: I wanted to speak to you first and inform you of everything.

DUL: You haven't done badly; but don't delay any longer. Go and bring him home and don't spare any expense in making him comfortable.

ERO: I go then. But, my goodness, isn't that him coming our way?

DUL: Is that him? I'll wait for him here to see if he looks as stupid as he seems.

SCENE TWO

The SIENESE; *his* SERVANT; *the false* EROSTRATO; *the false* DULIPPO

SIEN: He who travels about often encounters great and unforeseen dangers.

SERV: That's true. If the boat we were in this morning when we passed Pontelagoscuro[14] had split open and sunk, we would have all drowned, for none of us can swim.

SIEN: I'm not referring to that.

SERV: Then you must mean the mud that we encountered yesterday coming from Padua that twice almost made your mule fall.

SIEN: Oh, what an idiot you are. I speak of the danger that we nearly fell into coming to this city.

SERV: A great danger indeed to find someone who takes you from the inn and lodges you in his own house!

SIEN: Thanks to the gentleman you see there. But enough of this nonsense. Take care—and I say this to all of you—make sure that none of you mention that we're Sienese; and address me as none other than Filogono of Catania.

SERV: I'll never remember such a queer name, but I wouldn't forget [the word for chestnut]—Castagnia.

SIEN: What Castagnia? I said Catania, Catania, may the devil take you.

SERV: I'll never be able to pronounce it.

SIEN: Then keep quiet and don't mention Siena or any other place.

SERV: Do you want me to act dumb as I did once before?[15]

SIEN: It would be ridiculous to do so now. Enough! I know you like to joke.——Welcome, my son.[16]

ERO: Remember that these Ferrarans are most crafty. Be sure that they cannot tell either by your speech or your manners that you're anyone but Filogono, the Catanese, and my father.

SIEN: Don't worry.

ERO: It's you and your servants who have to worry, for you would immediately be despoiled, or even worse.

SIEN: I've just been admonishing them; they'll know how to pretend perfectly.

ERO: Pretend with those of my household no less than with others; all my servants are Ferrarans who never knew my father nor saw Sicily. Here's my house. Let's go in.

SIEN: I'll go in first.

ERO: That's the proper way for due respect.

DUL: An excellent beginning. I hope that the middle and the end are as good. But is that not my rival and competitor, Cleandro? Oh, the avarice, oh, the folly of men! In order to avoid a dowry for his gentle and virtuous daughter, Damone is ready to make this man his son-in-law, a man whose age suits him rather to be his father-in-law! He loves his own purse much more than his daughter's, and in order not to lose a single florin himself he doesn't care whether his daughter's remains empty forever, unless he expects the old man to put some of his doubloons in it. Ah, wretched me! I jest and I really don't wish to.

Scene Three

CARIONE, *a servant*; CLEANDRO; *the false* DULIPPO

CAR: What a time you pick to come to this district, Master! There isn't a banker in Ferrara who hasn't already gone for a drink.

CLE: I've come to see if I can find Pasifilo to take him to dine with me.

CAR: As if the six mouths that you have at home—and seven with the cat—aren't enough to eat a pound-and-a-half of perch, a pot of chick-peas, and twenty asparagus—for this is all that is prepared to feed you and your household.

CLE: Are you afraid that there won't be enough for you, you wolf?

DUL: (Should I not tease this old bird a little?)

CAR: It wouldn't be the first time.

DUL: (What shall I say to him?)

CAR: I'm not referring to this; it's just that your household will feel uneasy. Pasifilo won't be satisfied; he'll devour you together with the skin and bones of your mule. I would say the flesh as well, if she had any.

CLE: It's your fault [if she hasn't any], for you take care of her.

CAR: It's the fault of the hay and fodder, which are so costly.

DUL: (Leave it; leave it to me.)

CLE: Shut up, you drunkard, and look around to see if he's in the neighborhood.

DUL: (If I don't do anything else, I'll sow so much discord between him and Pasifilo that Mercury[17] himself couldn't make them friends again.)

CAR: Couldn't you have sent someone to look for him, without coming here in person?

CLE: Yes, since you servants are so diligent!

CAR: Surely, Master, you've come here to see someone other than Pasifilo, for if Pasifilo wished to dine with you he would have been waiting for you at your house an hour ago.

CLE: Be still while I find out from this fellow whether he's in his master's house. Aren't you one of Damone's servants?

DUL: Yes, if you please, at your service.

CLE: I thank you. Could you tell me whether Pasifilo came to speak with your master this morning?

DUL: Yes, he did, and I believe that he's still with him. Hah, hah, hah!

CLE: What are you laughing about?

DUL: About a discussion that he had with my master, a discussion that not everyone would laugh at.

CLE: What sort of discussion did they have?

DUL: Ah, I'm not supposed to say.

CLE: Was it something concerning me?

DUL: Uh!

CLE: Why don't you answer?

DUL: I'd tell you everything if I thought you would keep it secret.

CLE: Don't worry: I'll be silent. [To Carione] You wait there.

DUL: Woe to me if my master should learn of this.

CLE: He'll never learn of it, you can be sure.

DUL: What assurance do I have?

CLE: I give you my word of honor.

DUL: It's a bad pledge. The Jew wouldn't lend you a penny on it.

CLE: Among honest men it's worth more than gold and jewels.

DUL: Do you want me to tell you then?

CLE: Yes, if it concerns me.

DUL: It concerns you more than anyone else, and it grieves me that a boor such as Pasifilo should mock a man like you.

CLE: Tell me, tell me what is it?

DUL: First, I want you to swear to me on something sacred that you'll never mention this to Pasifilo, to Damone, or to anyone whomsoever.

CLE: I agree; wait, let me get a document.

CAR: (This must be some little story that he gives him from that young lady who has been driving him mad, and he hopes to get some profit out of it.)

CLE: Here, I found a letter.

CAR: (He doesn't know my master's stinginess; one would need pincers, not words, to get anything out of him. He would sooner have a tooth pulled from his jaw than a grosso[18] from his purse.)

CLE: Hold it in your hand. I swear to you that whatever you tell me I won't reveal to anyone unless you agree to it.

DUL: Fine. I'm sorry that Pasifilo makes fun of you and that you believe that he speaks and acts on your behalf, when, in fact, he continually urges my master to give his daughter to a foreign scholar named Rosorostro or Arosto.[19] I can't pronounce it; it's a devilish name.

CLE: Who is it? Erostrato?

DUL: Yes, that's it. It would never have found its way out of my mouth. And he speaks every evil imaginable about you.

CLE: To whom?

DUL: To Damone and even to Polinesta.

CLE: Ah, the scoundrel! And what does he say?

DUL: The worst that can be said.[20]

CLE: Oh, God!

DUL: That you're the greediest and most miserable man that was ever born and that you would let her die of hunger.

CLE: Pasifilo says this of me?

DUL: Her father doesn't pay much attention to it; he knows well that a man of your profession couldn't be other than extremely greedy.

CLE: I'm not really greedy, but it's just that today whoever doesn't have any wealth is considered an idiot.

DUL: He said that you're a bore, that you're the most obstinate man in the world, and that you'll make her die of anguish.

CLE: Oh, that malicious man!

DUL: And that night and day you continually cough and spit, so that even pigs would be disgusted with you.

CLE: I never cough or spit. Cough, cough, cough ... It's true that I have a little cold now, but who doesn't at this time of the year?

DUL: And he says much worse things: that your feet and armpits stink and your breath is even worse.

CLE: Oh, that traitor! The body that I . . .

DUL: And that you're exposed underneath and have a hernia larger than your head that hangs all the way to your knees.

CLE: I'll be damned if I don't punish him. He lies in his throat in saying this. If we weren't in the street I'd let you see for yourself.

DUL: And that you ask for his daughter more out of desire for a husband than a wife.

CLE: What does he mean by that?

DUL: That with her as bait you intend to attract young men to your house.

CLE: Young men to my house? For what purpose?

DUL: Because you suffer a certain infirmity for which a useful and appropriate remedy is to be with adolescent boys.

CLE: Can it be that he's said these things?

DUL: Yes, and countless others; not only now, but many, many other times.

CLE: Does Damone believe him?

DUL: More than you think; so much so that he would have rejected you outright a long time ago had Pasifilo not begged him to keep you guessing in the hope of obtaining some little thing from you.

CLE: Oh, that scoundrel, that faithless man! As if I hadn't considered giving him the very socks from my feet, after I had worn them a little longer! He wants to obtain something from me . . . Heh! I'll let him have a rope to hang himself.

DUL: Is there any other information you want from me? I'm in a hurry to get back to the house.

CLE: No, nothing else.

DUL: Remember, for heaven's sake, don't say a word about this to anyone; it would be the cause of my ruin.

CLE: I've already given you my word. But tell me, what's your name?

DUL: They call me Maltivenga.[21]

CLE: Are you from this city?

DUL: No, I come from a castle near Pistoia named Fustiucciso.[22] Good-bye, I must be off.

CLE: Oh, wretched me! In whom have I confided? What a messenger, what a spokesman I've chosen!

CAR: Master, let's go eat. Do you intend to continue looking for Pasifilo until dark?

CLE: Don't bother me now. May the two of you be hanged!

CAR: (He must have received unpleasant news.)

CLE: Are you in such a hurry to eat? May your hunger never be satisfied!

CAR: I'm certain that it never will be as long as I remain with you.

CLE: Let's go, and may God give you the plague.

CAR: A plague forever to you and to all the rest of you misers.

ACT THREE
SCENE ONE

DALIO, *a cook*; CAPRINO; *the false* EROSTRATO; *the false* DULIPPO

DALIO: By the time we get to the house I don't think I'll find a single unbroken egg in that basket you're carrying. But to whom am I talking? Where the devil has that glutton disappeared again? He must have tarried to chase a dog or to play some foolhardy and dangerous prank.[23] He stops at everything he finds in the street. If he sees a porter, a peasant, or a Jew, chains couldn't prevent him from doing some mischief.——One day you'll reach the end of your rope; every few steps I have to wait for you. By God, if I find a single broken egg, I'll break your head.

CAPR: Then I won't be able to sit down.

DALIO: Ah! Garbage, garbage.

CAPR: If I'm garbage, then it's not safe for me to go near a goat.

DALIO: If I weren't carrying a load I'd show you whether or not I'm a goat.

CAPR: I've rarely seen you when you're not loaded, either with wine or with blows.

DALIO: You little unspeakable!...

CAPR: Ah, you poltroon! You curse with your heart, but you don't dare use your tongue.

DALIO: I'm going to tell the master; either he sees to it that I'm not insulted by you or I'll leave him.

CAPR: Do me all the dirt you can.

ERO: What's all this noise?

CAPR: He wants to beat me because I reprove him when he curses.

DALIO: He lies in his throat. He insults me because I urge him to hurry up.

ERO: No more of this. You, Dalio, prepare what we need for dinner. When I return I'll tell you exactly what I want boiled and what I want roasted. And you, Caprino, bring in that basket and come keep me company.——Oh, how I'd like to find Pasifilo! But I don't know where. Here's my master; perhaps he'll be able to tell me.

DUL: What have you done with your Filogono?

ERO: I left him at the house.

DUL: And where are you going now?

ERO: I'm looking for Pasifilo. Can you tell me where he is?

DUL: No. It's true that he dined here with Damone this morning, but I don't know where he went afterward. Why do you want him?

ERO: To let Damone know that my father has arrived and that he has agreed to the wedding gift and to all the other things that he can do for us. I'll show you what I can do with that blockhead who turns everything into food for his stomach.

DUL: Go, my dear friend. Seek out Pasifilo so that all that is possible for our cause can be completed today.

ERO: But where should I look for him?

DUL: Wherever banquets are being prepared. Often you will find him at the butcher's and at the fish market.

ERO: What does he do there?

DUL: He watches whoever buys a good breast or a loin of veal or a large fish, and later he turns up unexpectedly, says, "Good health! Cheerio!" and worms his way into a meal.

ERO: I'll look in all such places. It will be surprising if I don't find him there.

DUL: When you return I'll tell you something that will make you laugh.

ERO: About what?

DUL: About a discussion that I had with Cleandro.

ERO: Tell me now.

DUL: I don't want to detain you. Now go and find him.

Scene Two

The false DULIPPO; DAMONE; NEBBIA, *a servant*

DUL: This amorous battle betwen Cleandro and him, which he pursues in my name, is like a game of dice[24] in which you see a player who has lost many times gamble all he has left. You expect him to be wiped out, but Fortune smiles at him and he wins the next throw, and two and four more until he recovers his losses. You now find that the other player, who previously had piled up all the chips, has his pile diminished so much that he's reduced to the situation of his adversary not long before. Then there's a resurgence and a let down; first one and then the other wins in turn and then loses, until they reach a point at which one of them has taken all and stripped his adversary cleaner than a glass doll. How many times have I thought that I had won the game against this cursed old man! And how many times also have I appeared to be the loser! Then within the space of a few days Fortune has so worked things that I could neither hope too much nor despair all. This plan that my cunning servant has devised at the moment seems safe enough; still I continue to worry that, just as in the past, some unexpected difficulty will arise. Oh, here's my master, Damone, coming out of the house.

DAM: Dulippo.

DUL: Yes, Master.

DAM: Go into the house and tell Nebbia, Rosso, and Moro to come out, for I want to send them to various places. And you go to the little room on the ground floor; look in the writing cabinet to see if you can find a deed drawn up by Lippo Malpensa, to the property called Serraglio that Ugo da le Siepi²⁵ sold to my great-grandfather, and bring it here to me.

DUL: Yes, Master. I'm going.

DAM: (Go, then, for you'll find a very different deed from what you expect. Oh, how unhappy is he who places his trust in anyone but himself! Oh, outrageous Fortune, who has sent this little thief from hell to destroy my honor and that of my entire household!)——[*To his servants*] You, come here and do exactly what I tell you, but be careful. Go into the room on the ground floor, where you'll find Dulippo; and while pretending to look for something, sneak up to him, seize him, and tie him hand and foot with the rope that I left on the table precisely for this purpose; then carry him to the small dark room under the stairs, and leave him there. Do this with as little noise as possible. And you, Nebbia, return here immediately after you've finished. Here's the key; bring it back.

NEB: I'll do that.

DAM: Alas! How should I avenge myself for such a grave insult? If I punish this miserable scoundrel myself for his terrible behavior, as my just wrath impels me to, I'll be punished by the prince according to law, for it isn't right for a private citizen to take justice into his own hands. But, then, if I bring my complaint to the duke and his officials, I make my shame public. Woe is me! What shall I do? Even if I make this miserable man suffer every possible pain it won't bring back my daughter's honor or remove my perpetual dishonor. But whom should I torment? I, I alone, am the one who deserves to be punished, for I entrusted her to this old whore of a nurse. If I wanted her to be well looked after, I should have seen to it myself. I should have had her sleep in my room; I shouldn't have kept young menservants around; I should never have been so lenient with her. Oh, my beloved wife, now I realize the damage that I've caused since I lost you! Alas! Why didn't I give her in marriage when I had the chance three years ago? I wouldn't have married her off so richly, but at least it would have been with honor. I waited year after year, month after month, for a good match for her, and see what has happened! To whom did I expect to give her? To a prince? Oh miserable, unfortunate, wretched me! This is really the greatest of sorrows. Compared to this what is it to lose one's wealth, one's children, or one's wife! This is the only grief that's mortal and, truly, it will kill me. Oh Polinesta, my kindness and my leniency toward you didn't deserve such a harsh reward.

NEB: Master, we've carried out your command; here's the key.

DAM: Very well. Now, go find Nomico da Perugia and ask him to lend me those shackles he has; and return immediately.

NEB: I'm going.

DAM: Listen, if he asks what I want them for, tell him that you don't know.

NEB: I'll say that.

DAM: And be sure not to tell anyone that Dulippo has been caught.

NEB: I'll not tell it to a living soul.

SCENE THREE
NEBBIA; PASIFILO; PSITERIA, *a maid*

NEB: It's impossible to manage someone else's money without part of it remaining in your claws. I wondered how Dulippo could dress so well on the small salary that my master pays him. Now I understand how. He was the purchaser; he was in charge of selling grain and wine; he took care of the accounts and was the factotum. Dulippo here, Dulippo there. He was the master's favorite; he was preferred by the children. Compared to him, we other servants were nothing. And see what has happened to him now! It would have been better if he hadn't done so many things.

PAS: You're so right; he's done too much.

NEB: Where the devil did you come from?

PAS: From your house; out the back door.

NEB: I thought you had left two hours ago.

PAS: I'll tell you. After dinner I went into the stable to . . . you know what, and I fell into the deepest sleep I ever slept; I lay on the straw and slept until now. But where are you going?

NEB: To do something that my master ordered me to.

PAS: Can't you tell me?

NEB: No.

PAS: You're very secretive.——As if I didn't know it better than he does. Oh God, the things I heard! Oh God, the things I saw! Oh Cleandro, oh Erostrato, both of you seek a wife and a virgin at that; it could easily be that you'll find them both together, for although Polinesta isn't a virgin, perhaps she has the virgin you seek in her womb! Who would ever have believed this of her? Ask the neighbors about her. They'll tell you that she's the best and the most pious girl in the world; that she associates only with nuns; that she spends most of the day praying; that very

73

rarely do you see her at the door or at a window; that she doesn't appear to be in love with anyone; that in short she's a little saint. Much good may it do! Whoever takes her as a wife will get more dowry than he thinks; if nothing else, he won't lack a nice pair of rather long horns However, this marriage won't be broken off because of my tongue; in fact, I'll do as much as I can to hasten it. Say, isn't this the mischevious old lady whom I just heard revealing everything to Damone?——— Where are you going Psiteria?

PSI: Nearby, to see a friend of mine.

PAS: Why are you going there? To gossip a while about the lovely doings of your young mistress?

PSI: Not at all; but how do you know about these things?

PAS: You made them known to me.

PSI: And when did I tell them to you?

PAS: When you told them to Damone, for I happened to be in a place where I both saw and heard you. Oh what a fine deed! To accuse that unfortunate girl and thus give the poor old man a reason to die of grief! And this is to say nothing of the ruin of that unhappy young man and the nurse, and of the other scandals that will follow.

PSI: It came out unintentionally, and I'm not as much at fault as you think.

PAS: Then whose fault is it?

PSI: I'll tell you how it happened. I knew for quite some time that by an arrangement with the nurse Dulippo slept with Polinesta almost every night; but I said nothing. Then this morning the nurse began to shout at me and at least three times she called me a drunkard. I finally answered her saying: "Shut up, you pimp, don't you think I know what you do for Dulippo nearly every night?" And truthfully I had no idea that I was being overheard. But fate would have my master hear me, and I was summoned to a place where I was forced to tell him everything.

PAS: And how well you told it to him!

PSI: Ah, wretched me! If I had thought that my master would take it so badly, I would rather have let him kill me before revealing it to him.

PAS: Small wonder he took it badly.

PSI: I'm sorry for that poor girl who cries and tears her hair and is so agitated that the mere sight of her moves one to pity; and she does this, not because her father has beaten or threatened her —on the contrary, the sorrowful old man has cried along with her—but because of the pity that she has for her nurse and most of all for Dulippo, both of whom are in a very bad way. But I

74

must go now, as I'm in a hurry.

PAS: Go then, for you really have fixed them well.

ACT FOUR
SCENE ONE
The false EROSTRATO, *alone*

ERO: Woe is me! What should I do? What means, what remedy, what excuse can I find to cover up the deception that until now has gone on for two years without the least difficulty? Now it will be known whether I'm Erostrato or Dulippo, since my old master, the real Filogono, has arrived unexpectedly.

While looking for Pasifilo, I was told by someone that he was seen leaving through Saint Paul's gate. I then went to find him at the port where I saw a boat arriving at the shore. I looked up and I saw Lico, my fellow servant, on the prow; and then I saw my master sticking his head out of the covering. Immediately I turned and hurried back to warn the real Erostrato so that both of us together could find a quick way out of this sudden misfortune. But what could we resolve in the end, even if we had plenty of time to deliberate? Everywhere he's known as Dulippo, a servant of Damone, and I likewise am known as Erostrato, the son of Filogono.——Come here Caprino, hurry, before that old lady enters the house, and ask her to see whether Dulippo is inside; ask her to tell him to come into the street because you want to speak to him. Listen: don't tell her that it's I who am asking for him.

SCENE TWO
CAPRINO; PSITERIA: *the false* EROSTRATO

CAPR: Hey, old woman . . . Hey, you deaf old hag . . . Don't you hear, you ghost of a woman?

PSI: May God keep you from growing old so no one will talk to you that way.

CAP: Go and see if Dulippo is in the house.

PSI: Unfortunately, he is. I wish he had never been!

CAP: Ask him for me to come out here, for I want to speak to him.

PSI: He cannot; he's tied up right now.

CAP: Give him the message, my beautiful one.

PSI: Eh, gallows-bird, I told you he's tied up.

CAP: You're crazy; is it so difficult to give him a message?

PSI: You know very well that it's difficult, you pesty glutton.

CAP: Oh, you indiscreet ass!

PSI: May you get the pox, you little rascal; you'll hang yet.

CAP: And you'll burn, you ugly old witch, if a cancer doesn't consume you first.

PSI: If you come near me I'll give you a blow with a cane.

CAP: If I throw a stone at you I'll crack that stupid old head of yours.

PSI: Go to hell! I believe you're the devil who has come to tempt me.

ERO: Caprino, come back here! What are you quarreling about? Alas! Here comes Filogono, my real master. I don't know what to do. I don't want him to see me dressed like this or before I have found the real Erostrato.

SCENE THREE
FILOGONO, *an old man;* FERRARAN; LICO, *a servant*

FIL: Certainly, my dear man, what you say is indeed true, that no love can be compared to a father's love. I wouldn't have believed, if someone had told me three years ago, that at my age I would leave Sicily, even if the most important business necessitated it. And now, just to see my son and take him back with me, I undertook this long and troublesome voyage.

FER: It must have been very exhausting and inconvenient for you at your age.

FIL: I came as far as Ancona with some noblemen, my compatriots, who had made a vow to Loretto. Then, with little difficulty I reached Ravenna by boat in the company of some pilgrims. But from Ravenna to here, going against the current, I had more trouble than on all the rest of the trip.

FER: You also found the accommodations bad.

FIL: The very worst, but that's nothing compared to the trouble the customs officials give you. How many times did they open the coffer that I have on the boat and this valise; how many times did they search them and turn all the contents upside down. They wanted to look in my pocket and to search down to my bare chest! At times I feared they would flay me to see whether I had something between my flesh and my skin.

FER: I've heard that they commit grave injustices.

FIL: You can be sure of it, and I'm not surprised, for whoever seeks such a position must either be a rogue or someone of bad disposition.

FER: Your past ordeal will be rewarded by even greater joy when today, as you rest, you'll be in the company of your dearest son. But I don't understand why you didn't make your son, who's young, come to see you instead of going through so much trouble to come here, for, as you say, you have no other business to attend to. Was it perhaps because you were more concerned about distracting him from his studies than about placing your own life in danger?

FIL: That wasn't the reason; on the contrary, I would rather he discontinue his studies, provided that he returns home.

FER: If you didn't want him to benefit from his studies, why did you send him here?

FIL: When he was at home he was hot-blooded as young men usually are, and the affairs that he had didn't seem suitable to me. Every day he did something that caused me more than a little displeasure. And I, without realizing that I would so regret it later, encouraged him to go study in any city of his choice; so he came here. I believe that he hadn't even set foot here when I began to have regrets, and from that moment until now I haven't been happy. I've written a hundred letters imploring him to return home, but with no results. In his replies he always begs me not to remove him from his studies from which, he assures me, he is profiting very much.

FER: Truly, I've heard him praised by men of good faith, and he's among the most noteworthy of scholars.

FIL: I'm glad to hear that he hasn't wasted his time; yet I don't care for him to become so learned if I have to be separated from him for many years. If I happened to die without him near me I would die in desperation. I won't leave this city unless he returns with me.

FER: To love one's children is human, but to have such tenderness is womanly.

FIL: That's the way I am. And let me say that my coming here was mainly prompted by what was told me by two or three Sicilians who at various times happened to pass through this city; I asked them about my son and they told me that they had been in Ferrara and that they had heard most wonderful things about him, but that they were never able to see him, although they had been to his house, some two, and others three, times. I fear that he's so occupied with his learning that he doesn't want to do anything else and avoids speaking to friends and fellow countrymen so as not to take even the least bit of time from his studies. For this same reason I suspect that he doesn't eat very well, and I fear that he stays up all night. He's young and has been brought up in ease and luxury; he could die, he could easily go mad, or meet some similar misfortune.

FER: All excesses, even virtuous ones, should be condemned. Now, here's the house in which your Erostrato dwells. I'll knock.

FIL: Knock.

FER: No one answers.

FIL: Knock again.

FER: I think they're asleep.

LICO: If that door were your mother you wouldn't bang on it more softly. Let me do it. Hello! Hey there, isn't anybody home?

SCENE FOUR
DALIO; FILOGONO; LICO; FERRARAN

DALIO: What madness is this? Are you trying to break down the door?

LICO: I thought you were asleep.

FIL: What is Erostrato doing?

DALIO: He's not at home.

FIL: Open up and let us in.

DALIO: If you think you can lodge here, forget it; there are other strangers who came here ahead of you, and there isn't room enough for all.

FIL: Oh excellent servant, you who would be the pride of any master! Tell me, who is inside?

DALIO: Filogono of Catania, Erostrato's father, who arrived this morning from Sicily.

FIL: He will be inside after you've opened up. Open, if you please.

DALIO: It's easy enough for me to open up; but I assure you that you cannot lodge here, for the rooms are full.

FIL: And who is there?

DALIO: Didn't you hear? I told you that Erostrato's father, Filogono of Catania, is here.

FIL: When did he arrive?

DALIO: About four hours ago he dismounted at the Crown's Inn, where he left his horses, and Erostrato went there and brought him back.

FIL: I think you're mocking me.

DALIO: And you take pleasure in keeping me here so that I won't be able to do my chores.

FIL: He must be drunk.

LICO: He seems to be. Don't you see how red his face is?

FIL: Which Filogono are you talking about?

DALIO: He's a fine gentleman, the father of my master.

FIL: And where is he?

DALIO: He's here in the house.

FIL: Can I see him?

DALIO: I think so, if you're not blind.

FIL: Please ask him to come out so that I may speak to him.

DALIO: All right.

FIL: I don't know what to think of this.

LICO: Master, the world is large. Don't you think there's more than one Catania and more than one Sicily, more than one Filogono and more than one Erostrato, and even more than one Ferrara? Perhaps this isn't the Ferrara where your son, whom we're looking for, is staying.

FIL: I don't know what to think other than that you're crazy and that fellow is drunk, and I don't know what to say. Look here, my good man, see if I've mistaken the address.

FER: Don't you think I know Erostrato of Catania and where he lives? I saw him here yesterday. But here's someone who can clarify the situation; he doesn't appear to be a drunkard like that servant.

Scene Five
SIENESE; FILOGONO; LICO; FERRARAN; DALIO

SIEN: Are you the gentleman who asked for me?

FIL: I would like to know where you're from.

SIEN: I'm Sicilian, if you please.

FIL: From what city?

SIEN: From Catania.

FIL: What is your name?

SIEN: Filogono.

FIL: What is your profession?

SIEN: A merchant.

FIL: What merchandise did you bring here?

SIEN: None. I came to see my son who is studying in this city and whom I haven't seen for the past two years.

FIL: Who is your son?

SIEN: Erostrato.

FIL: Erostrato is your son?

SIEN: Yes, he is.

FIL: And you are Filogono?

SIEN: Yes, I am.

FIL: A merchant from Catania?

SIEN: Why do you have to ask? I wouldn't lie to you.

FIL: On the contrary, you do lie and you're a cheat and a villain.

SIEN: You wrong me by calling me a villain, for I never offended you as far as I know.

FIL: But you're wicked and you lie when you say that you aren't.

SIEN: I am who I told you I am; if I weren't, why would I say it?

FIL: Oh God, what audacity—and with such a straight face! You are Filogono of Catania?

SIEN: How many more times must I tell you? I'm the Filogono that

I told you I am. What are you surprised at?

FIL: To find a man with such effrontery! Neither you nor someone greater than yourself could change you into what I am—rascal and liar that you are.

DALIO: Should I let you insult the father of my master? If you don't get away from this door I'll thrust this spit in your belly. Woe to you if Erostrato were here! Go back inside, Sir, and let this old bird caw in the street until he bursts.

Scene Six
FILOGONO; LICO; FERRARAN

FIL: What do you think of this, my Lico?

LICO: What do you want me to think except bad thoughts. I never liked the name Ferrara; but now I see that the thing itself is worse than the name.[26]

FER: You're wrong in speaking badly about our city; these people who are insulting you are not Ferrarans; I can tell by their accent.

LICO: All of you are at fault, especially your officials who allow such cheating in their city.

FER: What do the officials know about these things? Do you think they're aware of everything?

LICO: On the contrary, I think that they're aware of very little and they're not concerned where they don't see any profit. They should have their eyes and ears open wider than the doors of the taverns.

FIL: Shut up, stupid, and mind your own business.

LICO: I'm afraid that if God doesn't help us both of us will seem stupid.

FIL: What shall we do?

LICO: Well, I would look everywhere until we find Erostrato.

FER: I'll keep you company. First we'll go to the School; if he's not there we'll find him in the piazza.

FIL: I'm tired, and I had better rest rather than wander about. Let's wait for him here. He must return home sometime.

LICO: I am afraid you may find a new Erostrato also.

FER: Look, look I see him there ... But where did he go now? Wait here while I call him. Oh Erostrato, oh Erostrato, don't you hear me? Oh Erostrato, come back here.

Scene Seven
The false EROSTRATO; FERRARAN; FILOGONO; DALIO; LICO

ERO: (Well, I cannot hide; I must have courage, otherwise ...)

FER: Oh, Erostrato, Filogono your father has come from Sicily to see you.

ERO: You're not telling me anything new. I saw him and I spent some time with him. He arrived early this morning.

FER: According to what he told me, it doesn't seem to me that he has seen you.

ERO: And where did you speak to him?

FER: You don't seem to recognize him. Look, he's coming our way. Filogono, here is your son, Erostrato.

FIL: This is Erostrato? He doesn't look like my son.

ERO: Who is this fine gentleman?

FIL: Oh, he looks like Dulippo, my servant.

LICO: Who wouldn't recognize him?

FIL: My, you're dressed in a long robe! Are you also a student, Dulippo?

ERO: Whom is he speaking to?

FIL: It seems that you don't know who I am! Am I speaking to you or not?

ERO: Are you speaking to me, Sir?

FIL: Oh God, what have I come to? This rascal pretends not to know me. Are you Dulippo or am I mistaken?

ERO: You certainly have mistaken me for someone else, for that's not my name.

LICO: Master, didn't I tell you that we were in Ferrara? You see the faith[27] of your servant Dulippo who denies knowing you! He's picked up the customs of this city.

FIL: Oh shut up and go to hell.

ERO: Ask anyone in this city, for there isn't a gentleman who doesn't know my name. You who brought the foreigner here, tell me, who am I?

FER: I've always known you as Erostrato of Catania, and I've heard you called that since you came to this city from Sicily.

FIL: Oh God, I'm going crazy today!

ERO: I'm afraid that you already may be.

LICO: Don't you realize, Master, that we're among cheats? The one whom we thought was our guide is in collusion with that other fellow and thus he says that this is Erostrato when he is really Dulippo, my fellow servant.

FER: You shouldn't complain about me, for I've never heard this man called anything other than Erostrato of Catania.

ERO: How else could you have heard me called other than by my own name? But I'm certainly mad to listen to this old man who seems to have gone out of his mind.

FIL: Ah, you renegade! Ah, you scoundrel! Ah, you traitor! Is this the way to welcome your master? What have you done with my son?

DALIO: Is this dog still barking here? And you allow him to insult you, Erostrato?

ERO: Go back inside, you idiot. What are you going to do with that pestle?

DALIO: I'd like to crack the head of this enraged old man.

ERO: And you, put down that rock. All of you go back into the house. Don't pay attention to his insults; have respect for his age.

Scene Eight
FILOGONO; FERRARAN; LICO

FIL: Whom should I look to for help, since the one whom I raised and always considered as a son betrays me and pretends not to know me? And you, whom I took as a guide and held as a friend, are you in league with that most wicked servant of mine? Without having consideration for the fact that I'm a foreigner and at present am in misery, and without any reverence for God, that most just judge who knows all, you right away go ahead and falsely testify that this fellow is Erostrato—he whom the whole world and even nature itself couldn't make anyone but Dulippo.

LICO: If all other witnesses in this city are like this one, one can prove whatever one wishes.

FER: Sir, since he came to this city, I know not whence, I have always heard him called Erostrato, reputedly the son of one Filogono the Catanese. Whether or not he is I leave to your judgment and to others who knew him prior to his coming here. If someone testifies to what he believes is true, he cannot be condemned as a perjurer by man or God. I've only said what I heard from others and what I thought to be true.

FIL: Alas! This man whom I gave as a servant and escort to my dearest Erostrato has either sold or murdered my son or has made some awful agreement about him. And not only has he usurped the clothes, the books, and other possessions, which Erostrato brought with him from Sicily, but his name as well, so that without any difficulty he could profit from the bills of exchange and letters of credit that I gave to my son. Ah, wretched and unhappy Filogono! Ah, most unfortunate old man! Isn't there a judge, a captain, a *podestà*,[28] or some other official in this city to whom I can have recourse?

FER: We have judges and *podestà* and above all, a most just prince. Don't worry. You'll get justice provided your cause is right.

FIL: Take me, please, take me right now to a prince, to a *podestà*, or to whomever you wish, for I want to bring to light the worst cheating, the worst iniquity, the most wicked crime that was ever committed.

LICO: Master, someone who wishes to institute a suit needs four things and you know them: first, he needs a good cause; second, a good spokesman; third, influence; and fourth, someone to carry it out.

FER: Influence? I didn't know that the laws mention this.

FIL: Don't listen to him; he's a lunatic.

FER: Please tell me, Lico, what do you mean by influence?

LICO: To have someone to recommend your cause, for, as you expect to win, he'll see to it that the case ends quickly; but if the decision isn't in your favor, the case will be postponed or dragged out so long that your weary adversary, because of the excessive expenses, will give in or settle out of court.

FER: Don't worry on this score, Filogono, for although it isn't the custom here, I'll also provide you with influence. I'll take you to a lawyer who will suffice for all these things.

FIL: Must I then give myself as prey to lawyers and attorneys, whose insatiable greed I cannot satisfy with the means I have, and I couldn't do so even if I were in my own city? I know their methods very well. The first time I speak to them, they'll promise that without any doubt the case is won. After that, however, they'll seek you out every day to cast more doubts as to the outcome and they'll say that I've been at fault for not having informed them of everything at the beginning. And their object here is not only to draw the money out of my purse, but the marrow out of my bones.

FER: The man whom I have in mind is half a saint.

LICO: What's the other half—a devil?

FIL: Well said, Lico; I, too, have little faith in those who walk about with their necks twisted.

FER: Assuming that what you say is true and even assuming worse, the hatred and malevolence that this particular lawyer has for Erostrato or Dulippo, whoever he is, will make him take your case and pursue it vigorously without too much concern about what he'll gain from you.

FIL: What enmity is there between them?

FER: They are enemies in love; both are suitors for the same woman, the daughter of one of our better citizens.

FIL: Do you mean that this scoundrel enjoys such credit in this city at my expense that he dares ask for the hand of a daughter of one of your better citizens?

FER: That's right.

FIL: What's the name of his adversary?

FER: Cleandro. He's one of the best doctors of law here at the university.

FIL: Let's go find him.

FER: Let's go.

ACT FIVE
Scene One
The false EROSTRATO, *alone*

ERO: What a stroke of bad luck this is. Before I could find Erostrato, I had to run into my old master in such a ridiculous way. I had to pretend not to know him; I was forced to argue with him and answer him with more than one insulting word. I've offended him so grievously that no matter what happens in this affair he'll dislike me forever. Therefore, I resolve that, even if I have to go into Damone's house, I'll speak to Erostrato immediately; I'll renounce his name, give up his clothes, and flee from his house as fast as I can. As long as Filogono lives I'll never return to his house, the house in which I was raised since the age of five. Here is Pasifilo, who comes at just the right time to go inside and let Erostrato know that I have to speak to him.

Scene Two
PASIFILO; *the false* EROSTRATO

PAS: (I received two excellent bits of news: one, that Erostrato is preparing a lavish feast for this evening; the other, that he's looking everywhere for me. To save him further trouble in finding me, and because there's no one in this city more suitable than I am to indulge where there is abundant and tasty food, I've come to see whether he's at home. But, my goodness, here he is.)

ERO: Pasifilo, do me a favor if you don't mind.

PAS: Who has a better right to ask me than you? I'd go through fire for your sake. What do you want?

ERO: Go to Damone's house; knock and ask for Dulippo, and tell him . . .

PAS: I won't be able to speak to Dulippo.

ERO: And why not?

PAS: He's in prison.

ERO: What do you mean, "in prison!"? Where?

PAS: In the worst of places; here in his master's house.

ERO: How do you know this?

PAS: I was there.

ERO: Is it really true?

PAS: I wish it weren't!

ERO: Do you know why?

PAS: Don't ask any more questions. It's enough that you know he was caught.

ERO: I want you to tell me, Pasifilo, if you ever hope to have any favors from me.

PAS: Please don't force me to tell you. What does it matter if you know it?

ERO: It matters very much, more than you think.

PAS: And it matters more to others—even more than you think— that I keep quiet.

ERO: Ah, Pasifilo, is this the trust I've placed in you? Are these the offers [of help] that you've made me?

PAS: I wish I had fasted today instead of coming before you!

ERO: Either you tell me or this door will remain closed to you forever.

PAS: I would sooner have everyone in the world dislike me before suffering your enmity. But if you hear something that displeases you, blame no one but yourself.

ERO: Nothing could disturb me more than Dulippo's troubles, not even my own. So don't think that you can tell me anything worse than the news you gave me that he's been caught.

PAS: Since you order me to, I'll tell you the truth. He was caught in bed with your Polinesta.

ERO: Alas! Has Damone found out?

PAS: An old woman accused him; whereupon Damone took him, along with the nurse, who had been his confidante and accomplice in this, and put both of them in a place where they'll undergo a rather harsh penance for their sins.

ERO: Go into the house, Pasifilo, into the kitchen, and have them prepare and cook the food as you like it.

PAS: If you had been the chief justice[29] you couldn't have given me a sentence more in keeping with my desires. I'm going immediately.

SCENE THREE
The false EROSTRATO, *alone*

ERO: I wanted to get rid of this fellow as fast as I could so that he wouldn't see the tears in my eyes or hear the sighs of my breast that I can no longer hold back. Ah, cruel Fortune! The troubles that you've inflicted upon me in the past two hours, even if distributed throughout many years, would be sufficient to make someone extremely miserable! Nor have they reached the end; for I already foresee others worse than these, infinite in number and unforgettable. You've made my master, now that he's almost decrepit, come to Ferrara—he who, when he was a young man, never left Sicily—and this just today when we least needed him! You strengthened, diminished, and regulated the winds so well that he could neither have arrived here yesterday nor three or four days hence! Wasn't it enough to have thrown this obstacle in my way, without having young Erostrato's love-scheme discovered at the same time? You had kept it secret for two years just so you could reveal it on this awful day. Alas! What am I to do? What can I do? There's no time now to invent schemes. Every hour, every moment, that we delay in assisting Erostrato is perilous. I must go then and find my master, Filogono, and tell him the whole story without a single lie, so that he can provide a quick remedy to save the life of his unhappy son. That's the best thing to do. That's what I will do, even though severe torture will certainly follow for me. The love that I have for my young master and my obligation to him demand that I save his life, even at great personal risk. But what should I do? Should I go looking for Filogono throughout the city or wait for him to return here? If he sees me again in the street he'll shout and won't listen to anything I tell him. Then a crowd will gather around, and there'll be more than a little turmoil. I think it's better for me to wait here a while; and then, if he doesn't return, I'll go looking for him.

SCENE FOUR

PASIFILO; the false EROSTRATO

PAS: [To Dalio, inside] Yes, do that, but don't put it on the fire until we're ready to sit at the table. [To the false Erostrato] Everything is set, but if I didn't just happen to be here there would have been a great scandal.

ERO: What would have happened?

PAS: Dalio was about to put the thrushes and the veal on the spit at the same time, ignoring the fact that veal takes a while to roast while fowl cooks immediately.

ERO: Oh, I wish this were the greatest scandal that was happening.

PAS: And one of two misfortunes would have followed: if he had left them on the fire long enough to cook the veal, the thrushes would have been burned and ruined; if he had taken them out earlier, we would have eaten them cold or not properly done.

ERO: Your advice was good.

PAS: If you wish, I'll go buy some oranges and olives, for without them this meal would be worthless.

ERO: Nothing will be lacking; don't worry.

PAS: Hearing about Dulippo has made this fellow all nervous and irritable; he's so jealous that he's bursting. But let him be and burst if he will. As long as I dine in his house this evening, I don't care about anything else. Isn't that Cleandro coming this way? Now then, it's his head that we'll crown with a horn. Surely Polinesta will be his, for Erostrato, after learning about Dulippo from me, won't ask for her hand, nor will he want her any longer.

Scene Five

CLEANDRO; FILOGONO; PASIFILO; LICO

CLE: But how will you prove that this fellow isn't Erostrato, when everybody knows that he is? And how will you prove that you're Filogono of Catania, when that other man, supported by the testimony of the sham Erostrato, denies it and obstinately claims that he is?

FIL: Let me be put in jail and have someone sent immediately to Catania—and I'm willing to pay for it—to bring back two or three trustworthy people who know the true identity of Filogono and Erostrato. We'll abide by their decision as to whether I or this other fellow is Filogono; in the same way we'll see whether this impudent scoundrel is Erostrato or my servant, Dulippo.

PAS: (I'd like to greet him.)

CLE: This will be a long and very expensive procedure, but a necessary one, for I don't see a better way.

PAS: May God bring you happiness, my remarkable Master.

CLE: May He give you what you deserve.

PAS: He'll give me your favor and perpetual happiness.

CLE: He'll give you a noose with which to hang yourself, glutton and scoundrel that you are.

PAS: I confess to being a glutton, but not a scoundrel. You shouldn't call me that, for I'm your servant.

CLE: I want you neither as a servant nor a friend.

PAS: What have I done to you?

CLE: Go to the gallows, you faithless traitor.

PAS: Ah, Cleandro! Take it easy.

CLE: I'll make you pay for it, you can be sure, you drunken lout.

PAS: I don't know how I offended you.

CLE: I'll let you know at the right time. Get out of my way, you rascal.

PAS: I'm not your slave, Cleandro.

CLE: Do you dare open your mouth, you assassin? I'll make you ڊ . . .

PAS: What the devil! When I lose my patience, what will you do to me?

CLE: What will I do to you? If I didn't restrain myself, you poltroon . . .

PAS: I'm an honest man like you.

CLE: You lie in your throat, you gallows-bird.

FIL: [To Cleandro] Ah! Don't get into a frenzy!

PAS: Who's going to hit me?

CLE: I'll get you soon; let me go, let me go . . .

PAS: Good-bye, then. I won't stay here and quarrel.

CLE: Go then, and if I don't make you pay for this may my name
be changed.[30]

PAS: What the devil can you do to me? After all, I have no goods to
worry about if you sue me.

FIL: You've become enraged.

CLE: That villain . . . but let's forget it. Let's return to where we
were. I won't stop until I have him hanged as he deserves.

FIL: You're disturbed and you won't pay attention to me.

CLE: No, no. Tell me about your situation.

FIL: I was saying that if we send someone to Catania, and if we . . .

CLE: Yes, yes. I understand that, and it must be done. But how
come this man is your servant? Where did you get him? Tell me
the whole story.

FIL: I'll tell you. At the time the Infidels took Otranto . . .

CLE: Alas! You remind me of my sorrows.

FIL: How is that?

CLE: It was then that I left that place, my native city, where my loss
was so great that I can never hope to recover it.

FIL: I'm sorry about that.

CLE: Continue.

FIL: At that time some of our Sicilians, who were scouring the sea
with three armed galleys, spotted a Turkish ship returning from
the conquered city to Valona[31] laden with rich booty.

CLE: Perhaps a good part of it was mine.

FIL: They sailed toward the ship, fought and finally captured it, and
brought it back to Palermo whence they came. Among the things
they had for sale was this boy, a child of five or six at the time.

CLE: Alas! I left a child of that age in Otranto.

FIL: And, as I happened to be there and liked his appearance, I
bought him for twenty-four ducats.

CLE: Was the boy Turkish, or had the Turks kidnapped him
from Otranto?

FIL: They had carried him off from that city. But what does it
matter? The fact is I paid for him with my own money.

CLE: I'm not asking because of this. Oh, if only he's the one I hope he is!

FIL: Who do you want him to be?

LICO: We're in for trouble. Stop right here.

CLE: Was his name Dulippo, then?

LICO: Look after your own interests, Master.

FIL: What are you chattering about, presumptuous one? His name wasn't Dulippo, but Carino.

LICO: Sure, let him pull everything out of your mouth.[32]

CLE: Was his name Carino? Oh God, if you would only make me happy today! Why did you change his name?

FIL: We called him Dulippo because he used to call out that name when he cried.

CLE: Now I'm certain that this is my son, who was named Carino; and the Dulippo whom he used to call when he cried was one of my servants who fed him and to whom we had entrusted him.

LICO: Didn't I tell you, Master, that we're in Bari,[33] and we thought that we were in Ferrara? Just to deprive you of your servant this man would adopt him with stories about his being his son.

CLE: I'm not accustomed to telling lies.

LICO: Everything has a beginning.

CLE: Believe me, Filogono, I'm not cheating you in the least.

LICO: Not in the least, but in the most.

CLE: Be quiet for a moment. Tell me, did the child have any recollection of his family, or did he remember the name of his father or mother?

FIL: Yes, he did; and he told me, but I really don't recall it.

LICO: I do.

FIL: Tell us then.

LICO: I won't say it; he's already found out too much from you.

FIL: Tell us, if you know it.

LICO: I know it, and I'd rather have my throat slit than say it. Why doesn't he say it first? Isn't it obvious that he's groping for information?

CLE: You know my name; my wife and the mother of the child was called Sofronia; my family name is Da la Spiaggia.

LICO: I don't know all these things; but I do know that he said his mother's name was Sofronia. I'm not surprised that you know this, if you're working together. Has he informed you of everything?

CLE: I don't need any clearer signs than this. Without any doubt he's my son whom I lost eighteen years ago and for whom I've cried a thousand times. He must have a rather large mole on his left shoulder.

LICO: No wonder you know it, if he told it to you. Of course there's a mole; I wish he had . . .

CLE: Ah, Lico, what nice words. Hurry, let's go find him. Oh, Fortune, I forgive you fully, for you have restored my son to me today!

FIL: I'm much less obliged to her, for I don't know what has happened to my son. And now you, whom I chose as a lawyer, must have turned completely in favor of Dulippo and against me.

CLE: Filogono, let's go speak with my son, for I have hopes that we'll find your son with him.

FIL: Let's go.

CLE: Since I see the door open I'll enter informally without calling or knocking.

LICO: Master, be careful how you go in there. I'm certain that he's figured out some trickery to bring you to ruin.

FIL: As if I would care to remain alive if my son were lost!

LICO: I warned you; now do as you please.

Scene Six

DAMONE; PSITERIA

DAM: Come here, you chatterbox, you foolhardy woman; how could Pasifilo have learned of this if not from you?

PSI: He didn't hear it from me; he told it to me first.

DAM: You're lying, you rascal. You'll tell me the truth if I have to break every bone in your body.

PSI: If you find it to be otherwise, you can even kill me.

DAM: Where did he speak to you?

PSI: Here in the street.

DAM: What were you doing here?

PSI: I was going to Mona Bionda's house to look at a piece of cloth she's weaving.

DAM: How did he happen to speak to you about this, unless you began the discussion?

PSI: On the contrary, he started to reproach me and insult me because I was the one who told you everything. I asked him how he knew about it, and he told me that he had overheard us, for he was hidden in the stable when you called me there today.

DAM: Ah, poor me! What shall I do? You go back to the house. —— Before I die I'll pluck out the tongues of a couple of those chirpers. The fact that Pasifilo knows about my shame disturbs me more than the shame itself, a shame occasioned by a lack of care on my part. Whoever wants to keep something secret should tell it to Pasifilo; then no one will ever hear of it except those who have ears. By now it's common gossip in a hundred places.

Cleandro must have been the first to hear about it, then Erostrato, and then one person after another, until the whole city knows. Oh, what a dowry she prepared for herself! When will I ever be able to marry her off? Ah, poor me, I'm truly more miserable than misery itself! Oh God, if only what my daughter has told me is true, that this fellow who violated her is not of low origin as he pretended to be in my house until today; but that he's noble and wealthy in his own country. Even if what she told me were only half-true, I would be very happy to have him marry her; but I fear that this wicked Dulippo has deceived her with these stories. I'm going to question him further and by his answers I'll be able to tell whether this is the truth or merely a story that he invented to attain his goal.

Isn't that Pasifilo coming out of our neighbor's house? What makes him so happy that he jumps like a madman in the street?

SCENE SEVEN
PASIFILO; DAMONE

PAS: Oh God, I hope I find Damone at home so that I don't have to search for him all over the city! I want to have the honor of being the first to tell him. Oh happy day! There, I see him at the entrance to the house.[34]

DAM: (What news does he want from me?) What good thing has happened, my Pasifilo, that you're so cheerful?

PAS: Your good fortune is the cause of my happiness.

DAM: What do you mean?

PAS: I know that you're terribly saddened by what has happened to your daughter.

DAM: And how!

PAS: But you should know that the one who dishonored you is the son of a man of such quality that you'll not reject him as a son-in-law.

DAM: What do you know about it?

PAS: His father, Filogono of Catania, of whose riches you must have heard, has just arrived from Sicily and is in our neighbor's house.

DAM: Do you mean in Erostrato's house?

PAS: No, Dulippo's. Until now we've thought that this neighbor of yours was Erostrato, but he isn't; the one you hold as a prisoner in your house, whom you call Dulippo, is really Erostrato, and he's the master of this other one, who is really Dulippo, and who in this city has always been called Erostrato. They arranged this between them so that Erostrato, under the name of Dulippo and dressed as a servant, could easily accomplish what he has done in your house.

DAM: Then what Polinesta was telling me a while ago wasn't a story.

PAS: Did she also tell you this?

DAM: Yes, but I thought it was a story.

PAS: On the contrary, it's the very truth. Filogono will be coming to see you soon, and Cleandro is with him.

DAM: How come Cleandro?

PAS: Listen to another strange story. Cleandro has discovered that the Dulippo who called himself Erostrato is his son, who had been kidnapped by the Turks when they captured Otranto. He ended up in the house of Filogono, who raised him since he was a child and sent him to this city in the company of his son. There never was a stranger situation than this; one could write a play about it. They'll all be here in a moment, and you'll hear the full story from them.

DAM: I want to hear the whole story from Dulippo or Erostrato, whoever he is, before I speak with Filogono.

PAS: That will be fine. I'll go and delay them a little. But it seems that they're already coming.

Scene Eight

SIENESE; FILOGONO; CLEANDRO

SIEN: [*To Erostrato, offstage*] There's no need to apologize any more. Even though you tricked me, I received no greater injury than a few insults, so I consider it of little account. In fact, it was a useful lesson that I learned—and without any personal loss— to be more careful next time and not to believe anything right away. Furthermore, as it has been for the purpose of a love scheme, I dismiss it lightly and with a minimum of anger.——As for you Filogono, if I've done something that may have displeased you, take it in the spirit in which it was done.

FIL: The only thing that bothers me is the insulting words I said to you.

CLE: [*To the Sienese*] Enough has been said about this. Further discussion would be superfluous. Later on you'll find that you wouldn't for anything in the world have missed experiencing this fraud, or whatever you want to call it, for it will provide you with an interesting story to tell in a hundred places. And you, Filogono, can believe that heaven has ordained this, for in no other way would it have been possible for my Carino and me to recognize each other, considering the enmity that you heard existed between the two of us.

FIL: I know that what you say is true, because I believe that there isn't a single leaf that falls unless moved by the Divine Will. But let us find this Damone, for every moment that passes until I see my son seems like a year to me.

CLE: Let's go, then.——You, Sir, can remain with my son in the house, as these matters at first mustn't be dealt with in the presence of too many witnesses.

SIEN: I'll do as you please.

SCENE NINE
PASIFILO; CLEANDRO; FILOGONO; DAMONE; EROSTRATO

PAS: Cleandro, can you tell me how I've offended you?

CLE: I realize now, Pasifilo, that I insulted you unjustly, but the witness whom I relied upon distorted the truth for his own sake and led me into this error.

PAS: I'm glad that justice was not thwarted by malice; but you shouldn't have believed these things so readily and insulted me so.

CLE: I get angry very easily and I cannot help it.[35]

PAS: What anger? To insult an honest man publicly, to make accusations against him, and then blame it all on anger. This is a fine excuse!

CLE: Never again, Pasifilo; I am, as I always was, your friend, and, as the occasion arises, I'll give you the clearest proof of it. Tomorrow morning I expect you to dine with me. Here's Damone coming out of the house; let me speak first.—— Damone, we come so that your sorrow may be changed into gladness since we know how you suffer for what has happened. We come to assure you that the person whom you've thought until now to be Dulippo and a servant of yours is, in fact, the son of this gentleman, Filogono of Catania; he's not inferior to you in blood, and in wealth, as you have probably heard, he far surpasses you.

FIL: I'm prepared to amend, insofar as I can, my son's misdeed by making him your legal son-in-law, if it pleases you; and if there is something else that I can do for you, you'll find me ready and willing.

CLE: And I, who previously had asked for Polinesta as a wife, will be satisfied if, at my request, you grant her to this gentleman's son, who, because of his youth, his love for her, and a thousand other reasons, deserves her far more than I do. Besides, I sought a wife mainly to provide me with an heir; but now I neither need one nor want one, for today I have found the son whom I lost when my city was captured, as I'll tell you later.

DAM: There are many reasons, Filogono, why I should want a

family alliance and your friendship no less than you want mine. So I accept your proposal, and I'm more gratified with it than with any that were offered to me or for which I could have hoped. I receive your son as a son-in-law and you as a most honored relation. And how my soul rejoices to see you satisfied, Cleandro; I'm so happy that you've found your son about whom Pasifilo has told me everything. Now, Filogono, here's your Erostrato, whom you've longed for; and this is your daughter-in-law.

ERO: Oh, Father!

PAS: How great is the tenderness of fathers toward their children! Filogono is speechless with joy and tears come out instead of words.

DAM: Let's go inside the house.

PAS: Well said. Inside, inside.

SCENE TEN

NEBBIA; DAMONE; PASIFILO

NEB: Master, I brought the shackles.

DAM: Take them away.

NEB: What do you want me to do with them?

PAS: Shove them up your ass.——

He who has nothing to do with this can leave, for we don't want to be too many at this wedding.[36]

The *Pretenders*, written first in prose, received its debut at the ducal theater in Ferrara on 6 February 1509. Ten years later, on 6 March 1519, it was performed before Pope Leo X at Rome, where elaborate sets designed by Raphael were used. The intemperate delight of the pope on seeing the play has been described in a famous letter by Alfonso Paolucci (see Introduction, p. xxvi). Some time between 1528 and 1531 Ariosto recast the play in verse in a version that differed only slightly from the original prose; there is no evidence, however, that this second redaction was ever staged during its author's lifetime.

There are some variations in the names of the characters in the verse edition: Lico becomes Lizio; Nebbia is Nevola; Damone is Damonio; and the Nurse, who is called Balia in the prose version, becomes Nutrice in verse.

1. Minor variations appear in the prologues of the numerous printed editions of the prose version, which appeared during the author's lifetime. In the verse edition these differences were somewhat more marked:

"As you know, children are sometimes substituted for one another in our day, as they have been many times in the past. Besides having seen it in plays and read about it in ancient stories, perhaps there is someone in the audience who has actually experienced it. But it certainly must appear new and strange to you to see young men substituted for old men in this way; and yet even old men are interchanged. Why are you laughing? Oh, did you hear me say something funny? Ah, I believe I know why the laughter. You think that I'm going to say something risqué or to show you something lewd; for if you expected to see or hear something virtuous, you would sit with your eyes lowered and your mouths still, like wise brides when they hear themselves being publicly praised with fine words. And this shows that you are not saintly souls, for people never laugh at things that don't delight them.

"But I'm not so indiscreet as to say or show something reprehensible to anyone among you, let alone to an entire audience. And, although I speak to you about substitution, my substitutions are not like those ancient ones that Elephantis depicted in various actions, forms, and manners and that have lately reappeared in our own day in the holy city of Rome. These have been printed on fine paper as if they were the purest things, so that everyone in the world could have a copy. [The reference here is to the obscene imprints by Antonio Raimondi made from drawings by the contemporary decorator, Guilio Romano. The imprints were accompanied by descriptive sonnets composed by Aretino.] Nor are mine similar to those that the dreamy sophists have discovered in their dialectics. This substitution of ours signifies what in the vernacular would be called exchange. I'm explaining the meaning of the term in order to remove any evil thoughts and to make you understand that you haven't guessed correctly. Now, as both old men and youths are interchanged, our play will be called the *Pretenders*; and, if you will listen to it in silence, it may give you, along with these substitutions, an honest subject for laughter."

2. See the preliminary note to the *Coffer*.

3. There is no English word to convey adequately all the nuances of the Italian *suppositi*. The Latin participle, *suppositus*, itself translates into a number of possible Italian equivalents: *supposto* (supposed or assumed); *sottoposto* (submitted, subjected, or exposed); *sostituito* (substituted or

interchanged); *finto* (pretended or feigned); *scambiato* (exchanged or mistaken); and even *posposto* (placed after or behind). Obviously—and this is clearer in the prologue to the verse version—Ariosto was hoping that the minds of his audience would wander over a number of these meanings. Moreover, he places particular emphasis on two meanings of the word that are not contained in the above list: one has sodomistic connotations; the other refers to logical word substitutions, which became almost a game among certain scholastic writers.

4. Elephantis was a Greek poetess, the author of amatory verse and pseudomedical works in which various sexual postures, some depicting sodomy, were illustrated. The Emperor Tiberius had these reproduced on the walls of his palace. See Martial, *Epigrammata*, lib. XII, cap. xliii, and Suetonius, *Duodecim caesares*, *Tiberius*, cap. xliii.

5. The height of the Mount of Venus, the peak formed by the confluence of the two major lines in the palm of the hand, is, for the palmist, a determining factor in the length of one's love life.

6. After the capture of Constantinople in 1453, the Turks appeared as a constant, though remote, threat to the Italian states. The threat became very real, however, in 1480 when a large Turkish expeditionary force sailed from Valona in Albania to attack Otranto on the southern tip of the Italian peninsula. The city fell after nearly a month-long siege, and half its population was either massacred or taken as slaves. Only with the death of the sultan, Mohammed II, in 1481, did the Turks abandon Otranto as well as their plans for further attacks against the West. This example of Turkish barbarity, nevertheless, impressed itself deeply on the Italian mind, and the "cruel Turk" was to be a recurring topic in the literature of the period. See, for example, Machiavelli, *Mandragola*, Act Three, Scene Three. For a different view of the European reaction to the Turks see C. A. Patrides, "'The Bloody and Cruelle Turke': Background of a Renaissance Commonplace," *Studies in the Renaissance* 10 (1963): 126–36.

7. "Hence the saying: 'Justinian's law provides riches; from it you will gather grain, from other things you will get chaff.'" In the verse edition Cleandro's lines are split: "CLE: Nonsense! Well said. Hence we have that well-known verse and moral: *Opes dat sanctio Iustiniana.* PAS: Oh, how fitting it is! CLE: *Ex aliis paleas.* PAS: Excellent! CLE: *Ex istis collige grana.* PAS: Who wrote it? Vergil? CLE: Vergil? Hardly! It's one of our best glosses."

8. *Sopràdote:* a gift by the groom, who receives no dowry, to the father of the bride—in this case a bribe.

9. The verse version has: "I don't believe that all the eyes that Argo was supposed to have had would have sufficed . . . to find this man."

10. Of the ducal palace.

11. The allusion is to the classical themes of the deception of the Greeks and the disloyalty of the Carthaginians.

12. Hercules I of Este (1431–1505), second duke of Ferrara and Modena (1471–1505); Ferrante I (1431–1494), king of Naples (1458–1494).

13. In the 1525 prose edition the line reads: ". . . all of which the viceroy was sending to this prince as a gift"; whereas the verse version has: ". . . that the king of Naples was sending as a gift to his daughter and son-in-law, the duke." Hercules of Este had married Eleanor of Aragon, daughter of Ferrante I.

14. Garofalo in the verse edition. Pontelagoscuro is the port for Ferrara, located some four miles north of the city on the main branch of the Po; Garofalo is about eight miles downriver.

15. The verse version is more specific: "What would you think if I pretended to be dumb as I did in Crisobolo's house?" The reference is to Trappola's pretense in Act Four, Scene Seven, of the *Coffer*. Possibly the same actor played both parts.

16. The dialogue that follows proceeds somewhat differently in verse: "ERO: Welcome, Filogono, my father. SIEN: And I hope you are well Erostrato, my son. ERO: Always remember to keep up the pretense, so that these Ferrarans, all of whom have the devil in them, won't be able to tell that you're Sienese. SIEN: They'll never know; rest assured that we'll do what we have to. ERO: You'd be despoiled of everything and there would be other injuries done to you, for, *a furore populi*, you would immediately be expelled as rogues. SIEN: I was just admonishing them, and I'm sure that they won't fail me in this. ERO: And you must pretend the same way with my household, for my servants are all from this city; they never saw my father and never were in Sicily. This is the house. Let's go in; you follow me."

17. The reference is undoubtedly to *mercurius vitae*, the mercurial element in alchemy, which was thought to have the power of keeping extremes, such as body and soul, together.

18. *Grosso*: a silver coin, equal to twelve *denarii*, which first came into use in the thirteenth century when an increase in the value of silver led to a reduction in the weight and size of the *denarius*.

19. Obviously a pun on the author's name. Ariosto's surname derives from Riosto, a castle in the countryside near Bologna.

20. The variations in verse of the patter that follows are worth noting: "DUL: Imagine the worst things that can be said: that there isn't a more miserable and stingier man than you.... CLE: Pasifilo says this of me? DUL: And that coming to live in your house she would die of hunger because of your avarice.... CLE: Oh, may the devil take him! DUL: And that you're the most annoying and hot-tempered man in the world, and that you'll make her die of anguish.... CLE: Oh, that foul tongue! DUL: And that you continually cough and spit night and day, with such filth that pigs would be disgusted with you. CLE: I never cough and spit. DUL: Certainly, I can see this. CLE: It's true that today I have a very bad cold, but who doesn't at this time of year? DUL: And he says that your feet and armpits smell so that they pollute the air; and, furthermore, that you have intolerable breath.... CLE: I'll be damned if I don't make him pay for this. DUL: And that you have a hernia.... CLE: Oh, may he get Saint Anthony's fire! Everything he says is entirely false. DUL: And that you seek this girl more for want of a husband than a wife. CLE: What does this mean? DUL: That you hope through her to lure young men to your home. CLE: Young men? What for? DUL: Imagine it yourself." The last line of Dulippo is somewhat more precise and more vulgar in the 1525 prose edition: "Because you suffer a certain infirmity in your behind for which a good and appropriate remedy is to be with adolescent boys."

21. "Evil-befall-you."

22. "Drop dead."

23. *Scherzare con l'orso*: literally, "to play with the bear."

24. *Zara*: or "hazard," an old form of craps played with three dice. See Dante, *Purgatorio* canto 6, l. 1.

25. Ariosto reveals Damone's intentions vis-à-vis Dulippo through his choice of names: Lippo Malpensa—Philip the Evil-Minded; Serraglio—the Prison; Ugo de le Siepi—Hugh of the Fences.

26. See p. 81, lines 22–24, and n. 27.

27. A pun on the name Ferrara: *fé rara* (rare faith).

28. The institution of the *podestà* dates from the twelfth century, when internecine party rivalries forced many of the Italian city-states to transfer extraordinary power to an outside individual. By the fourteenth century the *podestà* had lost his political function and had become a sort of chief justice with police powers.

29. The text has *Iudice de' Savi* (Judge of the Twelve Sages), the title of the head of the Ferraran magistrature, a position held by Ariosto's father from 1486 to 1488.

30. This line and that of Pasifilo that follows are omitted from the verse version.

31. Valona, a strategic base in Albania facing Italy across the Strait of Otranto, was captured by the Turks in 1414 and subsequently was used for raids against the West. See n. 6.

32. This line was omitted from the 1525 edition.

33. A pun on the word *barare* (to cheat) or *baro* (a cheat); hence Bari—the city of cheats.

34. The verse rendition breaks this speech of Pasifilo into three parts and improves the opening of the scene from a dramatic standpoint by introducing more movement: "PAS: Oh, God, I hope I find Damonio at home. DAM: (What does he want from me?) PAS: May I be the first one to tell him! DAM: (What does he want to tell me? What brings on such happiness that he jumps so?) PAS: Oh, lucky me! I see him over there in the street! DAM: Pasifilo, what news do you bring me? How come you seem so joyful? PAS: I bring you quiet, peace of mind, and happiness. DAM: I could use it."

35. This line and that of Pasifilo that follows are omitted from the verse edition.

36. Ariosto varied the finale. In the verse ending Pasifilo says: "Shove them up as far as the hilt. You know what I mean, Nevola. Farewell, all of you. If you've enjoyed the story of the *Pretenders* give us an indication so that we may know." In the 1525 edition Pasifilo is more direct: "Shove them up where one farts. Farewell, all of you, and give us a sign of your enjoyment. Farewell."

THE NECROMANCER
Il Negromante

A Comedy Originally in Verse

CHARACTERS

MARGARITA	*A maid*
NURSE	
LIPPO	
FAZIO	} *Old men*
CINTIO	*A young man*
TEMOLO	*His servant*
MASSIMO	*Cintio's foster-father*
NIBBIO	*The necromancer's servant*
ASTROLOGO	*The necromancer*
CAMILLO	*A young man*
MADONNA	*Emilia's mother*
MAID	
PORTER	
ABONDIO	*Cintio's father-in-law*

The action takes place in Cremona

D ON'T THINK IT STRANGE IF YOU HEAR THAT WILD ANIMALS and trees followed Orpheus from place to place; and that by their singing both Amphion in Greece and Apollo in Phrygia imbued stones with such lust that they began mounting one another—as many of you here would do if given the opportunity. By this means they built the walls of Thebes and those of Priam's city.[1] And so [you shouldn't be surprised] to find that the whole city of Cremona, with its entire population, has come here today. I'm right in the midst of it; the city limits begin here and extend for a mile in that direction.

I know that some of you will say that she looks quite like Ferrara and was actually called Ferrara when the *Lena* was performed.[2] But you must remember that this is carnival time and people disguise themselves. The fashions that some wear today were worn by others yesterday and will be passed on to still others tomorrow. Tomorrow they will dress up in costumes that others have worn today. So, Cremona, that noble city from Lombardy, as I told you, has appeared before you with the gown and the mask that Ferrara wore when the *Lena* was performed.

I suppose that you would like to know what brought her here. I can truthfully say that I don't know, for I make little effort to pry into matters that don't concern me. If you want more information

Ariosto incorporated large portions of the first version of the *Necromancer* into the text of the second, and these borrowings have been indicated in the translation: by following the material set off between virgules and supplementing it with the variants below it is possible to reconstruct the text of the original version of the play.

There are a number of structural differences between the two versions, and some character names were changed. Act I, Scene 3, in the second version was originally Act II, Scene 1, and Act II contained five scenes instead of four; hence all of Act II comprises Scenes 2 to 5 of the original. Act I, Scene 3, as well as Act III, Scene 5, of the first rendition are incorporated into Act III, Scene 4, of the second. Act III, in fact, underwent the greatest alteration: Scene 1 became Scene 5 in the newer version, while an additional scene was created by dividing Scene 3 into Scenes 2 and 3. Act IV of the original contained seven scenes, reduced to six in the second version by combining Scenes 3 and 4 into Scene 3. In Act V the author added three final scenes to the initial three, which were kept virtually intact.

The character changes are as follows: NURSE was originally AURELIA; FAZIO was CAMBIO; NIBBIO was NEBBIO; MARGARITA was MARGHERITA; MASSIMO was MAXIMO; and MADONNA (Emilia's mother) was MADRE. The name of the necromancer was changed from FISICO to ASTROLOGO; hence wherever the term "the Astrologer" appears it would read "the Physicist" in the you'll find some money exchanges, some drapery shops, and some grocery stores in the piazza, which don't seem to be very busy. Those who want to hear the news hang out there, where they learn of events in Venice and Rome and whether France or Spain has hired Swiss or German mercenaries. These people know all that happens abroad; but they probably don't know and don't care to know about those things that most directly affect them—what their wives and the other women in their households are doing while. they stand there beating their gums. They'll be able to tell you what you want to know about Cremona's coming here. I cannot tell you anything else except that, to please you all the more, she has brought with her a new comedy called the *Necromancer*.

Now it will no longer seem such a miracle to you that she is here, for you have already come to the conclusion that the necromancer in our story has called upon the devil to transport her here through the air; but, even if it were so, it would be a miracle just the same. She tells us that the author of this new comedy is the same one who recently gave Ferrara the *Lena* and who some fifteen or sixteen years ago gave her the *Coffer* and the *Pretenders*. Oh God, how swiftly the years pass by!

---

first version. For economy's sake a number of minor differences in words and phrases that do not alter the meaning of the dialogue have been ignored.

PROLOGUE

Don't think it strange if you hear it said that rocks and trees followed Orpheus from place to place; and don't think it extraordinary that at one time Apollo and Amphion made stones pile themselves upon one another and thereby built the walls of Thebes and those of Priam's city. After all, at last year's carnival you saw Ferrara with its houses and majestic roofs, its private, sacred, and public places carried in its entirety here to Rome; and today you'll see Cremona brought here in the middle of winter by a difficult road, which is muddy and traverses steep mountains.

You mustn't think that necessity brings her here, that she comes out of a desire to be absolved of murders, vows, or other similar things; for she has no such need. And, even if she did, she would have expected the liberal pontiff to send a plenary indulgence to her at home. But she comes here in order to see and admire with her own eyes what she has heard about the celebrated reputation of the kindness, the candor of soul, the religion, the prudence, the supreme courtesy, the celebrated splendor, and the total virtue of Leo X.[24] And so that she may be no less pleasing and agreeable to you than was Ferrara, she has not neglected to bring with her an entirely new comedy, entitled the *Necromancer*, which will be performed for you today.

Now it will no longer seem so marvelous to you that Cremona is here, for you have already come to the conclusion that the necromancer in our

Don't wait to hear the plot or the prologue, which is always
annoying to do at the beginning. It's sometimes more beneficial to
vary the order and put it in the end—of the comedy, that is. If there
is anyone who wants to have it right now, he can run off to the
druggist here at the court and have him administer it, for he always
has enemas and concoctions on hand.

ACT ONE
Scene One
MARGARITA, a maid; NURSE

MARG: /Since the day Emilia was married—it must be over a month
by now—this is the first opportunity I've had /to get out of the
house long enough /to come and visit her./[a] Even if our house
had a hundred maids it would always be my turn to take care of
the cinders along with the cats. I never go to mass or to services
with my Lady; yet today I found her so pleasant, for as she was
leaving to come here and visit her daughter and son-in-law she
said to me: "Margarita, come for me when the bells ring four[3] as I
don't want to miss Vespers today." So I came somewhat earlier
in order to have a leisurely visit with Emilia and stay with her
a while. /Oh, here is her nurse coming out of the house. Where
are you going, Nurse?

NURSE: Nowhere. I came out because I thought I heard one of the
vegetable peddlers./[b]

MARG: Is my Lady getting ready to leave yet?

NURSE: Oh! You came very early for her.

---

story has called upon the devil to transport her here through the air; but,
even if it were so, it would be a miracle just the same. She tells us that the
author of this new comedy is the same one who gave Ferrara the *Pretenders*. And, if you don't seem to hear the proper and accustomed idiom
of Cremona, you can attribute it to the fact that she picked up a few terms
while passing through Bologna, where there's a university. She liked them
and remembered them. Then she tried to make them as elegant as possible
while passing through Florence, Siena, and all of Tuscany; but, in so short
a time she has not been able to learn enough to hide completely her
Lombard accent. Now, if you listen quietly to her comedy, she hopes to
provide you with as much to laugh at as did Ferrara.

[a] And I think that she must be disappointed, for in her goodness there
wasn't a neighbor whom she loved more tenderly than me.

[b] And where are you going, Margherita? MARG: I came to visit a while
with our Emilia. AUR: Please, if you love her, don't disturb her now, for
she's filled with melancholy and has locked herself in her room with
her mother.

MARG: What is our Emilia doing?

NURSE: She and her mother locked themselves in a room a while ago. A doctor—a foreigner—came today and is with them; they're speaking secretly.

MARG: I was hoping to visit a while with her.

NURSE: You won't be able to stay long today, for she's filled with melancholy.

MARG: /What has happened to her?

NURSE: That which the poor thing least expected. May whoever brought about this marriage get a cancer!

MARG: Everyone praised this from the start as the best match in the city.

NURSE: My dear Margarita, they couldn't have married her off worse.

MARG: And yet he's a fine young man.

NURSE: More than this is needed.

MARG: I understand that he's extremely rich.

NURSE: Even more than this.

MARG: Is he perhaps violent? She shouldn't oppose him or joust over matters of pride with him.

NURSE: Hah, don't worry about their jousting, for the lance is blunt and rather feeble.

MARG: Then he doesn't perform his duties by her?

NURSE: His duties, eh?

MARG: What! Is he incapable?

NURSE: The poor thing is just as much a virgin as she was before the wedding.

MARG: Oh, what a tragedy!

NURSE: It's one of the worst things that could happen to a woman.

MARG: She ought to let things be and not worry about it; perhaps he'll be able. . . .

NURSE: When will he be able to, if in fifteen or thirty days he couldn't?

MARG: I hear there have been cases where men have been incapable for years and then their ability returned.

NURSE: For years? Oh, Lord! Must she then wait with her mouth open until the grain/ sprouts and /ripens before she gets something to eat? Wouldn't it have been better for the poor thing to sit and idle away her time in her father's house than to be married/[c] if she only gets food, clothing, and similar things, all

[c] and get nothing out of it. Eating, drinking, getting dressed, and things such as these she was able to do in her own house.

of which she could have in abundance from her father?

MARG: /Some evil woman with whom the groom previously had relations must have reduced him to this condition out of envy; yet, there are remedies for such things.

NURSE: A number have been used and others are being tried, but all to no avail. A man has come to see him, /^d who, they say, knows all about these matters and performs miracles; however, so far he hasn't done him any good. /I'm afraid that it may be something worse than sorcery, and that he lacks ... you know what I mean.

MARG: It would have been better had she been given to Camillo, who had asked for her hand so many times. Why did they refuse him? Was it because Cintio is wealthier?

NURSE: There's very little difference in their wealth; actually they did so because from the very beginning there was always an extremely close friendship between the two fathers-in-law. Of course, they now regret it and if they could undo what they have done and do it again they would do better the second time than the first./^e But there's Fazio coming out of the house. Come inside. I don't want that nuisance to catch us here, for he always wants to know what goes on and what's being said. Lord, how indiscreet, how annoying, how unpleasant he is!

SCENE TWO
LIPPO, FAZIO, *old men*

LIPPO: /This is the first street on the left-hand side after passing Saint Stephen's; this must be Massimo's house and the one whom I seek lives nearby.^f Perhaps that fellow can inform me. But, by God, there he is; I see him! He's precisely the one I'm looking for. It's him.

FAZIO: Isn't this Lippo?

LIPPO: Oh, Fazio!

FAZIO: When did you arrive in Cremona?

LIPPO: Oh, my dear Fazio, I'm happy to see you.

FAZIO: I believe you are; and I'm glad too. What business brings you here?

---

^d a man called the Physicist, who has promised to perform wonders; however, so far we've heard nothing but stories.

^e MARG: Since you think it best, I won't disturb her. Good-bye. AUR: Go in peace, but come back on Sunday, for you'll find her more at ease then and you'll be able to stay with her longer.

^f If I'm not mistaken, he lives either in this house or in the next one.

LIPPO: Our Copo sent me here to collect some money that the heirs of Mengoccio de la Semola owe him.

FAZIO: When did you arrive?

LIPPO: I got here last evening.

FAZIO: How are things in Florence?

LIPPO: The same as usual. I hear that you have become Cremonese in body and soul, and that you no longer care about your own city. / [8]

FAZIO: What did you expect me to do? Taxes are so heavy in Florence that one cannot endure them. I moved to this city where I and my family live more comfortably.

LIPPO: How is your wife?

FAZIO: She's well, thank God.

LIPPO: Didn't you have a daughter? I seem to remember one.

FAZIO: Yes, you may remember a little girl whom we raised from childhood. We love her more than if she were our own daughter.

LIPPO: I thought she was your daughter.

FAZIO: No, she's not our daughter. She was left with us by her

---

[8] and that you've taken a pretty young wife. CAMB: Yes, indeed. What do you think of it? She was fourteen years old when I married her, and that was less than two years ago. LIPPO: And you must be over sixty. CAMB: I don't think I've quite reached that yet. LIPPO: I know that you're at least my age and perhaps even older. Well, let's forget it. It's no use reproving you for something that cannot be changed. Yet . . . CAMB: Go on. What do you mean "yet"? What are you implying? Do you think that I've done the wrong thing, having found so fertile a possession at an age when I should rest? LIPPO: Did you get such a large dowry? CAMB: The dowry was very small; but the income is so great and so useful to me that I've lived on it and am still living on it quite comfortably. LIPPO: I don't understand you. CAMB: She's such a kind, charming, and beautiful girl that she gives me a good income in every season. LIPPO: Ah, Cambio, but what about your reputation? CAMB: Things such as this are not considered shameful here. How many husbands do you think there are in this city who keep their wives more for someone else's use than their own? And, as a result, they go well dressed, they eat like abbots, and they suffer no inconvenience. LIPPO: Now this is what you really call a republic! Cambio, from what I knew of you as a child until you left our city, I always regarded you as being not at all like this, and I would never have believed that your exposure to the horrible customs here would have been sufficient to corrupt you so soon. But it seems to me that you only pretend to be so different from what you were in order to joke and that you aren't serious. CAMB: My dear Lippo, in the past I never wanted to hide anything that was on my mind from you, nor was I able to; and, as my love for you is the same as it used to be, I don't want to allow my absence of two years here in Cremona to have the effect of lessening the trust that I had in you while in Florence. LIPPO: I thank you for your kindness

mother who was gravely ill when she came to our house. She died after staying with us for ten or twelve days.

LIPPO: Have you married her off yet?

FAZIO: We married her off so well that one could hardly find a better match in this city; but then the devil intervened, with the result that I sometimes wish I were never born.

LIPPO: I'm sorry about your troubles.

FAZIO: I'm sure you are.

LIPPO: And if there's anything I can do, call upon me.

FAZIO: I thank you.

LIPPO: If I knew the situation I might be able to help you by doing something or giving you advice just as any of your other friends would so readily do.

FAZIO: Lippo, while in Florence I loved you as my very own self and I never wanted to nor could I hide anything from you that was on my mind. Now, I don't want my absence of five or six years to change my friendship with you; my trust in you here in Cremona is the same as it was in our own city.

LIPPO: I thank you for your kind words and your good will; /and you can be certain that I place the same trust in you. If there is something that you wish to confide in me, do so with the assurance that I'll be a faithful repository of whatever you tell me.

FAZIO: Now, listen./[h] Here in Massimo's house /there lives a polite

---

[h] LIPPO: Speak out. CAMB: It's true that a girl lives with me in this little house whom my neighbors think is my wife, but she isn't; the fact is she's the wife of a young Cremonese nobleman. Now, I'll tell you the reason why I want them to think as they do. LIPPO: Go on. CAMB: Do you remember Fazio, my sister's husband? LIPPO: I met him when he lived in Florence, and we used to be very close friends. CAMB: You must remember when he left Florence. LIPPO: Yes, I don't think that five years have passed since then. CAMB: Actually, it was nine years ago. LIPPO: That could be. Oh, God, how quickly the years pass by! CAMB: When they came here, he and his wife brought with them a pretty little girl whom they had adopted as their daughter. LIPPO: I remember seeing her and I always thought that she was their child. CAMB: No, she wasn't; she was the daughter of a woman who died in their house after coming from Calabria. It's a long story. LIPPO: Let's skip it. CAMB: But, as I was saying, Fazio came to this city where, with what he had brought with him from Florence and with his continued business activity—for you know he was a man of great industry . . . LIPPO: I know of no one else so keen on making profits. CAMB: He was able to buy this small house and a few other things as well. LIPPO: I believe it and he probably acquired more household goods than he did years of his life. CAMB: Without doubt. Now listen. LIPPO: I'm listening. CAMB: In the house next door

and noble young man named Cintio, whom Massimo has adopted as his son—because he has no other and he's very rich—with the intention of making him his heir. Now this youth shows him the obedience and respect that you would imagine to be proper for someone who expects such an inheritance, an inheritance that Massimo is induced to give him neither because of blood ties, nor of obligations, nor for any reason whatsoever other than his own free choice to so benefit him./[i] As I was saying, this young man, being a neighbor and occasionally seeing the girl—her name is Lavinia—at the door or at the window, /fell very deeply in love with her.

LIPPO: She must have turned out to be quite beautiful, judging from what she was like when she was small.

FAZIO: She's very pretty. Now, as I was saying, Cintio began from the first to tempt her by his pleadings and offers of money to give herself to him. She always replied with prudence and gave him to understand that she would not be his except as his legitimate wife and would not marry him without/[j] my permission, for she has great respect for me and always calls me "Father." /The young man would have married her/[k] without regard to his respect for the old man or to the risk of his being thrown out of the house. If I /had come to an agreement with him, the marriage would have taken place then; but I[l] saw that there would have been little good in giving Lavinia to him if it would lead to Massimo's resentment and disfavor. I prolonged the matter because I didn't want to refuse the youth altogether/[m] nor promise her to him outright.

---

[i] Now this young man, after seeing Lavinia—that's the girl's name—and occasionally speaking to her, as neighbors are apt to do

[j] the permission of my sister, Nanna, whom she always called "Mother."

[k] but he held off due to his respect for, and even more, his fear of Maximo, who would not have been amenable to this. If Nanna

[l] *Read "she" for "I" throughout the remainder of the paragraph.*

[m] nor destroy all his hopes. Meanwhile, Nanna informed me that Fazio had passed away—it all happened about the same time—and she asked me to come and stay here so that I could help her. To please her, as I should, I came here, and my sister informed me of the entire matter. I spoke with Cintio several times about the situation and, realizing that he loved Lavinia as much as anyone can love, I didn't let the opportunity pass; and, as a solution, I had him marry her secretly in the presence of two trustworthy witnesses. At the same time, I let it be known that I had come here from Florence expressly to take Lavinia as my wife, at my sister's suggestion, for she wanted both of us to benefit from Fazio's estate, which had been left jointly to her and Lavinia. I would be Lavinia's husband in name only, and

This affair went on for about four years. After seeing him persevere so long in his courtship and knowing what a fine young man he is, I didn't think that I should let such a rare opportunity pass. So, trusting in his discretion that he would keep the matter secret until Massimo is out of the way—in the natural course of events he shouldn't live much longer—I gave her to him with pleasure. I had Cintio marry the girl secretly in the presence of two witnesses. They were joined to each other secretly and have enjoyed each other secretly; and up to this point everything had been going along fine.

LIPPO: /I don't like this "had been"; [n] has this Cintio now changed his mind?

FAZIO: It wasn't that; he loves Lavinia just as before.

LIPPO: What is it then?

FAZIO: I'll tell you. Three months hadn't gone by, when Massimo, having no knowledge of this situation, with the help of some friends, convinced Abondio, a very wealthy man from this city, to agree to have his only daughter become Cintio's wife; and they exchanged vows to this effect. The old man arranged the wedding before we found out about it. They caught Cintio so completely unawares that they made him betroth her, marry her, and take her home all that same day; and the poor fellow wasn't able to say a word to the contrary.

LIPPO: So Lavinia will be left in the lurch; she'll be a widow while her husband is still alive. /[o]

FAZIO: I don't think so. Still, we're trying something which, if it succeeds, would invalidate the new wedding.

LIPPO: What's that?

Cintio would enjoy her in secret until old Maximo would be out of the way. So, to make the story short, Cintio secretly married Lavinia and they see each other on the sly, while I act as if I were her husband in public. LIPPO: Why did you have to pretend that she was your wife? Couldn't the young man have had her secretly without this? CAMB: No. If she became pregnant—and she did soon after the wedding—she could hardly have concealed her condition, and this would have brought nothing but censure and shame to herself and her mother. LIPPO: I'll keep quiet. CAMB: The affair had been going along very well.

[n] something unpleasant must have happened. CAMB: You guessed correctly. LIPPO:

[o] CAMB: No. Hear me out. We've figured out a way to bring this ship into the safest port, that is, if fate isn't completely opposed to us. LIPPO: May it be God's will. How?

FAZIO: /So far Cintio hasn't tasted/[p] this other woman.

LIPPO: /I don't believe this; it's impossible. But I do believe that he's telling you a story.

FAZIO: No, he's not telling me a story; you can be absolutely certain of it. If you knew him and were acquainted with him/, as we are, /you would not find it difficult to believe. What is more, the bride complained about it to her nurse, her nurse then reported it to her mother/[q] and to her father, /Abondio, and Abondio has complained about it bitterly to Massimo; and Massimo, not wanting to dissolve the marriage and thereby deprive Cintio of such a fine inheritance, has gone and found some astrologer or necromancer—I don't know which—an expert in such matters, and has promised him twenty florins if he can cure him. Now you can see whether or not Cintio is lying.

LIPPO: What do you hope to accomplish with this pretense?

FAZIO: After Cintio has abstained for/[r] six months or even a year, /Abondio will finally think that his infirmity is permanent and incurable and will take his daughter back[s]; and, if we can get out of this difficulty, we'll have nothing more to worry about. Anyone who would consider giving his daughter to Cintio once he has acquired the reputation for impotence and weakness would indeed be a fool and must really hate her.

LIPPO: This is a fine scheme and it could succeed, provided that Cintio remains firm in his purpose.

FAZIO: I'm not worried that he'll change.

LIPPO: If he perseveres I'll praise him as the most faithful and the finest young man I've ever heard of. Well, I'm glad to have seen you. May God grant all your wishes! Can I do anything for you?

FAZIO: Yes, you can stay as a guest at my house.

LIPPO: Thank you, but I'm staying with the Semolas; I have some business with them and it's not easy to get away. I just barely found time to come and see you, and right now they're waiting for me./[t]

---

[p] his bride, and he has slept with her for almost a month now, all the time pretending to be impotent; and he'll continue to feign this.

[q] , her mother related it to

[r] three or six or nine or twelve months

[s] and give her to another

[t] CAMB: I'll walk back with you. LIPPO: Come along, if it's not too far out of your way. CAMB: Well, here comes Maximo and he has the necromancer with him. He's willing to try anything to cure Cintio. LIPPO: I hope that everything turns out to the satisfaction of the patient. But let's go, for I have no time to waste.

FAZIO: I'll come and visit you this evening.

LIPPO: Please come and see me often; let's enjoy each other's company as much as possible while I'm here.

FAZIO: We'll do that.——Here comes Cintio along with Temolo. If all servants were as faithful to their masters as Temolo is to his, things would go much better for their masters than they now do.[u]

SCENE THREE [v]

CINTIO, a young man; TEMOLO, his servant; FAZIO

CINT: /Temolo, what do you think of this astrologer/,[w] this necromancer, I mean?

TEM: /I take him for a sly fox./[x]

CINT: Now here's Fazio.——I was asking him what he thought about our Astrologer.

TEM: I said that I take him for a sly old fox.

CINT: And what do you think, Fazio?

FAZIO: I consider him quite a shrewd man and very learned.

TEM: /In what science is he most learned?/[y]

FAZIO: In that which is called the Liberal Arts.

CINT: /Yet, in the Magical Arts he knows all that can be known, and I would think that there isn't his equal in the whole world.

TEM: What do you know about this?

CINT: His servant has told me marvelous things about him.

TEM: With God's help, tell us about some of them.

CINT: He told me that, when he wants to, he can make the night light up and the day grow dark.

TEM: I can do the same thing.

CINT: How?

TEM: If I light a lamp during the night and close the shutters during the day.

CINT: Oh, you blockhead! I'm telling you that he blots out the sun throughout the world and illuminates the night everywhere./

TEM: The grocers[z] /ought to pay him well.

CINT: Why?

---

[u] *Act One, Scene Three, is found in Act Three, commencing at note y,* p. 132.

[v] *Act Two, Scene One, begins here.*

[w] or necromancer, whichever he is.

[x] , Master, full of cunning. CINT: A fox, no; but cautious, yes.

[y] CINT: I can tell you that he's very learned in just about all of them.

[z] Those who grow olives and raise bees

111

TEM: Because he could lower or raise the price of oil and wax as he pleases. What else can he do?

CINT: He can make the earth move at his will.

TEM: I, too, move it sometimes when I put a pot on the fire or take it away; or when I shake the jug in the dark to see whether there's a drop of wine left.

CINT: Are you making fun of him, and do you think that these are stories? Well, what do you say to this? He can become invisible whenever he wishes./

TEM: Invisible? /Have you ever seen him/, Master?

CINT: /You idiot! How can you see him if he's invisible?

TEM: What else can he do?

CINT: Whenever he likes he can change men and women into various winged animals and quadrupeds.

TEM: That's no miracle; one can see it happen every day.

FAZIO:[a] Where does it happen?

TEM: Among our own people./[b]

CINT: Don't listen to his nonsense; he's making fun of us.

FAZIO: I want to know; tell us what you mean.

TEM: /Haven't you noticed that as soon as someone/[c] becomes a *podestà*, a commissariat, a provisioner, /a tax collector, a judge, a notary, or a paymaster he puts off his human form completely and takes on that of a wolf or a fox or of some bird of prey?

FAZIO:[a] That's true.

TEM: And when someone of a lower rank becomes a councillor, a secretary, or obtains a position where he commands others, isn't it true that he also becomes an ass?

FAZIO:[a] Very true.

TEM: I won't even mention all those who become cuckolds.

CINT: Temolo, you have a wicked tongue.

TEM: Yours is worse, for you relate fables as if they were true.

CINT: Then you don't believe that this fellow performs wonders?

TEM: On the contrary, I think that he does even greater things when, with simple words and without producing the smallest result, he's able to extract sometimes money, sometimes merchandise, from your avaricious old man. Now what can be more marvelous than this?

CINT: You're joking and not answering my question.

TEM: Tell me something that's true or at least something that one

---

[a] *This line is given to Cintio.*

[b] and it happens in every city in Italy. CINT: How is that?

[c] is placed in charge of public provisions or becomes

can believe, and then I'll answer you properly.

CINT: Tell me this: do you think that he's a great magician?

TEM: I can believe that he's a magician and an excellent one; but I don't believe that the miracles you told me about can be performed through the art of magic.

CINT: That's because you have such little worldly experience. Tell me, do you believe that a magician can do wondrous things?/ [d] Can he conjure up spirits which will answer the many questions you put to them?

TEM: /To tell you the truth, I, myself, would place very little credence in these spirits; but the example of great men—princes and prelates—who do, leads me, the humblest of servants, to believe also.

CINT: Now, if you admit this, you will also admit that I'm the most unhappy and unfortunate man alive today.

TEM: What do you mean? Go on.

CINT: If this man is able to conjure up spirits, won't he find out that I'm not impotent as I pretend to be? And won't he also discover the reason for my pretense? That by doing so I'm trying to get rid of Abondio's daughter? And that Lavinia is my wife? Once he learns of this and reports it to my old man, what will my situation be?/ [e]

TEM: There's no doubt, you'd be in trouble.

CINT: In very deep trouble.

FAZIO: Cintio, would you like me to tell you of an excellent plan that I've been considering these past few days? I've come to the conclusion that it can only help us.

CINT: /Go ahead.

FAZIO: [f] It seems to me that this fellow is very eager to reap ample gain.

CINT: I'm of the same opinion. So?

FAZIO: Then you can be sure that he would willingly take forty instead of twenty.

CINT: I'm most certain of it.

FAZIO: [f] The old man has promised, if he cures you, to give him

---

[d] TEM: Yes, but not such things as making someone go around invisible or transforming him into an animal or the like, which children could hardly believe. CINT: You're obstinate in your ignorance; but you will at least admit that spirits can be conjured up and that they can be made to answer the questions you put to them.

[e] TEM: Certainly a very difficult one. Shall I tell you something that comes to mind and might prove useful to you?

[f] This line is given to Temolo.

twenty scudi;[4] and I believe this is after expenses.

CINT: Well, continue.

FAZIO:[f] Go find him and tell him all about your situation; at the same time make him a magnanimous offer of forty ducats if he would see to it that this marriage of yours is dissolved.

CINT: But where will I find even forty pennies[5]—no less florins—at this moment?/[g]

FAZIO: Leave it to me. Even if I have to sell my bed and my sheets and every piece of furniture I have in the house, and even the house itself down to the last room, I'll take care of such requirements immediately.

CINT: In this and in everthing else, Fazio, I'll always place myself in your hands.

FAZIO: What do you think about it, Temolo?

TEM: I agree with you.

CINT: Since you feel this way, I'll speak to him.

FAZIO: Then speak to him, and soon.

CINT: Right now, for he's conveniently at home, and I won't have to look for him all over the city.

FAZIO: Is he in the house?

CINT: Yes.

FAZIO: Call him aside or else lock yourself in a room with him.

CINT: I'll do that.

FAZIO: But there's Massimo leaving just in time to give you the opportunity [to speak to him]. Temolo can stay with you. I'm going to see about getting the money we need.

SCENE FOUR
MASSIMO; CINTIO

MASS: /Cintio.

CINT: Yes, sir.

---

[g] TEM: Ask your Nanna and Cambio to help you find it. CINT: They're no more able to find it than I am. TEM: In order to bring about the desired effect, which would be more profitable to them than to you, I'm positive that they'd promptly put their beds, their furniture, all their property, even the house in which they live, up for sale. CINT: I don't care for your advice. Now, go see if Cambio is at home, for I'd like to discuss it with him. I won't say a thing to the necromancer or to anyone else before I hear his opinion. Is he at home? TEM: He's not in; they said he went to the piazza. CINT: He's gone to the piazza? Let's go there and find him. TEM: Is that the young man who told you about the necromancer's miracles? CINT: That's him. TEM: Oh, God, what a liar he must be! CINT: I don't consider him a liar; but I do consider you to be stubborn and unbelieving. TEM: Well, let's go. This isn't something that makes me a heretic if I don't believe it. *Proceed to Act Two, Scene One, of Text.*

MASS: Listen to me for a moment. I want to tell you something that on more than one occasion I had thought of telling you, but I've kept silent, not trusting my own judgment. But now that I see others in agreement with me, I've decided to tell you. Your relationship with our neighbor, Fazio, doesn't seem very proper or commendable to me. It's not right for young men and old men to be so close.

CINT: Sir, what you're saying is the opposite of what you used to tell me—that young men always learn by associating with older men.

MASS: One cannot learn very well where the pupil knows more than the teacher./ [h]

CINT: That may be so, but I don't understand you.

MASS: Must I explain it to you in detail to make you understand? /It doesn't seem very nice to me that an old man with such a young and pretty /daughter [i] /should be on such intimate terms with you that he permits you to frequent his house whether he's there or not. Previously, when you weren't bound by marriage, I always let you live as you pleased, and it didn't bother me that our neighbor's reputation suffered because of you; for, if he cared little about his honor, I cared even less. But now that you have a wife, and as your in-laws have complained to me about this matter and they suspect that this woman of his has reduced you to this condition, I have to break my silence and tell you that you're behaving very badly in keeping up this association.

CINT: It's not for any evil purpose that I frequent his house; and there is nothing sinful between that girl and myself—may God be my witness. But who can stop slanderous tongues from telling their stories?

MASS: So these are stories! What do you do there? What business do you have with them.

CINT: Nothing but good and honest friendship. And do you know of any homes where there are beautiful and charming women that noblemen don't frequent all day long to court them whether or not their husbands are home?

MASS: The custom is not commendable; this was not the usual practice in my day.

CINT: The youth of your day must have been more malicious than they are now.

MASS: This wasn't so; but their elders were more cautious. I'm

[h] CINT: Explain what you mean. MAX: Since you don't understand me, I'll state it more frankly.
[i] wife

surprised that the men nowadays are not fat like turtledoves.

CINT: Why?

MASS: Because they all have such good appetites./[i] Now, go back to the house and keep the Astrologer company. I want to go see if I can borrow a silver basin from a friend—one just like mine—for one isn't enough; the Astrologer wants two of them. As for the other things that are needed, I have plenty in the house, and I've given him money to buy quite a few things as he sees fit. I'm determined to try every means to have you cured soon even if I have to spend everything I have.

ACT TWO

SCENE ONE [a]

NIBBIO, *the Necromancer's servant, alone*

NIB: /My master, Jachelino, certainly has great confidence in himself; for while he hardly knows how to read and write, he nevertheless professes to be a philosopher, an alchemist, a doctor, an astrologer, a magician, and even a conjurer of spirits.[6] Although he's called the Astrologer/ par excellence, just as Vergil is known as the Poet and Aristotle as the Philosopher, /he knows as much about these and other sciences as a donkey or an ox knows about playing an organ. But with a face as motionless as marble, with stories and lies, and no other skills, he swindles people and confounds their minds. Thus, he benefits and makes me benefit from the riches of others—with the help of folly, which abounds in the world.

Like gypsies, we go from place to place, and wherever he passes he leaves his imprint like a snail or, for a more fitting comparison, like fire or lightning; and in each place, in order to disguise himself, he changes his name,/[b] his dress, and his country. /Now he calls himself Peter, now John; now he pretends to come from Greece, now from/[c] Africa. /In reality, he's a Jew, and he was among those who were expelled from Castile.[7] It would be a long story if I were to tell you how many men he has cheated and robbed; how many poor homes he has broken up, how many he has tainted with adultery by pretending that he would make barren wives pregnant or by pretending to remove suspicion and discord that arise between husbands and wives.

[i] *End of Act One.*

[a] *This is Act Two, Scene Two, in the first version. For Act Two, Scene One, see above, Act One, note v, p. 111.*

[b] *and says that he's from another country.*

[c] *Egypt, now from some other country.*

116

Now he has this gentleman in his grip and he's picking him cleaner than a/ᵈ monk ever picked a widow.

Scene Two

astrologo; nibbio

ASTR: /[*To Massimo inside*] I'll take care of everything; leave it to me.

NIB: Oh, yes, leave it to him; you couldn't have come across a better person.

ASTR: Oh, are you here, Nibbio? I was just going to look for you.

NIB: You would rather have someone like the person you just left inside the house; you'll get little profit out of me.

ASTR: I would rather have more of what I brought out with me. You see, you've guessed wrong.

NIB: How the devil did you do it?/ᵉ

ASTR: Massimo gave it to me just now to spend on certain drugs that we need. Here, take this and buy two pairs of fine capons. . . . Make sure, of course, that they're fat and juicy.

NIB: You'll be well served.

ASTR: You'll see that I'll have in my hands two silver basins worth no less than a hundred and fifty scudi. I think that Massimo will want a receipt for them and will only hand them over to me in the presence of witnesses.

NIB: /Take my advice, Master. As soon as you get them let's head for/ Ferrara or /Venice.

ASTR: You want me to leave with so little booty? Do you think that this is the only business that I have in this city, a city that has more stupidity than Rome has fraud and malice? If I leave with just this, I can truly say that I lose a thousand ducats, just as if I had deliberately gone and thrown them into the deepest part of the sea.

NIB: Apart from Massimo,/ᶠ what other business do you have?

ASTR: I have other business no less important with this Cintio. It

---

ᵈ hawk ever picked a sparrow.

ᵉ FIS: I'm about to buy the pentacle, the candelabras, and gums for the fumigations. NEB: We'll see what you'll buy! FIS: Let's go to the store to get the cloth and the drapery, for I have a letter of credit. I'll have them bring the calf directly to my house. NEB: I wish that you had the two flasks of silver, for they're worth more. FIS: I expect them this evening. I think that he wants to hand them over with written documents and in the presence of witnesses, as a cautious man would.

ᶠ what other good food do you have to nibble on? FIS: I'll tell you. Do you know Camillo Pocosale, a certain young man, rather short and dark?

will be much easier to extract a quick profit from him than from his old man. And then we have something else worth more than both of these put together, even if they were worth double what they are. They're all based on the same foundation. You must know Camillo Pocosale, that ·young man with the fair complexion, rather gallant.

NIB: /I should know him; I see him with you so often./

ASTR: What you don't know is that he has an enormous quantity of silver that was left to him by his uncle, a bishop, along with the rest of his inheritance. While I was in his room with him the other day he showed it to me. It's worth seven hundred ducats and perhaps more.

NIB: We mustn't let such an amount go untouched. It would be just right for us.

ASTR: It will be ours if certain plans that I'm devising succeed. /Camillo is so in love with Cintio's wife that he's almost going out of his mind. The poor fellow tried everything possible to obtain her as his wife before she was given to Cintio. Now that he's learned of the weakness and impotence of her husband, who cannot put the plow to the field, he has again taken heart and hope that they may now turn to him/[g] if they want /to prepare this field for planting. He came to see me/ a few days ago /after hearing that I had undertaken to straighten the handle of the plow. The moment he saw me he placed two scudi in my hand, and then, after telling me of his love, he begged me with tears to proceed with Cintio's cure in such a way that he will become weaker and more impotent than he already is, so that he will never be able to know Emilia carnally. And he promised to give me fifty florins if I break up the marriage./

NIB: Compared to the silver, this is a mere pittance; but fifty florins are nothing to scoff at, and I think that you'll easily pick them off,[h] /for as soon as you tell the father and the father-in-law . . .

ASTR: Please! Instruct me in anything else but in how to milk a purse, for that's my foremost skill./ I don't want to lose six hundred florins or more just to get thirty. That silver touches my heart. I must prolong this business until we get the opportunity to clear out. In the meantime, there's no shortage of other fools to live off. /There are some animals that are only useful for eating, like the pig. There are others which, if you keep them, provide for you daily; and, when in the end they can give no more, you eat them/ for supper or dinner. /Such are the cow,

[g] And, as he wanted
[h] The offer sounds fine, and you ought to consider it,

the ox, or the sheep. There are still others which, when alive, bring you handsome profits and are worthless when dead, like the horse, or the dog, or the donkey. In the same way one finds considerable differences among men: there are some whom you happen to meet while on a ship or at an inn and whom you will never see again; it's your duty to despoil and rob them right off. There are others such as innkeepers and artisans who always have a few carlins or julios[8] in their purse, but never a great many. The best thing to do is to take a small amount from them at a time and do it often; for I would gain little if I were to skin them all at once, and I would lose that which I could get from them almost every day.

There are others in cities who are well-to-do, with possessions, with houses, great merchants whom we must hold off biting, no less devouring, as long as one can now and then suck three, four, ten or twelve florins out of them; but if you're going to leave town,/ or if you get an unusual opportunity [you ought to] /shear them right to the skin or skin them completely. In this third category I place/ Cintio, /Massimo, and Camillo whom I'm stringing along with promises and stories and will continue to do so until the milk runs dry. Then one day, when I no longer find them soft and fat, I'll skin them and eat them.

Now, to make Camillo give more milk/ before I get a chance to skin him, /I feed him on the grass and leaves of hope, promising to so enkindle Emilia's love for him that, whether her parents like it or not, she will have no one else but him after she leaves Cintio. And I've given him to understand that I've already done such good work here that she pines for him because of her love. I have also simulated letters and messages from her.... /[i]

NIB: You never told me about this business.

ASTR: /And I also brought him a few small gifts from her, which he treasures./[j] This morning he gave me an exquisite little ring to present to her.

NIB: Will you keep it or give it to her?

ASTR: What do you advise?

NIB: /For goodness sake, don't [give it to her].

ASTR: There he is./[k] Stay alert, /play the fool, and don't interfere.

NIB: I'll be silent.

---

[i] NEB: You waited so long to inform me of this business.

[j] NEB: These gifts are like the salads monks send you in order to get pies in return. FIS: You can be sure that if I spend a soldo I expect to get a ducat back. This morning he gave me an exquisite ruby to give her in return. NEB: Will you give it to her? FIS: If you advise me to, I will.

[k] NEB: I see him. FIS:

Scene Three

ASTROLOGO; CAMILLO; NIBBIO

ASTR: Where's this young man going, this happiest of all lovers?

CAM: I come to pay my respects to the mightiest of all magicians, to bow to my idol, to whom I address all my vows, offerings, and sacrifices; for you're my good fortune./[1] Ah! Master, I cannot express the warm feelings I have for you.

NIB: (I think you'll soon change your mind.)

ASTR: You don't have to speak like this to me; in any way I can be of help, make use of me, for I'm always ready to serve you.

CAM: /I'm sure of it, and I'm forever thankful. But tell me, what is my dearest and sweetest one doing?

ASTR: [To Nibbio] You, go away; move away from us.

NIB: (When it comes to secrecy, this man surpasses all others. Oh, what shrewdness!)

ASTR: These things must never be said where servants can hear them, for they tell everything they know.

CAM: I hadn't thought about that. But what is my sweet and lovely Emilia doing?

ASTR: She's yearning for your love so much that I'm afraid that if I wait much longer to put her in you arms/[m] we'll see her melt like snow exposed to the sun or wax to fire.

NIB: (He's telling him a lie, but he embellishes it so well that he'll have him believe it.)

CAM: Then to prevent her from melting and me from dying of grief, finish [what you have to do]. I'm sure that if you clearly say that Cintio will never be able to consummate this marriage with her, her father won't deny her to me.

ASTR: /She also begs me to do the same thing. To you lovers, who allow youselves to be governed by your appetites, it seems easy to do, for you have no consideration except your own desires. But,/ tell me, /if I were to tell Massimo that Cintio's impotence is incurable, without first having tried a cure, wouldn't I be giving him an indication and perhaps the clearest sign of fraud?

CAM: I'll always abide by your judgment./

NIB: (How simple and innocent this youth is!)

ASTR: /At least you're more reasonable than Emilia is.

CAM: Does she not do so?

---

[1] my salvation, my life, my soul. FIS: Forget these words and let me serve you, for if you're willing to spend I'm always available.

[m] ... CAM: Oh, God! FIS: I'll see her melt like wax when it's exposed to fire or to the sun. CAM: Then don't let her melt because of me, for I would then die of grief. Cut short what you have to do; if you clearly say that it will never be possible for Cintio to possess her, I'm perfectly sure that her father will gladly give her to me.

ASTR: She do so? Hah. She gets angry, she won't listen to me, and she cries and tells me that I'm dragging this thing out on purpose.

CAM: I'll never say that anything is impossible for you after you've been able to make her fall in love with me in such a short time. For five long years I have constantly loved and served her and I have never had so much as a single indication that she liked me./

NIB: (When they baptized him, the world must have been without salt, for they couldn't find a single grain of it to put in his mouth.[9])

ASTR: I have a letter with me[n] /that she wrote to you.

CAM: Why are you waiting to give it to me?

ASTR: Should I let you see it?

CAM: I beg you to./

NIB: (This must be the letter that I saw him write a little while ago. Now he'll have him believe that Emilia wrote it in her own hand.)

CAM: /This letter comes from those hands that are whiter than milk, whiter than snow./

NIB: (It came from the mangy and dirty hands of my master; cherish it and kiss it.)

ASTR: /Before that it came from the alabaster/[o] or the Ligurian marble /of her bosom, where it lay between two small and fragrant apples.

CAM: Then this happiest of papers comes from the beautiful bosom of my sweet Emilia?

ASTR: Her lovely hand then took it from there and gave it to me./

NIB: (If only your mother had given you milk the same way!)

CAM: /Oh, you lucky paper, oh, you blessed letter; how fortunate is your lot! How much those other papers must envy you, papers that are used for writs, notices, inquiries, judicial citations, public testimonies, affidavits, processes, and a thousand other devices by which rapacious notaries legally steal from the public in the piazza! Oh, you fortunate linen, you who are more honored as fragile paper than you ever would be as cloth, even if you had become the tunic of some would-be prince, for my beloved mistress has deigned to write her thoughts upon you!/

NIB: (The antiphony will take longer than the psalm.)

CAM: /But why am I waiting to open you and experience the joy, the jubilation, the blessings, the salvation, the life that you bring me?

ASTR: Hold it. Take my advice.

CAM: What's that?

[n] What if I show you a letter
[o] and ivory

ASTR: Go read it at home.

CAM: Why not here?

ASTR: I'm afraid that, having uttered so many exclamations and formalities to a sealed and silent letter, the moment you open it and see the characters imprinted by that ivory hand and savor the sweetest words that proceed from her fervent heart, you'll swoon, possessed by that sweetness, and you'll fall to the ground or you'll let out such a cry for joy that all the neighbors will come running out.

CAM: No, that won't happen; let me read it,/P Master.

ASTR: Read it.

CAM: I'm reading it: "My dear Lord ..." She shouldn't have addressed me with this title, for I'm her servant.

ASTR: Continue.

CAM: "My only hope ..." Oh, what a honeyed word!

ASTR: Rather, sugared, for honey is impure.

CAM: You're so right.

ASTR: Go on.

CAM: "Oh my soul, oh my life, oh my light!" These words rend my heart. "I beg you, I beseech you out of your feelings for me ..." What a strong plea!

NIB: (It must be difficult subject matter, for he's commenting on it one part at a time.)

CAM: "And because of the deep and inestimable love I have for you, to do, for my sake, whatever you hear from the lips of our Astrologer. Don't think about finding an excuse, for what I ask of you is not impossible or difficult. This will clearly prove to me whether or not I'm yours and you're mine. Stay well and continue loving me."

NIB: (*Cuius figurae*? One can truly say, *simplicis.*[10])

ASTR: Have you finished?

CAM: Yes, but why did she have to beg me? Isn't she convinced that she can drive me into the fire by her mere nod? And if she asked for my heart, I would be ready to rip open my chest and give it to her. What do I have to do?

ASTR: As you can see, the letter serves as my credentials. I'll let you know today what I have to tell you on her behalf. Come see me later.

P FIS: No, you won't; go and read it at home and also take my advice: have someone tie you to a marble column so that you cannot get loose. CAM: Are you afraid that I'll go mad? FIS: I'm afraid that your joy will lift you into the air and that you'll rise up to heaven and we'll lose you. Close it. Look, Emilia's mother is coming out there. If you really care for me, go read it elsewhere. CAM: I'm going to fly home in a hurry, for no one will bother me there. FIS: Let's go to the store for the silk and the white linen.

CAM: Wouldn't it be better to tell me now?

ASTR: It's a delicate matter and not to be settled with three or four words. Let's postpone it a while until I have more time than I have now. Cintio is expecting me. I want to finish something that I began with him a while ago, something that will be completely to your advantage. There's Emilia's mother coming outside. Don't let her see you with me! Follow me, Nibbio.

SCENE FOUR
MADONNA, Emilia's mother; MAID

MAD: /[To Emilia inside] Cheer up, my daughter, wise women find a remedy for everything other than death. Now, God be with you.——Ah, human misery! To how many strange and unusual circumstances is this life of ours subject!

MAID: Upon my faith, one shouldn't take a husband before trying him out.

MAD: Ah, you idiot!

MAID: Why an idiot? What I said is true. You don't buy something without first examining it inside and outside several times. If you spend your money on a simple spindle, you look at it and rotate it in your hand; yet, should men, who are so necessary, be selected with only a dim light?

MAD: I think you're drunk.

MAID: On the contrary, I was never more sober. I knew of a wise neighbor of mine who took a young man to bed every night for more than sixteen months and tried him out in every possible way; only after she found him qualified for the job did she give him to her only daughter as a husband./

MAD: Get out of here, you old sow,^q /you should be ashamed of yourself.

MAID: Why should I be ashamed to tell you the truth? If you had made this experiment with Cintio things wouldn't have come to such a pass. But what more do you need? The situation is the same, as Emilia has tried him out for so long. Let him go, along with his bad luck, and find yourself another son-in-law. But do it my way—try him out first yourself./

MAD: Lord, ^r/what sort of advice is this one giving me!

MAID: If you don't like it, I'll make another suggestion. Let me try him out. If I test him, I'll be able to tell whether or not Emilia will be satisfied.

MAD: Oh, you horrible, deceitful, and evil woman; shut your mouth, damn you, and come with me.

^q Shut up, you pig,
^r Oh, go to hell!

ACT THREE
SCENE ONE [a]
ASTROLOGO; CINTIO; NIBBIO

ASTR: /Cintio, you can be certain that you haven't told me anything that I didn't already know perfectly well. And, if I have pretended to prescribe cures for you, cures generally salutary for those who are impotent in the service of women, it's not because your pretense led me to believe that you needed them. Rather, I[b] had compassion for you, and even though you had not asked me to do anything, everything that I have done so far has been more in accord with your wishes than contrary to them.

CINT: If you've already done me a good turn/ without my asking it or my knowing it, /I'm obliged to you and always will be;/[c] if you say that you did it without my pleading, I believe you. /Now that I ask you and beg you, and now that I'll be aware of the benefits, should you not continue to help me all the more?/[d] It would be much easier for you to do [what I ask] than what Massimo would like you to do. All that you have to do is tell my old man, and the others as well, that my impotence is incurable.

ASTR: If I were to tell the old man and the others that your impotence is incurable, do you think that he'll so easily believe me and return the bride to her house? Cintio, people don't readily believe things that displease them; he might suspect that I was saying this at the urging of someone who envied something of yours and wanted to divert it to his own house. But I see another way to get her out of your house and back to where she came from immediately, a way that will more likely succeed and is faster than this.

CINT: Tell me about it, if you will.

ASTR: I don't want this fellow to hear me.——You move away; leave us alone for a while. You shouldn't always try to hear what's being said.

NIB: (As if he hasn't already told me his plans and what he intends to do!)

ASTR: One shouldn't discuss important matters in the presence of servants.

NIB: (There isn't a *secret*ary like him in the whole world. If princes

---

[a] *Act Three, Scene One, of the first version begins at note q, p. 136.*
[b] regretted your troubles and
[c] but, if you have been well disposed and benevolent to me without my asking you and without my knowledge of your good deeds,
[d] FIS: I'll do it most willingly; and rest assured that you'll be free of her within two days. CINT: Lucky me if you'll do it. FIS: Most certainly I will.

knew him, as I do, they would certainly want him—hanged, that is.)

ASTR: Now, as I was saying, what I'm going to do will immediately remove her from your house.

CINT: /Tell me how, if you please.

ASTR: Before I tell you/[e] I want you to promise not to repeat it to a living soul; not to those two confidants of yours—your servant and your father-in-law—nor even to your wife. If you mentioned it to anyone, I would run the risk of death and both of you of public shame. /Actually, if I were able to do the job without your knowing about it, I would feel much better.

CINT: If I promise you to be silent, do you think that I won't keep my promise?

ASTR: I believe that you intend to now; but as soon as you're with Lavinia, without meaning to do so, you'll tell her what I say to you. And when a woman knows something it cannot remain secret for a whole day.

CINT: I won't say a word about it to her or to anyone else; you can be sure of this./ [f]

ASTR: Then do you promise?

CINT: /I give you my word.

ASTR: Then I'll tell you. Listen./[g] Tonight you'll find a man in your room in bed with Emilia.

CINT: /What did you say?

ASTR: That you'll find a young man in bed with Emilia/ tonight. /Didn't you understand me?

CINT: Perhaps I'll find myself there.

ASTR: I said that there will be another fellow there who'll give her plenty of what you deny her.

CINT: Will she then be an adulteress?

ASTR: Not really. She's chaste and most pure; but soon she'll be considered an adulteress by the old man, and you'll have a legitimate excuse to repudiate her, an excuse acceptable to him and to everyone./[h] And even if you objected, Massimo would not let her remain in the house and would immediately send her back to

---

[e] I ask that you repeat it to no one.

[f] FIS: Then promise it to me. CINT: I promise it and

[g] If I were to say to your father that your malady is incurable, it would be difficult to get him to believe me. This is so not only because people are unwilling to believe that which is unpleasant, but also because he would suspect that I'm saying this at someone else's request or that I envied his possessions or that I wished to remove this profit from his house. But I'm thinking of doing it this way: tomorrow night you'll find someone in your room who'll come to sleep with Emilia.

[h] Maximo will be the first to send her back home to her father.

her father.

CINT: /Ah, there will be a scandal and unending disgrace for the young lady!

ASTR: Why should it bother you as long as she's taken from your house and/ⁱ will never be returned to you? Don't hesitate to hurt someone else, Cintio, if it's to your advantage. We live in an age when it's rare to find those who don't when they have the opportunity. The more important the men, the more they do so. You cannot blame someone who goes along with the majority.

CINT: I leave it up to you; direct me as you will. Of course, I would feel much better if it were possible to do otherwise and avoid such shame and dishonor to the girl.

ASTR: You'll come by yourself to my room ...

NIB: (If you go there he'll pull a fast one on you.)

ASTR: / ... so that I can prove to you that there's no risk here of scandal or dishonor, as you imagine./ʲ

ⁱ you're assured that she'll never be returned to you? CINT: I don't like it. FIS: Then let me take care of it. CINT: I don't want this. FIS: Let me convince you; there isn't a better, a faster, or an easier way than this. CINT: Frankly, I don't have the heart. FIS: Come see me at my place

ʲ But, if you want to make this scheme completely foolproof, see to it that you find me—eight and eight is sixteen, and eight is twenty-four, and then fifteen and fifteen is thirty, and another fifteen is forty-five—if I'm not mistaken that makes seventy-three florins. I'll melt these in your presence so that you won't think that I intend to steal them. From them I'll make three leaves on which I have to write certain letters as I recite a particular prayer.... I'll hide one of them under the threshold of your house, another beneath Abondio's threshold, and the third beneath Lavinia's. Then I have to fashion three images, for each of which I need fifteen florins: I'll dedicate one of them in your name, another in the name of Abondio, and the third in the name of your old man. I'll keep all three of them at my house and pray to them continually for seven hours during the day and seven hours at night and within three days your old man, and Abondio as well, will have changed their minds. In this way they'll undo the marriage themselves, without any effort or any other action on your part. Bring me the gold this evening; before then, if possible. CINT: You need seventy-three florins and no less? FIS: No less. CINT: How will I be able to put together such a sum today? FIS: How did you expect to pay me the fifty florins that you had promised me? CINT: I was going to sell all the furniture that my relatives have in the house. FIS: Whatever you counted on to pay me with will be excellent for this purpose. Now see if you can add another twenty-three, and the job will be done; once the job is done—and it will take no longer than three days—I'll take my fifty. You can keep the rest. So don't waste any time; go find the money so that I can melt the gold and make the three leaves and the three images this evening. CINT: I'll do what I can to bring it to you today. FIS: Now don't tarry any longer; go and get it. CINT: I'm going. ——I'm beginning to see today what Temolo has seen all along. I was going to give him forty scudi; but by means of his maneuvering he increased it to fifty. Now he wants me to add another twenty-three to that. At first he told me that he didn't want

NIB: (My master's plowing with both ox and donkey.[11])

ASTR: Urge your father-in-law to get the money ready this evening so that I can have it as soon as your wish is fulfilled. I don't want it to take more than this night to accomplish what I promised.

CINT: I'll go find him.

ASTR: Remember, let's keep these things secret among ourselves.

CINT: They'll be more than secret.

Scene Two
ASTROLOGO; NIBBIO

ASTR: Since I find Fortune so favorable to all my plans, there's no possibility that Camillo's silver will escape my grasp today. Compared with that all these other little gains seem like trifles. I had thought that if I managed to get hold of it in ten or even fifteen days I would be accomplishing a Herculean feat. But after Cintio spoke to me and informed me of the state of things, I realize that if I wait until tomorrow to make it mine I could be accused of being ignorant and inept. It's necessary to alter my initial plan and turn it upside down. I intended to have Emilia's letter serve me for one thing; now I have to use it in a worthier and more profitable way.

NIB:[k] /Well, then, which of the three partridges that you're holding are you intending to eat?

ASTR: You'll see me pick at them one by one and then settle on the juiciest one and eat it up.

NIB: Here comes/[l] one, and it's the best; /if you're hungry, sit down at the table whenever you please.

ASTR: Who is it? Camillo?

NIB: Yes.

ASTR: I'll devour him so thoroughly that I don't think even the bones will be left./[m]

payment until the job was done; but now he wants to have it, under the pretext of making images and leaves of gold. He must really think that I'm frivolous if he expects me to run without any other incentive.

[k] *Act Three, Scene Three, begins here.*

[l] a fine dish;

[m] Oh, Camillo. CAM: Oh, Master. FIS: Have you read the letter? CAM: Yes. FIS: What do you think of it? CAM: It seems to me a difficult and very dangerous thing. May I be damned! She wants me to come to her bedroom tomorrow night. FIS: You sound as if she were asking you to go into a den of hungry lions. CAM: And, finally, she threatens to come to my room if I refuse to go to her, and she wants me to speak to you about it, for you can best inform me about the whole thing. FIS: Do you think that she's joking? Camillo, I want you to know for certain that your Emilia has such a longing . . . a longing? She has such a passion to be with you that she has finally decided that tomorrow night she'll flee from her husband's bed and come to you at your house.

Scene Three
CAMILLO; ASTROLOGO; NIBBIO

CAM: I'm back.

ASTR: I see.

CAM: Now, explain what my mistress wants of me.

ASTR: She wants you in bed with her tonight; she wants to hold you in her arms and kiss you more than a hundred thousand times. The rest she leaves to your discretion.

CAM: Come on, tell me what she wants; the stars are not so favorable to me to allow me such happiness so soon.

ASTR: I tell you the truth, and you won't believe me. She wants me to place you in her bedroom tonight.

CAM: And where will Cintio be?

ASTR: I'll have Cintio stay the night at my inn under the pretext of having to give him certain baths, which might help cure his impotence. Now what do you think?

CAM: I think it's very difficult and dangerous.

ASTR: Dangerous, eh?

CAM: It's like sending me into a Babylonian lion's den.

ASTR: And she added that if you refuse to go to her she would come to you. Do you think I'm joking? I can assure you that she has such a longing ... a longing? She has such a passion to be with you that she's decided to flee from her husband tonight and come to you at your house.

CAM: /Oh, no! Dissuade her from such a thought, for it would bring on the worst scandal, the worst shame, the worst disgrace that can ever come to a woman.

ASTR: Believe me, I've done everything possible to dissuade her and I could find no other remedy than to give her my word that I would place you with her this very night.[n]

CAM: Do you really advise me to do this?/

ASTR: Without doubt, for if you go there you can °/convince her to wait ten or twelve days at least until she can come to you with her father's permission and with the satisfaction and consent of her relatives and friends, legitimately and with honor./

NIB: (Do you think that the swindler will be able to put it over on him?)

CAM: /And won't I be in danger if I go there?

ASTR: Undoubtedly you would if you went there without my knowledge; but, since I know about it, you can go there as safely as you can go into your own house.

---

[n] I'll have Cintio sleep in my room under the pretext of having to take certain baths that might help cure his impotence. So I want you to go there.

[o] I give you this advice in order to

CAM: How should I go there?

ASTR: I have a hundred sure and easy ways to send you. If I want to, I can make you take the form of a dog or a cat. Now, what would you say if you found yourself transformed into something very small like a mouse?/ [p]

CAM: Could you perhaps also change me into a flea or a spider?

NIB: (I'd better move away a bit so that I won't hear this nonsense, for I couldn't listen to it without bursting out laughing.)

ASTR: /I can change you into any kind of animal and then change you back to your original form, and I can even make you invisible. But think of it: if I were to transform you into a dog or a cat you would receive a few blows and would be locked out of the room at the most inopportune time./ [q]

CAM: Wouldn't it be better if you sent me there invisible?

ASTR: Invisible for certain; but not in the way you think. If you want me to send you invisible, as you say, we would have to find a heliotrope and we have little time left to consecrate it and prepare it the right way. But I've saved the enchantments for when they're needed most, and I thought about sending you in a box, which I'll have brought to her room. I'll make them all think that the box is full of spirits, and no one will come within four yards of it, except Emilia, who knows all about it. Then she'll quietly come and get you out of the box.

CAM: I understand, but it seems very dangerous to me.

ASTR: Just a while ago you were ready to cast yourself into a fire and rip open your chest at her mere nod; and now, when she asks you to do such a simple thing, something that will give you

[p] or into a spider or a flea?

[q] CAM: I don't want to be a mouse, a spider, or a flea, for any little accident could be disastrous for me. FIS: You're a man of foresight. CAM: It would be better if you sent me there invisible. FIS: We would have to find a heliotrope, and we have little time left to consecrate it and prepare it the right way. I'll do it in such a way that not only will you be unseen by mortal eyes, but even the eyes of the sun itself, which see everything, will not see you. CAM: Then you'll send me there invisible? FIS: Invisible for certain; but not in the way you think. CAM: Tell me how. FIS: I'll enclose you in a box. CAM: Enclose me in a box? FIS: What are you afraid of? If I enclose you in a box, don't you think I know what I'm doing? I'll make them all think that the box is full of spirits and no one will come within four yards of it, except Emilia and her nurse who are aware of what's going on. CAM: What will happen then? FIS: As soon as the others in the house have gone to sleep, the nurse will come to you quietly, will take you from the box and will lay you in bed beside Emilia. Why are you so sad and timid—as if I were placing you in great danger? CAM: Don't you think that this is very dangerous? FIS: Do you have so little faith in me? What's the use of letting you know how much I care about you and how much my studies and experiments can do?

pleasure, do you stand there dumbfounded? And do you think it's so dangerous?

CAM: I fear for her, not for myself.

ASTR: Oh, what mistrust! Where do you think I'll be? Knowing that I'm near you, how can you fear danger?

CAM: /Couldn't you place me with her some other way, instead of enclosing me in a box?

ASTR: Easily, but not in so short a time./ʳ

CAM: Then let's postpone it for three or four days.

ASTR: /As for myself, I'm willing to/ˢ postpone it six days, ten days, or a year, /provided that Emilia would be willing to do so. But she's not;/ᵗ and you can be certain that she intends to leave this very night, as I told you. I cannot describe her passion, her desire, her frenzy, her impetuousness. In any case, wait for her tonight.

CAM: /Before I would suffer this I would have myself enclosed not only in a box, but in/ᵘ an oven hot enough to melt glass.

ASTR: Have no fear. /Tell me, does your room face on the east?

CAM: Yes, it does.

ASTR: That's perfect for my purposes. Tonight I'm going to/ᵛ lock myself in it . . .

CAM: /What for?/ʷ

ASTR: . . . and never close my eyes. I'll say prayers and recite certain powerful exorcisms that will make everyone in Massimo's house, except Emilia, sleep—even the mice.

CAM: How can you stay in my room tonight, if you plan to keep Cintio with you in your room?

NIB: (Whoever wants to be a liar must have a good memory.)

ASTR: The dormice don't sleep as soundly as I'll have Cintio sleep as soon as he gets there. I've already prepared the sleeping potion. Tell your servants to open the door for me tonight and to obey me as they would you. I want them to keep a vigil with me and to help me do the things I tell them.

CAM: /I'll do that.

ASTR: But we don't have any time to lose. Go and find a box into which you can easily fit and wait for me in the house.

CAM: Is there anything else?

ʳ CAM: Why not wait one or two days?
ˢ wait as long as you want,
ᵗ so be sure that you find yourself in her house this very night.
ᵘ a lighted oven. Well, then, I put myself in your hands
ᵛ stand watch there
ʷ FIS: Just to recite certain powerful exorcisms to prevent anyone from finding out about you; so please tell your servants to obey me, for I'll have to use all of them in different ways.

ASTR: No, nothing else.

NIB: Here you are, as soon as one dish is taken from the table, another is brought in.

ASTR: Let it come, then, for I have a good stomach to digest it. Now pour me a drink and listen to me.

Scene Four

MASSIMO; ASTROLOGO; NIBBIO

MASS; Oh, Master, I found you just in time; I was coming to see you.

ASTR: And I wanted to see you also./ˣ

ˣ MAX: I came to let you know that everything I was supposed to do is ready. FIS: And I to give vent to a little anger which only a short while ago had induced me not to meddle any more in your affairs; then I got over it. MAX: In what way have I offended you? FIS: For God's sake, Maximo, you shouldn't allow your servants to say the things they do about me—that I asked for the calf in order to eat it. MAX: Who said so? FIS: And the flasks in order to steal them. MAX: Who said that? FIS: I've had custody over the storeroom and the treasury of His Catholic Majesty and, if I've been trusted with them once, I've been trusted with them a hundred times; and they're afraid that two flasks, which hardly weigh six pounds, would lead me to do that which a hundred-thousand florins never was able to induce me to do on a hundred occasions. MAX: Please, tell me, who is it who spoke about you in any way less than honorable; I'll show . . . FIS: It has never been my policy to accuse anyone. MAX: That I'm more disturbed by an insult to you than one to myself. FIS: Enough. Let's forget it. I won't allow evil tongues to dissuade me from keeping the promise I made you. MAX: Master, you're doing the duty of an honest man, and I thank you for it. I've sent to the countryside for the calf that you want for the sacrifice, and I'm surprised that it's not here yet. The flasks are ready, clean, nice, and polished. Take them and carry them wherever you please. And, if there is anything else that you want from me for this job—something that I have in the house or that money can buy—ask me for it and see whether or not I trust you. FIS: Listen to me. I want to help you in any way I can; but in serving you I'll do it in such a way as not to give these vicious tongues cause to croak about how I intend to deceive you. And, in order for them to see that it's not to eat the calf that I'm asking for it, I'll perform the sacrifice in your house. For this I'll need six cups, plates, the flasks, and other such things, for we need many more than I told you, as I'm not taking them out of your house. Now they won't say the things they've been saying. My only regret is that Cintio's cure will take longer, for if the flasks were already in my house before it gets dark I would have them consecrated, and by tomorrow morning I would have shown you the deed done. MAX: Why not take them home! Come and get them. FIS: Send them to me instead, and your servants won't return until they're consecrated. MAX: I'll send them. Then you can keep them and send them back when you please; and you can perform the sacrifice either in your house or mine, whichever is more convenient. FIS: I've decided to do it in your house because of what I have already told you, which would be superfluous to repeat, and also (*Act Three, scene Four, continues at note g, p. 134.*)

MASS: I came to tell you that I found a basin just like mine and about the same weight.

ASTR: I'm pleased. Now that there are two of them I can do something that's useful and will bear fruit. But listen to me. ʸ/ Before we do anything else, Massimo, I want to do something that few other magicians or astrologers would attempt, or if they did, would they be able to do.

MASS: What's that?

ASTR: I want to see, before the expenses begin to mount, whether the illness is curable or not; for if there's no remedy—*quod praesupponere nolo*[12]—it would be more honorable for me and more useful to you if I frankly let you know it.

MASS: I know that it's not incurable. By all means, proceed with your cure with confidence. This is a spell someone—a man or a woman—out of envy has placed him under, and it should be easy for you to remove.

ASTR: I think you're right; but this also could be the work of/ ᶻ such a learned and experienced enchanter /that the cure either will take a long time or will be impossible.

MASS: I hope to think that it isn't of such a bad nature.

ASTR: And what if it is?

MASS: If it is, too bad.

ASTR: If it is, wouldn't it be better to know about it before the expenses begin to mount?

MASS: Yes.

ASTR: For this purpose I'll put a spirit into a cadaver, a spirit with an intelligible voice that will tell me the cause of your Cintio's impotence. Then I'll be able either to promise you a cure or to remove all hope.ᵃ Now, where can we find a new surplice that has never been used before?

MASS: I don't know.

ASTR: We could make one with twenty yards of cloth, but it must be fine and the very whitest.

ʸ *Act One, Scene Three, begins here.*

ᶻ someone so well versed in enchantments

ᵃ MAX: Do what you please. FIS: If I had a black calf available, one that's very young and tender, which I need for a sacrifice, I would do the thing this very night. NEB: (My master wants to provide a meal for some of his young disciples.) MAX: Give me some time. FIS: Provided it's only slightly black and fat, it would suffice. NEB: (I expect to sink my teeth into it also.) MAX: I'll send someone to choose the best there is in the herd. FIS: It would be fine if its head were black, or its shoulders, or any other part. NEB: (Even if it were white as snow he'd like it, as long as it's young and tender.) MAX: You'll have it this evening. FIS: And I'll sacrifice it tonight. NEB: (To Saint Gaudentius.) FIS:

NIB: (He needs shirts,/[b] not a surplice.)

ASTR: We also have to make the stole and two maniples out of black silk; and we have to put two squares [of black silk] at the bottom of the surplice, two on the chest, and another on the front of the amice, just as priests wear on religious holidays. The whole thing could be made with four yards.

NIB: (Yes, of a rope [for hanging]. /His doublet is threadbare; he'd like a new one.)

ASTR: Ah! I almost forgot the pentacle.[13]

MASS: I have plenty of pots and pans in the house.

ASTR: Not pots and pans; I said a pentacle.

NIB: (He's preparing the ground to obtain some stockings.)

MASS: We'll see if we can borrow one./[c]

ASTR: You cannot borrow such a thing.

MASS: What shall we do, then?

ASTR: I'm thinking about it. I recall that a few days ago a monk told me that he had one for sale, and the price didn't seem unreasonable. I know that its original cost was not less than six florins; but I think that he would let it go for twelve of your lire.

NIB: /(This way he'll not only get his stockings, but his cap and even his slippers.)

MASS: Do these panaches cost that much?

ASTR: I didn't say panaches; I said pentacles.

MASS: Who cares about the name; I'm concerned with what they cost.

ASTR: If I can get him to give it to you for eleven and a half lire, buy it sight unseen, for I can always get you eleven for it; and you can always get your money back for the cloth and those other things with little loss./[d] Have the basins ready on time for consecration, so that we can use them when needed.

MASS: The basins are ready.

NIB: /(We'll get more than stockings and a doublet out of this.)

MASS: [e]Is there anything else that I have to provide?

ASTR: We also need two torches, plenty of candles, various herbs,

---

[b] FIS: For the maniple and stole and to adorn the surplice and the outer gown a large piece of black silk cloth is necessary.

[c] FIS: It's very difficult to borrow such things. MAX: How will we get one then. FIS: I'm thinking about it. Ah! I just remembered that about ten days ago a priest came to see me and wanted to sell one at a good price. He paid less than six florins for it in the first place; and he would have let me have it for fifteen imperial lire.

[d] MAX: Do you need anything else? FIS: I won't ask for anything else now. It's true that I also need two large flasks of the purest silver; but we can easily borrow these.

[e] MAX: I have these at home, and there's no need to ask anyone for them.

and gums for the fumigations, all of which will cost about fifteen
or sixteen carlins. You can either see to it that they're bought/
today /or give me the money and I'll take care of it.

NIB: (The leech has penetrated the skin and won't let go as long as
there's any blood left.)/[f]

MASS: Meanwhile, go see whether the monk still has that pentash[14]
of his.

ASTR: No, a pentacle.

MASS: It's the same thing. Come to an agreement about the price.
I'll send Cintio with the money as soon as he gets home, so that
whatever is needed can be bought while he's with you.

ASTR: Have him come soon, [g] /because I want you to hear with your
own ears a spirit that will answer in very plain language. You'll
find this a wonderful and marvelous experience.

MASS: It will be a great pleasure./

ASTR: I'll send you a cadaver in a box; now don't let the others
know what's in it. [h]/Have it placed beside the bed in which the
newlyweds sleep. Its main feature is that as soon as they get close
to the bed they'll make love even if it there were mortal hatred
between them. Then, I'll come tomorrow morning, when the
surplice is ready, to/ [i] conjure up the spirits.

MASS: Whatever you think.

ASTR: But be careful and warn everyone in your household, if they
value their lives, not to open the box or move it from the spot
where I'll have it placed. /One fool who didn't believe me dared
to touch a similar object of mine. Ask him what happened.

MASS: Tell me about it.

NIB: Immediately he was seen to burn up.

ASTR: And he burned in such a way that not even the ashes were
left./

NIB: What about those who wanted to see whether you had dutiable goods hidden in your valises?

ASTR: Heavens! Tell him what happened to them.

NIB: They were transformed into frogs and they're still at the gates

[f] MAX: Come inside for a while. I'm determined that there'll be no lack of
diligence or expense on my part to prevent me from finding out today
whether or not he can be cured. FIS: [To Nebbio] Now you, go and arrange
what I told you and return here immediately. MAX: Go inside, for I see
Cintio coming, and I want to speak to him without witnesses around. *End
of Act One, Scene Three: proceed to Act One, Scene Four, of text.*

[g] *Act Three, Scene Four, continues here.*

[h] FIS: Within the hour I'll send you the altar.

[i] finish the job in your presence. MAX: Whatever you say. FIS: But I want
to warn you and all your servants, if you value your lives, not to dare
touch this altar, which will be in the form of a box.

croaking at foreigners who pass back and forth.

MASS: Where did this happen?

NIB: At Adrianople. Perhaps you'll come across a couple of men in Venice, and also in Genoa, who know the story in detail.

MASS: Oh, how I wish our customs officials would annoy you some day, so that I could see them punished. I don't think there are more troublesome ones in the world.

NIB: He would fix them so well that Cremona would always remember him for this.

MASS: /Oh how good of you to warn me about this! What if someone touches the box without knowing it?/ [i]

ASTR: Just to touch it, knowingly or unknowingly, can do little good and much harm; but whoever opens it or touches it intentionally places not only himself but you and everyone in your house in great danger.

MASS: Anyone who would dare open it or touch it intentionally would be bold and foolhardy! I'll certainly inform all in my household about this danger.

ASTR: I'll send it along with this fellow. Have it placed in the room where the newlyweds sleep, as I told you, beside the bed, and then have the room locked.

MASS: I'll be very careful.

ASTR: I'll have it brought here.

MASS: I'm going to warn all my servants right away so that no mishap will occur because they didn't know in time.

NIB: This is quite an affair. What will come of it?

ASTR: /I want to shear and milk these sheep one by one, some of their golden fleece, others of their silver./ [k] I'll take one of the basins from Massimo; I still don't know what to do with Cintio. /As for Camillo, I'll leave him cleaner than a glass doll/ or a sparkling shaving basin. /I'll lock myself in his room as soon as I have sent him out enclosed in a box. I'll give his servants some work to do so they won't see me while I open and break boxes, safes,/ coffers, /and wardrobes and remove/ [l] the silver /and

---

[i] FIS: As long as he doesn't open it, touching it won't harm him. MAX: Anyone who would open it would be foolhardy. Then I'll inform all my servants of this danger so that they'll be careful. FIS: I'll go back to the inn and I'll send it along with this fellow. Have it placed down with care. MAX: I won't leave the house. Send it over then, and I'll have it locked up in Cintio's room; and I'll stand guard over it myself. Scene Five. NEBBIO; FISICO. NEB: This is a grand hodgepodge; now what are you thinking of doing?

[k] First I'll take Maximo's flasks and the seventy-three florins from Cintio.

[l] all the clothes, linens

whatever/ valuables /they hold./[m] I want you to be waiting for me in the street on which the windows face, so that by conveniently tying the goods to a rope I can slowly lower them into your hands one by one. Having done this, /what else is there to do but to leave through Garfagnana[15] headed for the Near East with our booty?

Meanwhile Camillo will be hidden quietly in the box waiting in vain for/[n] Emilia /to come and get him out; and this will give us plenty of time to get away. Neither Massimo nor Cintio will realize that we're gone until we've reached Francolino.[16]

NIB: What will become of Camillo?

ASTR: I'm giving him up to the devil. Undoubtedly, he'll be found in the box and taken for a thief or an adulterer./[o] After he's waited quite a long time for Emilia to come and get him out of the box, finally /he'll come out on his own if he doesn't want to die of hunger; and, the greater the scandal, the greater the confusion, the greater the din, the easier our escape will be. Let's go find him and shut him in the box.

NIB: Go ahead; I'll follow you./[p] ——My master is really a glutton and full of cunning; but he isn't the most prudent and sensible man in the world, for when he sees a small possibility of gain he doesn't worry about whether the enterprise is safe or dangerous. It's a miracle that he hasn't been hanged a hundred times considering the risks to which he has exposed himself. Some day he won't be able to get away with it, and I, too, may be caught if I continue to follow him much longer in his schemes.

SCENE FIVE [q]
FAZIO, *alone*

FAZIO: /I'm afraid that I gave Cintio bad advice when I suggested that he disclose the secrets of his heart to the Astrologer./[r] I'm

---

[m] for I know that there is a great abundance of everything. What valuables there are I'll conveniently lower out the window on a rope to you in the street; and you'll take them one by one to the inn. And, then, after we have a reasonable load,

[n] the nurse

[o] Even if Cintio doesn't come to take him out

[p] *Act Three ends here. Proceed to Act Four, Scene One, of text.*

[q] *Act Three, Scene One.*

[r] TEM: Ah, have no fears that he'll reveal them, for he has heard them in confidence and under oath. CAMB: I'm not saying this for fear that he'll reveal them; but because I'm afraid that now that he's aware of the situation the necromancer will employ his diabolical skills for the wrong purpose, that he'll take Cintio's mind off Lavinia and turn it in the direction of Emilia's love. TEM: The fifty florins that he offered him—believe me—have more power over him than he and his magic have over others. Go, then, bring the money and give it to him. CAMB: I'll go to Nanna and get it

not saying this because I believe or can believe that he would reveal them. After all, he heard them in confidence and under oath.
But I say this because I'm very much afraid that the rascal might
work against us. I see certain tendencies that I don't like very
much. However, I'm not going to hesitate to gather the money
together. I can easily do so, for when Lavinia's mother died she
left a jewelry box full of rings, necklaces, and other gold pieces,
which together are worth a hundred scudi. I never wanted to sell
them, hoping that some day they would enable Lavinia to be
recognized by her father. Now that we're in this predicament I've
changed my mind and will pawn or sell as much as is needed to
get the right sum. But the Astrologer won't get the money until I
see Emilia out of the house and the marriage broken up.

ACT FOUR
Scene One
FAZIO; TEMOLO

FAZIO: /[*To Lavinia inside*] Rest assured that I won't give him a
   penny unless I first see him do a job worthy of reward.——But
   here's Temolo./[a] I'm afraid you were right when you said that
   the Astrologer is a sly old fox full of cunning and deceit.
TEM:[b] /You wouldn't believe me, would you?/
FAZIO: And I'm afraid we gave Cintio horrible advice when we told
   him to disclose that which, if we had any brains, we should
   never have had him reveal, even under torture.
TEM:[b] /What's new?/[c]
FAZIO: Well, I'm afraid that, since he knows how things stand, he
   may try, by some diabolical trick, to take Cintio's mind off
   Lavinia and turn his attentions toward Emilia. A little while ago

---

from her. TEM: Fifty florins, can she...? CAMB: Yes, easily, for when
Lavinia's mother died she left a jewelry box full of rings, necklaces, and
other gold pieces, which together are worth a hundred scudi or there-
abouts. My sister has continued to save these in the event that her father is
ever found; for then they would serve as proof that Lavinia is his daughter.
Now that we're in this predicament she'll change her mind and will immediately pawn or sell as much as is needed to get fifty florins. TEM: That just
suits our purpose! CAMB: Now I'm going inside. TEM: Here comes Cintio
and his mentor. CAMB: Leave them alone, for whatever they decide on
Cintio will tell us when he has a chance. *Proceed to Act Three, Scene One,
of text.*
   [a] TEM: You were right. We gave Cintio bad advice indeed when we told
him to disclose his secrets to the Physicist.
   [b] *This line is given to Cambio.*
   [c] TEM: That scoundrel is trying nothing other than to make him take his
mind off Lavinia and turn his attentions toward the other girl. Just now as
he left Maximo he said that he would send over a box or a cabinet, that is, a
certain enchanted altar, which is to be

Cintio came to see me and with great urgency asked me for fifty scudi with which to pay the Astrologer—that's how much he had promised him. I tried to find out from him precisely what they had talked about and what the Astrologer had promised to do. He barely condescended to answer me, and said: "Get the money for me today and don't worry about the rest; you'll know what we have agreed upon from the results." Having said this, he went away pale, his expression having changed, and with a very different air about him; he didn't seem like the usual Cintio. I'm really worried that this blackguard is going to deceive us and that he's already begun to do so, having half-ruined such a good soul.

TEM: I, too, am worried about the same thing because of other signs. Among them is the fact that the rogue, as he left Massimo, ordered that a box be sent there, a box that has miraculous powers. He wants it /placed beside the bed where the newlyweds sleep; and it will have the power to have them make love together even if there were mortal hatred between them.

FAZIO: When did he say he would send it?

TEM: I'm surprised that it's not already here. He said that he would send it as soon as he returned home.

FAZIO: He has undoubtedly deceived us. Hah, the scoundrel!

TEM: Worse than a scoundrel!

FAZIO: But, just the same, we were fools for having given him the opportunity to come and do us harm. He would never have found a way had we remained quiet.

TEM: Now that we didn't keep quiet, what shall we do?

FAZIO: We must find Cintio and warn him. What the devil do I know? But tell me: is he at home?

TEM: No.

FAZIO: Can you tell me where he is?

TEM: No.

FAZIO: We must find him wherever he is, to get him to come and calm down Lavinia, who does nothing but cry, so much so that it seems to me that she's going to melt with tears; and it's all because of me, for today I told her that I was afraid the Astrologer, by some diabolical means, would cool off Cintio's love for her.

TEM: You were wrong in saying this! Go back and allay her fears, for the danger that you described doesn't exist.

FAZIO: She needs more than I can give her! She won't be consoled until she sees Cintio.

TEM: Well, go find him.

FAZIO: I'll go to the piazza.

TEM: Then go. Perhaps you'll find him.... Aren't you paying attention? Listen to me. You're more likely to find him if you go toward the inn where the Astrologer is staying, for he probably is with him. But why are you rushing off in such a hurry?

FAZIO: Ah! They're bringing the box that you told me about.

TEM: Where is it?

FAZIO: Come over where I am and you'll see it.

TEM: Who's bringing it?

FAZIO: A porter.

TEM: By himself?

FAZIO: The Astrologer's servant is with him.

TEM: Is the Astrologer also there?

FAZIO: No, he's not.

TEM: He's not there?

FAZIO: I told you, he's not.

TEM: Then leave it to me.

FAZIO: What are you going to do?

TEM: Here they are. Now, pay attention and make sure that you give the right answer.

FAZIO: What are you talking about? But to whom am I speaking? Where the devil is he running to? Why did he leave me so suddenly? I think he's gone mad.

SCENE TWO
TEMOLO; FAZIO; NIBBIO; PORTER

TEM: Oh, this evil city!

FAZIO: What the devil is he shouting about?

TEM: It's impossible to live here; it's full of traitors ...

FAZIO: What are you shouting about?

TEM: ... and assassins./

FAZIO: Who wronged you?

TEM: Oh, the poor man!

FAZIO: /I think that you're ...

TEM: Oh, Fazio,. what a great pity.

FAZIO: What's a pity?

TEM: What a horrible thing! I couldn't help crying out of compassion.

FAZIO: For what?

TEM: Alas! For a poor stranger whom I just now saw being killed by a cruel stabbing in the head, which he received from an assassin who was waiting for him as he turned the corner.

FAZIO: Why do you care about it?

TEM: I had come to like him because he was a friend of the family. [d]

[d] and a good man.

Didn't you know him?

FAZIO: How should I know him unless you tell me his name?/ᵉ

TEM: I don't know whether he's a Spaniard or an astrologer or a necromancer. They call him the Astrologer.

NIB: /Oh, woe is me! What did you say about the Astrologer?

TEM: Oh, I hadn't noticed you. Aren't you his servant? Your master has been seriously wounded, and I believe that he was left for dead by a rogue who was waiting for him as he turned the corner.

NIB: Oh, woe is me!

TEM: The wound on the back of his head is extremely serious. Everyone is running there to see him.

NIB: Ah! For God's sake, tell me where he is.

TEM: Go straight to the ᶠ corner; then turn to your left and run until you reach Saint Dominic's. Turn to your right and ask someone there to show you where the Buffalo Inn is. But what's the use of directing you? It's impossible to miss it. Just follow the others; the old and the young are all running there.

NIB: Oh, God!

TEM: I don't think you'll find him alive.

PORT: Where shoud I put this box?

NIB: Oh, Master Jachelino, you poor soul. I warned you!

FAZIO: What are you raving about?——Where did you dream up these stories in the short time that you were away from me?

PORT: Let him go where he pleases. I won't run after him. If only I knew where/ᵍ to put this. . . .

TEM: You're supposed to put it inside. Go and get rid of your load where he tells you. /Show him where the master said to put it— in the upstairs room, beside Lavinia's bed.

FAZIO: Lavinia's?

TEM: You know what I'm talking about.

FAZIO: I understand you.

TEM: Then pay him and send him away; I'm going to find Cintio.

SCENE THREE
CINTIO: TEMOLO; FAZIO; PORTER

CINT: ʰ I see that there really is no other solution than to make

ᵉ TEM: He's that learned Spaniard, the one who is an astrologer by profession and whom we call the Physicist.

ᶠ delicatessen store that you'll find at the

ᵍ this fellow lives; I forgot his name. TEM: I know it; I'll refresh your memory. It belongs to Maximo. Here's his door; leave it here. PORT: Yes, he told me Maximo. Come and show me where to put it. TEM: This fellow is from the house.

ʰ CINT: I went to see him again and I've resolved that he won't get a penny from me until he has freed me from my difficulties; but

Emilia appear to be an adulteress.

TEM: (Here he is, thank God!)

CINT: He'd like me to believe that afterward he can easily hush up the entire affair so that no disgrace will result./[i]

TEM: I think /you always hide when we need you most.

CINT: What do you need me for?

TEM: If you don't hurry and console Lavinia, I'm afraid you may find her dead.

CINT: Ah! What has happened to her, Temolo?

TEM: The poor thing is so afraid that this necromancer, with his black magic, will make you alter your love for her that she's consumed with grief and has gone into a fainting spell. . . .

CINT: She shouldn't worry.

TEM: She's very ill.

CINT: I'm going to her.

TEM: Go, for heaven's sake.

FAZIO: Cintio, has he told you how Lavinia . . .

CINT: Well, here I am./ I came just for that.

FAZIO: Comfort her.——You couldn't have come up with a better idea, Temolo.[j]

TEM: /Pay the porter and send him away; send him far away, immediately.

FAZIO: Hey there, here's a grosso.[17] Would you also do me a favor?/[k]

PORT: Yes, I'll do it.

FAZIO: /Go to [Saint Mary of] the Graces and tell the vicar that I sent you to get/[l] those radishes /that I spoke to him about yesterday./[m]

PORT: I believe it's more than two miles away.

FAZIO: So it is. /What do you care as long as you're paid?

PORT: On whose behalf should I ask?

FAZIO: Ask on behalf of/[n] Bertel the mask-maker.

PORT: /I'm going.

FAZIO: Go so far away that you never come before me again. Now you'll see. If this enchanted box is useful and beneficial to any woman next to whose bed it's placed, then it will be so to our Lavinia,/[o] but not as the Astrologer intended.

TEM: /That's true; but I'll give you even better advice.

[i] I'm still confused and I cannot make up my mind what to do.

[j] *Scene Four begins here.* CAMB: We couldn't have found a better opportunity than this.

[k] PORT: What do you want?

[l] the two flasks of oil

[m] PORT: It's two miles away. CAMB: And what if it were six!

[n] Maximo's steward.

[o] and not to Emilia, as the Physicist intended.

FAZIO: What is it?

TEM: Let's go/ upstairs /and chop it into pieces and bury it at the bottom of a cesspool; or burn it instead so that no one will hear of it any more. And, if by chance they come back here with the porter to retrieve it, you can reply forcefully that the porter is lying, that you don't know what they're talking about, and you could open the doors and let them look everywhere.

FAZIO: We would run the risk then of ruining the house, for I'm positive that it's completely filled with spirits.

TEM: Do you believe in such nonsense? Oh, you foolish man! Let me worry about the danger. Give me an ax; I'll make the spirits fly through the air along with the splinters. But look, the Astrologer's servant is returning. He mustn't find me here. Feed him some other story, Fazio, and send him away. I'm going upstairs and I'm determined not to let them ever find the box.

Scene Four

NIBBIO; FAZIO

NIB: What sort of people one finds in the world today; for without getting any profit out of it they nevertheless delight in bothering this man or that one! But I, blockhead that I am, who considered myself a master at playing pranks, find myself to be a rather poor pupil, for an idiot made me run around so foolishly. I was running as fast as my legs could carry me and with shouts and cries I asked everyone whom I met where it was that my poor master lay wounded or dead. Behold, I heard his voice calling me; and I turned and saw him as safe and sound as I had left him. He asked me whether I had delivered the box/ according to his instructions. /In my joy I couldn't answer him. Then, finally,[p] I told him what some glutton had given me to understand. On hearing this he/ made quite a scene; he /reproached me[q] and sent me back/ immediately /to look for the box that I had left/[r] with the porter without telling him where to bring it. /Yet I look around and I don't see it. Where the devil could he have gone? Perhaps this/ good /man will be able to tell me.——What happened to that fellow who made me run?

FAZIO: You shouldn't be surprised, for he usually keeps Arabian horses in his stable and makes them run; in truth, he must have taken you for a horse.

NIB: I may render the same sort of service to him sometime when

[p] having gotten hold of myself

[q] —I deserved it—

[r] in the street without thinking. I hadn't even remembered to say to the porter: "Take it to Maximo's house."

I have the opportunity. But can you give me any information
about the porter whom I left here carrying a load?

FAZIO: For quite some time he wasn't sure where to put the box;
he finally decided to take it to the customs house, and he went
there.

NIB: Ah, that ass of a porter, that impertinent fellow, the poltroon!

FAZIO: You can catch up with him if you run a bit.——Run, then,
you'll win the Palio.[18] But isn't that Abondio,/ˢ Emilia's father?
I don't think that you could ever finish counting the old miser's
ducats.

SCENE FIVE
ABONDIO; FAZIO; CAMILLO

ABON: /To hear this coming from people's mouths bothers me more
than anything else that might have happened. I must complain
about it to Massimo who has been the main reason why people
gossip in the piazza. [19]/ᵗ He's gone to look for doctors, astrologers, /and enchanters and has done such foolish things that
children would hardly do them.

FAZIO: (If I were to hold you as a prisoner, I would get six thousand
florins from you before . . .ᵘ Who is this servant leaving in such
a hurry with only his doublet on?)/

CAM: Oh, what great danger!

FAZIO: /(It's Camillo/ᵛ Pocosale. Who brought him here? /God
help me!)/

CAM: Oh, the perfidy of wicked men!

FAZIO: /(When the devil did he come in?)

CAM: Oh, what a dreadful thing! Oh, what great danger! What
great danger I've endured here. Whom can I trust any more if
those who have received benefits from me and who still receive
them . . .

FAZIO: (What's he yelling about?)

CAM: Betray me? Oh, Divine Goodness, you prevented such disgrace and so much evil from coming to pass! Oh, Divine Justice,
you have made me understand things that I cannot regret having
learned—even though I have been in danger of losing my life
today.

FAZIO: (I imagine that some calamity has overtaken him.)

CAM: But from whom can I borrow at least a small mantle to put

---

ˢ How many ducats does that miserly old man have?
ᵗ The fool has gone to look for herbalists
ᵘ But what's all this noise? Oh, God, what's this uproar I hear? Temolo
must have ruined me by filling the house with spirits.
ᵛ What's he doing around here?

over my doublet so that I can go find Abondio right away ...

ABON: (Who's that mentioning my name?)

CAM: ... and make him realize how hard these rascals are trying to bring about his eternal shame, ...

ABON: (May God help me!)

CAM: ... the dishonor of his daughter, and the infamy of his household.

ABON: (I think it's Camillo Pocosale; it's him.)

CAM: Abondio. You're just the one I'm looking for.

FAZIO: (The only thing that can come out of this is injury and misfortune.)

ABON: I see that you're wearing your doublet. Are you perhaps ready to play ball? Find someone else who is better than I am in that sport, for I'm not very agile.

CAM: I didn't come to play ball with you Abondio, but to make you realize that you're being bounced around more than a ball is, and that they're betting high stakes on your and your daughter's honor. I want you to know that your son-in-law has another wife in this house. But, for God's sake, let's go into one of the nearby houses, for I'm ashamed to appear in public undressed as I am.

ABON: Let's go into Massimo's house.

CAM: I would sooner go into Massimo's house than anywhere else so that he can hear me.

FAZIO: Temolo, Temolo, quick, follow them; try to hear what Camillo is complaining about. Wait, wait, for Cintio is coming out.

SCENE SIX
FAZIO; CINTIO; TEMOLO

FAZIO: What's going on, Cintio? How the devil did he get inside?

CINT: Indeed, the devil brought him in! But who had this box brought up here when it should have been delivered to our house?

FAZIO: Temolo and I had it put there/ just now.

CINT: /Well you and Temolo have just ruined me; you've pushed my and Lavinia's hopes over a precipice, hopes that we had sustained until now with so much difficulty. Why did you do it?

FAZIO: To thwart the plans of the Astrologer, for we were absolutely certain that he intended to betray you by means of that box.

CINT: Then why didn't you at least say a word to me about it instead of letting me make such a mistake? I have been betrayed by you, not by the Astrologer, for a young man was hidden in the box; and because of what you did he heard the whole plot as I was telling it to Lavinia. Now that it's known, by God, it will put me in a position in which I would be better off dead.

Now tell me, where did Camillo go—the fellow who ran out of here? Perhaps by begging him, by giving him gifts and offering to become his slave forever, I may be able to move him to have pity for my situation so that he won't reveal what he heard. But it will be impossible to placate him, for he has too good a reason to hate me.

FAZIO: You're too late—believe me—for as he was rushing out of the house he ran into Abondio and told him everything; that is, he told him as much as he could briefly, for he could hardly express himself due to his anger and irritation.

CINT: There isn't a miserable man in the world with whom I wouldn't change places the moment that the old man learns about this—and it's a certainty that he'll find out right away. Oh, God! What a predicament I'm in.

FAZIO: You had better assume that he already knows about it, for Camillo and Abondio went directly to see him and undoubtedly they have already told him the whole story.

CINT: Did they go together to see Massimo?

FAZIO: Yes, they did.

CINT: I've had it. I'm as good as dead! Open up earth, open up, by God, and let me be buried.

FAZIO: You mustn't despair, Cintio.[w] Think about it and consider whether there is anything, any remedy, that can be used here.

CINT: I know of no solution; I cannot find any but to run so far away that Massimo will never see me again. I don't want to face his anger. Farewell, Fazio, I place my Lavinia in your trust.

FAZIO:[x] Ah, you fainthearted one, where are you going?——He's gone. Go into the house, Temolo. Find out exactly what's going on and report it to me.

TEM: I'll do that. Wait for me inside.

ACT FIVE
SCENE ONE
MASSIMO; CAMILLO; ABONDIO; TEMOLO

MASS: If I find this to be true, you can rest assured that I'll make such a fuss about it that you'll be able to see how much it disturbs me; you'll see that I consider the injury no less mine than yours.

CAM: If you find that it's not true then you can tell everybody that

[w] Get hold of yourself
[x] Wait a moment.

I'm the most villainous, the most malicious, the most envious person in the world.

ABON: If it weren't more than the truth, / Massimo, /not only would he not say it—I know this young man—he wouldn't even be able to imagine it. I'm convinced, therefore, that this must not go unpunished; and I don't want it passed over so lightly.

MASS: Listen, Abondio, please don't be in such a hurry; let's find out more about this.

CAM: Who could inform you better than I can, for I heard with my own ears and I saw with my own eyes that your Cintio has/ [a] another wife.

MASS: Take it easy. /I'd like to clarify this a little better.

CAM: Let's go inside. Have him confront me, and if you find that I've added a single word to the truth you can tear out my tongue, my eyes, and my soul.

MASS: Come on, let's go. [b]

CAM: Let's all go in; let's clear up this matter completely.

MASS: Please wait here. Let me go in alone; don't make an uproar and don't make the affair more public than it already is. Let's not bring on our own dishonor.

ABON: You go then, and call us when you're ready.

MASS: I'll do that.   Wait for me./

TEM: (I'm going to follow him and witness the final calamity that will destroy us all.)

Scene Two
NIBBIO; ABONDIO; CAMILLO

NIB: /(I think that these gluttons have taken me for a cricket ball today; one of them hits me with a story, and the blow sends me as far as Saint Dominic's. . . .)

ABON: It was certainly foolish of you to let yourself be shut up in a box and placed in such great danger.

NIB: (I return and find the other one waiting for me . . .)

CAM: When I think about it, I'm astonished at myself.

NIB: (. . . with another story that makes me roll all the way to the customs house. And there they throw me out the door.)

CAM: In truth, Abondio, I don't attribute this so much to my foolishness as to the will of God, who by this means has made me aware of the snares that were set for both of us. There goes one of the fellows who shut me in the box and betrayed your daughter and myself.

---

[a] a wife and children in this house.
[b] ABON: Yes, let's go. *Camillo's line that follows is part of Maximo's next speech.*

NIB: (I don't know where to turn. But there's the fellow who was enclosed in it. Oh, God; I'm afraid that we may have stirred up a scandal.)

CAM: Ah, you glutton, you thief, you betrayer, you perfidious one, you and your master! Is this the way you treat those who trust you?

NIB: Neither I nor my master ever did anything except for your benefit and pleasure.

CAM: It would have been a real benefit and pleasure for me if you had had me caught as a thief in someone else's house at night.

ABON: Aren't you scoundrels ashamed of yourselves? Don't you have any scruples about making decent young ladies seem adulteresses? And about heaping shame and disrepute on noble families by your fraudulence?

NIB: Ask my master; he'll know how to answer you.

CAM: I'll speak very plainly to him, you can be sure of it, but somewhere else; and a rope will make you answer about this and all your other misdeeds....

NIB: You can say what you will, but it's not proper for you or for gentlemen to say or do things injurious to foreigners. My master will be able to give a good account of himself.

CAM: Fine, if he can.

ABON: Let him alone; don't say anything else to him.

CAM: Now go to the devil, you little thief; go to the scaffold and hang yourself.

ABON: Let him go and don't get so excited. By now Massimo should have called us inside; maybe that's him. No, it's not. This fellow is coming out in such a hurry! He seems full of joy.

Scene Three
TEMOLO; ABONDIO; CAMILLO; MASSIMO

TEM: ——Oh, great Luck, oh excellent Fortune! How rapidly you did turn so much fear and such a horrible storm into such a safe and placid stillness.——

ABON: Why is he so happy?

TEM: ——Where should I run, where should I fly to find Cintio?——

ABON: What can this be?

CAM: I don't know.

TEM: ——So that I can tell him of the greatest joy, the greatest happiness he could ever have.——

ABON: What is it?

TEM: ——His Lavinia was found to be Massimo's daughter.——

CAM: Did you hear that?

ABON: Yes.

CAM:[c] How can it be?

TEM: ——But why am I waiting to go and find Cintio?——

ABON: He never had a wife that I knew of.

CAM: Men can also have children from women who aren't their wives.

ABON:[d] But here he comes and he'll tell us the whole story.

CAM: Did you find me a liar, Massimo?

MASS: No, by God. /

ABON: Explain this to us: What is this about a daughter of yours whom Temolo says you found?

MASS: I'll explain it if you'll listen.

ABON: Both my ears willingly lend themselves for this purpose.

MASS: You probably remember when the Venetians took over Cremona[20] how I was accused by some malevolent people and banished from the city with a price of three thousand ducats on my head.

ABON: I remember that.

MASS: I fled and didn't stop until I reached Calabria where, for safety's sake, I dressed humbly, I lived alone, and I changed my name to Anastasius and pretended that I came from Alexandria. I concealed [my identity] so well that all the time the city was in their possession nobody knew what had happened to me. While I was there, I took a wife, I got her pregnant, and this girl was born. Then, on hearing that the French had joined with the emperor to drive the Venetians out of their conquered territories, I decided to be present when my city was retaken. But, in case things took a turn for the worse, I didn't want the way back to my hiding place closed. So I told Placidia—for Placidia was my wife's name—that I was returning to Alexandria to see about an inheritance of mine; and that, if my plans produced the desired effects, I would send some trusted persons to fetch her and bring her to me. I cut a ring in half as a token; I gave one half to her and I took the other half, and I ordered her not to budge unless she saw the token.

I then returned here, and more than fifteen months passed before I could settle my affairs. As soon as they were settled, I went to Calabria myself to get her instead of sending someone else; but I found that, after having waited quite a while beyond the time that we had agreed upon, and not seeing me or hearing any news from me, she had set out to look for me in Alexandria, just like a woman, moved by her own desires rather than reason. On learning of this, I rushed off and journeyed by stages[21] to

---

[c] ABONDIO *not* CAMILLO.

[d] CAMILLO *not* ABONDIO.

148

Alexandria. There I found that she had come with her little daughter looking for a certain Anastasius; and, hearing no news and finding no traces of him, and knowing nobody there, she had hurried back toward Calabria. I returned there once again and sent out letters and innumerable messages every so often. I have never told anyone the reason for my searching; not, in these sixteen years, was I able to find any trace of her until now.

And now, Abondio, ᵉ/I beg that with your kind and charitable heart and out of our long friendship you will forgive my Cintio for the very grave injury he has done you; excuse him for his youth./ᶠ

ABON: So you found out that Cintio has taken her as his wife?

CAM: /Who doubts it?

MASS: One must attribute this, not to the temerity of the youth, but to unfailing divine providence, which determined from the beginning that this had to happen. If not for this I would never have known my daughter, whom I had lost when she was a little girl of five; it has been sixteen years since I had any news of her. Now, whereas Cintio feared that he had offended me by taking a wife without my permission, he has actually given me great pleasure, for I couldn't have chosen a more gratifying son-in-law than him, nor could I have given him a woman more dear to me than my only daughter. Only your concerns, my Abondio, taint my joy and prevent it from being complete. If this had happened without injury to you, you can be sure that my joy would be the greatest any man could have. And I beseech you, if I may, to put up with my happiness and not to/ᵍ object to it. /Take back your Emilia, who is as much a virgin as when she came to us and whom you'll easily marry off to a young man as honorable and as rich as ours. I place myself always at your disposal with all that I have in the world.

ABON: Ever since childhood I have always had a love and reverence for you, Massimo, and I don't need anyone but you to be my witness. That my love for you now is just as it used to be, may God be the judge, for we cannot hide our souls from Him. But I cannot say that I'm not sorry to see this marriage dissolved and Emilia returned to my house. While dishonor will not rightly fall on Cintio and her, nevertheless this will be a subject for gossip among the common people; and so marrying her off will be a greater problem than you think.

ᵉ But listen to me. You, dear Abondio, I pray,

ᶠ and for the advice that he received from evil ones. ABON: Are you convinced, then, that your Cintio has another wife?

ᵍ oppose God's wishes.

MASS: Here is a son-in-law already available; he's a handsome, noble, rich, and well-mannered young man who loves her more than himself and who wants to have her. Now, how can you place her any better?

CAM: May his mouth be eternally·blessed by God!

ABON: Let him speak out and I'll be able to answer him.

CAM: I'll be happy to have her; and so I pray for this with all my heart and I beg you to give her to me willingly.

ABON: And I promise her to you.

CAM: I accept her as my legitimate wife.

MASS: May God guide and bless this marriage, and may it always be without quarrels.

ABON:^h Are we agreed?

MASS: Agreed.

CAM: Agreed, indeed.

ABON: Now, if you please,/ⁱ tell us where she was hidden for

^h *Abondio's and Maximo's lines are interchanged.*

ⁱ Maximo, tell me how it is that she's your daughter; where was she hidden these twelve years? How did you come to recognize her today? MAX: I'll explain it to you, if you'll listen. ABON: My ears willingly lend themselves for this purpose. MAX: When the Venetians first captured Cremona from [Lodovico] the Moor and I was banished from the city, they put a price of three thousand florins on my head, thinking that I had been negotiating to give over the citadel to the Germans. You know that I fled, and all the time the city was in their possession nothing was ever heard of me. During that time I was reduced to hiding in a small village in Calabria where for safety's sake I wore humble dress, I changed my name to Anastasius and pretended that I came from Alexandria.

Now, while I was there I became very friendly with a widow from the village and, partly because I loved her, partly because being alone is unpleasant, and partly because she had a house and furniture, I took her for my wife; I got her pregnant, and this girl was born. I remained there quietly until news reached me from a number of sources that the French, together with the papacy and the emperor, were preparing to take the Venetian possessions away. I decided to be present when my city was retaken, but, in case things took a turn for the worse, I didn't want the way back to my hiding place blocked. So, I told Ginevra—for Ginevra was my wife's name—that I was returning to Alexandria to see about an inheritance that some of my relatives were disputing; and I also said that, if my plans produced the desired effects, I intended not to remain in Calabria any longer, and that I would come back to take her with me or would send some trusted person to fetch her.

But, in case she had to go with anyone but me, I cut a ring in half as a token. I gave one half to her and I took the other half; and I ordered her not to budge unless she saw the token. I then returned here. But things took longer than I had expected, and fifteen months passed before I could settle my affairs. As soon as they were settled, I went to Calabria myself to get her instead of sending someone else; but I found that, after having waited six months beyond the time that we had agreed upon, and not seeing me or

sixteen or eighteen years. How is it that you found this out today
and not before?

MASS: I had gone in there to inquire further about what Camillo had
told us. I was so angry with this poor family and in such a rage
that I wished them all dead. I had turned to my daughter and was
insulting her as one would insult a hussy; with a menacing face I
threatened to put her to public dishonor and shame. Then my
neighbor's wife /threw herself at my feet and, weeping, said:
"Have pity on her, Massimo; she was not lowborn as you perhaps may think, for her father and mother were of noble birth."
On inquiring into her origins, I learned that her father's name
was Anastasius, that he had come from Alexandria, and that he
had lived at one time in Calabria where he had taken a wife.

ABON: You're a prudent man, Massimo; yet I would remind you
that this could be a trick, for, having heard this story from
Cintio, she could pretend to be your daughter.

MASS: And how would Cintio know if a single word about it didn't
come out of my mouth until now?/ⁱ I never told even you, who
are so close to me, /for I considered it a great burden to have a wife
and not to know where she was. I have several other indications
besides this. I recognized the ebony beads that she was wearing
around her neck, and then she showed me necklaces, rings, and
other such things that belonged to her mother, all of which I had
given her. But what? Do you need any better indication? She
showed me her half of the ring/ that I had given Placidia when
I left her. /This would suffice for me if there was nothing else;
but the fact that she is the image of her mother makes me even
more certain.

ABON: What happened to her mother? Was she able to tell you?

MASS: Yes, of course, But it was the others [in the house] who told

---

hearing any news from me, she had set out to follow me, just like a woman
who thinks of nothing but her own desires. She had sold the house and
whatever she couldn't easily carry and had loaded everything on three or
four donkeys.

On learning this, I rushed off and journeyed by stages to Alexandria.
There I found that she had come with her little daughter looking for a
certain Anastasius; and, hearing no news and finding no traces of him, and
knowing nobody there, she had hurried back toward Calabria. I returned
there once again and sent out letters and innumerable messages, I believe
everywhere throughout Italy; but never, in these twelve years, was I able
to find any trace of her.

And now, I had gone in here to find out about this matter with great
anger, with a threatening expression, and with menacing words, when
the old woman

ⁱ Never was anything kept more secretly,

me more—that while returning to Calabria her mother had taken ill in Florence, where Fazio [k] gave her shelter. Here she came to the end of her troubles and she left them the little girl. As they had no other children, they raised her as their own daughter. They changed her name from Ippolita to Lavinia, I believe they said in memory of one of their ancestors.

ABON: I'm extemely pleased with your happiness.

CAM: And so am I.

MASS: I thank you.

CAM: What shall we do now?

ABON: You can marry Emilia whenever you wish.

CAM: Why not finish what has to be done right away?

MASS: He's right; let him marry her now.

ABON: Then marry her; let's go.

CAM: Please, let's go. /[l]

Scene Four
TEMOLO; ASTROLOGO

TEM: I had gone to find Cintio with the hope of getting him to buy me a drink for bringing him the wonderful news. But my hopes weren't realized; in fact, quite the opposite happened. I met some friends of mine who, on seeing the joy on my face and in my actions—joy that I couldn't hide—asked me why I was so happy. I told them, and because of my happiness they made me buy them wine. As I didn't have a penny to pay for it, they took my cloak and they're going to pawn it for more money than I get in a month's salary. But, if I can find Cintio and be the first to bring him such happy news, this loss will indeed be a very small one.

There's that cheat. I won't call him the Astrologer any more. The glutton apparently doesn't know that his frauds have been discovered; otherwise he wouldn't return here with such audacity. It would be a commendable thing and a pious deed to see to it that he gets caught.

ASTR: I don't know what Nibbio has done with the box that he left with the porter. I shouldn't have left him until he had it placed in the room and had [the door] locked. But just then a fellow came to see me and offered me three scudi to tell his fortune. I kept talking to him hoping that he would go as high as four. In the

---

[k] who was the husband of this widow,

[l] ——Hey there! Don't wait for Cintio to return, for he already went into the house quietly through the back door. And whoever wants to find out about the necromancer can run after him; but hurry, for he's running as if he were being carried by the devil. Farewell, my fine audience, and indicate your pleasure to us so that we'll know you enjoyed our story.

end, I couldn't get a penny out of him and I ran the risk of a serious scandal and of ruining everything. Since I haven't heard anything to the contrary, I'd like to believe that Nibbio has found the box and has left it with the person I told him to.

TEM: (I'm going to try my hardest to play a trick on him that will never be forgotten.)

ASTR: But I see someone who can tell me.——Say there, young man, has my servant—you know who he is—has he brought a box here?

TEM: A porter brought it, and if I weren't here he would have run the risk of creating quite a disturbance.

ASTR: As a matter of fact, he told me that one of you had played a prank on him.

TEM: One of us? He didn't tell you the truth. It was another fellow, one who's half a clown and who seems to think of nothing else than to play a trick on this person or that one, on anyone who appears a little stupid. But, as I happened to be there, I had the porter go into the house—he wanted to return—and put his load down in the room where the newlyweds sleep. Soon after that my master came, closed the door, and took the key away with him on his belt.

ASTR: You did the right thing! Massimo and his entire household should be grateful to you. Had the box remained in the street, the spirits would have escaped. They would have entered the house tonight with fury and maltreated you.

TEM: Oh, Master, I hope that these spirits of yours stay in the box and don't run through the house and harm us in some way.

ASTR: Don't worry, there isn't any danger.

TEM: You can say what you will, but my insides shake with fear.

ASTR: Trust me; I won't let any harm come to you.

TEM: Will you promise this?

ASTR: Yes, if you don't open it.

TEM: Oh, whoever dares open it or merely touch it would be a fool. God forbid that I should want to! I wish you would do me a favor and tell the old man that you received the two silver basins. He instructed me to go and get them today and take them to you under cover so that they won't be seen. Now, it happened that one of our neighbors asked me to lend him my cloak for about a half-hour; but four hours have gone by and he hasn't returned it. As I have nothing to cover the basins with, I didn't go get them; but as soon as I get my cloak back I'll go and bring them here. In the meantime, tell my master that you have received them.

ASTR: Wouldn't it be better to go and get them rather than tell a lie?

TEM: I won't go if I have to carry them uncovered, for Massimo would be angry with me if he found out. If it weren't for the fact that you might consider it presumptuous, I would have asked for your gown, which would be excellent for this purpose; but I'm not so stupid as to think that this is not an improper request.

ASTR: If you think it suits your purpose, then take it. Why shouldn't it be all right? Take it anyway and be quick about it.

TEM: That would be just perfect; but it would seem to me an indignity to take it from you.

ASTR: It would be worse if I didn't take advantage of the favorable conjunction of Mercury and Venus that is occurring right now. Take this gown then and return immediately. I'll wait for you here at Massimo's house.

TEM: It seems funny for me to leave you here dressed only in your undershirt; still, if you insist, I'll take it.

ASTR: Take it.

TEM: Now I'm the Astrologer and not you.

ASTR: You look like a gentleman in that gown.

TEM: And you look like ... I'll tell you when I return.

ASTR: Go on, hurry up and return quickly.

TEM: (I almost told him that he looked like a glutton and a thief. Let him wait just long enough for me to run to the *podestà* and inform him about what he seems to be and what he is. I don't intend to return this gown I took from him; it will serve as partial payment for what the little thief made us spend money on uselessly.)

Scene Five

ASTROLOGO; NIBBIO

ASTR: I was quite certain that Camillo's silver would be mine. Since I sent him enclosed in the box and had him locked in the room, I'll have plenty of time to empty out his house and get away safely. As for the basins that Massimo was going to give me, I had my doubts—not that he would change his mind about giving them to me, but that he wouldn't give them to me today. And if he intended to give them to me tomorrow, I wouldn't be here, for I plan to leave tonight. I don't know when there will ever be such a fine opportunity. When Fortune begins to smile at you, things continue to improve for a while; and whoever doesn't take advantage of this has only himself and not her to blame. I'll surely take advantage of her. Ah, there's Nibbio.

NIB: What are you doing here in your undershirt? Did you perhaps gamble away your gown?

ASTR: I lent it to one of Massimo's servants, who went to get those two basins, and I'm waiting for him to bring them to me.

NIB: Basins? Hah. You'd better get out of here, Master! That rascal has really played one on you. You poor wretch, don't you know that we've been exposed and that the young man got out of the box?

ASTR: He's out? Oh, hell! Did he get out?

NIB: He got out and he heard from Cintio about the whole fraud and how you were going to use him. Go away, leave here, for God's sake! There's no time to lose.

ASTR: I would like my gown first.

NIB: Master, I don't think that whoever took it intends to return it. To whom did you give it?

ASTR: To that fellow who usually goes around with Cintio. What's his name?

NIB: You must have given it to Temolo.

ASTR: Yes, to Temolo; it was to him I gave it.

NIB: Oh, he's the very one who chased me today and made me run. Write it off as an expense.

ASTR: This pains me, and so much the more since I'm used to profiting and not losing.

NIB: Watch out, Master, that you don't lose more than your gown. Let's leave right away; get out of here. Do what I say; let's head toward the Po. We'll find a boat there that will take us down-river. I think that the police are coming at any moment to throw us in jail.

ASTR: Shouldn't we first go to the inn and get our belongings?

NIB: You go to the port right away and find a boat—any one, large or small—to take us; wait for me there, for I'll run to the inn and bring all our belongings.

ASTR: Then be off.

NIB: Turn down this street.

ASTR: I'm going. But listen, don't leave any of our things in the innkeeper's room; in fact, if you can, take a few of his things.

NIB: You didn't have to tell me.

SCENE SIX
NIBBIO, *alone*

NIB: If I follow him, I run the risk that one day, when I think I'm in Italy, I'll find myself in Picardy.[22] So, this is the last time I'll see him, for I won't follow him. I'll go to the innkeeper to get our things and then I'll head toward Tortona[23] and then on to Genoa. If he intends to proceed on to Venice or Padua, as he said he would, I don't know whether we'll see each other very soon.——
Now don't worry about seeing the Astrologer wind up un-

happy at the end of the play; for art, which imitates nature, doesn't ever suffer the deeds of a scoundrel to lead anywhere but to catastrophe. Don't wait for Cintio to return, for he has already been with his Lavinia a while; he went in through the garden gate, and Temolo is searching for him in vain throughout the city. Now, my audience, let us know by your cheerful applause whether you enjoyed our story.

Although the *Necromancer* was the third play written by Ariosto—the first to be written entirely in *sdrucciolo* verse—it was the fourth to be produced on stage. He had outlined the plot as early as 1509 following the successful debut of the *Pretenders*, but the play remained unfinished for some ten years because Ariosto was not satisfied with what he had written. It was only at the bidding of the pope that the play was completed. Leo X, after delighting in a performance of the *Pretenders* at the Vatican (see preliminary note to the *Pretenders*), requested that Ariosto send along another play, and the poet hurriedly finished the *Necromancer* in time for the carnival of 1520. However, it was not produced: the comedy apparently failed to please the pontiff, possibly because of the author's remarks about indulgences in the prologue. Ariosto had to wait until 1529 to see his *Necromancer* on stage; and the play that premiered in Ferrara at the carnival of that year was a revised and longer version of the comedy. It is this second version, representing a more mature Ariosto, that forms the basic translation here; one can, nevertheless, reconstruct the first version by following the indications in the text and the additional notes.

1. Amphion and his twin brother, Zethus, were co-kings of Thebes. Zethus showed disdain for Amphion's musical talents and was surprised when his brother suggested that they jointly build a wall around the lower city. While Zethus staggered under the weight of his stones, Amphion's share of the stones, charmed by the music of his lyre, followed him and fell into place by themselves. Apollo charmed stones in the same manner when he and Poseidon hired themselves to Laemedon, king of Troy, to build a wall around the city.

2. See preliminary note to the *Lena*.

3. *. . . come suonano vent'ore . . .* For the method of determining modern time equivalents see the *Lena*, n. 6.

4. The *scudo* was a coin of either gold or silver used as late as the nineteenth century, roughly equivalent in value to the crown or the dollar. Apparently the *florin*, the *ducat*, and the *scudo* had approximately the same value at this time, for Ariosto uses them interchangeably.

5. The text has *picciolo*, an old Florentine coin of extremely small value, worth perhaps a farthing.

6. The term "necromancer" is used in its generic sense by Ariosto to refer to a practitioner of any of the black arts. Hence Jachelino is given the title of *Fisico* (Physicist) in the first version of the play and *Astrologo* (Astrologer) in the second. His reputation for necromancy—that is, for conjuring up spirits and questioning the dead—serves him best in his swindles; but, as Nibbio tells us, he is ready to employ any of the occult or pseudosciences for his purposes. A discussion of the influence of superstition and the occult on Ariosto's Italian contemporaries is found in Jacob Burckhardt, "Mixture of Ancient and Modern Superstition," in *The Civilization of the Renaissance in Italy.*

7. As many as 200,000 Jews were expelled from Spain in 1492, a considerable number of whom came to settle in Italy, particularly in Venice.

8. The *carlino* (carlin) was a small silver coin first struck at Naples in 1278 by Charles of Anjou whose effigy appeared on one side. The *julio* was a silver coin of small value first minted by Julius II in 1504 as a substitute for the papal *grosso* or *carlino*.

9. Nibbio is playing here on Camillo's surname, Pocosale, meaning "of little salt [wit]." The pinch of salt administered at baptism symbolized wisdom.

10. *Cuius figurae*?: a Scholastic formula meaning "What figure of speech?"; to which the reply is *simplicis*: "that of a fool."

11. That is, he employs every possible means to achieve his purpose. Gabriele Ariosto uses the same metaphor in his prologue to the *Scholastics*.

12. "Which I won't presuppose."

13. A five-pointed star used as a magical symbol.

14. The text has *spantacchio*, a deformation of *pentacolo*, a pentacle.

15. Garfagnana: a province in the Apennines, northeast of Tuscany, where Ariosto ruled as governor from 1522 to 1525. It is appropriate for the necromancer to head in that direction, since the region was known as a haven for brigands and cutthroats. Under Ariosto's governorship the area experienced a measure of stability.

16. Francolino: a village some six miles northeast of Ferrara on the Po. The first version has Villafranca. In both cases there is a play on the word *franco* (safe).

17. See the *Pretenders*, n. 18.

18. Palio: a race, usually a horserace, that was held annually in a number of Italian cities. The race takes its name from the *pallium*, a precious cloth or banner given as a prize. The most famous Palio is the one still held in Siena every 2 July and 16 August in which horsemen representing various wards compete in the Piazza del Campo.

19. The text has . . . *che se ne fanno in piazza i circoli*: ". . . why people form circles in the piazza."

20. Prior to his invasion of Italy in 1499, Louis XII of France secured Venice as an ally with a promise to allow her to extend her borders into Milanese territory. When the French captured Milan (see *Students*, n. 19), Venice moved in and took possession of Cremona. She kept control of the city until driven out in 1509 by the forces of the League of Cambrai, an alliance of France, the emperor, the pope, and virtually all of Italy directed against Venice.

21. . . . *a grandissime giornate*: "by forced marches." Clearly, then, the city referred to is Alexandria of Piedmont, located some fifty miles northwest of Genoa.

22. ". . . in Picardy"; that is, "hanged." The author is punning on the word *impiccato* (hanged).

23. A town in northwestern Italy, forty-five miles due north of Genoa.

24. See preliminary note.

LENA [or THE PROCURESS]
La Lena

A Comedy Originally in Verse

Characters

CORBOLO	*Flavio's servant*
FLAVIO	*Young man*
LENA	*Procuress*
FAZIO	*Old man*
ILARIO	*Flavio's father*
EGANO	*Old man*
PACIFICO	*Lena's husband*
CREMONINO	*Giulio's servant*
TORBIDO	
GEMIGNANO	*Surveyors*
GIULIANO	*Pacifico's relative*
BARTOLO	*Pacifico's creditor*
MAGAGNINO	
SPAGNUOLO	*Policemen*
FALCIONE	
MENICA	*Fazio's housemaid*
FOOTMEN (*two of them*)	
MENGHINO	*Fazio's servant*

The action takes place in Ferrara

First Prologue

UST NOW, AS I SAW THESE GENTLEMEN AND SO MANY BEAUTIFUL
ladies assembled here, I thought for certain that they had come
to dance, for the occasion seems to call for it;[1] and so I
put on a mask. But then, as I walked into one of these rooms and
saw some sixteen people dressed in various costumes talking back
and forth and reciting various lines, I realized that they were
intending to stage one of those ridiculous things that they call
comedies and that they think they do well. I know from what my
teacher taught me that among all poetic invention there is nothing
more difficult [than comedy]. The Latin poets wrote very few new
ones; instead they translated those of the Greeks. Of the comedies
we read today, none of those of Terence and hardly any of Plautus
are original. I cannot help but be amazed and laugh at our contemporary authors who have the temerity to do that which was not
done by the ancients, who knew more than we do about this and
other learning.

Nonetheless, as we are already gathered here, let us be quiet and
watch. In any event, we'll not lack a subject for mirth, for if we
don't laugh at the humor of the comedy, at least we'll be able to
laugh at the presumption of its author.

Second Prologue of the Lena After it Had Been Augmented by Two Scenes at the End

ERE IS LENA, WHO WOULD LIKE TO MAKE A SPECTACLE OF
herself a second time. She doesn't think that because she
pleased you last year she should be content and not risk
displeasing you now; for people's minds change many times, and
the opinion of the morning is not necessarily that of the evening. If
she didn't please you before, when she was younger and fresher,
then she should please you less now. But the silly thing imagines
herself to be more beautiful now that she's had a tail tacked on to
her end; and she claims that in coming before you with this tail
she has more charm than she had last year when she allowed herself
to be seen without it, wearing a simple dress and attired very
differently from what we see today.

And what would you expect? *Lena* is like all other women who
want to feel a tail behind them and who despise—as if they were
peasants, baseborn, or ignoble—those who don't want one, or, to
put it better, those who cannot have one, for no one, either rich or
poor, who can put one on refuses to do so. In short, *Lena* now has a
tail and she'll come out in public once more to show it to you. She's

certain that you women will praise it and that the young men will do the same, for she knows that tails are not displeasing to them; they rather like them and accept them as fashionable and becoming to noble persons.[2]

But she's fearful of some severe and disagreeable old men who always disapprove of all modern fashions and only praise those that date from ancient times. Of course, there are some amiable old men who don't consider tails annoying and who are delighted with things that are in fashion. Thus, in order to please these people and others who like new fashions, *Lena* comes with her tail to show herself off. And those attached to the past would do well to get up and make room for those who want entertainment.

ACT ONE
Scene One
CORBOLO; FLAVIO

CORB: Flavio, if the question is appropriate then tell me: where are you going so early, for Matins have just rung? There must be a reason why you've dressed and adorned yourself so meticulously; you smell like a phial of perfume.

FLAV: I'm going where my love takes me—to feast my eyes upon an incomparable beauty.[3]

CORB: And what beauty do you think you'll see in this darkness? Perhaps you want to see the star that Martin of Amelia liked.[4] But even that doesn't ordinarily rise so early.

FLAV: Neither that, nor any other star in the sky, Corbolo, not even the sun, is as bright as the beautiful eyes of Licinia.

CORB: Nor are the eyes of the cat; you should have included these also, for, as they are eyes and they shine, they would provide a better comparison.

FLAV: May God give you the plague. Comparing the eyes of an animal, a brute, to angelic lights!

CORB: The eyes of Cuchiulino, of Sabbatino, Mariano, and other drunks when they come out of the Gorgadello[5] provide a more suitable comparison.

FLAV: Oh, go to hell!

CORB: I'd rather go to heaven and lie down in bed to finish that sweetest of sleep you interrupted.

FLAV: Now come here and listen, and forget this silly humor. Corbolo, you can tell from many things that I have always had great confidence in you; but I'll give you a better indication of it now, for I'm going to let you in on a secret of such importance that I would rather lose my wealth, my honor, and my soul than have it revealed. And, although I need your help, I want you to know that I won't ask for it unless you first promise to keep the matter secret.

CORB: You don't have to give me a discourse on the subject; you know well from past experience that when it's necessary I can be quiet.

FLAV: Good, listen: I know that you're aware, without my repeating it, that I'm in love with Licinia, the daughter of our neighbor, Fazio, and that she returns my love. You've been a witness to our words, our sighs, our tears when we've chanced to speak to each other, she at that little window and I in the street; our love lacks nothing except a place where we can relieve our anxieties. She has finally shown me such a place, for she made me become friendly with Pacifico's wife, Lena, who lives next door. When Licinia was a little girl Lena taught her how to read and sew; and now she's teaching her embroidery, needlepoint, and other such skills. Licinia is with her all day long until sunset, so that Lena can easily bring us together without anyone knowing about it. She's willing to do so and intends to try it the first time today; and, because the neighbors may get suspicious if they see me entering her place, she wants me to come there at night.

CORB: It's convenient.

FLAV: The girl will come and go as she usually does. But today I won't be able to budge until nighttime. Then tonight I'll quietly go out.

CORB: By what means were you able to convince Pacifico's wife to be the pimp for her own protégé?

FLAV: I convinced her by the same means that one uses to induce the most steadfast persons to give up castles, cities, armies, and sometimes even the person of their prince—with money. There isn't an easier means than this. I promised her twenty-five florins, and I was going to take the money to her now, for I thought that I would get it from Giulio. He had promised to give it to me yesterday, and he kept me waiting until the last moment. Then late last night he informed me that he wouldn't give it to me, but that a friend of his would let me have it without interest for four months; however, as it was a stranger who was going to lend it to me, he wanted security, which at that moment I couldn't give him. And since I had an appointment to come here, I didn't want to break it and I came. I somehow doubt that Lena will believe me; yet I'm compelled to tell her how the thing went to keep her quiet until tomorrow.

CORB: If she believes you, it would be a good thing to deceive her. The pig! May she roast in hell! She has no scruples. To sell the daughter of the man who confides in her!

FLAV: How do you know that she doesn't have a good reason? For your information this old miser was once in love with her and he has satisfied his desires with her many times.

CORB: It's a miracle! I suppose he's the first one!

FLAV: I believe that her husband either tolerates it or pretends he doesn't know. How many times has Fazio promised to pay off all his debts, for the poor fellow doesn't dare put his foot out of the house for fear that the creditors would have him rot in jail; but when the time comes to keep his promise the villain denies that he has promised anything and says: "It ought to be enough that you have the house rent-free"—as if Lena didn't deserve anything for teaching Licinia!

CORB: Truly, if up until now she didn't deserve anything she will in the future, for she'll teach her how to do the pleasantest work there is—pumping her treadle up and down. She's more than right in doing so.

FLAV: What should I care whether she's right or wrong? Since she pleases me, I'm obliged to her. Now, what I want you to do is to buy me as many as three pairs of quails or turtledoves. If you cannot find them, then get me two pairs of pigeons and roast them; also have a fat capon boiled and bring them all along with fresh bread and the best wine at a suitable time. Make sure that there's plenty to drink. Here's a florin; take it and don't bring me any change.

CORB: You won't have to remind me.

FLAV: I want to give a sign to Lena.

CORB: Yes, do so, but mark it on her face, for by God, she deserves it.

FLAV: If she does me a favor, why should I offend her?

CORB: Do you call it a favor to make twenty-five florins tinkle out of your pocket like the notes of a cembalo? But tell me, once you've borrowed it, how will you be able to pay it back?

FLAV: I have four months to think about that; who knows what will happen during that time? Could my father not die within three months?

CORB: Yes, but he could also remain alive; and if he lives, which is more probable, how will you pay the debt?

FLAV: Won't you always find a way to help me steal it from him?

CORB: I'll find more than ten ways.

FLAV: I hear the door opening.

CORB: And you'd better get ready to open your purse.

Scene Two
FLAVIO; LENA; CORBOLO

FLAV: Good day, Lena, good day.

LENA: It would be more appropriate to say good night. You're very prompt!

CORB: You should greet him again and this time be more courteous.

LENA: I'll greet him again with good deeds and not with useless words.

FLAV: I'm well aware that my happiness today is in your hands.

LENA: And mine in yours.

CORB: I'd also like to put mine in yours.

LENA: Oh what profit! Tell me, Flavio, do you have it with you?

CORB: You can be sure that he wouldn't have come if he didn't have it. I can tell you that it's nice and ready.

LENA: I don't mean that; I'm asking him whether he brought the money.

FLAV: I thought for sure I'd bring it . . .

LENA: You thought? This is a bad beginning!

FLAV: A friend of mine was going to lend it to me yesterday; then last evening he told me that, as it was already nighttime, he would give it to me today or tomorrow for sure. But trust me. I'll have it for you tomorrow before midafternoon.[6]

LENA: If you have it tomorrow, then I'll allow you to come in here the following day at the same time. Meanwhile, be sure you stay out.

FLAV: Lena, consider yourself as having it.

LENA: These are words, Flavio; consider yourself not believed without the money.

FLAV: I give you my word.

LENA: It would be a poor exchange to take one's word instead of money, for you cannot spend it; the tax collectors place it in the class of worthless coins.

CORB: Are you joking, Lena?

LENA: I'm not joking; I'm speaking very seriously.

CORB: Can you be so beautiful and yet so unpleasant?

LENA: Whether I'm beautiful or ugly the loss or the profit is mine. At least I'm not so stupid as to be taken in by words.

FLAV: May God be my witness.

LENA: I don't want a witness whom I cannot bring in to testify.

CORB: Do we enjoy so little credit with you?

LENA: Let's not stand here and waste time; I'm determined that he'll not set foot inside until the money gets here first to open the door for him.

FLAV: Are you afraid that I'll rob you?

CORB: Yes, Master, rub her down, for then it will give you more pleasure.

LENA: I don't have rheumatism.

CORB: (May you be rubbed on your back with an ashen club two yards long, you ass!)

LENA: I tell you, I want money not humbug; he knows very well that this was our agreement. He cannot complain.

FLAV: What you say is true, Lena; but can it be that you're so cruel as to exclude me from your house?

LENA: Can it be that you consider me such a simpleton, Flavio, as to believe you; it has been so many days since this affair began that if you wanted to you could have found twenty-five florins. People like you are never without money. If your friends won't lend it to you ask the brokers, for they're always dealing with a hundred moneylenders. Take off this velvet gown, remove your cap, and send them to the Jew; you have other clothes to wear.

FLAV: Let's do it this way, Lena. Take these clothes as a deposit until tomorrow, and if I don't bring you the money or have him bring it in the afternoon you can pawn them.

LENA: Take them off and send them to the pawnshop yourself.

FLAV: I'm determined to please you and to convince you that I don't intend to cheat you. Corbolo, take this cap and this gown; help me so that it doesn't fall on the ground.

CORB: Are you going to take them off?

FLAV: I intend to satisfy her in every way; what the devil does it matter?

CORB: Now all the butchers can go hang themselves, for no one can skin [an animal] better than Lena.

FLAV: I want you to go see Giulio between ten and eleven o'clock and ask him to find someone right away who will advance me the money that he knows I need, with these clothes as deposit. If he beats around the bush, go to Sabbioni's exchange[7] and pawn them for twenty-five florins; as soon as you get the money from one place or the other, bring it here.

CORB: And will you remain undressed?

FLAV: What else? Oh yes, bring me a small cap and a woolen doublet.

LENA: Hurry up and remember that, although he enters here, he mustn't think that I'll allow the girl in before you count out the cash.

FLAV: Then I'll go inside.

LENA: Yes, enter, but under the condition that I've specified.

SCENE THREE
CORBOLO, *alone*

CORB: Screw her! I'm almost ready to take her in. In my youth I had a thousand dealings with pimps, whores, and other such women who live on dishonest gains; but I never came across one like this, who carries on her wretched trade so avidly and with so little shame. But the day is dawning. Surely it wasn't Matins that rang; it must have been the *Ave Maria* or the *Predica*. Maybe the priests had too much to drink last night and this morning *erant oculi gravati eorum.*⁸ I don't think that I'll be able to see Giulio, for he usually sleeps until ten or eleven o'clock. In the meantime I had better go to the piazza to see if I can find some quails or turtledoves to buy.

ACT TWO
SCENE ONE
FAZIO, *an old man;* LENA

FAZIO: Whoever doesn't arise early and take care of the important things in the morning wastes his day; and his own affairs never succeed very well.——Menghino, I want you to go to Dugentola⁹ and tell the steward to load the cart this evening and bring the firewood here tomorrow. Tell him to be sure that he does, for I have no more left to burn. Don't return until you see that everything is in good order; let me know how the sheep are and how many male and female lambs were born. Have them show you how many holes have been dug and how many trees have been planted, and make a note of whatever still has to be done. Now go, don't waste time. Listen, if they have a tender lamb ... Eh, no, it would be better to sell it. Go, go ... Too bad ...

LENA: Yes, it would have been a miracle if you had become such a spendthrift!

FAZIO: Good day, Lena.

LENA: Good day and good year, Fazio.

FAZIO: Do you arise so early? This isn't your usual way.

LENA: Since you clothe me so nobly and feed me so well it would be appropriate for me to sleep in at my ease until noon¹⁰ and to spend my day in idleness.

FAZIO: I do what I can, Lena. To provide for you I would need a greater income than I have; yet, insofar as I can, I try to be good to you.

LENA: What good do you do me?

FAZIO: That's just like her; she always forgets the benefits. Only when I'm giving you something do you thank me; as soon as I've given it to you, you do the opposite.

LENA: What have you ever given me? Perhaps you're going to repeat that I live here without paying you rent?

FAZIO: Does that seem small to you? It's still twelve lire a year without counting the benefit of having me as a neighbor; but I won't speak of that, for I don't want it to seem that I'm flaunting it in your face.

LENA: Flaunting what in my face? The fact that when some soup or broth is occasionally left over you send it to me?

FAZIO: There are other things, Lena.

LENA: Maybe you mean the one or two loaves of bread a month or the few drops of sour wine? Or perhaps the small piece of wood that you let me have when the carts are unloaded here?

FAZIO: There are still other things.

LENA: What other things? Heh, tell me, a satin or velvet tunic?

FAZIO: It wouldn't be becoming to you to wear it nor right for me to give it to you.

LENA: Show me a dress that you've given me.

FAZIO: I won't answer you.

LENA: Occasionally you give me an old pair of shoes or slippers for Pacifico after they've been worn down.

FAZIO: And for you there were new ones.

LENA: I don't think that you have given me more than three pairs in four years. Aren't the virtues that I've taught your daughter and continue to teach her worth anything?

FAZIO: They're worth very much, I won't deny it.

LENA: When I first came to live here she couldn't read the *pater* from a tablet, not even by syllabifying it, and she couldn't hold a needle.

FAZIO: That's true.

LENA: Nor could she turn a spindle; and now she recites the office and she sews and embroiders as well as any girl in Ferrara. There isn't any stitch so difficult that she cannot duplicate it.

FAZIO: I confess that this is true. I won't be like you and deny the obligation that I have toward you; yet I won't hesitate to reply that, if you hadn't, someone else would have taught her and would have been satisfied with ten julios[11] a year. It seems to me that there's a great difference between three lire and twelve.

LENA: Haven't I done other things for you that merit nine lire more? In the devil's name, if you gave me twelve lire twelve times a year it wouldn't be a sufficient reward to compensate for the shame you cause me; for our neighbors publicly say that I'm your mistress. May the plague come to Master Lazaro who brought me to this little house! But I won't stay there any longer; let someone else have it.

FAZIO: Watch what you're saying.

LENA: Give it to someone else. I don't want you always reproaching me for living in your house and not paying any rent. Even if it means that I have to take up residence in the neighborhood of the Paradiso or the Gambaro,[12] I won't stay here.

FAZIO: Think it over and let me know.

LENA: I've thought about what I want; give it to whomever you please.

FAZIO: I'll find a buyer, and I'll sell it.

LENA: Do what you want with it; sell it, give it away, or burn it. As for me, I'll try to find another place.

FAZIO: (The more I mollify her, the more I humble myself to her, the more proud and haughty she becomes. I can truly say that she doesn't appreciate anything I give her. She's ungrateful to me; she'd like to suck out my soul.)

LENA: As if I wouldn't be able to live without him!

FAZIO: (And, really, besides not paying me any rent for the house, she and her husband cost me more than another twelve lire a year.)

LENA: Thank God that I'm still young enough to help myself.

FAZIO: (I'd like to demolish her arrogance; I really don't want to sell the house, but I want to make her think that I will.)

LENA: I'm neither cross-eyed nor lame.

FAZIO: (I'll bring Biagiolo or one of the Abbacos to make an estimate of the house and I'll discuss the price in her presence and pretend that I have a buyer. She and her husband haven't the money or credit to find another place; they would die of hunger elsewhere. I'm going to poke this beast all over with so many prods—I'm determined to put a rein and a saddle on her.)

SCENE TWO
LENA, *alone*

LENA: He wants the sweet without the bitter; he would taint me with his foul breath, drag me about like a fine donkey, and then pay me with a "Thank you very much." Oh, what a man, oh, what a lover is this who would have me give in to him without any reward! Oh, what a foolish woman I was to let myself be convinced by his stories and his promises! But it was due to the continual nagging of that good-for-nothing Pacifico who never stopped saying: "Please him, wife; it will be our good fortune. If you treat him right, he'll pay all our debts." And who wouldn't have believed him at the beginning? He promised me *Maria in monte*—[the whole world][13]—as these scholars say; then all he gave us was a rope. May it hang him as he deserves.

Since Fazio didn't give what he had promised, I'll do as servants do when they don't get the wages their masters owe them—cheat, steal, and murder. I, too, am determined to be paid through any means, licit or illicit; and neither God nor the world will find fault with me. If he had a wife all my attention would be

devoted to making him what he makes Pacifico; but, as this isn't
possible, for he doesn't have any, by means of his daughter I'll
make him become—I don't know what you call it.

Scene Three
CORBOLO; LENA

CORB: (One man is worth a hundred, but a hundred men aren't worth
one. This morning I had proof of the truth of this proverb.)

LENA: That seems to be Corbolo coming over there; it's him.

CORB: (When I left here to do what Flavio had ordered I went to the
piazza and looked all over; and then I proceeded along the
loggias looking for the fruit vendors. From there I went to find
out whether the delicatessen vendors in front of the castle[14] had
any quails or turtledoves.)

LENA: He's walking very slowly; he seems to be counting his steps.

CORB: (I didn't find a thing; I saw some pigeons so lean and so small
that they looked as if they had had a quartan fever for a
whole year.)

LENA: If only he has the money!

CORB: (Another person would have taken them and said to himself:
"There weren't any better ones; what do I care whether they're
lean or fat, for they're not being cooked for me.")

LENA: He's walking with a heavy load on his left arm.

CORB: (But I didn't do that. I'm not like those to whom you can give
an assignment but not any discretion. I stopped in front of the
gate to the courtyard to see whether some farmers or others
would pass by with better ones. There, standing in a circle, were
some of the duke's followers whom I believe were waiting to be
called into the Gorgadello for a drink by those noblemen who
delight in hawks and dogs. One of them, a friend of mine, said
to me: "What are you looking for, Corbolo?" I told him, and I
also complained to him that they never in any season sell game
here as they do in every other city; that there is a scarcity of good
food and that all there is to eat is coarse meat that never cooks.
And even this was expensive enough! They all agreed with what
I said.)

LENA: I'll wait for him and find out what he's done.

CORB: (I left and one of them followed me. At the corner where the
Orafi begins he accosted me and whispered: "If you want a pair
of plump pheasants you can have them for fifteen bolognini."[15]
I said: "Yes, yes, indeed," to which he replied: "Wait for me by
the bishop's palace; but don't say a word about this;" and I
answered: "I'll be as quiet as the statue of Duke Borso[16] there."
In the meantime I bought a fat capon that I had seen; I picked up

six Seville oranges and went into the bishop's palace. My friend arrived, hiding the pheasants, which weighed as much as a pair of ducks. I reached in and took out fifteen bolognini, which I counted out for him on the altar. Then he ended by saying: "If you need four, six, seven, or ten pairs, let me know, provided that we keep this between the two of us." And I thanked him. . . .)

LENA: He seems to be daydreaming and talking to himself a good deal.

CORB: (I gave him my word that I would keep it secret. But I felt like laughing. To think that the duke protects his forests with such care by decrees that carry such harsh penalties; yet those who take care of them are the very ones who steal from them.)

LENA: Hurry up, may your soul be plucked out!

CORB: (Because of these decrees one cannot serve pheasants at weddings and public banquets; yet they are eaten by whores and gigolos in their rooms. I had the pheasants roasted and the capon boiled; and I'm bringing them here warm in a basket. Here's Lena.)

LENA: Do you have the money, Corbolo?

CORB: I'll have it.

LENA: I don't like to hear an answer in the future tense.

CORB: You're different from other women, who all love the future.

LENA: I like the present.

CORB: Here, I give you a present of a capon, pheasants, bread, wine, and cheese. Take them inside. It would seem unnecessary to bring pigeons, for I see that you have two beautiful plump ones in your bodice.

LENA: May the devil take you!

CORB: Let me put my hand in to see how soft they are.

LENA: I'll give you a fistful. What about the money?

CORB: Every psalm finally ends with a *gloria*. You don't forget such a thing. I'll bring it in half an hour. I found Giulio still in bed and I gave him the message; he made me leave the clothes on a chest, and he told me to return at noon. Meanwhile, I had dinner cooked and got everything ready. But, Lena, what reward will I get for my troubles, for I'm the main reason why you're getting the twenty-five florins?

LENA: What do you want?

CORB: Do you want me to tell you? It's something that you couldn't lose if you gave it to me or to a hundred others.

LENA: I don't understand.

CORB: I'll say it plainly.

LENA: Bring me the money, for without it I cannot understand you.

CORB: Does money help, then, to make one understand?

LENA: Yes, it makes me understand, and I believe this is no less true of all people.

CORB: Would this be a good remedy, Lena, to make a deaf man hear?

LENA: There's a big difference, you blockhead, between hearing and understanding.

CORB: Explain the difference to me.

LENA: One can hear donkeys braying when they're pulling a mill-stone, yet one cannot understand them.

CORB: It always seems easy for me to understand them when I hear them; they'd like exactly what I want from you.

LENA: You're more wicked than the devil. Now that the roast is done just right, let's go inside and eat.

CORB: I'm coming. Tell me, where's the girl?

LENA: Where's the money?

CORB: I think I can let you have it within an hour.

LENA: And I think I can have the girl come here as soon as the money arrives. Let's go, for the food is getting cold.

CORB: All right, I'm coming.——May it be the last thing you eat. I hope you choke on it! Did I have to take so many pains to buy this and cook it so that a whore and a cuckold could eat it? But they won't get the portion they think, for I, too, am going to grease my mouth and hands with it.

ACT THREE
SCENE ONE
CORBOLO, *alone*

CORB: Now, of the two tasks, I have done one well and to my satis-faction: the capon and pheasants came out juicy and tender, the bread was fresh, and the wine excellent. Flavio doesn't stop praising me as a man who knows how to spend his money. I'll now do the other task, but not with the same enjoyment that I did this one. It bothers me to see him spend—I should say lose—twenty-five florins, and it's too much to bear. It's easy to borrow; it's difficult to return. I don't know how he'll manage unless in the end he sells his clothes; but if he sells his clothes—and I know that he won't be able to hide the fact from his father for very long—the shouting, the noise, the uproar will be heard everywhere, and he runs the danger of being thrown out of the house. What is needed is a cunning servant who would be able to draw this amount out of the purse of his old master by means of fraud and deception as I have sometimes seen done in plays. Alas, although I am neither Davus nor Sosia, and although I was not born among the Getae or in Syria, don't I also have some tricks in this silly head of mine? Can I not also come up with a plot that Fortune will favor—Fortune who, as they say, smiles on the daring? But what shall I do? I'm not dealing with a credulous old man in a way that Terence and Plautus had their Chremes and Simo duped.[17] But won't my glory be greater the more cautious he is, if I catch him in the trap? Yesterday he went by boat to Sabioncello[18] and he's expected back this morning. I had better think about what to say when I see him. Oh, here he is now! This is just typical of a comedy: To mention his name and to have him arrive in town at the same time. But I don't want him to see me until I've laid the net in which I hope to envelop him today.

Scene Two
ILARIO; EGANO; CORBOLO

ILAR: One should never prize anything so much that one wouldn't sell it if he could do so profitably, the only exception being wives.

EGANO: These as well, if it were allowed by law or custom.

ILAR: Not only should they be sold, but they should be exchanged and given away as gifts.

EGANO: You mean the ones who aren't acceptable to you.

ILAR: Naturally. It isn't customary to sell them, but it seems permissible to lend them out. Now to get back to the subject I was speaking about—a pair of oxen that I sold yesterday for thirty Hungarian ducats . . .

CORB: (These would do for our purposes.)

ILAR: . . . to a farmer from Sandalo.[19]

EGANO: They must have been beautiful.

ILAR: You can be sure . . .

CORB: (I want them; I will have them.)

ILAR: . . . that they were very beautiful.

CORB: (They're ours.)

ILAR: Beautiful indeed! I like this money much more, though.

CORB: (I've made up my mind.)

ILAR: At least I'm sure that the requisitioner of oxen[20] won't whip them.

EGANO: You did well. That's the way. I'm at your command if I can be of any help to you.

ILAR: Good-bye, Egano.

CORB: (The quail is under the net; I'd better run ahead and make sure that it becomes entangled and is caught.) I don't know what to do or where to turn since my master isn't here.

ILAR: (Oh! What can this be?)

CORB: But why did Flavio have to leave?

ILAR: (This must be something unpleasant.)

CORB: It would have been better to have written a letter and to have sent a messenger immediately ...

ILAR: (Alas, some misfortune must have occurred!)

CORB: ... rather than to go to him in person.

ILAR: (What can it be?)

CORB: It would have been better for him to have told the duke about it.

ILAR: (God help me!)

CORB: The moment Ilario finds out he'll come flying home.

ILAR: Corbolo!

CORB: He won't stand for it, and he'll raise hell.

ILAR: Corbolo!

CORB: But what can he do?

ILAR: Corbolo!

CORB: Who's calling me? Oh, Master!

ILAR: What's the matter?

CORB: Did Flavio meet you?

ILAR: What happened to him?

CORB: It wasn't even eight o'clock when he left the city saying that he was going to look for you.

ILAR: What was so important?

CORB: You don't know what danger he was in!

ILAR: Danger? Tell me: what happened to him?

CORB: He can claim that he was born again, Master. Some thieves left him for dead; yet thank God, the injury ...

ILAR: Is he hurt?

CORB: Not seriously.

ILAR: What madness was this for him to come to the farm if he's hurt, seriously or not?

CORB: Going there cannot aggravate his injury.

ILAR: How come?

CORB: It won't, I tell you; rather it will make him more agile.

ILAR: Tell me, is he wounded?

CORB: Yes, and his recovery will be difficult; it's not that the wound is bleeding ...

ILAR: Alas, I'm dead!

CORB: But let me tell you where it is.

ILAR: Tell me.

CORB: It's neither in his head, nor in his shoulders; it's not in his chest or in his side.

ILAR: Where, then? Out with it. He's hurt, isn't he?

CORB: Yes, he is, and it's very painful.

ILAR: He must be hurt very seriously.

CORB: No, very superficially.

ILAR: Oh, you're torturing me! Is he hurt or isn't he? Who can understand you?

CORB: I'll explain.

ILAR: Explain it, may the devil take you!

CORB: Listen.

ILAR: Go on.

CORB: His wound is not in his body.

ILAR: Is it in his soul, then?

CORB: He's wounded in someplace like that. Last night at supper Flavio found himself in the company of a group of young men. As he went to supper he told me to come with a lantern to call for him when the clock struck eleven; but—and I don't know why —he left at ten o'clock. While walking alone without a lantern he had no sooner reached the portico opposite Saint Stephen's when he was surrounded by four men with clubs who beat him up.

ILAR: And wasn't he wounded? Oh, what danger!

CORB: As God willed it, they never caught him on his body.

ILAR: Oh, God, I thank you for this.

CORB: He turned around and started to run as fast as his legs could carry him. One of them tried to hit him on the head.

ILAR: Alas!

CORB: But the blow struck the gold medal that he was wearing, and his cap fell off.

ILAR: Did he lose it?

CORB: No. Those rascals took it.

ILAR: Didn't they return it to him?

CORB: Return it, eh?

ILAR: It cost me more than twelve ducats with the gold pointed trimmings. Thank God they didn't do worse than that.

CORB: His gown, which was falling to one side and was entangling his legs, almost made him fall three or four times; finally he freed himself by throwing it off with both hands.

ILAR: Did he lose it, then?

CORB: The little thieves took that also.

ILAR: And if the little thieves took it, don't you think that Flavio lost it?

CORB: I didn't think you consider things lost that other people have found.

ILAR: Oh, you are thick! It cost me eighty ducats with the lining. Then Flavio is not wounded?

CORB: Not in his body.

ILAR: Where the devil then? In what other place could they wound him?

CORB: In his mind. He's very upset, for, apart from his injury, he's concerned about the annoyance that you'll feel when you find out.

ILAR: Did he see who it was that attacked him?

CORB: No. His great fear and the extreme darkness of the night prevented him from recognizing anyone.

ILAR: We can write them off as a debit, then.

CORB: I'm afraid so.

ILAR: You lazy loafer! Why didn't you wait for him if you had to pick him up?

CORB: You see . . .

ILAR: But you are indeed an ass, for you weren't prompt in going after him.

CORB: This is just like you; you always reproach me for his mistakes. He should have waited for me or, if he didn't want to, he should have taken his companions along with him; they all would have gone had he asked them. But let's not lose any time; now, while the damage is fresh, let's try to do something about it.

ILAR: Do something about it? What could we possibly do?

CORB: Speak to the *podestà*, to the secretary, and, if necessary, to the duke himself.

ILAR: And what the devil do you expect them to do?

CORB: Have them proclaimed outlaws.

ILAR: So that in addition to the loss there would also be mockery. Everyone will say that he wasn't caught alone and unarmed, but that he was attacked as an equal and that his clothes and arms were taken from him without any resistance. Now, even if I go to the duke and tell him the situation, what will he do if not send me to the *podestà*? The *podestà* right off will look at my hands and, not finding a donation, will pretend that he has more important things to do; and, if I have no proof or witnesses, he'll take me for a fool. Besides, who do you think the criminals are, if not the very same ones who are paid to catch the wrongdoers? The *podestà* divides the spoils with their chief or with the leaders;[21] and everybody steals.

CORB: What shall we do, then?

ILAR: Be patient.

CORB: Flavio never will.

ILAR: He ought to be, whether he wants to or not; since he got out of it alive he should consider himself favored by God's grace. He's free from fear and danger and has received no other injury; but it's I who feel badly wounded—wounded in my purse. The damage is mine, and I'm the one who should feel sorry, not he. I'll have a cap made for him right away, just like the other one, and a respectable gown as well; but there's no one who would be willing to incur a loss by replenishing my purse with the money that I'll have spent.

CORB: Don't you think it would be a good idea to warn the second-hand dealers and the Jews? In case these assassins come to pawn or sell the clothes, they could hold them at bay until you got there to recover the goods and have them arrested.

ILAR: This could be more useful than harmful. Yet I'm not very hopeful, for those who lend money at interest are undoubtedly scoundrels themselves. Those others, the secondhand dealers, are fraudulent and never tell you the truth; and they accept nothing more readily than stolen goods, for they can buy them very cheaply. If they lend you money on an item, they see to it that you never get it back.

CORB: Still, let's warn them; let's do our duty.

ILAR: If you think so, then go ahead and warn them.

Scene Three
CORBOLO; PACIFICO

CORB: The affair is going well, and I can consider it successful; the only thing left for me to do is to get Giulio to give back the clothes and then to send them to be pawned for as much as possible with someone else. I'm sure that the old man will redeem them as soon as he finds out where they are. I want to tell Flavio about all this so he'll know how to act with Ilario and so that our stories will be identical. Here's Pacifico coming out of the house.

PAC: Flavio wants you.

CORB: I came to see him and bring him the good news.

PAC: He knows it, for we overheard what you said from beginning to end; both of us have been listening from behind the door, and we didn't miss a word.

CORB: What do you think of it?

PAC: We give you the glory and the praise of being able to invent a lie better than any poet. But stay where you are; I don't want Fazio to see you enter the house. Come in as soon as he's inside and turns his back.

Scene Four
FAZIO; PACIFICO

FAZIO: I don't want you to be surprised, Pacifico, so I'm telling you now to find yourself a house within a month, for this one is up for sale.

PAC: It's yours; dispose of it as you wish.

FAZIO: The buyer and I have agreed to let Torbido settle the matter, and he has gone to get his rod to survey the place. I doubt whether we'll part before reaching an agreement.

PAC: Had I known about it yesterday, I would have straightened the place up a little; you caught me with an untidy house.

FAZIO: Go then and do what you can to tidy it up immediately; it won't be long before they arrive.

PAC: Not today; make them come back tomorrow.

FAZIO: The man who's buying it cannot be here tomorrow; he's going to Modena.

SCENE FIVE
PACIFICO; CORBOLO

PAC: How are we going to conceal your master, Corbolo, so that these people won't see him? If Fazio sees him, surely he'll realize what's going on and there will be an enormous scandal.

CORB: Is there a place where we can hide him?

PAC: Where in a house like this can we be sure that he won't be found? They're going to measure everything.

CORB: Isn't there a chest or a wardrobe?

PAC: We have only two small chests, which wouldn't even hold Santino the dwarf[22] in his underwear.

CORB: Then we have to get him out of here before they come.

PAC: Undressed as he is?

CORB: I'll go home and bring him another gown.

PAC: Go then and return quickly; I'll wait for you here.

CORB: I see Ilario coming out.

SCENE SIX
ILARIO; CORBOLO; CREMONINO

ILAR: It cannot hurt if, besides having sent Corbolo, I go myself; I shouldn't think that anyone else would be more diligent than myself in my own affairs. Ah, here he is. What have you done?

CORB: I've warned Isaac and Benjamin at the Sabbioni; now I'm going to the Carri. Those at the Riva[23] will be the last.

ILAR: What does that fellow want—the one who's about to knock on our door?

CORB: It's Cremonino. (Oh, damn it, we're discovered!)

ILAR: What do you want, young man?

CREM: I'm looking for Flavio.

ILAR: Oh, that seems to me to be his gown.

CORB: And to me also. Look, there's his cap too. (Oh lies, help me now or else we're ruined.)

ILAR: Corbolo, what's going on here?

CORB: His own companions must have played a trick on him, and I believe that they took pleasure in seeing him run.

ILAR: A fine trick indeed.

CREM: My master, Giulio, is returning his deposit and wants him to know that this friend of his . . .

CORB: What friend? Listen to this story!

CREM: . . . the one who would lend money on this collateral, Corbolo . . .

CORB: What prattling!

CREM: . . . the money that you . . .

CORB: Oh, what sham!

CREM: . . . came to ask for today.

CORB: Who, me?

CREM: Yes, you.

CORB: Look at him! See how well he tells a lie!

ILAR: Corbolo, take these and put them away. Go, I mean you, go and tell Giulio that such tricks shouldn't be played on friends. . . .

CREM: What tricks?

ILAR: They're not proper for someone like him.

CREM: I don't think that my master has done . . . Why are you making faces at me, you idiot? I'm going to tell the truth. . . .

CORB: I, make faces?

CREM: . . . and defend my master whom you wrongly slander. If he had had the money he would have lent it and willingly.

CORB: Money? Keep on joking! Are you dreaming perhaps, or do you take us to be drunk or raving mad?

CREM: But didn't you bring this gown to Giulio this morning?

CORB: On foot or on horseback? We understood you.

CREM: Then why are you still making faces at me?

CORB: Am I making faces?

ILAR: Oh, may you get Saint Anthony's fire! Didn't I see you making faces?

CORB: Of course I'm making faces to show that we're aware of his tricks and that we don't buy them.

CREM: It's you who are playing tricks.

ILAR: I want to know what's going on. Where did you get these clothes?

CORB: Yesterday Giulio was waiting for Flavio.

ILAR: I want to hear it from him, not from you.

CORB: He'll feed you some story; he knows too well how to deceive.

CREM: But it's you who deceive.

CORB: Now, look at me and don't laugh.

CREM: Who's laughing? Why look?

CORB: Go, go tell Giulio that some day Flavio will be able to repay him for this.

ILAR: No, don't go. [*To Corbolo*] You, get out of here; I want to find out from him and not from you.

CORB: I won't stand for having this man mock you.

ILAR: What are you afraid of—that perhaps his words will enchant me? But tell me, these clothes ... [*To Corbolo*] Go away; get out of here.

CORB: Are you really going to listen to him? All the winepresses used at vintage time couldn't squeeze a single truth out of him.

CREM: I'll tell the truth.

CORB: That's about as likely as a donkey saying a paternoster.

ILAR: Let him speak.

CREM: I'll tell you the gospel truth.

CORB: Let's remove our hats, for it's not right to hear the gospel with one's hat on.

ILAR: You're trying to interrupt in every way; if you speak once more ... [*To Cremonino*] Please come in; let's leave him outside. Go inside. I'm determined to find out about this swindle, for it cannot be anything else; but let's lock this nuisance outside.

SCENE SEVEN
CORBOLO; PACIFICO

CORB: We're done for. The twenty-five florins are running away by leaps and bounds; they're running so fast that there's no longer any hope of catching them. What a great favor Giulio did for us! By God, we'll always be obliged to him! He said to me: "Come back in an hour and see how we've made out"; and then he changed his mind and sent this blockhead to ruin the web that I was in the midst of weaving.

PAC: How come you were arguing so long? Where's the gown that you were bringing to Flavio? A plague on you! Let's not lose any time in getting him out of the house. What are you waiting for? For Fazio to come in and see him?

CORB: I couldn't get into his room! Ilario has locked me out!

PAC: What shall we do?

CORB: Try and hide him in the house.

PAC: There isn't any place.

CORB: Then send him out in his shirtsleeves. Choose one of the alternatives: either hide him in the house or send him out in his shirtsleeves.

PAC: I don't want to choose either one.

CORB: What will you do then?

180

PAC: I just remembered that I have a large barrel in the house that was lent to me at this year's wine-harvest by a relative of mine who wanted to get rid of its stale odor by using it as a vat. He left it with me, and I still have it. I'll hide him in it until those who are coming with Fazio will have looked over everything at their leisure.

CORB: Will he fit inside?

PAC: Comfortably. I cleaned it thoroughly a few days ago, and I can easily remove and replace one end of it.

CORB: Let's go then and discuss it with him.

PAC: I think that these are the men who want to see the house. It's them for certain; I know Torbido. Let's finish what we have to do ourselves.

CORB: All right.

PAC: Then come inside.

CORB: Go ahead; I'll follow you.

Scene Eight
TORBIDO; GEMIGNANO; FAZIO

TORB: Once I've measured it, the rod will tell me how much it's worth down to the last penny.[24]

GEM: Then do rods sometimes speak?

TORB: Yes, and they also make other people speak when they're laid on their backs. But here's Fazio.——What are we supposed to do?

FAZIO: What I told you. Start measuring whenever you wish; the property line begins here and doesn't extend beyond that mark.

TORB: Then let's start here.

FAZIO: Begin over here.

TORB: One; mark the end of it with your knife.

GEM: Done.

TORB: Two; and the remainder lacks about two-sixths so it can barely be three feet. Let's go inside now.

FAZIO: You can take chalk and mark that.

TORB: Here, I'm doing it.

Scene Nine
GIULIANO, *alone*

GIUL: Just now, as I was in the palace, I saw the mayor sign a warrant permitting Pacifico's property to be attached to the amount of forty-three lire, which he owes Bartolo Bindello. I'm certain that there won't be enough to amount to half or even a third of such a debt. Because of this I'm afraid that they may take a barrel of mine that I lent him at vintage time to ferment the wine. I had better go pick it up before the police get a hold of it, for then I would have to go to court and argue and prove that it's mine. Since the door is open, I'll go in without knocking. Come on, porter, come inside; follow me.

ACT FOUR
Scene One
CREMONINO, *alone*

CREM: Now I realize how foolish I've been. When my master learns about it he'll reproach me harshly for having revealed to Ilario the snare set by Corbolo to enable Flavio to get money from him; but I failed him only out of carelessness and not out of malice. How was I supposed to know, since I hadn't been told anything? It's my master whom they should complain about, for he should have warned me. Then again, it was because of my great stupidity that I didn't realize the mistake until it was too late. But where are these policemen going? They must be going to bother some poor citizen. What a breed! The dregs of mankind!

Scene Two
BARTOLO, *alone*

BART: I've sent bailiffs ten or twelve times to attach his property; but those rascals are hardly interested in carrying out any sequestration as long as they're paid for the trip. He originally owed me forty lire and fifteen soldi; and when I tried to collect this he kept the lawsuit going for four years. I received two judgments, both favorable, but the amount that I spent in fees for lawyers, solicitors, and judges was twice that amount, while the summonses, the copies of legal papers and articles, cost me only slightly less. On top of this there was the intolerable bother and the heavy expenses of the examiners, the transcriptions of the processes, and the verdicts. The number of times that I've had to take off my hat to this one or that one, the shoes that I've worn out in the palace of justice following after solicitors who are always on the run—this I think is worth more than forty lire. Then, after going through all the trouble and expense, the judges sentence him to pay me only forty lire; as for my expense, I can scratch my bottom. See how justice is done in Ferrara! At least if I could get those forty lire! But just when I think I'm making good my losses with some pieces of household furniture, which aren't worth forty lire altogether, his wife appears with an inventory of items in her dowry and it includes them all. I won't believe, nor can I believe, that he's as poor as they say.

182

Scene Three
BARTOLO; MAGAGNINO

BART: Go, do your duty, Magagnino; knock on that door.

MAG: Why should I knock it, if it hasn't offended me?

BART: It offends me because the law prevents me from getting at the man who lives behind it.

MAG: Avenge yourself, and since you've been denied other satisfaction, let out your anger. Beat it with your hands and feet.

BART: I hope to get other satisfaction; let's go in. But I hear the door being opened.

MAG: It has wisely obeyed you and has avoided being beaten.

BART: It seems that many people are there; let's move over here to the side a bit. I think they're carrying out the furniture and clearing the place.

Scene Four
GIULIANO; PACIFICO; BARTOLO

GIUL: If the barrel is mine, why are you preventing me from taking it?

PAC: How come, after leaving it here for six months, you want to take it away from me all of a sudden?

GIUL: Because, if I leave it here today, I run the risk of losing it, for the reason I gave you.

BART: (They must have been warned; we couldn't have come at a more opportune time.)

GIUL: Unless you tell me, I cannot understand what harm or benefit it can do you whether I take it or leave it.

PAC: If you take it now you'll do great harm to me.

GIUL: And you to me.

PAC: Please leave it with me for another half hour.

GIUL: What if the police come to search your house? And here they are; here they are, to be sure. Now I won't be able to get it without a contest; you see, I shouldn't have left it with you.

Scene Five
BARTOLO; MAGAGNINO, SPAGNUOLO, *policemen;* GIULIANO

BART: I want that as part of the debt. Falcione and you, Magagnino, put it on your shoulders; and you also Spagnuolo.

MAG: I'm not used to being a porter.

SPAG: Neither am I.

BART: Great help you give.

GIUL: Don't any of you dare touch it, unless you want . . .

BART: Then are you going to prevent me from carrying out the order that I have to remove the property that was pledged?

GIUL: I'm not preventing you from taking his property; but, I tell you, the barrel is mine.

BART: What do you mean, yours?

GIUL: It's mine, by all means; he borrowed it from me a while ago.

BART: Hey, what kind of stories are these? When I see it coming out of his house, I take it as his.

GIUL: You take it? Yes, but only if I allow you to. Leave it, or else I'll . . .

BART: Be my witnesses that this man prevents me . . .

GIUL: What do you mean prevents? Let it be.

Scene Six

FAZIO; GIULIANO; PACIFICO; BARTOLO; CORBOLO

FAZIO: Say, why all the noise here? What's the uproar?

GIUL: The barrel is mine, and I want to take it home; but this man is trying to prevent me.

PAC: He's telling the truth; it really is his.

BART: On the contrary, both of them are lying.

GIUL: You're the liar.

FAZIO: Speak without insulting each other.

BART: You're lying to me.

GIUL: You're lying, since you say that I'm not telling the truth.

BART: What do you think, Fazio? If it's being taken out of Pacifico's house should I believe him when he tells me that it's not his?

GIUL: If it were Pacifico's we wouldn't be bringing it into the street.

BART: That's not true; you were taking it out to hide it.

PAC: Not at all, by God! We were taking it out to return it to him; he lent it to me during the year.

FAZIO: May I express my opinion?

BART: Yes, I'll abide by your judgment.

GIUL: Me, too.

FAZIO: Bartolo, leave this barrel in trust with me, and if Giuliano proves to me that it's his within two days he can have it; but if he doesn't bring me convincing evidence, then he'll have to be patient.

GIUL: I'm satisfied.

BART: And so am I.

GIUL: I can very easily prove to you that it's mine.

BART: If you can prove to him that it's yours with genuine and concrete evidence, then take it away when you please.

PAC: It doesn't seem very sensible to me for you to leave it to an arbiter and allow your clear right to become clouded.

CORB: He's right. You're better off leaving it where it was, in Pacifico's house.

BART: This advice doesn't benefit me.

FAZIO: What business is this of yours? Why are you getting mixed up in this if it's not yours?

CORB: I'll answer for myself, for maybe I do have an interest in it.

GIUL: I'm not willing to concede that to you.

CORB: It belongs to me more than you think.

FAZIO: Sure, it belongs to you.

GIUL: What do you mean? That's not true.

FAZIO: Let it belong to him. Don't you think that it would be safe in my house? As if I were only friendly with Bartolo and not with Giuliano!

GIUL: We've already agreed to let Fazio arbitrate the matter; let him be the custodian and the judge.

BART: I agree.

FAZIO: Then roll it inside my house; and don't worry, I won't let it be moved until I'm absolutely certain as to whom it rightfully belongs.

PAC: (Flavio is hidden inside. See how bad luck and disaster always follow me!)

FAZIO: Pacifico, it would be best for you to look after your house so that the police won't take away anything else or even do worse to you.

PAC: What can they take? What little there is they know all belongs to my wife; they've been here before. Well, I want...; but here they're coming out.

SCENE SEVEN

MAGAGNINO; TORBIDO; GEMIGNANO; GIULIANO; FALCIONE;
SPAGNUOLO; FAZIO

MAG: I guess there's nothing else, except what we usually find, and that's in the inventory.

TORB: Ah, thieves, scoundrels, you've stolen my cape!

MAG: You wrongly accuse us and insult us.

TORB: You contemptible gallows-bird, may the plague take you! What's this that you have hidden underneath?

MAG: I took it for my expenses. I didn't steal it from you.

TORB: I'll really give you expenses if this rod doesn't fail me.

GEM: I'll help you out.

GIUL: And I don't see any point in keeping my hands at my side.

TORB: You see that stone, Gemignano? Take it and break his head; after all, you, too, are from Modena.[25]

FALC & SPAG:[26] Is this the way to treat officers of the duke?

TORB: The duke doesn't keep thieves in his service. Away with you thieves; away with you poltroons; away with the devil. If I had hesitated a little longer before realizing it, I would really be in a fix—I would have had to go out in my doublet. If that were the case this pole that I brought would have come in handy, for, by carrying it on my shoulder, I would look like a *Landsknecht* or a Swiss soldier.[27]

FAZIO: Is there anything else to be measured?

TORB: I've measured everything down to the last brick and the last board and I've written it all down and brought the figures with me; I'll finish the calculations and let both of you know how much it will come to.

GEM: When will that be?

TORB: Today, if you wish. Is there anything else, Fazio?

FAZIO: No, not now.

TORB: Good-bye.

FAZIO: Good-bye. [*To Licinia, inside*] Hey there Licinia. If anyone comes to see me, send him down to Master Onofrio's shop. I'll be there until suppertime.

SCENE EIGHT
LENA, *alone*

LENA: With all this bad luck it's our good fortune that Fazio has left the house. If he hadn't gone it would have been difficult to get Flavio out of that barrel today. As I watched him being rolled into that house my heart was so seized with fear and trembling that I don't know how it is that I didn't die of a stroke. Had he moved ever so little he would have given away his presence; a sigh, a sneeze, a cough would have ruined us. Now that this danger has passed without any damage let's see to it that something else won't happen. All we have to do now is to get him out right away so that no one will see him. I'll send Corbolo to bring him a gown; but first I'll send out the servant, for if she were to remain there's the risk that she'll see or hear the young man.——Listen, Menica. Whom am I speaking to? Licinia, tell Menica to get her veil and come see me. Oh, there she is.

SCENE NINE
MENICA; LENA; CORBOLO; PACIFICO

MEN: What do you want, Lena?

LENA: Dear Menica, please do me a favor, and I'll always be indebted to you.

MEN: What do you want?

LENA: Will you do it for me?

MEN: I'll do it provided I can.

LENA: If you love me, dear mother, go to the Church of the Angels.[28]

MEN: Now?

LENA: Yes, now.

MEN: At least let me put supper on the fire.

LENA: No, go ahead. I can put a pot on the fire without you. Go, and when you're right in front of the church turn in between the Mosti gardens and the monastery; keep to the right, and after you make a left turn, you'll come to a place, I think, called Mirasol.[29] Go now.

MEN: Goodness me, what do you want me to go there for?

LENA: See what a scatterbrain I am! Find out where the wife of Pasquino lives—I think it's the third door. She's the woman who teaches girls how to read; her name is Dorotea. Go there and say to her: "Dorotea, Lena sent me to get the metal pieces used for winding silk on spools";—and ask her to send them along, because I need them. Go now, dear Menica, and I'll give you enough cloth to make a bonnet.

MEN: The meat in the basin is washed and ready; it only needs to be put in the pot.

LENA: [*To herself*] I think it's far too ready; but he won't put it in the pot until he gives me twenty-five florins.[30] I know all about the love of these young men; it lasts only while they crave the object of their love. And while they're in this state of desire they would give you, not only their fortunes, but their hearts. But once in possession their love is like fire that has had water thrown upon it—it immediately is extinguished; and now that they lack passion they wouldn't give you a thousandth part of what they had promised. With this in mind, I had better go inside and put a stop to anything they intend to do without me. ——Come on, Corbolo, hurry up and bring him a gown, so that we can let him out while there is the chance.

CORB: Instead, while there is a chance, I beg you and Pacifico to let him put it in.

LENA: No, in heaven's name, he won't; and don't think that I'll let him satisfy his desires unless he gives me the money first. I'm going to guard her myself.

CORB: Guard her so well that your eyes become glued to her.——Must I suffer Flavio to leave Licinia without enjoying her? After all, he's gone to the trouble of getting up before five o'clock, of being shut up in a barrel in such peril, just like the eels or the mullets of Comacchio.[31] But what shall I do when I find myself opposed by this whore of a woman and her cuckold husband upon whom prayers are worthless and threats have no effect? How could I use force when the situation is already too dangerous without making more noise? Well, I guess we need twenty-five florins and we'll have to give it to them; they won't give in and they won't give us credit. Where can I find the money? I've tried borrowing it on our word of honor, and it hasn't worked; we cannot borrow on collateral, for Ilario has deprived us of this. It would be a foolish thing to try to set another trap for him; he would never fall for it. And yet sometimes birds that have been caught in the net and then freed themselves have been caught again. Perhaps it will be easier to deceive him now, for it would seem to him unlikely that I would gather my courage so soon to try it again after having failed the first time. But what shall I do? What shall I do this time? I had better decide on something soon, for there is precious little time to think about it. I'll ... what? I'll say ... yes, of course; and will he believe me? He will believe me. But Pacifico is coming outside.

PAC: Where's the gown?

CORB: What gown? Do you take me for a tailor? Oh, it seems that you don't know my profession. I mind the mint and I'm going to strike twenty-five florins now to give you.

PAC: If only it were true!

CORB: Now do as I tell you. Do you have any arms in the house?

PAC: Fazio's coat of arms is painted over the fireplace in my bedroom.

CORB: I mean offensive ones.

PAC: There are many that offend me: poverty, worries, my wife's anger, and her constant insults.

CORB: I mean a spear, a pruning hook, a sword, or something like that.

PAC: Yes, there's an old spear that's all rusty. It's so bad, and in such horrible condition, that the police weren't interested in taking it away.

CORB: Enough; come and show it to me. Now don't you think it will be a fine work of alchemy if I were to change this rusty piece into twenty-five florins?

ACT FIVE
Scene One
CORBOLO; PACIFICO; FOOTMEN

CORB: Come on out; come a little closer; a little closer. Get away from the house a bit. You seem as timid with that weapon in your hand as you would be if it were in your breast. What are you afraid of?

PAC: Of the captain of the piazza who might catch me with this spear and put me in prison.

CORB: No, I'd make him think that you're a policeman or a hangman; and he'd believe it, for you certainly have the appearance
of both. Hold your head up high. You look as if you're going
to cry! Stand up straight, stand firm, look fierce, act like
a bravo.

PAC: How does one act like a bravo?

CORB: Curse God and the saints often. Hold it like this; turn this
way and make a fierce and menacing face. This is really ridiculous, trying to make a sheep look like a lion. But I see two of
Don Ercole's[32] footmen coming this way; perhaps they can
supply what this man lacks. I'll approach them. Good day,
brothers.

FOOT: Oh, Corbolo, good day and good year. How are things?
Would you give us a drink?

CORB: Yes, willingly; but I'm thinking about giving you something
better than a drink.

FOOT: What?

CORB: If you stay with me here for half an hour I'll lead you to
some contraband from which you'll get at least a couple of
scudi[33] each.

FOOT: Here we are ready to serve you for the benefits you'll
provide us.

CORB: I'll tell you about it. Those Jewish moneylenders at the Riva
bought a large quantity of cheese yesterday. They loaded it on
two carts and covered it with straw in such a way that no one
would realize what it was—except for me, for I learned about it
from the person whom they bought it from. They're bringing
it along this street without a customs certificate and without
paying any duty on it. Now, as I didn't want to let them know
who I am, I told my neighbor about it and I placed that spear
in his hand so that, as the carts pass by, he could poke through
the straw to find the contraband. I'll be ready to act as a peace-
maker to enable them to come to an agreement, so that he won't
go and accuse the Jews of smuggling. But he's fainthearted, and I
don't want to be hindered by him. Now, if you want to join me
in this, I'll willingly accept you.

FOOT: As a matter of fact, we beg you to accept us and we promise
to split the gains like good companions.

CORB: Now, hold it. You stay here and keep a lookout so that if
the carts pass by you can run to them; and you keep watch on
this other street. ——(I've posted the artillery at the corners. Now
may the lies that were fleeing, pursued and in disarray, make
their stand and vigorously counterattack against Ilario, who had
put them to rout. There he is coming outside; provided that they

can withstand this rather difficult beginning, I have no doubts
that the victory will be mine.)

SCENE TWO
ILARIO, *alone*

ILAR: Oh, how neatly that little thief would have deceived me if the
Lord God hadn't sent that young man in the nick of time. He
came by chance, and not of his own free will, and he directed
my eyes to the trap into which I almost fell. I think that Corbolo
was going to induce Flavio to sell his clothes secretly and
squander the proceeds in lasciviousness, while withholding the
greater part of it for himself; and I, believing him and thinking
that Flavio would become worried, intended to make him
another gown and another cap so as to change that worry into
gladness, as if the loss had been a real one.

I cannot understand why my Flavio employs such methods
with me, for I'm the most indulgent father, and what is more, I
try to satisfy his every honest desire more than anyone in the
world. I only blame that glutton, Corbolo, whom I don't want in
my house another minute. I'll dismiss him, for he deserves it.

SCENE THREE
ILARIO; CORBOLO

ILAR: Do you still have the audacity to come before me, you low-
down scoundrel?

CORB: Please put aside your anger and, for God's sake, don't let pity
overwhelm you.

ILAR: Oh, you're crying?

CORB: And you should cry even more, because your son . . .

ILAR: God help me!

CORB: . . . is in danger.

ILAR: In danger?

CORB: Yes, in danger of being killed unless we make amends
right away.

ILAR: How, how? Tell me, tell me, where is he?

CORB: Pacifico caught him committing adultery with his wife. Look
at him, he wants to kill him with that spear and he's called in
those two young relatives of his to help him. He's also waiting
for three brothers-in-law to come.

ILAR: Where is he?

CORB: Who? Flavio? Inside the house where these rascals are
beseiging him.

ILAR: Inside where?

CORB: There, in Fazio's house.

ILAR: Is Fazio there?

CORB: If he were there the danger wouldn't be so great. The only one there is a girl, his daughter; there's no one else. Now just think, what kind of help can he get from a woman!

ILAR: If Pacifico caught him in his house with his wife, how come he's in Fazio's house?

CORB: I'll tell you the whole story from the beginning.

ILAR: Tell it, but don't leave out or add anything.

CORB: I'll tell it exactly as it happened; but first I want to assure you that the story that I told you before—that Flavio had been assaulted and that his clothes had been stolen—was not made up to hurt you. I devised it only to get you to give me the money with the least opposition, money to free your son from the danger in which he now finds himself. Now that this scheme has failed his life is in much greater danger than it was before.

ILAR: Tell me the whole story.

CORB: Flavio, thinking that Pacifico would be away today, and his wife thinking the same, had come to the house and had gone into the bedroom with her; and, while they were enjoying themselves, that cuckold, who was hiding I don't know where, sprang up with a spear to kill him.

ILAR: My heart is trembling.

CORB: Flavio begged him and entreated him so much that, with a promise of money, he agreed to spare his life.

ILAR: Now you revive me—if the matter can be solved by money.

CORB: I haven't told you everything yet.

ILAR: What else is there? Go on.

CORB: They agreed on twenty-five florins, which were to be paid before they parted. Flavio sent for me and, taking off his cap and gown, he entrusted me to go and ask Giulio to lend him that amount with the clothes as a deposit; he would remain as a hostage. Then, as you know, that young man ruined our plans; and because of him Flavio is in extreme danger unless you make amends. May God help him!

ILAR: Why should he harm him if they've come to terms?

CORB: Now listen. Pacifico, thinking that he was being deceived, became angrier than before; he grabbed the spear and without listening to any explanation, he tried to kill him.

ILAR: You made a mistake in not coming immediately to tell me. What happened finally? Continue.

CORB: I don't know how he didn't kill him. Believe me, God and the saints must have been favorable to Flavio.

ILAR: A villainous poltroon has dared to threaten to kill my son?

CORB: Had your son not leaped outside, after shielding himself with a bench and gradually withdrawing toward the door, he would have killed him.

ILAR: So then he was saved?

CORB: I don't consider him safe yet.

ILAR: You're killing me.

CORB: As that rogue continued to chase him without letting him get too far away, Flavio was forced to take refuge in Fazio's house, where he's now being beseiged.

ILAR: See the audacity of that beggar, that scoundrel, that impudent one!

CORB: And, furthermore, Pacifico is trying to round up more men so that he can enter the house.

ILAR: Enter the house? I'm not so lacking in means and friends that I cannot defend my son and make Pacifico appear a villain.

CORB: Don't get yourself involved in this, for you have another remedy. [As you know], organizing a gang is against the decrees of the duke, and the penalties are up to the judge; besides, someone may get killed. If you were to [use force to] prevent Pacifico from harming Flavio physically—which should be easy for you, for I believe that you and Flavio can harm him more— and if he complains to the *podestà*, as I think he intends to, then you will not be able to prevent the *podestà* from proceeding against Flavio. You know very well what the penalties are, by law, for adultery; and you know that the *podestà* has the authority to increase the penalties according to the wealth of the accused and not according to the seriousness of the offense.

Master, take care that your tears and sorrows don't provide an occasion for laughter for those at court who always have their eyes open for such cases so that they can run and ask the duke for the fines as a gift. It's better to spend twenty-five florins without a struggle, in reaching an agreement, than to place yourself at the risk of losing five hundred or even a thousand.

ILAR: I think it would be better if I spoke to Pacifico myself to see what he has in mind.

CORB: No, in the devil's name! Don't go, for, moved by his anger, he might say something insulting, which you'll always be sorry about. Let me go, for I hope with two words to be able to make him quiet and humble. And it will be more to your honor if I can bring him here.

ILAR: Go, then.

CORB: Wait for me here.

ILAR: Listen. Make him offers, but don't mention any sum; I want to settle the amount myself. Make him general promises, you know what I mean.

CORB: I understand. However, don't hesitate to spend one or two florins more.

ILAR: Leave it to me, for I'm more experienced in this than you are.

SCENE FOUR
ILARIO, *alone*

ILAR: I think that it would be a good thing for me to find Fazio before I talk to Pacifico. I want to ask him whether he ought to allow these people to do violence to my son in his house; and he could also serve to bring harmony between us, since Pacifico is a good friend of his. I'll find him at the barbershop where he usually plays chess all day long.

SCENE FIVE
CORBOLO; FOOTMEN; PACIFICO

CORB: Brothers, you can go now; don't waste any more time here. My master, from whom the Jews buy their cheese, tells me that they've changed their minds: they've gotten a customs certificate and have paid the duty.

FOOT: It would have been a miracle if we had been so lucky.

CORB: Accept my good will; I tried everything possible to be helpful to you.

FOOT: We realize this, and we'll always be obliged to you.

CORB: I'm always yours, brothers.

FOOT: Good-bye, Corbolo.

PAC: How did you make out?

CORB: Wonderfully. The twenty-five florins will be given to you by Ilario, begging you and asking you to please accept them; however, you must continue to behave as I tell you and follow my instructions about what to say, instructions that I'll give you as soon as you've put away the spear. Now don't waste any time; put it away and return to me immediately. Listen.

PAC: What do you want?

CORB: Since you no longer have any doubt that the money promised you will be paid, have your wife come outside and give the two lovers a chance to enjoy themselves before the servant or Fazio returns.

PAC: There'll be time enough; even if Menica returns, I'll be able to send her somewhere else. You don't have to worry about Fazio, for he never returns home before the bells ring seven o'clock.

CORB: Well then, put away the spear and come with me, so that Ilario can give you the twenty-five florins.

Scene Six
CORBOLO, *alone*

CORB: The enterprise is proceeding very well. The army of lies, after experiencing so many dangers, after so much travail, will finally be victorious despite Fortune, who had undertaken to deter me from tapping Ilario's purse. But where does that man think he's going?——Pacifico, come here, come out, run quickly, help!

Scene Seven
PACIFICO; CORBOLO

PAC: Here I am, here I am.

CORB: Run, Pacifico; don't let that fellow see Flavio.

PAC: What fellow?

CORB: What's the name of that young servant of yours? What are you waiting for? Go inside and get him. Menghino, that's his name.

PAC: Menghino? Damn it!

CORB: Menghino, yes, Menghino.——See the negligence of an idiot! But it's I who am stupid for trusting someone who's slower than a sawhorse. And here's Menica returning. I see the enemy's strength increasing in so many quarters that I'm losing all courage to resist his assault.

Scene Eight
MENICA, *alone*

MEN: By the cross of God! I'll never do another favor for Lena. She sent me half a mile beyond the Church of the Angels, and I almost had to run all the way to get back on time; now I feel so weak and tired that I can hardly move. My going there wouldn't have bothered me had I found the woman I was looking for. I went around like a beggar pleading for alms in the name of God from door to door; and I wasn't able to find any sign of a Dorotea who teaches people how to read. Nor, from what I learned, is there anyone named Pasquino living in Mirasol or even nearby. Worse still, my master saw me and is coming here with Ilario; he's angry, but I don't know why. When he asked, I told him where I had been and that Lena had sent me; then he screamed at me and threatened me with a good beating if I ever do anything for her again. I'll certainly obey him. If I can, I'll sit down. As long as I only hear words, I don't think they'll make me move.

Scene Nine
ILARIO; FAZIO

ILAR: I had gone to find Fazio, thinking that this would be a good way to bring about an accord between Flavio and Pacifico and to

194

pacify him. I didn't realize that he was so in love with this woman that he's thoroughly corrupted. The moment I told him that Pacifico found her having relations with my Flavio he got so angry, so enraged by jealousy, that it will be more difficult for me to placate him than her husband. But here he is.——Quicken your pace a bit so that we can get there before another scandal occurs. You'd better hurry up if I ever expect to get any help from you.

FAZIO: I cannot bear it, Ilario, and, even if I could, I wouldn't stand having that bitch betray me after she has received and was about to receive so many benefits from me. I'm ready to avenge myself.

ILAR: If she has offended you, then avenge yourself. I'm not asking you for her sake; I only ask so that you don't let my Flavio be harmed by Pacifico in your house.

FAZIO: She chose a fickle young man who's young enough to be her son and from whom she could expect no reward except to have him boast about it and bring disgrace on her.

ILAR: My son didn't intend to offend you; if he had realized that she was your mistress I know that he would have been very respectful, for he has great reverence for you.

FAZIO: That's the reason why she has become so wild during the past couple of weeks.

ILAR: Speak to me with a little less anger.

Scene Ten
MENGHINO; ILARIO; LENA; FAZIO

MENG: I saw him; it's no use hiding him.

ILAR: Ah, we delayed too long! They're shouting in your house. For pity's sake, Fazio, help me!

MENG: I'm going to find him and let him know about your wonderful deeds.

PAC: Menghino, listen to me.

MENG: I've already seen and heard enough.

PAC: Don't be . . .

FAZIO: What's going on here?

PAC: . . . the one to start up such a fire.

MENG: I'm going to tell even if I have to lose my head.

FAZIO: Hold it. Let's stay here a while and hear what they're quarreling about.

PAC: Wait, Menghino; stop, listen to me.

MENG: Let me go, Pacifico. Don't think that I won't tell because of you.

LENA: What the devil can you say in a hundred years? May you get a cancer! And what did you see, you stupid ass?

MENG: I saw Licinia and that young man, Ilario's son ...

ILAR: He means Lena, not Licinia.

MENG: ... embracing each other.

LENA: You lie in your throat.

MENG: There's Fazio. Master, I'm telling the truth; I won't betray you. Your daughter ...

FAZIO: Hey, stupid, I heard you. Do you want the whole neighborhood to hear all about it? By God, Ilario, I can never allow your son to wrong me so without taking revenge. What tales, what stories did you give me to believe about Lena and Pacifico?

ILAR: That's the way I heard it from Corbolo.

FAZIO: This isn't an affront that one can pass over lightly; it's too important.

ILAR: By your faith, Fazio.

FAZIO: Please, Ilario, I really wonder at you; does this insult seem to you to be of such a nature that I should bear it so easily? Even though you're richer and more noble than me, I'm not inferior to you in nobility of spirit. Before Flavio gets out of my house I'll make an example of him to show that those in my situation mustn't be taken advantage of.

ILAR: For the sake of filial love, which I see you feel as much as I do, I pray you, I beg you, to have pity on me and Flavio.

FAZIO: It's precisely my filial love that moves me to vengeance.

ILAR: For the sake of our long friendship!

FAZIO: If you were in my position it would be difficult for you also to forgive. I care more about my honor—forgive me if I speak frankly—than your friendship. I would sooner lose everything that I have in the world before that, and without it I wouldn't care to live.

ILAR: What if there were a way not to lose it?

FAZIO: I'm willing to make a bargain with you. As soon as your son marries my Licinia and she regains her honor we'll be friends; otherwise ...

ILAR: Enough said. I believe that by now you have known me for more than fifty years and you know the way I live as well as anyone else. You know very well that I always like things honest and lawful; and you know that I've always been well disposed toward you and ready to do you honor and a good turn, for I've shown you examples of this. Now don't think that I can be or wish to be different from usual. Let me speak to Flavio and find out about the whole thing; and rest assured that I'll do whatever is appropriate to make amends for this injury.

FAZIO: Let's go inside.

ILAR: Go ahead, and I'll follow you.

Scene Eleven
PACIFICO; LENA

PAC: Now do you see, Lena, where your wicked and whorish dealings have got you!

LENA: Who made me a whore?

PAC: You might at well ask those who are hanged every day what makes them thieves. Attribute it to your own free will.

LENA: Rather to your insatiable greed, which has reduced us to this miserable state; if it weren't for the fact that, to provide food for you, I allowed myself to become a donkey with a hundred scoundrels you would have died of hunger. Now, as a reward for the good that I've done, do you reproach me, you poltroon, for being a whore?

PAC: I'm reproaching you because you should pursue your trade with more modesty.

LENA: Ah, cuckold, you speak of modesty? If I had accepted all those to whom you had recommended me I know of no prostitute at the Gambaro who would be more public than me; this front door hardly seemed wide enough for you to receive them all, and you even advised me to make use of the back door.

PAC: In order to live in peace with you I was only suggesting something that I know you liked very much; if I had tried to prevent you, it would have been impossible to live with you.

LENA: Oh, may you get the plague!

PAC: I have it continually with you. You should be satisfied, Lena, that you always do as you please with your own body—and that I see this and tolerate it. Must you also seek to disgrace us by being a pimp for honest men's daughters?

LENA: If I were always to remain young, it would be easy to support both of us by the same means that I've used until now. But, just as ants provide for themselves for the winter, so it's only right that poor ones like myself provide for their old age. When they have the opportunity they become skilled in a trade so that when the need arises they don't have to learn it, but are expert and experienced in it. And what trade can I pursue that would be more profitable than this one and would be easier for me to teach? Do you expect me to wait until the last moment, when I'm in need, to learn it?

PAC: If you had behaved this way with anyone other than Fazio, to whom we are too obligated, it would be more tolerable for me.

LENA: Ah, you miserable cur, may you get a cancer! As if you weren't aware of the whole thing! Now that the scheme has ended in failure you blame me alone for our common sin. But if the money had appeared you would have wanted your share and more.

PAC: Enough, Menica is coming outside.

Scene Twelve
MENICA; LENA

MEN: So this is the way you act, Lena? Do you think that Fazio deserves this sort of abuse from you?

LENA: What abuse? What the devil have I done to him?

MEN: Nothing!

LENA: Nothing, indeed. For the suffering that he causes me there isn't an injury known in the world that he doesn't deserve from me.

MEN: You revealed your bad intentions, Lena, but you've done him a service rather than an injury. It was because of you that he has been able to marry his daughter to a rich and noble young man such as he himself would have chosen.

LENA: Is he going to give her to him as a wife?

MEN: He has already given her. He and Ilario came to an agreement in a few words.

LENA: Even though I hate that wretched old man more than I do snakes, I'm glad for Licinia, and I wish her every happiness.

MEN: If you persist in your anger, Lena, you would be the most ungrateful woman in the world. Although he has every reason to feel exactly the opposite, Fazio cannot help loving you. He cannot hide the passion that burns within him, and he cannot but repent the harsh words that he had with you this morning that he thinks moved you to plan this indignity against him. He also told me that when he heard from Ilario that your husband found you with that young man he almost died of anguish on the spot. And then, when he found out that he hadn't done it to you but to Licinia, which was indeed the case, he was consoled again, and it seemed to revive him. Now you can see that he will undoubtedly become reconciled with you soon, especially as this error of yours turned into his good fortune.

LENA: Let him be and let him do as he pleases. If he feels the same toward me as before, he'll find that I feel the same toward him.

MEN: Now, Lena, here's the truth. Fazio sent me to tell you that he's yours just as he used to be, and he begs you similarly to be his. He invites you and Pacifico to a wedding this evening, and he doesn't intend Licinia and Flavio to be the only honeymooners tonight.

LENA: I'm ready to do whatever pleases him.——Now, my audience, tell us, has this story been pleasant and agreeable or has it been boring?

The first performance of the *Lena* took place in Ferrara at the ducal palace during the carnival of 1528. The play may have been performed again in December of that year when Duke Alfonso's son, the future Hercules II, brought his bride, Renée of France, back to Ferrara. A year after the premiere the expanded version mentioned in the second prologue was staged in Ferrara, once again during carnival time.

1. See preliminary note.

2. Through the use of the word *coda* (tail) in the image of a woman's train, Ariosto not only is able to effect a bit of salacious humor, but in his praise for "modern fashions" he also takes an oblique thrust at his conservative critics. One can also detect a reference to sodomy. Cf. the *Pretenders*, prologue and n. 4.

3. The Venetian edition of Marchio Sessa (1533 or 1536?) has: "I'm going where Love, my most pleasing Lord, takes me—to feast my starving eyes upon an incomparable beauty."

4. The moon.

5. Cuchiulino, Sabbatino, and Mariano were notorious drunks. Ercole Bentivoglio mentions Cuchiulino in his fourth satire; the two others were employed at the Este court. The Gorgadello was a tavern located on the street of the same name. See Ariosto, *Satira* 2, l. 67.

6. *Vent'ore.* The numerous references to hours of the day in the *Lena* only become meaningful when placed in the framework of medieval chronology, according to which the day begins at sunset, and darkness and light are each divided into twelve hours. At carnival time (mid-February), when the plays were usually presented, the day would thus begin at about 5:30 P.M. and sunrise (the twelfth hour) would be somewhere between 7:00 and 7:30 A.M. By this reckoning, *vent'ore* would occur between 2:00 and 2:30 P.M.

7. The Banco dei Sabbioni was one of Ferrara's leading lending institutions.

8. "Their eyes were heavy with sleep."

9. A village to the southeast of Ferrara, situated about halfway between Ferrara and Portomaggiore.

10. *Nona.*

11. See the *Necromancer*, n. 8.

12. The lanes behind the Paradiso Palace (later the seat of the university) and Gambaro Street contained a number of bawdy houses.

13. *Maria in monte* (Mary on the mountain) was a popular distortion of the saying *maria et montes* (seas and mountains).

14. The piazza near the ducal palace is a prominent marketplace.

15. The name given to coins of various sizes and weights issued by the commune of Bologna after 1191. Corbolo is most likely referring to the silver *bolognino grosso*, which was worth about twelve *denarii*.

16. Borso d'Este (1413–1471), natural son of Niccolo d'Este, was duke of Modena (1452–71) and became the first duke of Ferrara in the year of his death.

17. The names of Davus and Sosia came to epitomize the cunning slave in the Latin theater. They were supposed to have been captured from the Getae in Syria. Davus is found in Terence's *Phormio*; Sosia appears in his *Hecyra* and in Plautus's *Amphitryo*, while both are together in Terence's *Andria*. Chremes and Simo, prototypes of the gullible old man, generally

served as foils or as contrasts to the above. See Plautus, *Pseudolus, Mostellaria*; Terence, *Phormio, Heautontimorumenos, Andria.*

18. A hamlet situated about fifteen miles east of Ferrara.

19. A village located some fifteen miles southeast of Ferrara.

20. *Giudice alle fosse*: literally, the "judge of the ditches"—the person who supervised ditchdigging operations in Ferrara. He had the authority to requisition oxen from local owners once a week for work in progress.

21. "With the nobleman who is their leader" in the Sessa edition.

22. The Este court dwarf from 1512 to 1519.

23. The Sabbioni, Carri, and Riva were local banking institutions. Benjamin da Riva was a prominent Ferraran moneylender who was instrumental in financing the wars against Venice.

24. See the *Necromancer*, n. 5.

25. The Modenese had a reputation for ferocity and obstinacy. See Ariosto, *Orlando Furioso*, canto 3, stanza 39, and *Satira* 5, l. 29.

26. The text has *sbirri* (policemen).

27. The distinguishing feature of the German *Landsknecht* (mercenary infantryman) and the Swiss footsoldier was their long pike.

28. Saint Mary of the Angels.

29. The district of Ferrara in which Ariosto lived.

30. The Sessa edition has: "I think it's far too ready—I mean Flavio's; but he won't put it in Licinia's pot before I get the twenty-five florins."

31. The lagoons of Comacchio near the Adriatic are well known for their eels.

32. Hercules II (1508–1559), the son of Alfonso I, became fourth duke of Ferrara and Modena in 1534.

33. See the *Necromancer*, n. 4.

THE COFFER
La Cassaria

A Comedy Originally in Verse

CHARACTERS

NEBBIA CORBO }	*Crisobolo's servants*
CORISCA EULALIA }	*Young ladies*
EROFILO CARIDORO }	*Young men*
LUCRAMO	*A procurer*
FURBO	*Lucramo's servant*
VULPINO	*Erofilo's servant*
FULCIO	*Caridoro's servant*
TRAPPOLA	*A cheat*
BRUSCO	*A farmer*
STAMMA	*Lucramo's maid*
RICCIO BRUNO ROSSO }	*Crisobolo's servants*
CRISOBOLO	*Erofilo's father*
NESPOLO (*silent*)	*Crisobolo's servant*
CRITONE	*A merchant*
CRITONE'S SON-IN-LAW (*silent*)	
GALLO (*silent*) NEGRO (*silent*) }	*Crisobolo's servants*
SERVANT	*of Crisobolo*

The action takes place in Sibaris[1]

I N CASE YOU DON'T KNOW IT, THE COMEDY BEING PRESENTED TODAY is the *Coffer*, which made its debut on this very stage twenty years ago. At that time it rather pleased everyone. But it didn't receive a worthy reward, for it became the prey of pesty and greedy printers who tore it apart, doing what they liked with it; then they sold it everywhere—in shops and public markets—to whomever would buy it, at bargain prices. In short, they so mistreated it that it no longer resembled the play as it was originally written.[2] The play itself was most sorrowful and complained to its author many times; and he, moved to pity by its miseries, decided in the end not to let her sufferings continue any longer. So, he recalled his play and made her more lovely than ever. He has refashioned her to such an extent that anyone who had previously seen her would scarcely be able to recognize her at first glance now.

Oh, ladies, if he could only do the same thing to you that he has done to his story: make you more beautiful than ever, and, by completely renewing you, restore you to the prime of life! I'm not speaking to those of you who are young and beautiful and who have no need to multiply your charms or to turn back the years, for you are now experiencing the best years of your life; so be aware of this and live them to the fullest before they pass! But I address myself to those of you who aren't satisfied with your beauty and would like to be lovelier. What would you give if you could increase your beauty and improve it? And what would so many others pay, others whom I won't name? I'm not saying that they're not pretty; I only say that they could be much more beautiful. If they had sound judgment or a mirror in their house they would see that I'm telling the truth and that one could find innumerable women prettier than they are. The jars and makeup from the Levant that they always carry with them are of little help. If their mouths or their noses are too large or too small, if their teeth are yellow, crooked, sparse, or larger than ordinary, or if their eyes are crossed or some other part of their body in which beauty resides is poorly formed, all their efforts can never change this.

How much would these women pay—I'm speaking of those of you who used to be so beautiful in your prime, whether at sixteen or at twenty. Oh, what a sweet age! Oh, cruel memory! How quickly the years go by! I speak of those who have reached the regretful age of forty or even more. Oh, this fleeting life of ours! Oh, how it passes; oh, how we find our beauty and charm fall away as if off a precipice! There's no way to retrieve them. Putting on powder and rouge will never turn back the years; nor will perfume smooth the skin. No, not even if we stretched it with a winch would we ever be able to hide the cursed wrinkles that so shrivel the face and chest—which, I believe, have even a worse effect on those parts of the body that don't show.

But I shouldn't always touch upon women. I shouldn't continually put them down, even though they allow themselves to be touched and put down without much complaining—such sweet and pleasant natures do they have! I'd like to say a few words also to the men, principally to those at court who want to be lovely and graceful as much as women do; and rightly so, for they're well aware that at court they will never obtain favors or riches without beauty and grace. Others want to be handsome for a different purpose, and I'm not going to seek the reason why.

Such desires are more tolerable in young men than in old; and yet some old men, nonetheless, try their best to be good-looking and well-groomed. The more feeble their bodies become—and they would be decrepit if they lived but a few days more—the more fresh and daring they feel and the more arrogant and libidinous their minds become. They utter the same words, they think the same thoughts, they have the same feelings, the same desires, as when they were young men. Thus they speak of love; they boast of accomplishing great deeds. They perfume themselves and show off their fringes and embroideries more than ever. To hide their ages they pull the white hairs from their chins and heads; some dye them black, but two or three days later they grow in a different color. Some hide their hoariness or their baldness by wearing wigs; others shave twice daily.

But there's no denying their age when their faces accuse them and reveal their years by the wrinkles around their eyes, by the redness of their eyelids, and the tears constantly flowing; or by the great number of teeth that are missing or have fallen out—in fact, all of them would be gone if they didn't retain them in their mouths by ligatures and with considerable difficulty. What would these men pay if our author would do for them what he did for his comedy? Any treasure, any amount, would seem a small price to them. But, if the author of our comedy were able to perform this service for men and women—a service, as I told you, he has done for his play, as he has enhanced its beauty and changed it completely— then he would do it for you, ladies, without payment or any other reward; because he would like to please you no less than himself.

Yet, there are many things that are easy to do to one person and impossible to do to another. If it were in his power to make men and women younger, as he is able to do to his stories, then he would

have made himself so young, so handsome, and so charming that
he would be pleasing to you no less than he expects his *Coffer* to be.
But if he cannot do this for himself, don't think that he can do it for
you; if he could, I tell you on his behalf, he would gladly do so.

ACT ONE
Scene One
NEBBIA; CORBO; *servants*

NEB: I'm leaving. You don't have to take up a sword or a cudgel to
chase me out. All of us are going immediately; we'll leave the
house to you. Come on, let's all go; let him alone, so that he can
take what he wants and ransack the place without witnesses.

CORBO: Your foolishness is indeed unbelievable, Nebbia; of all of us
servants you alone always oppose Erofilo's wishes. You, yourself, should realize by now whether this has been harmful or
beneficial to you. What the devil, obey him and please him in
what he wants. After all, he's our master's only son and, in the
natural course of events, we'll be serving longer under his
command than under that of the old man. Why the hell do you
insist on staying in the house when he wants to send you out
with us? Why do you try to make him a worse enemy than he
already is?

NEB: If you had received the strictest orders from the master as I
did, I'm sure that you would have done the same.

CORBO: Perhaps.

NEB: And if you saw things as I see them, you would see that I'm
not doing enough.

CORBO: How do you see them?

NEB: I'll tell you: you probably know that pimp who's been living
on our street for a short time.

CORBO: Yes, I know him.

NEB: If you know him, then I'm sure you've seen the two gorgeous
girls he has in his house.

CORBO: I've seen them.

NEB: Our Erofilo is so taken with one of them that in order to have
her he's ready to give everything he has in the world, and even
sell himself. But the pimp, who's aware of his desire and who
knows that he's the son of Crisobolo, one of the wealthiest
merchants in Sibaris, is asking him more than twice the price
and more than would be considered reasonable.

CORBO: How much is he asking?

NEB: I cannot say exactly; but I do know that he's asking him much
more than usual and that Erofilo couldn't gather together such
a large sum by himself or even with the aid of his friends; he

would need his father's help.

CORBO: What is he going to do?

NEB: A great deal of harm to his father as well as to himself. I think that he has his mind set on selling either the wheat that arrived from Sicily a few days ago or the silk, the wool, or other such merchandise with which the house is bulging. His adviser in this matter, as you know, is that thief, Vulpino; you can imagine the rest. The opportunity that they've been awaiting came this morning when the old man left very early to go to Procida;[3] and they want us out of the house so that no one can witness their scheme. Now they've sent us to find Filostrato with the excuse that he needs our help around the house.

CORBO: Let him do what he wants. Why should you care about it more than we do? Even if they robbed and emptied the house, Erofilo will be heir to what remains, not you, stupid.

NEB: It's you who are stupid; you have no more sense than an ass. Tell me, Corbo, if Crisobolo returns, what will happen to me? When he left this morning he entrusted me with the keys to his bedroom where the other keys are kept; and he ordered me, if I valued his good will and my life, to keep them on my belt or in my sleeve, not to give them to anyone, especially not to Erofilo, and never to dare set foot out the door. Now you see how I obey him! He probably hadn't even reached the port when Erofilo asked me for the keys and finally demanded them, saying that he wanted to look in the closets for a certain hunting horn of his. He got them—perhaps you were there.

CORBO: I could easily hear the sound of about ten or twelve blows of a cudgel ...

NEB: There were more than fifteen, more than twenty!

CORBO: ... which flattened your back before you agreed to give them to him. But I wasn't right there when it happened.

NEB: I wish I, too, hadn't been! He would have killed me had I not given them to him.

CORBO: I believe he would have.

NEB: What should I have done?

CORBO: You should have given them to him as soon as he asked for them and left the house the moment he ordered you to. You would always have had a legitimate excuse for the old man—that you were forced to do so. Do you think he's so unrealistic and unreasonable that he's not aware of the fact that you're hardly fit to be a match for a rash and ardent young man like Erofilo, his only son?

NEB: Yes, by God, as if it would be difficult to place all the blame on my shoulders! After all, he's the master, and all of you servants in the house despise me! This truly isn't due to my faults, but to my merits, for I don't allow the master to be robbed.

CORBO: It's due to your bad disposition, for you don't know how to make friends.

NEB: Have you seen anyone in any household who has my job and isn't also hated by all the others?

CORBO: Because those like you are wicked and you're all scoundrels. In choosing stewards, whose job it is to provide for the household, masters always select the worst man they have in the house so that they can shift the blame to him for every hardship the servants suffer. But let's change the subject. Tell me something: who's that young man who just entered the house—the fellow Erofilo honors so much?

NEB: He's the son of the captain of justice.

CORBO: What's his name?

NEB: Caridoro. He wants the other girl in the pimp's house; but I don't think he's any more able to raise the money unless he, too, tries to steal from his father. And, just as Erofilo has Vulpino as his adviser, he likewise has a little glutton of a servant, one named Fulcio, as his. The two of them would seem as natural on a gallows as wine on the table. Oh, look, Corbo, the girls are coming out of the pimp's house.

CORBO: Which one is Erofilo in love with?

NEB: With the one closer to the door. Caridoro is in love with the other one.

CORBO: Let's get going; if Erofilo came out and found us here, he'd accuse us of negligence and he might get angry.

SCENE TWO
CORISCA, EULALIA, young ladies

COR: Please! Come on, Eulalia; Lucramo's not home. Come out for a while. Let's take this small pleasure.

EUL: What pleasure could compensate for a thousandth part of our misfortune, Corisca? Oh, how miserable we are! We're servants, and while this is a hard and distasteful condition, it would be tolerable if we belonged to someone who showed some humanity and moderation; but of all the procurers in the world there's none who is as unpleasant, greedy, godless, mean, and bursting with anger as the one to whom our cruelest fate has made us slaves.

COR: Have patience, sister. We're not going to remain like this forever. I have hopes that some day our friends will take us out of this misery.

EUL: And when are they going to do this if they haven't already done so? How do you expect them to, if we're leaving at dawn tomorrow?

COR: I know too well what Caridoro has promised me many times, and you know what Erofilo has promised you also; and we both know how much they love us.

EUL: I'm well aware of what they promised; but I don't know whether they intend to keep those promises. Neither you nor I really know whether they love us, for we cannot look into their hearts. This much we do know—they should be in love with us.

COR: They should love us indeed! Simply because they're fine young men you assume that they're in love with us, and because they're in love with us they'll do what they promised us a thousand times.

EUL: I would rather that they had denied it a thousand or two thousand times and then promised only once, for I would find them more credible. If they're going to do it what are they waiting for? They don't intend to, Corisca, and they're enjoying themselves by teasing us. In this they've done us much harm: If they weren't around perhaps others might have come who would have provided us with fewer words and more deeds. Besides, they so angered Lucramo—who has seen the whole affair dragged out and himself deceived—that under no circumstances will he stay in Sibaris any longer; and we're going to leave tomorrow come what may. But we'd better go inside; let's get our things ready and do what our master ordered us to do. Let's not give him reason, because of our neglect, to vent his anger and irritation on us.

COR: Sister, since we have to leave, are we going to depart without speaking to our boyfriends?

EUL: Alas! If they were our boyfriends, as you say, sister, I don't think that they would have let this come to such a pass that we would have to say good-bye and take leave of them; they would have rescued us from our servitude and kept us with them here in the city.

COR: I'm not going to abandon the hope that they still may do it.

EUL: Let's return to the house. Since they won't come out, it's not proper for us to go knocking on their door.

COR: Let's stay a while, Eulalia. They shouldn't be much longer now. I hear the door opening; it must be them.

EUL: It is them.

COR: Here they are.

SCENE THREE
EROFILO; CARIDORO; EULALIA; CORISCA

ERO: Oh, Caridoro, we're going to have great success in all our plans after having experienced such a happy encounter, such a lucky omen.

CARI: Here they are, Erofilo. Here are the serene and salutary stars whose appearance calms the stormy and dismal sea of our thoughts.

EUL: We could more truthfully say this about you, for you indeed could be our happy encounter, our lucky omen, and our serene and salutary stars if actions would follow the words we hear being said. You make great promises when you're with us: "Give me your hand, Eulalia." "Give me your hand, Corisca." We give you our hands; then one of you says: "May I be cut into pieces," and the other, "May I burn like wood if I don't free you by tomorrow, my soul." Alas, how wretched you would be if you were to suffer the punishments to which you condemn yourselves for not keeping your promises!

ERO: You're wrong in saying this.

EUL: Even though you're rich and noble, you shouldn't scoff at us poor women and make fun of us; for, although misfortune has brought us to this condition, we were not lowborn in our own country.

ERO: Don't make my anguish more bitter by these complaints, Eulalia. Please! Don't think that our words aren't in accord with our intentions and that we desire anything else other than to free you from your servitude to this beastly man; but we cannot do this as easily or as rapidly as we had planned and intended. Because you see me dressed in respectable clothes and hear that my father is an extremely rich merchant you imagine that I can lay my hands on his money whenever I want and spend it as I please. And what I say about myself is true for him also: we both have the same object in mind. It's true that we have considerable wealth, but its not in our power to dispose of it. I want you to know that we both have fathers who are as stingy as they are rich; they show no less diligence in conserving their possessions than in acquiring them. Until now, by God, I haven't been able to lay my hands on a penny.[4] But now that my father has left me alone for a while, for he set out this morning to go to Procida, I'm sure I'll prove to you that I'm speaking from the heart and not pretending. You can publicly denounce me as the most uncivil, the most ungrateful and perfidious man in the world if by tomorrow . . .

EUL: Ah, Erofilo, cursed be the day that I put so much faith in you. All the todays and yesterdays pass by, but your tomorrows never come.

ERO: Please let me finish! Listen to what I have to say. I cannot tell you everything, but you can be certain—and rest assured—

that I'm not going to take longer than tomorrow to free you.

EUL: Even if you're telling the truth, for I cannot believe that you are—although I would like to believe that you have the means as well as the intention of doing it—even if it is the truth, what good will it do when I'm dead to give me the medicine that you wouldn't administer to me when I had a soul in my body? Don't you realize that Lucramo wants us to leave Sibaris tomorrow?

ERO: I don't believe it.

EUL: Why should I lie to you?

COR: We're going to leave, believe us.

ERO: I believe that Lucramo told you so, but I don't think he told you the truth.

CARI: What harm is there in believing what he said? Let's see if we can possibly get done today what we're supposed to do tomorrow.

EUL: Or else have Lucramo discover your plans in such a way that he can believe you. I think if you assure him that the money will be forthcoming tomorrow, he'll stay.

ERO: Since my old man is no longer around and won't be able to keep his eyes on me continually, I have no doubts about being able to accomplish everything. Rest assured, Eulalia, for you're not going to leave Sibaris and you'll never belong to anyone but me.

CARI: And I say the same to you, my Corisca.

EUL: May God hear you and may He have you persevere in your determination and turn your words into deeds. Your duty should be to love us and to act for our benefit, for ever since the very day we became acquainted we have loved you with all our hearts and have revered you as our gods. But enough for now; we don't want Lucramo to return and find us here.

ERO: I don't think that many hours will pass before you'll be free and be able to be with me.

EUL: May it be God's will!

COR: And what of me?

CARI: We seek your well-being no less than that of Eulalia, my life.

COR: I go in hope of it.

CARI: Go with your mind at ease.

EUL: Good-bye, Erofilo.

ERO: Good-bye, my dear Eulalia.

Scene Four
EROFILO; CARIDORO

ERO: Should I not show her how much I love her? And should I not assure her that I love no one else—not even my father ...

my father? I won't even exclude myself—as much as the least part of her! In some way I'm going to remove the suspicion from her mind that I'm mocking her. Today will be the last time that she'll reproach me for such a thing. I'm prepared to set her free today even if I have to change places with her. I'm not going to let myself be taken in any longer by Vulpino's stories, which make me appear to be, in her eyes, what I'm not and never intended to be—ungrateful, disloyal, and unloving.

If Vulpino doesn't resolve this matter today—rather, if he doesn't do something more than he has been doing—I'll no longer listen to his prattling, prattling with which, from one day to the next, for fifteen days, he has led me on. First he promises to play a trick on the old man who, without realizing it—that is, while thinking he was spending his money wisely—would give me the money that I need to redeem her; then he changes his mind and tells me that he's going to devise such a scheme that we'll have the girl in our power without my father giving me a penny or anyone else lending it to me. And now he wants to humble this Lucramo, who has been so arrogant, and shear him like a sheep. Should I continue to listen to these dreams and these stories? By God, I won't. If I cannot obtain my desires secretly, I'll do it openly. There's no shortage of silver and other things in the house, which can be converted immediately into thousands of scudi.[5] Am I to be like Tantalus and let myself die of thirst while in water up to my chin?

CARI: If only I were in your situation, Erofilo! If my old man was away from Sibaris for a while and left me a house full of goods, as your father has done, he'd find it so clean when he returned that it would seem as if the Spaniards had lodged there for some time. Oh, here he comes.

ERO: Who's coming.

CARI: The procurer.

ERO: I wish he were being carried, but in the manner he deserves.

SCENE FIVE

LUCRAMO, *a procurer*

LUCR: When you hear a woman's beauty, a prince's liberality, a friar's sanctity, a merchant's riches, the good life and enjoyment of a city, or similar things being lauded or, as they say, being praised to the skies, you wouldn't be mistaken if you believed little of it; and at times I have found it best to believe the opposite of what one hears of their reputation. Nor would you be wrong if, on hearing someone being condemned for thievery or greed, or it being said that he's a swindler, a cheat, a forger, or a traitor, you believed more than what you heard; for, in practice, you'll always find the vices worse and the virtues, the good and praiseworthy qualities, less than what their public image is. I cannot explain why this is so; but the experience I've had with both types prompts me to say this. Right now I'm encountering one more than the other. I'll tell you about it.

These past few days I found myself in Genoa, where on many, many occasions I've been able to sell my mechandise—for no other merchandise is there a more stable market—and where I came away with a hundred florins after expenses. While I was there I heard it said that in Sibaris more than anywhere else in the world every sort of pleasure is prized, and, above all, the pleasure that comes from amorous entanglements. [I also heard it said] that the young men here were wealthier and greater spendthrifts than in any city you could name. Attracted by its reputation, I came to this city; and, when I first arrived, I rejoiced on hearing that the gentlemen—most of whom were called counts—used the title of "Lord" when speaking with one another. I said to myself: "In other cities there's perhaps one person of this quality and in many places none; now, if there's so many of them here, there's no doubt that money must flow through the streets and it must rain gold." But I wasn't here three days when I regretted having come; for, apart from their titles, their boasting and their vanity, their ostentation and their fables, I found very little that's splendid about them. They spend whatever they have in adorning themselves, in polishing and perfuming themselves like women. They spend it in feeding mules and page boys who follow them around all day long while they go here and there running through the streets and the piazzas waggling more than coquettes and making more gestures than a monkey. They think that by dressing in brocades and fancy clothes, by dressing fashionably and ostentatiously, they'll get others to esteem them as they esteem themselves, that is, as generous, munificent, and important men; but, in reality, they're like new boxes—painted on the outside and empty within.

One might think that if they're lavish in adorning themselves, then perhaps they would have their women be parsimonious; and, by staying at home and working and exhausting themselves, they would try to restore what their husbands or sons squander in their foolish and ridiculous ambition. But, instead, one finds husbands and wives, mothers and daughters, all working together to the detriment and ruin of their houses. We'll ignore the fact the these women want new dresses and new hats like women in any other city. [But the truth is that] you couldn't find a woman in this city whose husband is an artisan and who deigns to walk. They abhor going out of the house on foot and they won't even cross the street unless they have a carriage underneath their buttocks. They want their carriages all painted in gold, covered with brocades, and drawn by great big horses; and they must have two damsels, a personal maid, footmen, and pages to accompany them. It isn't only the rich, but the poor as well, who engage in such foolishness and who draw the bow so tight that they never have a carlin⁶ left to spend for any unusual desire.

And so it happens that when a foreigner comes to this city he rarely finds someone who invites him to his house and uses terms of courtesy that are commonly used elsewhere. Someone who comes from abroad and isn't acquainted with their custom of penurious living considers them as prodigals, immoderate and hardly discreet; for, if they were misers, they would engage in commerce and the other occupations that make men rich. But these people consider all employment as lower class and they'll only call someone noble who lives in idleness and doesn't work. And this itself isn't enough: it's necessary for his father and grandfather also to have spent their time scratching their bellies. See what a mistaken custom, what a queer idea this is; see what discipline, what fine organization for a sensible city that intends to expand its riches and power! Let them do as they please. What? Am I supposed to introduce reason? Let them live and behave as they will. If my interests weren't involved I'd take the same care that bishops do for the souls that were entrusted to them by Christ.

I came to this city about three months ago with the hope of profitably selling my girls, whose beauty, whose youth, and whose charm seemed to me—and still do—to deserve to have all the gentlemen compete for them, with no price seemingly too high. But I found myself greatly mistaken. Many of them came to see me—the old more than the young; one or another of them tells me that he wants to buy this woman or that one and asks me the price. I tell it to them. Some abandon the idea; others stay a while and bargain. They make me an offer; I make a counter-offer, and finally we come to an agreement. Then, when I expect them to pay me the money, they lack the means and ask for an extension, some until the sheep are sheared, others until the hay or the wheat is harvested, and still others ask to postpone it until vintage time; and they won't give me any guarantees except their word or a promissory note signed in their own hand.

Elsewhere, when you sell something, the cash appears; here it's invisible. Not mine, however, for if I want bread, wine, or meat to live on I have to put my hand in my purse, take out money, and show it. If I could pay for the various things that I need with words, notes, and promises, then I'd be happy to sell my women to whomever wants them for the same price. Who would believe that here, where there's such a splendid court, where there are such gallant men, one wouldn't find a thousand customers for two girls tender as babes? I could almost say that these young men seem to be of such quality that there are no women in the world worthy of being loved by them; and I rather think that they yearn for one another and make love together and do other things that I won't mention.

I no longer have hopes that someone from Sibaris will take my girls. There are two youths, foreigners, on whom my entire plan hangs. They've taken a fancy [to the girls], and any price would seem small to them. If their audacity were as great as their desire and they would venture to steal from their fathers, as they promised they would do—they could easily do it—we could come to an agreement; but they're leading me on from day to day without concluding the deal. One of them is the son of a merchant who lives in that house and who came here from Procida not long ago to carry on his commercial activity. The other is the son of a Catalan who is a judge here and who is called the captain of justice in charge of criminals. In order to hurry them along, I'm pretending that I'm going elsewhere, and I hope that this pretense will work.

Now I'd better return to the house, for I never can leave it for even a moment or go the least bit away from it without experiencing some loss. It's impossible to get these rascals of mine and these whorish asses to do something they're supposed to do without my getting angry and without threats—in fact, not unless I employ an abundance of punches, kicks, and canings.

ACT TWO
Scene One
lucramo, *a procurer;* furbo, *his servant*

lucr: Furbo hasn't returned yet. I left him in the piazza a while ago to buy me a denarius's worth of radishes; and I thought he would be home ahead of me, for I stopped at a number of places on my way. Ah, here he's finally returning.——Must I always hold a cane or a spur behind you, you ass, for in no other way can I ever get you to hurry. Stop right there and listen to me

214

if you value your eyes and your tongue—I know that you care
little about your shoulders, and I rather think you dislike them,
for every day, in fact every hour, you find a reason to have
them thrashed. To the extent that you value your head, and so
that I won't see it cracked open and your brains scattered at my
feet, open your ears and listen to me.

FURBO: I'll open my mouth also, so that your words can enter more
easily.

LUCR: Close it instead. As for your other parts, above or below,
open them as much as you wish. If you say anything about
what I'm going to tell you, I'll tear out your eyes and cut out
your tongue.

FURBO: I won't say a thing.

LUCR: Now, listen to me. You know that for the past six days I've
been continually saying that I want to go to Sicily as soon as the
master of the ship who's returning to Drepano[7] is ready to
leave. I've been saying this in such a way that you believe it,
the girls also believe it, and everyone who has had anything to
do with me or with my household believes it as well. But my
intentions have always been contrary to my words, for I'm
not going to leave. I'm pretending to do so in order to hurry
those young men who want our women or say they do. They'll
either accomplish in one day what should be done in twenty or
else they'll make [their intentions] clear to me. When I get within
hearing distance of the girls or of anyone else whom I want to
think that I'm going to leave, I'll give you a great many errands
to do. Remember, I have no intention of having them carried
out; above all, make sure that you don't spend a penny of what I
give you. Act solicitous and diligent, but don't make your
pretense at my expense. Do you understand?

FURBO: I understand you.

LUCR: Now let's go back toward the house. Get close to the door;
a little closer; now stop. Did you say that the ship's master
wants me to load all our belongings today?

FURBI: That's what I said.

LUCR: And that he wants to set sail and start the journey tomorrow?

FURBO: That's what he told me.

LURC: Well, then, we'd better hurry and do what has to be done.
Listen, you women of great expense and little use; you who are
so beautiful and pleasant that you cannot find someone to free
you from your servitude. Other men aren't as blind or as stupid
as I, who went and spent my money on two pieces of glass
thinking I was buying two precious jewels. But rest assured that
I'm not going to let this remain a loss, and, if I'm not able

to recover what I spent all at once, I'll be forced to put it
together little by little. There's no doubt that you'll be able to
bring in four or six carlins a day by means of which I'll be able
to clothe you or at least feed you. As soon as we arrive at our
destination I'll have you open your shops. I won't undertake this
here, for I don't want the lords of Sibaris to have this satisfaction. They're lords without dominions and they're more
puffed up with wind than balloons. Oh, you ugly woman, to
whom am I speaking? You little rascals, you good-for-nothings!
Strip all the beds, fold up the sheets and covers, and put away
the shirts and aprons whether or not they're clean; and do the
same with your curlers and bonnets, your towels and napkins
and your other trash. But place the mirrors and phials among the
clothes and, if you don't want your rumps broken by a whip,
make sure that they're arranged in such a way that they won't
break in transit.

Here, Furbo, go buy me several feet of rope and tie up the
boxes, coffers, matresses, and quilts. Then go get six porters; no,
get eight of them, so that we can clear out everything at once.
What are you waiting for? Why haven't you gone? What a lazy
ass you are! Didn't you hear me? I want you to go to the customs
house and ask one of those wolves to send someone here to
see the goods before they're packed so that they won't make us
unload them and open the boxes and won't give us any trouble
when I pass through the gates. Hold it. Wait there for me.
Listen to the music! It's all for love.

FURBO: I'll play the counterpoint.[8]

LUCR: Don't return until late so that it will seem as if you actually
had been to the port. Then come and report to me that the
ship's master met you and told you that his departure, which was
to take place tomorrow, has been postponed and is uncertain.
Tell me this so that the girls can hear. There, I got Erofilo to
come out of the house and Caridoro is with him. Surely they
must have heard me and perhaps they're coming to make a
deal, for now more than ever they should have the means to
do so. But I'm not going to wait for them on the street; I
don't want them to think that I'm out here just to have them
speak to me.

SCENE TWO

CARIDORO; EROFILO

CARI: What are we going to do, Erofilo, now that we're sure that
he's leaving? Do you think we ought to go find him? If we pro-
pose various alternatives to him, alternatives that are more

appealing, and if we plead with him and point out what profits
there'll be—actually have him touch them with his hand—if we
show him how close we are to settling the matter, don't you at
least think we could convince him not to leave so soon?

ERO: Oh, Caridoro, I think we should try everything possible to
keep him here; but I'm not going to make any decision until I
inform Vulpino about the matter and hear his advice. I don't
know what to think or imagine about why he's so late in
returning.

CARI: If Fulcio cannot find him, at least he ought not to waste time.
I wish he would return!

ERO: Unless I first speak to him and tell him about the procurer's
departure, I wouldn't know what to do.

CARI: My goodness, here they are. Both of them are coming together. Take a look.

Scene Three
VULPINO, FULCIO, *servants*; CARIDORO, EROFILO

VULP: Could one possibly devise a more remarkable scheme than
this, Fulcio, in order to save two young lovers and punish
a greedy and knavish pimp like him?

FUL: Vulpino, despite all the self-confidence I have, this plot
reminds me of an artichoke, which has more toughness, thistles,
and bitterness than tastiness.

VULP: At least we can take comfort in this, that if it doesn't work
out we won't be punished for some small thing. What more can
we get than a beating?

FUL: Who is more capable of receiving it than you; no shoulders
in the world are more suitable than yours.

VULP: Yours are the only ones that are better; they would tire
the arms of ten men and would wear out a hundred canes a day.

CARI: ——It seems that they're laughing as they come.

ERO: Fools laugh at every little thing.——

VULP: There they are, waiting for us.

CARI: ——Yet their gaiety gives me high hopes.

ERO: You hope in vain, for they don't realize that Lucramo is
leaving so soon.——

VULP: May God preserve you, Masters.

ERO: Indeed, we need Him as well as the saints to save us.

VULP: Right now there's no necessity for God or the saints to take
the trouble to save you. I can save you myself. My name is no
longer Vulpino; it's Salvation.

ERO: Alas! Don't you know that Lucramo is going to leave
tomorrow morning?

VULP: May he leave in a storm.

CARI: For pity's sake no, for the girls would also be in danger.

VULP: Then let the girls remain on land and him be drowned in the sea. Just as I'm Fortunate Salvation to you, so I'm Misfortune to the procurer. I'm determined to destroy that glutton and save you any way I can. But don't think that he's leaving.

ERO: He is leaving; believe one who knows.

VULP: The rascal is pretending to leave in order to scare you.

CARI: Without seeing us or realizing that we were where we could hear what he was saying, he ordered his women to fold up the sheets, the covers, and the gowns, and even the dirty shirts, and to pack everything in boxes. He sent Furbo to the customs house so that they can ship out their goods; and he ordered him to bring some porters to carry their belongings to the ship this evening. Have no doubts about it, Vulpino, he's going to leave.

ERO: Alas! What will become of me if he leaves? Wherever Eulalia goes my heart will go with her.

CARI: And my heart will likewise go with Corisca.

VULP: If you decide that your heart is going to leave tomorrow morning, let me know, so that I can get a bill of lading before the office closes; then they won't hold it up at customs.

FUL: And it wouldn't be inappropriate if you made a gown for yours so that the nasty crows and eagles won't find it naked and peck at it.

ERO: See, Caridoro, how these wise guys make fun of us!

CARI: Ah, how wretched is he who is the servant of Love.

VULP: We who serve unhappy servants, Fulcio, are doubly wretched servants. Erofilo, I didn't think you had such little faith that, knowing Vulpino is around, you would let such a trifle scare you.

ERO: Is this a trifle? If this is a trifle, then what can be important?

VULP: Listen to me carefully. The procurer is leaving, right? I'll accept what you say. My response is that, if you do as I tell you, I'll place Eulalia in your arms, and Corisca in yours, before tomorrow arrives; and as for Lucramo, that arrogant fellow, I'll shear him like a sheep.

CARI: Oh, my good Vulpino.

ERO: The very best.

VULP: But tell me, did you prepare the shears with which to clip him, as I asked?

ERO: What shears did you tell me about?

VULP: Didn't I ask you to get the keys to your father's room?

ERO: I have them.

VULP: And to send all the servants out of the house, especially

Nebbia?

ERO: Everything is done.

VULP: These are the shears that I asked for. Now pay attention and listen to me. I came across a prudent and able fellow here in the city who just suits our needs. We became close friends when I spent some time with your father in Naples. He's the servant of one of the noblemen there. Now, then, his master sent him here on some business, and he has to return tomorrow. He only arrived yesterday, and he's never been here before.

ERO: What has this to do with me?

VULP: I'll tell you. Listen. I'll have him dress in your father's clothes. I'll have him put on a coat, a cap, stockings, slippers, and a long gown—the complete attire of a merchant. He makes a good appearance, and I'll dress him in such a way that everyone, on seeing him, will imagine that he's a great merchant. Disguised in this way, he'll go to see Lucramo; we'll give him the coffer filled with fine gold brocades that those Florentine litigants deposited with your father.

ERO: What is he going to do with it?

VULP: He'll take it to Lucramo and leave it as security for giving him Eulalia.

ERO: And leave it in Lucramo's hands?

VULP: Yes, Lucramo's.

ERO: With that pimp?

VLUP: Yes, with the pimp. Listen to me a moment. I'll have him give the coffer to Lucramo or the pimp, whatever you want to call him; he'll tell him that he'd like to leave it with him for a day or two as a pledge until he brings the amount that he'll pretend to agree upon with him.

ERO: I understand all right. What the devil! Leave it with a pimp?

VULP: And get the woman. Then we'll go immediately . . .

ERO: Think of something else. [Are you going] to place such valuable goods in the hands of a cheat, of a perfidious fellow, of the greatest little thief in the world?

VULP: Let me take care of it. Now listen.

ERO: It's too risky.

VULP: It's not, if you'll listen. We could then easily . . .

ERO: Easily do what?

VULP: If you'll be quiet, I'll tell you. Erofilo, it's necessary for anyone who wants . . .

ERO: What's this prattling; what are these stories you're creating?

VULP: If you won't listen it's your hard luck. I must be mad . . .

CARI: Let him speak.

ERO: Go ahead.

VULP: . . . to bother helping someone who doesn't want me to. May I be eaten away by plague if I ever . . .

CARI: Don't go away; he'll listen to you.——Listen to him.—— Don't go away, Vulpino; come back.——Now listen for a moment.

ERO: What do you want to say? I'm listening.

VULP: What do I want to say? All day long you beg me, you urge me, to contrive to find a way for you to get this girl. I've found a hundred ways, but not one of them pleases you. One seems difficult, the other too perilous. This one is too long; that one too obvious. Who can figure you out? You want it and you don't want it; you desire something, but you don't know what. Oh, Erofilo, believe me, you cannot do something memorable without effort and without great risk. Do you think that you can get this procurer to relent and give her to you by your sighs and tears?

ERO: Still, it would seem rather foolish to place a thing so valuable in such obvious danger. Don't you realize that the brocades in that coffer, which was given to my father on deposit, are worth two thousand ducats, or even more? If they were ours, perhaps I would more readily risk them. These are shears with which to clip us rather than the sheep you were telling me about.

VULP: Do you think that I have so few wits about me, Erofilo, that I would try to lose something so precious as this without figuring out a way to get it back at once? Leave it to me. I'm in more danger than you are. If my plans don't succeed—which I doubt very much—you would only be punished with words; I would receive severe bodily torture, or I would be thrown in jail to die of hunger.

ERO: If we place the coffer in his hands, how are we going to get it back from him unless we first produce the money? And you know how little we have of that. What if my father returns before we get the cloth back, or—and this is the real danger— what if the procurer leaves tonight and takes it with him? Tell me, where will we find ourselves then?

VULP: If you'll have enough patience to listen to me, you'll find that my plan is good—excellent, in fact— and that there's an easy way to get it back this very night.

ERO: Go ahead, I'm listening. Speak out.

VULP: As soon as our merchant has given the coffer to Lucramo and has delivered the girl into your hands, I want you to go to the captain of justice, Caridoro's father, and complain to him that the coffer has been stolen from your house and that you suspect a procurer who lives nearby.

ERO: I understand.

VULP: This is certainly plausible, for since he's a pimp he could be a thief. You'll ask the captain if he would please send his bailiff along with you to search the house. Caridoro will influence his father in your favor, and he'll send the bailiff immediately.

CARI: That will be easy to do; if necessary I'll go myself.

VULP: We'll be upon him so fast that we'll find the coffer; he won't have time to put it somewhere else. He'll say that a merchant left it with him as a guarantee of payment for a woman whom he sold to him. But who will believe that someone would leave goods worth two thousand ducats as a pledge for something barely worth, let us say, a hundred ducats? Now, after the stolen goods have been found in his house, undoubtedly he'll be taken for a thief and dragged off to jail; and if he's then hanged or drawn and quartered, what concern is it of ours? Anyhow, he deserves this and even worse for his wickedness.

ERO: By God, it's a fine plan, and it could work!

VULP: As soon as Lucramo is taken, you, Caridoro, being the man that you are, can accomplish your purpose by yourself. Speak to the bailiff and arrange with him to have the girl brought to you as soon as that glutton is thrown in jail. Whatever happens, whether they hang him or let him go, it doesn't matter. If he survives, Lucramo will be only too happy to give her to you as a present, provided you show that you're ready to use your influence with your father and the others in his favor.

CARI: By God, Vulpino, you deserve a crown.

FUL: Rather a fine miter.[9]

VULP: Not everybody can rise to your rank, Fulcio.

ERO: Where is this fellow of yours whom we're going to dress up as a merchant?

VULP: I'm surprised he's not already here; but he won't be long.

ERO: Do you expect him to carry the coffer on his back by himself?

VULP: We've also taken care of that. He has a peasant with him, a fellow who works for the same master as he does. That gentleman sent both of them here to find two or three pairs of bullocks and buy them. This peasant will be the porter. Now go get the gown and whatever else is needed ready, so that he won't have to wait when he gets here.

CARI: Is there anything else you need me for?

VULP: You can go home, Caridoro; we'll let you know the results.

CARI: I'll go then. Good-bye.

FUL: If you don't need me any longer, I'll go with my master.

VULP: Go ahead.

Scene Four
VULPINO; TRAPPOLA, *a cheat*; BRUSCO, *a peasant*

VULP: I should have remembered that Trappola rarely tells the truth. It was rather foolish of me and lacking in foresight to let him stay behind. If he's cheated me again, as usual, I won't be able to do what I had planned; and I cannot find a substitute, for it's already evening. Ah, here he is, thank goodness! Now that he's here, I have hopes that all my plans will succeed.

TRAP: Isn't it great, Brusco, that you can never do a favor for anyone without expecting something in return!

BRUS: It's even greater, Trappola, that you never have enough to do yourself that you have to take on other people's business that doesn't concern you.

TRAP: I consider Vulpino's affairs to be nothing less than my own; and it has always been my practice—it's my nature—to seek out new friends.

BRUS: If it's your habit and your nature to acquire new friends, acquire them with your own labors, without troubling me or others who don't have such desires.

TRAP: What else have we got to do?

BRUS: We have to load some hay on the boat for the bullocks and provide the things we need to sustain us.

TRAP: There's time for that.

VULP: Trappola, I thought that you had deceived me.

TRAP: Good Lord, Vulpino, I'm sorry that I led you to jump to the wrong conclusion, but I didn't think about it.

VULP: You were walking very solemnly.

TRAP: If I'm going to have to be a serious man today, it's only right that I learn how to walk in a serious manner.

VULP: Who should know better than you—you whose merits have made you used to walking around with irons on your legs.

TRAP: Who's used to it more than you? There isn't an animal so obstinate that it wouldn't learn to slow down from a trot to a gentle amble if its master had made it tote heavy loads for so long, as your master has made you do.

VULP: Come inside. Forget this nonsense; we have no time to lose.

Scene Five
BRUSCO, *alone*

BRUS: For God's sake, I have a good mind to return to the inn and leave that idiot here without me; he wants to do someone else a favor with my labor and thus earn one or two scudi. I know that he wouldn't be so ready or eager to do so without a reward, but he won't let me partake of it. And from what I gather they intend to cheat someone—I don't know who. If this thing is discovered, I'll be considered no less guilty than he is; if we're caught, I'll receive my share of the punishment, perhaps the greater portion, since I have much more to lose than he has. All he has to do is save himself; he has no other worries. This isn't the case with me; if I save myself, the bullocks won't be saved. My master will make good his losses out of me, for I own cows, sheep, goats, and pigs and have so many possessions that one couldn't buy them with a hundred lire.

Yes! It would be better if I turned back. Oh, I'd better not, for I did promise him, and if I don't wait for him I'll be behaving badly and giving him cause to be my enemy forever. I know that he has a thousand ways to hurt me through my master. He'd do it, too, for his tongue is as sharp as a razor and the master gives him credence as does nearly everyone who listens more attentively to those who speak evil than to those who speak good. Those who say nice things are so few that you can count them on the tip of your nose; but the sowers of evil are infinite in number. It's a general rule that whoever wants to get into the good graces of his master must accuse others and relate all the bad things he knows about them and conceal or minimize their good works as much as he can. He must demonstrate that all others have little or no worth, that they're lazy and idle, that they have no love for their master and don't care whether his affairs go badly or well, and that they steal all they can. He must show that he alone is faithful and loving, that only he is diligent, careful, and prompt. So, be that as it may, I'm determined not to give him cause to complain about me. As soon as we've done what we have to, I'm going to return to the inn so I won't be caught with him if some disturbance results.

ACT THREE
Scene One
VULPINO; TRAPPOLA; EROFILO

VULP: Before you leave, make sure you remember well what I told you so that you'll know where you have to bring the woman and won't mistake the house. Come along this street until you reach a portico; go past that and beyond the church nearby, and when you come to the first corner turn left; then go to the fifth door.

TRAP: Why are you repeating it so much? By now a donkey

would understand you. If you're afraid that I'll forget, then wait for me here and I'll bring her to you; then you can take her where you please.

VULP: Lucramo might see us together, or someone else might see us and report it to him; and so through mere foolishness our plans would be discovered, and everything would be spoiled.

TRAP: Then don't instruct me any more.

VULP: It's a small door that was recently built.

TRAP: I remember that.

ERO: The lady of the house ...

TRAP: I know.

VULP: ... is called Lena. There's a shed across the way.

TRAP: You're annoying me.

ERO: Don't give him any more instructions. Let's go now and wait for him. He cannot possibly miss it.

VULP: When you get to the corner, give us a signal. Whistle, and we'll come and meet you.

TRAP: My mouth is so dry that it will be difficult to whistle.

VULP: You'll have plenty to drink.

TRAP: I wish I had some already.

VULP: You're better off sober; you'll have your wits about you. Go then, and remember, you're not dealing with a fool; be careful that in thinking we're deceiving him, we're not the ones being deceived. Open the coffer and show him the brocades; then close it tightly and bring back the key. Make sure you can tell us in what room he puts it, so that I can lay my hands on it right away.

TRAP: I understood you; don't bother me any more. If you're as generous with drink at supper as you've been with words, everything will go smoothly.

ERO: Now, then, let him go, and if there's anything else to do, let's do it.

SCENE TWO
BRUSCO; TRAPPOLA

BRUS: Hurry up; don't make me waste any more time.

TRAP: What's the hurry? Who's rushing you?

BRUS: Do you think that the bullocks can be without me all day long without a particle of hay before them?

TRAP: They can feed to their hearts' content all night long. We would be as dumb as bullocks and even more so if we miss this supper just to give them some hay, for it's a supper we'll enjoy, with girls and merriment.

BRUS: You can stay there if you want; as for me, may I break my neck if I wait around another minute after I get this box off my back.

TRAP: Keep still; I hear the door being opened. This must be our pimp; he looks like a scoundrel.

SCENE THREE
LUCRAMO; TRAPPOLA

LUCR: ——I'd better leave the house before those chatterboxes deafen me, before they split my head, before they destroy me, overwhelm me, kill me.——

TRAP: Others have the signs of their trade on their chests; this man has his very clearly written on his face.

LUCR: ——As long as you remain with me, you women will do what I tell you, even if it breaks your hearts.——

TRAP: It shows even more in his speech.

LUCR: ——How arrogant, how insolent these whores are! They're always looking for a quarrel or a fight. All their efforts are directed at opposing your wishes; they're always trying to steal, and they constantly think of ways to defraud and betray you. Their sole intention is to bring you to ruin.——

TRAP: From what I hear, he must have realized that I want to buy his merchandise, for he's praising it so much to make it attractive to me.

LUCR: ——If someone had committed every possible crime and he kept women as I do, and tolerated their ways without flying into a rage every minute, without anger, without irritation, without wrath, without fury, without screaming and cursing and turning heaven and earth, sea and air, upside down, he would merit greater forgiveness than the saints in the monasteries with their prayers, their scourging, their fastings, and their vigils.——

TRAP: If they can put up with you without hanging themselves they have more patience than Job.

LUCR: (That fellow who's coming this way must have just disembarked, for a porter with a heavy load is accompanying him.)

TRAP: According to all indications, he must live in this neighborhood. There's the large house, and there's the narrow street and the two sheds in the rear.

LUCR: (He must be looking for a place to stay without going to the inn; he would just as soon stay at Francolino.[10]

TRAP: Here's someone who'll give me information. Tell me, my good man, I'm not very well acquainted with this place . . .

LUCR: You're certainly not very well acquainted! The name you called me by is not mine, nor was it my father's name, nor that of my grandfather or of anyone else in my family.

TRAP: Forgive me for not knowing better. If I've offended you, I'll correct myself. Tell me, wicked man, from a long line of wicked men ... Good heavens, you could be the very one I'm looking for or one of his relatives.

LUCR: Whom are you looking for?

TRAP: I'm seeking a glutton, a cheat, a fraud, a thief, a perfidious fellow.

LUCR: Hold it; you're on the right track. What's his name?

TRAP: His name ... his name ... I just had it on the tip of my tongue. I don't know that became of it.

LUCR: You either spit it out or swallowed it.

TRAP: I must have spit it out, for I couldn't have fed my stomach such rotten food without immediately vomiting it up.

LUCR: Well, then, gather it out of the dust.

TRAP: I can describe him in so many ways that there'll be no need to know his name. He's one who screams, goes back on his promises, and blasphemes.

LUCR: Who wouldn't if he had females in the house as I do.

TRAP: He's a liar and a perjurer.

LUCR: These are precisely the attributes of my trade.

TRAP: He's a counterfeiter, and he clips and shaves coins.

LUCR: If one knows how to do it, there's no better way to make a profit.

TRAP: He's a thief and a cutpurse.

LUCR: Do you consider it an insignificant skill to know how to manipulate one's hands?

TRAP: He's a pimp.

LUCR: That's my principal activity.

TRAP: He's an informer, a slanderer, a sower of discord, and a scandalmonger.

LUCR: Don't trouble yourself any more. I'm positive that you're looking for me. I'll also remind you of my proper name. I'm called Lucramo.

TRAP: Lucramo with the pox.

LUCR: May you be the one to get it.

TRAP: Lucramo, that's just whom I'm looking for.

LUCR: I'm the one you're seeking. Now, tell me: what do you want from me?

TRAP: First let him place his load in your house, and then I'll tell you what I want.

LUCR: Go inside and put it where you like.——You women, help him unload.

TRAP: The day before yesterday, while I was in Naples, one of the great lords they have there, knowing that I was preparing to come

to Sibaris, gave me an errand to do. He asked me to look over two
girls whom you have in your house for sale and to buy the one
whom I thought was prettier, if you were willing to sell her at an
honest and reasonable price. I'm to deliver her to the helmsman
who brought me here. Now, contrary to what he originally told
me, the helmsman intends to return tonight, and because of this
I'm caught unprepared, for I made a deal today that emptied
my purse. So as a deposit, until I bring you the money—
you'll have it before Vespers tomorrow—I'll give you something
with which one could buy fifty women, even if they were all
Helens and Venuses. Let's seal the bargain.

LUCR: They're already sold, and I have the down payment. The
purchasers are coming with the full amount tomorrow; however . . .

TRAP: I understand. What you mean is that the lure of profits can
lead men into a galley.[11]

LUCR: You get the point. My duty is to serve whoever pays me
more, regardless of who it is. Let's go into the house.

TRAP: I'm never afraid to spend, provided that the merchandise is
worth the price.

Scene Four
STAMMA, *a maid*; LUCRAMO

STAM: Since we're going so early, Master, I don't want to leave my
shoes at the shoemakers. Remember to tell Furbo, as soon as he
returns, to go get them; or else give me five quattrini,[12] for that's
how much he asked to fix them.

LUCR: Don't bother me, you idiot.

STAM: I'm always an idiot when I ask him for something. There's
no one more close-fisted toward his poor servants than he is.
He'd let us die of hunger if not for the fear that he would lose us
or would be denied the use of our labor if we became weak or
infirm. It does us little good if there's an abundance of wheat or
some other crop, for he has us eat moldy bread full of tares
and vetch and made with bran. He looks around for the worst
wine possible or for putrid fish or meat that the butchers
weren't able to sell; and the old miser buys carrion at bargain
prices and feeds it to us, food that would be loathsome to wolves
and ravens. But there's no one more prodigal than him in giving
out punches and kicks or in breaking our backs with a cane or
marking them with a whip and often drawing blood. Poor me!
The other women have hopes that some day they'll be delivered
from their servitude to this devil, either by changing masters or
by freeing themselves; they can hope, for the young and the

beautiful are never without their luck. But I, who was born ugly and am now old, have no hope of finding someone to take me away from him, even if my master was willing to give me as a gift rather than sell me. Cursed be my unhappy lot!

SCENE FIVE
BRUSCO, *alone*

BRUS: He's inside there engaged in a conversation that isn't about to end very soon. I'm not going to wait around any longer, no matter what the consequences. I'll lose payment for the service I've already done for him, but it doesn't matter; I've lost it on other occasions. It makes no difference whether one does him a favor or not: he gives the same reward to those who serve as to those who injure him. Whatever is done him out of kindness he thinks is done out of obligation. Just because he knows how to read and write and keep records of profits and expenses—and so the master often confers with him, as he must—he's become so haughty that he thinks he's a hundred-thousand times better than we are. We can no longer live with him: he screams and reprimands, and he scolds us and abuses us as if we were donkeys. This evening I'll have him at my ears. I don't care. I'll know very well how to answer him, for this time we won't be in Naples or in my master's house where, out of respect and fear, I keep quiet and tolerate it. Now, who are those jolly fellows coming out of there? What have I to do with them? I don't care who they are.

SCENE SIX
RICCIO, BRUNO, CORBO, NEBBIA, ROSSO, *servants*

RIC: Filostrato is truly a kind and liberal young man.

BRUNO: Men like him are the ones to serve, for they give you little work and plenty of drink.

NEB: And what an abundance of meat on that table!

CORBO: What about the wine, which has touched my heart.

ROSSO: I've never seen any that was clearer or more like topaz.

CORBO: Have you ever tasted any that was more fragrant, that was sweeter than this?

RIC: Didn't it seem somewhat strong and tangy?

CORBO: How sweet that tanginess is! It's worth more than the kisses from the vermilion lips of painted women.

ROSSO: I wish I had a decanter full in my room tonight!

CORBO: And I'd like a pitcher of it at the head of my bed!

RIC: I'd like to have the whole barrel to myself!

BRUNO: I only wish that Erofilo would decide to send us to work for this fellow every day.

RIC: Yes, provided he treats us this well.

CORBO: I don't know how all of you feel; but, as for me, I'm so happy I can hardly contain myself.

ROSSO: I think we're all in the same condition.

NEB: I only wish it were so when the old man returns! We're all together when it comes to drinking and gulping down food; but when the master returns I'm afraid that I alone will digest it all and pay the bill.

CORBO: Don't worry about trouble that hasn't yet arisen, stupid; don't kick back before you've been stung. How do you know what may come up?

NEB: I'm neither a prophet nor an astrologer; but you'll see. As soon as we get home everything that I predicted today will happen.

CORBO: I, too, am neither prophet nor astrologer, but I predict that things will go badly for you if Erofilo becomes your enemy; and, if you persist in behaving the way you have been and don't change your ways, you'll have him after you continually with punches and kicks. At times he'll crack you on your face or break your head, perhaps with footstools and trestles or whatever is handy at the time. I'm afraid he might maim you or tear out your eye; and maybe one day he'll kill you. But if you ignore a few minor things in order to serve him, you'll find the old man, who's wiser and more discreet, easier to pacify than he is. He would realize that you would be crazy to oppose a passionate young man, his son, whose mind revolves like a spinning wheel. I tell you this as a friend.

NEB: I've been giving a great deal of thought to this since earlier today when you told me something similar; and I've finally concluded that what you say is right. In any case, I'm going to follow your advice.

CORBO: You'll benefit from it.

SCENE SEVEN

TRAPPOLA; CORBO; NEBBIA; ROSSO; BRUNO; RICCIO

TRAP: (Has that peasant left? Oh, what an ass, what a stupid fool!)

CORBO: Look, Nebbia, do you see who's there?

NEB: I see. Isn't that Erofilo's sweetheart?

CORBO: It looks like her.

NEB: It looks like her, because it is her.

TRAP: (The big fool left without saying a word.)

NEB: That fellow must have bought her.

CORBO: Perhaps the pimp lent her to him.

NEB: If he begins by tapping the barrel, our master will have plenty to drink and will be able to quench his thirst without spending too much.

ROSSO: I could quench mine much better with the wine we had today.

CORBO: Me, too.

TRAP: (It got dark rather fast, and it's not very safe escorting this girl by myself).

BRUNO: Hold it. Let's see where he takes her.

CORBO: You hide around the corner; we'll withdraw into this entranceway, and when they get some distance from that door we'll follow them very, very quietly so that we can tell Erofilo all about it.

TRAP: (Now that I find myself alone, I'm sorry that I got involved in this.)

RIC: Oh, Erofilo, you unfortunate fellow! Oh, what bad news we're going to bring him! Shall we do him a good turn?

NEB: What?

CORBO: Take her away from him.

TRAP: (Still, I'd better go on and have courage.)

BRUNO: The plague to him who hesitates.

CORBO: May I get it if I hesitate.

RIC: And me too.

CORBO: Nebbia's going to get it, because he doesn't answer.

NEB: I'll do whatever the others decide to do.

CORBO: There's no better way than this to begin making Erofilo your friend.

TRAP: ——Don't vex yourself, my beautiful girl, you're not among enemies.——

CORBO: Let's wait until he gets further away from Lucramo's house; then we'll do it.

NEB: What if he shouts and people come running?

CORBO: They won't be able to get here soon enough; besides, you'll find few people who would stir at night when they hear a noise outside.

TRAP: ——Don't stain such beautiful cheeks with your tears.——

NEB: Where are we going to take her once we have her? We cannot take her to the house without endangering both the master and ourselves: someone could easily see her enter and have us arrested. We'd be too conspicuous.

TRAP: ——Does it seem so painful for you to leave Sibaris?——

ROSSO: Where shall we take her then?

CORBO: How the devil should I know?

NEB: Then let's not bother about the whole thing.

CORBO: You won't make me change my mind and get the plague.

TRAP: ——Don't cry, don't shed tears because of this; you won't be taken far away.——

CORBO: Let's take her to Galante's house. Erofilo doesn't have a closer friend than him, and, as you know, he lives in a solitary place, near the [city] walls.

RIC: That's a good idea. The place is just right and the person even more so.

CORBO: Let's get a move on. You hold him at bay and, if he resists, beat him with punches and kicks. Nebbia and I will get the girl away.

BRUNO: Enough talking: Forward, my brave men.

TRAP: ——Good grief! Who are these people following us in such a hurry?——

CORBO: Hold it, merchant. What merchandise is this?

TRAP: I'm not going to tell you; I don't have to pay a duty to you.

CORBO: You haven't obtained a customs certificate or a receipt and you intend to take the goods out as contraband. If you have a certificate, let's see it.

TRAP: Look down below and you'll find the ring with which to stamp it. What certificate?

CORBO: If you don't have a certificate, then you're smuggling.

TRAP: One doesn't need a certificate for such things, nor does one pay duty when the loss exceeds the gain.

CORBO: The loss. Well said, for you've lost it because you tried to defraud customs. Let go of her.

TRAP: Do you think you'll take her from me this way?

CORBO: I told you to let go of her.

BRUNO: Let go.

RIC: If he doesn't let go, cut off his arm.

TRAP: Is this how you murder foreigners in Sibaris?

NEB: Eulalia, let's go find your Erofilo.

CORBO: Tear out his eyes if he doesn't shut up.

BRUNO: Break his head.

TRAP: Help! Help! Citizens, come to my aid.

ROSSO: What are you doing? Why haven't you cut out his tongue already?

BRUNO: He's defending himself with his teeth.

ROSSO: Hold him until I get that stone. I'll knock them all out one by one.

TRAP: Is this the way you take my woman away from me, you scoundrels?

BRUNO: Let's go and let him croak.

TRAP: (Woe is me, what shall I do? I'll follow them to see where they take her, even if they kill me.)

BRUNO: Where are you going? If you don't get away immediately and go down another street, I'll mince that fat head of yours into more pieces than one cuts a turnip when preparing to cook it. If you want to demand your rights to this woman, present yourself to the collector of customs.

TRAP: (I'm in bad shape: They've taken the woman from me; they've thrown me to the ground and rolled me in the mud; they've disheveled my hair; they've struck me in the face and eyes; and now they jeer at me.)

Scene Eight
EROFILO; VULPINO; TRAPPOLA

ERO: We've been walking quite slowly and now we've reached the house; yet we haven't met Trappola with the girl.

VULP: We cannot go on any further, for if we allow ourselves to be seen, we might cause some commotion.

TRAP: (How can I possibly face Erofilo?)

ERO: I think I see him, but the girl isn't with him.

TRAP: (What can I say to justify myself?)

VULP: I don't see the coffer.

TRAP: (How can I begin to tell him that they took her from me?)

ERO: Let's go meet him.

TRAP: (How will I convince him that they took her by force and that I didn't give her up willingly?)

ERO: What's this? Weren't you able to get the girl?

VULP: Where did you put the coffer?

TRAP: I got the girl. I took her from the house, and I was bringing her to you.

ERO: Good grief!

TRAP: When I reached this spot I was surrounded by more than fifteen people ...

ERO: See if the devil himself isn't involved in this!

TRAP: ... all of them armed, who beat me up severely and took the girl away.

ERO: They took her away from you?

TRAP: They knocked me to the ground senseless with three blows; then they gave me a hundred more and another hundred after that. They finally left me, thinking I was dead.

ERO: And they took Eulalia away?

TRAP: I cannot say for certain, but I think so; as soon as I got up ...

VULP: Did you deliver the coffer to the procurer?

ERO: Let him answer me; this is more important.

VULP: It's more important to find out about the coffer, for it's clear that they've taken the girl from him.

ERO: Why am I waiting to run after them?

TRAP: I delivered the coffer to Lucramo.

VULP: Where are you going? What are you thinking of doing?

ERO: I'll either get her back or I'll die.

VULP: Don't go off in such a hurry, Erofilo. Remember, we run the risk of losing the coffer. Let's first take care of that, and then . . .

ERO: What should I take care of? What coffer? My Eulalia is more important to me than all the riches in the world. Which way do you think they went?

TRAP: I think they went that way.

VULP: Don't go, Master, for they'll hurt you.

ERO: What more can they do to me when they've already taken my heart and soul away?

VULP: I'll follow him and see if I can convince him to do that which, if it isn't done, will result in our losing the coffer. Now you, Trappola, go and wait for me in the house so that in addition to our other losses we won't lose Crisobolo's clothes. Hurry up and go inside so that Lucramo won't see you with me, for there he is coming out of the house. You keep watch until I return from the wine shop.

SCENE NINE
LUCRAMO; FURBO

LUCR: Of all the fowlers, there's none more fortunate than I am; for, having prepared my snare for two paltry little birds who hung around and sang all day, a partridge got caught in it while in flight. By a partridge I mean a certain merchant who's more partial to loss than to gain. He asked me to sell him one of my women, and not only was he ready to agree to the amount I asked without bargaining, but, until he brings the money, he left me as collateral a coffer full of the finest gold brocade that is worth more than my women or than all the women that a procurer could ever buy and sell.

This is an opportunity that rarely comes, and, if I'm so foolish as to let it go, I'll never come across a similar one. If I wait until that fellow returns to reclaim the coffer, I may as well pull the hair from my chin and hang myself; but, if I take it with me someplace else and sell it, I'll never be poor for the rest of my life. I'll leave tonight, if possible, or as soon as the gates open at dawn. I won't let myself be found here tomorrow. So, the pretense that I made was actually a forecast of what was going to happen; and what was a fable this morning has now become an historical fact. If that merchant doesn't find me when he returns to redeem his coffer, he would be wrong in complaining about

me, for I told him all my attributes before he came into the
house; rather, he told me that I was a glutton, a fraud, a thief, a
cheat, a perfidious fellow, and that I was guilty of every vice. If
after knowing me he was still willing to trust me, he can only
blame himself. Ah, here's Furbo. Did you buy the rope? Where
are the porters that I asked for to pack our belongings?

FURBO: Weren't you just singing about sailing?

LUCR: Hurry up. I sold the wine to the mark; I have the flower
in my hand and tonight, if I can, I'd like to buy the whole
bouquet and leave.[13] Now, I'll sing to you off-key. Go get two
porters. Do you have three grossi?[14] Buy some good packing
rope and bring it here. Run to the piazza; the stores there won't
close until eight o'clock.[15]

ACT FOUR
SCENE ONE
VULPINO, *alone*

VULP: Ah, poor Vulpino. You're assailed on all sides by so many
adversaries, by so many misfortunes, that if you're able to
defend yourself against them you could boast of being an excellent swordsman. Oh envious Fortune, how you always gaze at
the designs of men with fixed and watchful eyes in order to
choose the right moment to interrupt them! How I've tired
myself out, how I've turned and racked my brains these past
fifteen days! I've searched for, considered, and imagined a means
by which I could either lift the money to buy the girl out of
Crisobolo's hands or swindle and trick this Lucramo so that
he'll let her go without us have to spend anything. With what
longing, with what concern we waited for the day when the
master, by leaving the city, would give us the opportunity to
do one or the other! Well, he left today; we managed to trick the
procurer and we took the girl from him without expending any
money. And just when we thought we had finished our weaving
a few loose threads remained. There, in ambush, lay malevolent
Fortune who, suddenly, and I don't know from where, conjured
up some men who took her away from us. I thought that we had
provided for and taken care of all contingencies; however, we
hadn't thought about or provided for this. Not only will this
impede Erofilo in fulfilling his desires, his pleasures, and his love,
but it will affect his interests and the things that really matter;
for, if he fails now, he could go from rich to poor.

He's so intent on finding out where they took her that he
doesn't listen to anything I tell him. I reminded him, but in vain, to
go complain to the captain of justice as we had agreed and [I

pointed out that] if he doesn't do it or postpones it, he's likely
to lose the coffer just as he's lost the girl. Some day he may be
able to recover the girl; but not the coffer if he gives the
procurer a chance to carry it away tonight. If this happens, not
only will it bring on certain ruin to himself and his father, and
his own dishonor, but it will give rise to perpetual warfare in the
house. It will be the cause of my rotting in prison, poor wretch
that I am, where I'll continually waste away in pain and torment.

Alas! Perhaps I could stave off this misfortune, serious as it is,
if I only had a little more time to think about it, only enough
to gather my wits again. But I'm troubled on the one hand by
the fear that the procurer may pack up tonight and on the other
that Crisobolo may suddenly return—I can almost see him
coming now—and keep me so busy that I won't even have
time to tie a rope around my neck and kick my feet in the air. I
just learned from one of Pontico's servants who was coming
from the pier that a considerable number of ships have returned
to port and are still returning, because of a sea wind that
prevents them from leaving and drives them landward. But
what's this light I see coming toward me? God help me, I hope it
isn't the old man! Oh, my goodness; it's him all right. It's my
master; it's Crisobolo! You're a dead man, Vulpino! What will
you do, you poor fellow; you wretch, what will you do?
To whom should I appeal? To whom should I turn? Where can
I hide? Where can I flee? Where can I rush off and fling myself
to escape from the torments that I see being prepared for me
tonight?

Scene Two

CRISOBOLO, *Erofilo's father;* VULPINO, *a servant*

CRIS: I really shouldn't complain that this foul weather prevented
me from going to Procida.

VULP: (It's your son and I who should complain.)

CRIS: By remaining here, even though against my will, I gained
more than I would have had I left.

VULP: (You'll soon see whether there's a gain or a loss.)

CRIS: For as I landed I met someone whom I hadn't see in twelve
years . . .

VULP: (Alas, why didn't we have the same luck with you?)

CRIS: . . . and whom I thought was dead. While in Alexandria I
had lent him a hundred saraffi[16] and merchandise worth two
hundred. I gave him a year's credit; but shortly after that he
went bankrupt, and I thought that . . .

VULP: (I, too, am bankrupt.)

CRIS: . . . I would never recover a grosso. He told me that he had been to Arabia and India . . .

VULP: (If only we had such a master who goes so far away that it takes years and even centuries for him to return.)

CRIS: . . . and that he's now rich. We didn't take leave of each other before he counted out a hundred and eighty ducats, and he promised me the rest as soon as he sells some merchandise that he was clearing through customs today. While we were engaged in talking about these things we didn't notice that night fell and the sky became dark and overcast.

VULP: (Ah, Vulpino, you coward and fainthearted wretch. Where's your boldness, where's your enterprise, where's your ingenuity? You're seated at the helm of the boat. Will you be the first to let himself be dismayed by such a small storm? Cast all fear aside and demonstrate that you're the same Vulpino who showed his mettle before in the face of danger. Find your old cunning and put it to work here, for you're in need of it now more than in any previous undertaking.)

CRIS: It certainly is quite late.

VULP: (On the contrary, it really is much earlier than it need be for us or than we want it to be. He couldn't have come at a more opportune time. Come, come then, for I've already prepared the neatest bag of tricks and the finest and most marvelous sleight of hand that was ever seen.)

CRIS: Since the weather prevented me from going to Procida today, I won't go there at all. I'll accomplish the same thing by means of letters, and it will be more profitable for me if I stay here.

VULP: (It's a little late for him to realize it.)

CRIS: Especially when one has a prodigal son such as mine who's never satisfied unless he has friends at the table day and night and for whom ordinary things aren't good enough. He wants to buy the best that there is in the piazza regardless of what it costs.

VULP: (You would have been quite content if, on this occasion, all we had done was prepare meals.)

CRIS: But this time I returned so fast that, if he had thought about causing some trouble, he wouldn't have had time to do it.

VULP: (You'll soon find out. If you had run faster than a deer, I don't know whether you could have arrived in time. But why am I waiting to take out my little balls and begin the game?) Oh, poor us! Oh, how unfortunate we are!

CRIS: That seems to be my Vulpino.

VULP: Oh this city, full of deceit, full of thieves and villains!

CRIS: God help me!

VULP: Oh, the foolishness of a drunk; oh, the negligence of a rascal!

CRIS: What is it?

VULP: How will the master take it when he finds out?

CRIS: I tremble and sweat with fear that some misfortune has come upon me.

VULP: He entrusts his rooms, which are filled with so many things, to the custody of a senseless idiot who leaves them open all day long and never stays at home.

CRIS: Vulpino!

VULP: If they don't find it this evening, it's gone.

CRIS: Hold it, Vulpino.

VULP: The master is ruined.

CRIS: I would sooner your tongue be dry than this be true, Vulpino!

VULP: I hear someone calling me.

CRIS: Vulpino!

VULP: Oh, it's the master!

CRIS: What are you shouting about?

VULP: Oh, Master!

CRIS: What's the matter?

VULP: I'd like to think . . .

CRIS: What's wrong?

VULP: . . . that God, by some miracle . . .

CRIS: What is it?

VULP: . . . has brought you back. . . .

CRIS: Come on, tell me, what misfortune has occurred?

VULP: I can hardly catch my breath.

CRIS: What's the matter with you?

VULP: But now that I see you I can begin to breathe. Goodness me, I didn't know to whom to turn.

CRIS: Whom are you complaining about?

VULP: I was dead.

CRIS: What did you die of?

VULP: But now that I see you, Master, I'm revived.

CRIS: What's the matter?

VULP: I no longer have to abandon hope . . .

CRIS: Come on, speak up; out with it.

VULP: . . . that you'll recover it.

CRIS: What do you want me to recover? What the devil is the matter? Am I not going to . . .

VULP: Oh, Master!

CRIS: . . . find out from you today?

VULP: Your servant . . .

CRIS: What servant?

VULP: . . . your Nebbia . . .

CRIS: What has he done?

VULP: He's done an enormous amount of damage.

CRIS: What did he do?

VULP: I'll tell you; but let me rest a while, for I've done nothing but run around all day long. I can hardly move, and I'm having difficulty getting the words out.

CRIS: Tell me just one; that will suffice. What did he do?

VULP: He's ruined you through his negligence.

CRIS: Finish me off; don't hold me in suspense any longer, you rascal.

VULP: He allowed someone to steal from the room ...

CRIS: What did he allow to be stolen from the room?

VULP: ... from the room, Master, in which you sleep, the one whose keys you had handed over to him alone, the one you had entrusted him with ...

CRIS: What was stolen from my room? Tell me at once; speak up.

VULP: The coffer.

CRIS: The coffer?

VULP: The one that those men—I think they were Florentines— put there.

CRIS: That one?

VULP: Yes, that one.

CRIS: Oh, God! The one I have in trust?

VULP: You should say "you had," for you no longer have it.

CRIS: Ah, woe is me! Ah, Crisobolo, you're the unhappiest man in the world! To leave the city and entrust your house to poltroons, idiots, drunkards, scoundrels, and gallows-birds! I could just as well have entrusted it to so many donkeys.

VULP: Master, if you find the wine cellar in a mess, punish me and make me suffer whatever torments you please; but what have I got to do with your room?

CRIS: Is this how Erofilo uses his discretion? Is this the care and concern that he has for my things and his? Is this the duty of a good son?

VULP: You shouldn't find fault with him for this either. What more can a young man do than imitate his father? If you trust Nebbia no less than you do yourself, why shouldn't he also trust him? Why shouldn't he believe, as you do, that Nebbia would be just as diligent in the care and custody of your things and that he wouldn't go out and leave the door to your room open as soon as you turn your back?

CRIS: I'm undone! Oh, poor me, I'm ruined!

VULP: Master, do something about it while the damage is still fresh. Now that I see you here I won't lose hope that your coffer will soon be recovered; and I believe that the Lord brought you back in the nick of time.

CRIS: Have you any clue, any lead, that can aid me in recovering it?

VULP: I looked for it all day long, and I went around searching here and there like a bloodhound, with the result that I think I can show you where the hare is located.

CRIS: If you know it, why didn't you tell me?

VULP: I didn't say that I knew it for certain; I said that I think I know.

CRIS: Whom do you suspect has taken it?

VULP: I'll tell you; but come a little closer to me, a little closer. Move far away from that door.

CRIS: Who are you afraid will hear us?

VULP: The one whom I think may have it.

CRIS: Is he close enough to hear?

VULP: He lives in that house, that one on your right.

CRIS: Do you think that the procurer who lives there has taken it?

VULP: I think so; in fact, I'm certain of it.

CRIS: What proof do you have?

VULP: I didn't say that I had proof; I said I'm certain of it. But, for God's sake, let's not waste time by asking me to relate with what skill, with what difficulty, by what means I found out, because any delay could be disastrous. I can assure you that the scoundrel is preparing to flee at dawn as soon as the gates are open.

CRIS: What do you think I should do? Advise me, for this sudden turn of events has so overwhelmed me that I don't know where to turn.

VULP: I advise you to inform the captain of justice immediately that the coffer is missing and that this procurer, your neighbor, has stolen it. Ask him to send a bailiff with you so that you can break into his house. If you get there soon, without giving him a chance to flee or tamper with the coffer, you're sure to find it.

CRIS: But what evidence can I give him? What proof can I bring?

VULP: Isn't it proof enough that, being a pimp, he's also a thief? And if you say so, wouldn't the captain believe you more than ten other witnesses?

CRIS: If we have no other proof than this we're in a sad state. Whom do the authorities give more credence to than pimps and villains? And whom do they scoff at more than law-abiding and virtuous men? Whom are they out to get if not merchants like me who have the reputation of being wealthy?

VULP: Let me come with you. I'll give him so many indications and conjectures that he'll believe us. I'm not telling them to you now in order not to waste time. Let's hurry, let's quicken our pace so that we won't give the procurer time to flee or to hide the goods somewhere else.

CRIS: Let's go, then. No, wait a moment; I just thought of another way and I'd like to try it.

VULP: What other way could be better and more certain than this?

CRIS: Come here, Nespolo. Go to Critone's house and ask him for me to come here immediately and to bring his brother with him, and his son-in-law as well, if he's there, or any others in his household. Tell them to come quickly. I'll wait for him here. Hurry up; run.

VULP: What do you want them for?

CRIS: As my witnesses when I go inside the house; and I'm determined to enter without waiting for the bailiff. I'll descend upon the procurer unexpectedly and, if I find my coffer, I'll take it without anyone else's help. I have the right to seize my merchandise wherever I find it. If we were to go to the captain at this hour I know that it would be useless. He would either inform us that he was going to have supper or they would say that he had withdrawn to deal with important matters. I know very well the habits of those who govern us. When they're by themselves in idleness, or when they waste their time playing chess, taroc,[17] backgammon, or, more often, playing cards, they try to appear the busiest. They place a servant at the door who lets in gamblers and pimps and sends away honest citizens and virtuous men.

VULP: If you gave him to understand that you had something important to tell him, I doubt that he would deny you an audience.

CRIS: And how would you get him to listen? Don't you know what the doorkeepers tell you? "You cannot speak to him." "Please let him know that I'm here." "He's ordered me not to give him any messages." Once they've said this there's no other reply. So it will be better if I go in there myself, without other help, and take my own goods provided they're there.

VULP: They're there for sure, so go in with confidence. Your idea is excellent.

CRIS: While we're waiting for Critone, tell me something: how did you find out that the procurer had stolen the coffer? What evidence do you have?

VULP: It would be a long story, and there wouldn't be enough time. Let's try to recover it first and then when we're more at our leisure I'll tell you the whole story.

CRIS: We have time enough, and, if you cannot tell me the whole story, at least tell me part of it.

VULP: I can begin, but I won't be able to finish.

CRIS: You could have told me part of it already.

VULP: Since you want me to tell you, I'll do so. (What the devil will I say to him?)

CRIS: Aren't you going to say something?

VULP: I'm afraid that Critone will delay too long and the procurer will get a chance to hide or transfer the goods. It would be better if I went to urge them to hurry. (Still, I'd like to hold him at bay with a few lies until they arrive.)

CRIS: No, don't go. I don't think they'll be very long. Tell me: did it take you long before you realized it had been stolen?

VULP: Listen. If you really want to know, I'll tell you. Erofilo had returned home after we had lunch—he had been invited out by some of his friends this morning. Nebbia then came to see him and said: "I have to go out on an errand; here, these are the keys to your father's room in case you need to go inside." And he gave them to him without being asked.

CRIS: This was a fine way to begin obeying me!

VULP: Erofilo took them, without suspecting anything, and Nebbia left.

CRIS: Why did he do that? Didn't I expressly forbid him ever to leave the house or to stop guarding the room?

VULP: You see. We stayed a while chatting about various things; and we went from one subject to another, as usual. Finally, we got to talking about hunting. Erofilo then remembered a horn that he used to have and that he hadn't seen or heard for some time. He wanted to see whether it was in your room; so he took the keys that Nebbia had left; he opened the door and went in. I followed him. Your son looked around, and he was the first to notice that the coffer was missing; then he turned to me and asked if I knew whether those who had left it on deposit had reclaimed it. I looked around and I was more than astonished— I was mortified—when I didn't see the coffer. I told him that I remembered that when you left I had seen it at the head of the bed where it used to be. Immediately I realized the stupid ploy of your Nebbia, who, as soon as he realized that the coffer had been stolen, brought the keys to your room to your son to make him share the blame, although he alone is guilty. Do you see what I mean?

CRIS: I understand. Go on. I'll treat him as he deserves.

VULP: He played dumb, but he has more malice than the devil himself. You don't know him.

CRIS: Continue.

VULP: (They're so late in coming that I'm afraid I'm running out of stories.)

CRIS: Your mind is on something else.

VULP: I'm preoccupied with those dawdlers who haven't yet come, and I forget. Now, as I was saying, my dear Master, as soon as I realized this, Erofilo and I began to discuss the matter, to think about and consider who could have taken it. Erofilo gave me his opinion, and I gave him mine. We deliberated a long time without being able to decide on how to go about this or what course to follow to get evidence. We were more confused than ever: we didn't know where to run, to whom to turn—we were at a complete loss. Oh, dear Master, I found myself so downcast today that I wished I were dead and buried; in fact, I wished I were never born. Ah, here comes Critone—damn it, it's about time—and he has his brother and son-in-law with him.

CRIS: With all your chattering you haven't given me a single indication by which I can deduce that it's the procurer rather than anyone else who has my coffer.

VULP: Enter [his house] with assurance, and if you don't find it then hang me. If I wasn't sure of it, I wouldn't dare affirm it with such conviction.

SCENE THREE
CRITONE; CRISOBOLO; VULPINO

CRIT: (Every place has its thieves, but there are more of them here than anywhere else. Where can citizens be safe, if they're robbed in their very own homes? Oh, there's Crisobolo.) We're sorry about what happened; and we're ready to help you in whatever you want.

CRIS: Thank you. I'm sorry to bother you at this hour; you can impose upon me some other time when I can be of benefit to you.

CRIT: You don't have to say that to us.

CRIS: I'd like you please to come with me and be my witnesses. I'm going in here where I was told that I'll find my goods.

CRIT: We'll be happy to come.

VULP: Enough said; let's go in.

CRIS: Yes, let's go in.

VULP: All of you line up along the wall and hide the torches. I'll knock, and when they open up everyone come in. I'll stay at the door so that while you're searching for the coffer in one place he won't take it out of another and hide it elsewhere.

CRIS: Come on, knock, and have us do what you think best.

SCENE FOUR
FULCIO; VULPINO

FUL: There are many braggarts who try to hoodwink you by

boasting that they can do all sorts of things; but when put to the test they don't dare even attempt them. Among these is that drunkard, Vulpino, who promised us today that, with the help of one of his friends, he would play a really cunning and well-conceived trick on the procurer that would work. He was to let us know as soon as he begins so that we, on our part, could follow up what we had agreed upon. Caridoro and I have been waiting all evening, and we still haven't heard any news. I'm going to find out whether the plans have been changed or whether something has come up to interrupt them.

VULP: (I hear someone coming this way; he seems to be approaching our door. He's about to knock on it.) Who are you? Hey there, what are you looking for? Whom do you want?

FUL: Oh, Vulpino, I seek no one but you.

VULP: Oh, Fulcio, I didn't recognize you.

FUL: Should we continue to wait for you and Erofilo to come and do what we had agreed, or have you changed you mind?

VULP: Oh, Fulcio, the devil must not only have put his tail in, as they say, but his head and his horns as well; he's messed up all our plans.

FUL: What has happened?

VULP: Listen, I'll tell you. Hold it; be quiet, shh, shh.

FUL: What mob is this coming out of Lucramo's house with so much noise and such an uproar?

Scene Five
LUCRAMO; CRISOBOLO; CRITONE; FULCIO; VULPINO

LUCR: My good man, is this the way to treat foreigners?

CRIS: Is this the way to treat citizens, you thief?

LUCR: Don't think you'll get away with this so easily; I'll cry to high heaven.

CRIS: I won't take my complaints to such a high place, but rather to a place where your wickedness will be punished.

LUCR: Don't think that just because I'm a procurer I won't be listened to . . .

CRIS: Do you still have the audacity to speak?

LUCR: . . . and that I don't have a tongue with which to express my rights.

CRIS: The hangman will make it stick nine inches out of your mouth. Listen to him! Wouldn't he be even more indignant if he had found his merchandise in my house just as I found mine in his?

LUCR: I'll undergo torture and I'll have all in my household do the same in order to prove to any judge that a merchant gave me this coffer. He left it as security until be brings me the sum we had agreed upon for a woman he had just bought from me.

CRIS: Do you still dare to open your mouth, you common and notorious thief?

LUCR: Who's more common and notorious than you, you who come here to steal and bring witnesses with him?

CRIS: If you don't speak with moderation, you glutton . . .

CRIT: Don't bother answering him; don't reply to his tittle-tattle. It's not fitting for someone like you to argue with this idiot.—— If you think he's done you an injustice, take him to court tomorrow; he's not a fugitive like you. Show up before the captain of justice.

LUCR: You'll see me there; be certain of that. You won't get away with this as easily as you think. Right now there are too many of you against one; but we'll meet in a place where I can answer you as an equal.

CRIS: Did you ever see such insolence? Have you even seen a thief as arrogant as this one?

CRIT: No, never. You've been very fortunate, Crisobolo.

CRIS: Most fortunate.

CRIT: Is there anything else you want from us?

CRIS: Only that you call upon me if you need me, as I called upon you. Vulpino, take that torch and accompany them home; you, hand it to him.

SCENE SIX
FULCIO; VULPINO; CRITONE

FUL: Shall I wait for you, Vulpino?

VULP: Yes, wait for me; I'd like to speak to you.

FUL: Try to get back soon.

VULP: I'll be back in a flash.

FUL: Do you have far to go?

VULP: No, just a short distance.

FUL: I'll keep you company.

VULP: That would be better. I'll be able to talk to you about our affairs. Oh, blast it!

FUL: May you break your neck! What's the matter?

VULP: Alas, woe is me! I've had it; I'm dead!

FUL: What's the matter, you idiot? What's going on?

VULP: Here, take the torch, Fulcio, and accompany these gentlemen. Damn my short memory!

FUL: Please, hold it yourselves and light the way for each other. I want to find out whether what just happened to him is good or bad.

CRIT: Both of you certainly are fine servants and courteous young men! You indiscreet poltroons, by God, we would certainly give you back your torch were it not for the fact that the police would arrest us if they found us without a light at this hour. Then, tomorrow morning, without knowing who we are, without allowing us recourse to the captain for pardon, they'd have us hanging from a rope with our arses exposed to the crowds. Come, then, let's provide the light ourselves and be like the poor knights who accompany one another.[18]

FUL: What happened to you just now?

VULP: Alas! I left Trappola with Crisobolo's clothes on and I forgot to run on ahead and have him undress and give him back his own gown, which is in my room, before my master gets home.

FUL: Oh, you scatterbrain, you good-for-nothing! Run quickly and at least have him hide someplace so that your master won't see him.

VULP: I'm afraid I'll get there too late. In fact, I am too late, for I already hear the shouts. He must have found him. There he is outside. God help me.

SCENE SEVEN
CRISOBOLO; VULPINO; TRAPPOLA

CRIS: Where do you think you're going? Don't move, you false-faced little thief. Where did you get this gown of mine?

VULP: (What will you do now, wretched and pitiful Vulpino?)

CRIS: You must be the fine fellow who also stole my coffer!

VULP: (Oh! If I could only get close to his ear!)

CRIS: Do you think I won't get you to answer, you scoundrel, you cheat? Hey there, help me so that he won't flee. This glutton pretends not to understand me and he won't speak. He's either a mute or he pretends to be one.

VULP: (One couldn't have found a better remedy for this unexpected turn of events. Now is the time to help him.) Master, what are you doing with that mute?

CRIS: I found this fellow dressed in my clothes, as you see him.

VULP: Who the devil gave him your gown and brought him into the house?

CRIS: I can't make him answer at all.

VULP: How do you expect him to reply if he's dumb?

CRIS: Is he a mute?

VULP: What? Don't you know him?

CRIS: I never saw him before.

VULP: Don't you know the mute who hangs around the Monkey's Tavern?

CRIS: What tavern? What mute? What monkey do you expect me to know, you rascal? Do I look like a man who frequents taverns?

VULP: I see he's dressed in your clothes.

CRIS: Why the devil do you think I'm so angry?

VULP: I see that he's put on your hat as well.

CRIS: You mean everything he's wearing, from his shirt to his shoes, is mine.

VULP: So it is, by God. This is the strangest thing in the world! Did you ask him who gave him your clothes?

CRIS: Of course I asked him; but how do you expect him to answer me if he's dumb?

VULP: See if you can get him to tell you by means of signs.

CRIS: I cannot understand someone who doesn't speak.

VULP: I can.

CRIS: If you understand him, then you question him.

VULP: I understand him very well, no less than I do anyone else.

CRIS: Then ask him.

VULP: Who gave you these? I mean these clothes; these, where did you get them?

CRIS: See how well they converse with their hands, as well as everyone else does with their tongues! Tell me, do you understand what he's saying?

VULP: He indicates that someone from this house took his rags and gave him your gown and your other clothes in exchange; and he told him to wait here until he returns.

CRIS: Motion to him to let you know, if he can, who in my household it was.

VULP: That will be easy.

CRIS: I could watch him for a thousand years and I still couldn't comprehend what he's saying; in fact, I couldn't decipher a single phrase. What does it mean when he raises his hand or when he touches his head and face, and often his nose, and when he puffs out his cheeks?

VULP: He indicates that it was a short fellow with a large nose, curly hair, a pallid face, who speaks somewhat hurriedly.

CRIS: I think he means Nebbia. But how does he know that he speaks hurriedly? Can a mute hear?

VULP: I didn't say that he speaks hurriedly, but that he left in a hurry. There's no mistaking it; he means Nebbia. You understood it sooner and better than I did.

CRIS: What did that fool hope to accomplish by dressing in this fellow's clothes?

VULP: I imagine that, having noticed that the coffer was missing and realizing that it was his fault, he decided to flee. He switched clothes because they might recognize him and hold him at the gates.

CRIS: Why did he give him my clothes rather than his own?

VULP: How the devil should I know? He's somewhat reckless at times.

CRIS: Now go take him in the house and have him put on some clothes that would be suitable for him so that he doesn't soil mine.

CRIS: (By, God, it could be quite otherwise: one shouldn't go into this with one's eyes closed and believe everything Vulpino says. One shouldn't take his word as gospel.) Don't go yet, Vulpino; wait a moment. Didn't the procurer say that a merchant had given him the coffer? And didn't he describe him, if I remember correctly, as being dressed precisely in this manner?

VULP: What? Would you rely on what the procurer said?

CRIS: I don't consider you a better foundation on which to rely, Vulpino; and now I'm going to do otherwise. Gallo, Negro, Nespolo, hold that fellow still and tie him up.

VULP: Why?

CRIS: I'm going to send him to the captain of justice to see whether a rope is a good remedy to cure speechlessness.

VULP: Master, don't I know for certain whether he's a mute? Yet, if you want to clarify this further, I'll take him to the procurer so that when he sees him he'll be able to tell if he's the merchant who gave him the coffer. Who would know him better?

CRIS: I'll have the captain's rope clarify it, and that will suffice. Hurry up and if there's nothing else to tie him with, take the rope from the well. That's fine; tie his hands behind his back. But damn you, first take my gown off him.

TRAP: Forgive me, Vulpino. I served you as long as the words and threats didn't turn into actions.

VULP: (Oh, God, woe is me, wretched Vulpino!)

TRAP: But I won't be maimed or killed because of you.

CRIS: By God, this rope deserves to be included in the list of the saints, for it heals a mute. Do you think, Vulpino, that if it's placed around your neck it can perform the miracle of curing your villainy? Now, answer me: who gave you my clothes?

TRAP: Your son gave them to me.

CRIS: And not Vulpino?

TRAP: The two of them were in it together.

CRIS: For what purpose?

TRAP: To send me dressed this way to pick up a woman from the procurer's house.

CRIS: Were you the one who took my coffer there?

TRAP: They gave me a chest, which I brought there and left as security as they told me to do.

CRIS: So this is how you have the audacity, Vulpino, to place so much valuable merchandise in such danger, in the house, in the hands, in the power, at the discretion of a fleeing pimp, of a perfidious man? You almost ruined me, you rogue! Are these the exemplary morals, are these the fine deeds you teach my son whom I asked you to look after? And then you mock me and try to make me believe such nonsense, which even donkeys would see through by now, no less men? You'll not boast of it, by God. ——Untie that fellow immediately and tie up this rascal.

VULP: Oh, Master, your son ordered me and forced me to do it. You left me here to take orders from him and not to command him.

CRIS: Tie him up firmly. If God allows me to live until tomorrow, I'll make such an example of you to others that they'll never again dare deceive me.

VULP: Have pity on me, Master!

CRIS: You scoundrel!——You, come and get your clothes; come in, for I want to hear all about this business.

SCENE EIGHT
FULCIO, *alone*

FUL: Everything is going badly for all of us, but especially for Vulpino, as fickle Fortune has put everything in disarray. She had been treating us so favorably for a while, and would have continued to do so, had she not been interrupted and reversed by the short memory of this fool. Now what other course should I pursue than to persuade my young master to abandon this project and turn to something else that would be more profitable and would bring him greater honor? If he cannot have his desire, then he ought to desire what he can have.

But what will I accomplish by this? I would need more eloquence and more valid reasons than I have available in order to remove such firm conviction from his mind, a conviction that Vulpino and I reinforced by giving him such high hopes and getting him close to realizing his objective. Now if, on the contrary, I persuade him to give up this undertaking, it will more likely lead the poor thing to desperation than induce him to undertake something honest and profitable. Besides, if I don't find some way for him to reach his objective, won't I incur shame, blame, and infamy? Won't I always have the reputation of being a fool? It will seem as if I'm not able to hatch a plot without Vulpino; and, despite my successes in the past, if I fail here, now that I'm by myself, the glory will go to Vulpino. May

God prevent me from being known as Vulpino's disciple and may He save me from such dishonor, from having such an ugly blemish mar my face!

What shall I do, then? What shall I do? If I try it this way . . . , it would be very difficult. And this other way . . . ; it would be much easier. Yet it's not that simple, and I have many reservations. How about this other . . . ? It's almost the same thing. But what if I take precautions by . . . ? That's fine, but I'm afraid that I'll be discovered. What if I take precautions by . . . ? That's not bad, Now if I complete it this way . . . ; that's it. How will it be if I add this twist . . . , and then this . . . ? It might be good enough; in fact, very good . . . ; as a matter of fact, excellent. It will be perfect. I've found it. I'm going to do it in any case, and it cannot help but succeed. I figured it out. I decided to do it this way; and I'll show then that I'm not a disciple, but the master of masters. Now I'll advance against this pimp with an army of lies. I'm going to destroy him and put him to the sack. So favor me, Fortune, and, if my plan succeeds, I vow to stay drunk in your honor for three whole days. Behold, she must have heard me, for the procurer is not waiting for my assault; he's opening the door and coming to surrender.

Scene Nine
LUCRAMO; FULCIO

LUCR: (The more I delay in complaining, the more I weaken my case. I wanted Furbo to come with me, but he's so late returning that I'm forced to go alone.)

FUL: Oh, God! I hope I find Lucramo at home so that I can inform him . . .

LUCR: (Who's that mentioning my name?)

FUL: . . . of the ruin descending upon him.

LUCR: (What is he talking about?)

FUL: So that at least he won't lose his life.

LUCR: (Oh, God!)

FUL: However, he's more likely to lose it than have it saved. Anyway, I'm going to warn him.

LUCR: Don't bother to knock, Fulcio; here I am if you're looking for me.

FUL: Of, unhappy, oh, unfortunate, oh, pitiful Lucramo! Why don't you flee?

LUCR: Why the devil should I flee?

FUL: Oh, you poor beggar! Go; get away from here right away. Run away and hide.

LUCR: Why do you want me to run away?

FUL: You'll be hanged at once, immediately, you poor fellow, if they catch you. Flee. What are you waiting for?

LUCR: Who would have me hanged?

FUL: My master, the captain of justice. I warn you, run away. Are you still here? Flee, you poor soul.

LUCR: What have I done that merits the gallows?

FUL: You've stolen from your neighbor, Crisobolo.

LUCR: That's not true.

FUL: And he has witnesses—what witnesses!—to prove that he found the stolen goods in your house. You're still hanging around? Go, get away, run away immediately. Aren't you moving yet?

LUCR: Maybe your master will listen to my part of the story . . .

FUL: Don't waste your time; don't stand around talking, you poor man. Go, run like the devil, for the chief of police isn't fifteen yards away; he has a warrant to hang you on the spot and he's bringing the hangman with him. Now see whether you have the time to chatter. Flee, disappear.

LUCR: Ah, Fulcio, I place myself in you hands. Help me; advise me. You know very well that I like you and have always liked you ever since our friendship began.

FUL: That's why I came to warn you and I did so at the risk of being punished.

LUCR: I thank you for it.

FUL: If my master knew it, I'm afraid he would hang me along with you. So get out of here and don't croak any more.

LUCR: But what will become of my poor family and my possessions?

FUL: What family? What possessions? It's better to lose everything else you have than your life. Run! What are you waiting for?

LUCR: But, alas, where can I flee? Where can I hide?

FUL: How the devil should I know? I've done my duty; if they hang you, it's your fault. I don't want to be found with you and follow you to the gallows.

LUCR: Ah, Fulcio, Fulcio!

FUL: Shut up and don't mention my name, may you be drawn and quartered! Let no one hear you and report to my master that I came to warn you.

LUCR: I place myself in your hands. Please don't leave me!

FUL: Place yourself in the hands of the hangman, not in mine. I wouldn't want my master to find out that I spoke to you, not for a hundred-thousand ducats.

LUCR: Oh, for God's sake, listen a moment.

FUL: I can't wait a moment longer; I think I hear something and I'm afraid it's the chief of police.

LUCR: I'll come with you.

FUL: Go somewhere else; I don't want them to find you with me.

LUCR: I want to come.

FUL: No, don't come.

LUCR: Wherever you go I'm determined to follow.

ACT FIVE
SCENE ONE
FULCIO; EROFILO; FURBO

FUL: With these and other words, along with various and appropriate gestures, which worked with great success, I put so much fear into the poor fellow that he came running after me. He followed me for quite some time as I ran here and there all over the city as if I, too, were afraid. At every little sound he heard he shook more than a leaf in the wind, as if he had the chief constable constantly on his trail, with the police force not far behind.

ERO: I'm amazed that, knowing himself to be innocent, as in truth he is, he's such a coward that he wouldn't have the courage to show up [before the captain of justice].

FUL: What? Does it seem so strange? I already had told him and convinced him that the chief of police had the strictest orders to hang him on the spot as soon as he was caught, without examination or trial!

ERO: I don't see how he could believe you so readily.

FUL: Why shouldn't he believe me? He knows my master—he's seen him elsewhere—and he knows very well that he often plays such tricks on others like him; and he knows how quick he is to anger and how much he has always hated the name of procurer.

ERO: Yet, knowing his innocence . . .

FUL: What? Granting that he's completely innocent of this, as he is, of how many other untold crimes of every sort do you think he's guilty, the smallest of which deserves not one, but a thousand hangings? He knows he's a scoundrel, and it would be madness for him to go to jail and suffer torture; for, even if he were to acquit himself of one false accusation, he would run the risk of uncovering other crimes that would easily condemn him to death.

ERO: Did you say that he went to see Caridoro in his bedroom? How did he find the courage to go there?

FUL: I gave him to understand that my master decided to have him hanged right off, no matter what, and if he were not found in the course of the night, he wouldn't let the gates be open tomorrow; and that he was going to issue a decree requiring anyone who knew or had any indication of his whereabouts to bring it to the attention of the authorities under the threat of harsh punishment. With this story and an infinity of other lies I brought the poor man to such a state of desperation that there isn't a precipice in the world so high that he wouldn't have leaped from it in order to escape. And then, pretending that I wanted to save him, I suggested that it would be best if he took refuge with Caridoro, who could hide him without the fear that others might have of being punished by his father for sheltering him. I told him that, as Caridoro was a nice and amiable friend, he wouldn't refuse to hide him until his father's anger abated somewhat.

ERO: And so you brought him there?

FUL: I jabbered so much that I finally got him there. I wish you could have seen him when he came before Caridoro—trembling all over and pale. His tears were streaming down like those of a child; and how humbly he begged and pleaded with him to have compassion in his misfortune! He embraced his knees, he kissed his feet, and he offered to give him, not only the girl, but all his worldly goods and to be his slave forever.

ERO: Hah, hah, hah! You're making me laugh.

FUL: You should also have seen Caridoro pretending to be very reluctant and afraid of incurring his father's wrath, and begging him, in turn, to go elsewhere and not to cause him to fall into disfavor with the very person whom he should love and revere above all others.

ERO: Hah, hah, hah!

FUL: If only you had seen me trying to convince Caridoro, proposing ways by which he could help him without incurring censure.

ERO: Hah, hah, hah! Good Lord, it would have been impossible for me to refrain from laughing.

FUL: Finally, I advised Lucramo to send for the girl, as her presence would do more to get Caridoro to help him than would prayers and offerings. He agreed to my suggestion; and he wrote this note himself and gave me this ring as a token. So now I'm going to get the girl whose arrival will have a beneficial effect.

ERO: I'm sure it will. Then the procurer is waiting for you in Caridoro's bedroom?

FUL: Oh, I didn't tell you the best part! So that he wouldn't be seen by others in the household as they come and go, we had him hide under the bed. He's so frightened that I can hardly describe it to you and he doesn't dare breathe lest he be heard.

ERO: I rejoice that Caridoro has had such fine success in his love affair; and it doubles my happiness in having found Eulalia. The enormous worry and fear that I had lost her forever—I couldn't imagine who had taken her from me—makes my pleasure greater than it would have been had our Trappola brought her to me without any difficulty, for I had already dissipated a good part of my joy in a particular expectation. Now, I have her back; and it was my servants, who had taken her away, thinking that they were pleasing and serving me, who restored her to me.

FUL: So it is that the more trouble, the more danger one encounters in obtaining things and the more one lacks hope of getting them, the more enjoyable they are.

ERO: And, conversely, it's most disturbing if misfortune comes when you least expect it, when it interjects itself into the midst of pleasure and ruins your enjoyment. I have proof of this right now with the horrible news you brought me that my father has returned instead of going to Procida, that he's discovered our plans and that he's imprisoned our adviser, Vulpino.

FUL: You can easily find a remedy for this misfortune. With a few humble words to the old man he'll be happy to forgive you and make peace. Show him that you have respect and reverence for him, for that's all he expects of you. Once peace is established between you, you'll be able to free Vulpino from all danger. So, Erofilo, it's up to you to do everything you can to save him. And then there remains one more debt—no less important—to satisfy.

ERO: What debt?

FUL: We have to get Lucramo to leave town tomorrow morning.

ERO: Let's have him leave tonight.

FUL: We need money for that; at least we ought to pay him what the two girls cost. It's better for him to gain than lose, so that should he later realize that we duped him, he'll keep quiet. See if you can put together fifty scudi and let's have them now, if possible. I'll ask Caridoro for the same amount. Let's send him on his way immediately with a hundred scudi, and let's not hear any more clamor.

ERO: Speak to anyone but me about this; you won't be able to get a carlin or a picciolo[19] from me.

FUL: You must really be poor. Borrow it from someone.

ERO: I don't have enough credit to borrow such a sum.

FUL: The Jews will lend it to you if you don't have a friend to whom you can turn.

ERO: What collateral can I give them?

FUL: At least find thirty, if you can't find more. Don't waste any more time.

ERO: I don't have it and I don't know where to find it. Since my old man has returned and our scheme has been discovered, don't expect me to be able to help out with a soldo.[20]

FUL: What shall we do then?

ERO: You think of something.

FUL: I'm thinking about it. If you can't give me anything more, couldn't you at least give me fifteen [scudi]? Still, it won't be very much. I know that this poor procurer hasn't a penny[21] to his name. He has to leave with his household and support himself during the voyage. See if this can be done without spending!

ERO: I couldn't even give him one; you find the money.

FUL: I'm thinking about where to find it.

ERO: Think harder.

FUL: I'm still thinking and I believe I can find it at last.

ERO: I have such confidence in you ingenuity that even if none existed in the world you would create some out of nothing.

FUL: Come on, then, leave it to me; I hope to find it for you before midnight. First I'll hurry and take the girl to Caridoro; then I'll concentrate on making the money sprout up from somewhere. ——Hey, you going in there; stop, whoever you are. I want to talk to you.

FURBO: Even if you owned me, you shouldn't have commanded me with such arrogance. If you need me for something, then follow me.

FUL: Oh what an ass! His manners are just like those of his master.

SCENE TWO
EROFILO; CRISOBOLO

ERO: (I'll go into the house and do what I can to appease my father; if it weren't a matter of helping Vulpino, I wouldn't dare face him for a fortnight. There's our door being opened. It's him. I feel my blood surging and my heart pounding in my bosom.)

CRIS: I wonder what's keeping those other rascals! I don't see them coming from any direction. Where can they be at this hour? If I find my things in such a fine state when I'm gone for only one day, and not even the whole day at that, what would have happened had I stayed away for two or three months! The next time that villain deceives me I'll surely forgive him. Oh what a fool I was to fall for his stories!

ERO: (I'm still not sure whether or not I ought to show my face.)

CRIS: If, with his cunning, he manages to slip out of the shackles in which I placed him, I'll be happy to let him put me in his place.

ERO: (I must finally take courage; otherwise Vulpino will be in a sad state.)

CRIS: Oh, my fine fellow!

ERO: Didn't you go to Procida, Father?

CRIS: (See with what temerity this rascal comes before me!)

ERO: Oh, Father, I'm extremely sorry and I regret having upset you.

CRIS: If this were really true, Erofilo, you would try to live better. Oh, well, I'll remember this and when you think I've forgotten, I'll remind you of it.

ERO: Forgive me, Father. Next time I'll be better advised, and I won't give you anything to complain about.

CRIS: Ah, Erofilo! I don't want you to promise me with words what you try to take away from me with deeds. It would have been difficult for me to believe that the perfect child whom I raised with such care would, in his adolescence, when his wisdom should have increased with the years, turn out to be one of the wickedest and most dissolute young men in Sibaris. I expected you to be the cane to sustain me when I'm decrepit; instead you have become the cane with which to beat me and break my bones one by one, to bury me before my time.

ERO: Oh Father!

CRIS: You call me "Father"; but then you show with your deeds that you're my enemy instead.

ERO: Forgive me, Father.

CRIS: If it weren't for the fact that I don't want to offend your mother's honor, Erofilo, I would deny that you were my son. I don't see any resemblance to me in your actions or manners; and I would very much rather you resembled me in your virtues than in your physical features.

ERO: Father, my youth and my carelessness made me fall into this error and offend you.

CRIS: Don't you think that I, too, was young once? At your age I was always at your grandfather's side, and with hard work and diligence I helped him increase our patrimony and property, which you, prodigal as you are, try to consume and destroy with your deceit and lust. In my youth, my concern, my intention, my desire, was to gain the esteem of upright men; with them alone I associated, and I tried whenever possible to emulate them. You, on the contrary, think it disgraceful to be seen with me; and you're always to be found with pimps, drunkards, cheats, or other such riffraff. You ought to burn with shame and not just blush if you were seen in their company by the birds, let alone by men.

ERO: I was wrong, Father, I confess it. Forgive me and rest assured that this will be the last time you'll have cause to be angry with me.

CRIS: I swear by God, Erofilo, that if you don't mend your ways and turn to living virtuously you'll know my resentment and you'll suffer for it. I'm not as stupid as you would have me be. If sometimes I pretend not to see, don't think that because of this I'm blind. If you won't do your duty, I'll do mine. It's better to be without a son than to have one who always torments me, afflicts me, and doesn't let me live.

ERO: In the future, Father, I'll try to be more obedient.

CRIS: If you seek out good things you'll be doing that which not only pleases me very much and is becoming to you, but which will benefit you more than anyone else. Believe me.

SCENE THREE

FULCIO, *alone*

FUL: [*To Furbo, inside*] If I wait here for her to finish beautifying herself I won't be able to do another task or accomplish anything else all evening. Keep hurrying her along until I return; in the meantime, there are other matters, no less important, that I had better settle.——

Oh, how much time these females waste in getting dressed and making themselves up! Wait for them, wait, for they never finish: they have to use three hundred pins and move each one to three hundred different places, and even then they won't let them be; they change each curl a hundred times and still they're not content to let it stay. And then come the cosmetics: oh, what patience is needed here! First they put on the white, then the red; then they take it off; they adjust it; they wipe it off and they begin again, returning to the mirror more than a thousand times to look at themselves. Oh, how long they take in plucking their eyebrows! Oh, what care they use in lifting their breasts so that they'll be firm and won't sag! What do they do to their nails with their files and scissors, and to their hands with lotions and lemons? They spend an hour washing their hands and another hour oiling and rubbing them so that they'll stay soft! How much attention they give to picking their teeth and brushing them with a variety of toothpowders! How much time is wasted, how many little boxes, phials, and jars, how many paints they put to use! I couldn't count them all. One could fully arm a naval vessel in less time. But what the devil! If one must be truthful, why reproach them for following their instincts, which are to seek every means possible to appear beautiful and to provide with their skill what they were denied by nature. Their desire is quite understandable, for if you take away their beauty what else do they have that's worthy of attention?

But what will we say about our young men, who should be

256

known and honored for their manliness? Instead of devoting
their time to acquiring it, they too waste time in beautifying
themselves and in putting on greasepaint and rouge. They copy
the women in all things: They have their mirrors, their combs,
their tweezers, their small cases with various instruments; they
have their little boxes, their phials and jars. They're experts in
making up, not heroic or elegiac verses, but with moss, amber,
and civet. They too wear hoopskirts to broaden their hips, and
they puff themselves out by filling their doublets at the chest with
wool-batten; and with cardboards or felt they expand themselves
and broaden their shoulders as they wish. Many whose legs
resemble those of a crane give form to their thighs and calves by
means of a double lining. Now, if one is going to waste time in
adorning oneself, it's more excusable for women to do so; and
thus it's only right that I give Corisca time to beautify herself. I'll
use this time to assail Crisobolo whom I'll get to surrender just as
the procurer did.

Well, then, let the army of lies come before me and let's despoil
this rather tenacious old man. In any case, it's fitting for him to
become my tributary. Favor me, Fortune, for I reaffirm my vow;
let all the glory be mine alone. Forward, onward. I want to
approach the enemy's doors, and by knocking on them, I'll catch
the guards unawares.

Scene Four
SERVANT; FULCIO; CRISOBOLO

SERV: Who's that knocking?

FUL: Tell Crisobolo that a servant of one of his best friends wants to
speak to him about something important.

SERV: If you want to speak to him, why don't you come inside?

FUL: There are good reasons why I want to wait for him out here;
he won't regret this inconvenience when he hears what I have to
say.

CRIS: Who is it that wants me at this hour?

FUL: Forgive me if I disturb you, but the person who sent me doesn't
want me to be recognized by your servants nor does he want
them to know who sent me. Have them go back inside.

CRIS: Go into the house and wait for me.——Now tell me what you
have to say.

FUL: I was sent to see you by my young master, the son of the
captain of justice, who, because of his close friendship with
your son, esteems you and loves you as a father; and, for this
reason, when he can do something useful for you and to your
honor and can help you avoid censure, he will never fail to do so.

CRIS: I thank him, and I'll always be obliged to him.

FUL: Now, listen. As he was leaving the house to take a stroll, as young men are accustomed to do—and I was with him—we came upon a certain procurer, as luck would have it, at the foot of the stairs, and he claimed to be a neighbor of yours.

CRIS: Well, then?

FUL: He was shouting angrily and complaining a great deal about you and your Erofilo to some people who were with him.

CRIS: What was he saying?

FUL: If Caridoro hadn't stopped him he was going to go straight to the captain of justice to complain and inform him about a fraud that it seems your Erofilo committed against him; and if he's telling the truth, it's a very serious charge.

CRIS: Now see how much trouble is in prospect for me because of the imprudence of that silly fool!

FUL: He said that earlier today he had dressed up a cheat in the clothes of a merchant and had sent him there with a certain deposit.

CRIS: See how the devil still meddles in this!

FUL: Having left the deposit, the cheat took one of his women. I didn't hear all the details, for Caridoro sent me off in a hurry to warn you.

CRIS: We're much obliged to him; he's done the duty of a gentleman and a friend.

FUL: The two persons who I told you were with the procurer seem ready to testify on his behalf and accuse you.

CRIS: What could they accuse me of?

FUL: They claim that the cheat is in your house and that the fraud was carried out with your knowledge.

CRIS: With my knowledge?

FUL: So they say; and, if I remember well, I think they also said that you entered his house with some people and removed a coffer or a strongbox. Caridoro sent me off in such a hurry to see you that I couldn't hear the details. Now, what my master sent me to tell you is that he'll do everything in his power to ensure that the procurer doesn't get to see the captain of justice tonight. Meanwhile, try to calm him down and do what you can so that he won't complain to the captain, for if he complains to him not only will you suffer, but your son will be publicly shamed.

CRIS: What provision can I make? What remedy can I find?

FUL: Have him give back the girl.

CRIS: He can't, for he doesn't have her and he doesn't know who took her away.

FUL: Oh, that's too bad.

CRIS: It couldn't be worse.

FUL: What shall we do, then?

CRIS: How in heaven's name should I know? No one is more miserable than I am.

FUL: The easiest and best thing to do is to pay the procurer for the girl; at least give him what he could have gotten for her, and that would keep him quiet.

CRIS: It seems strange to me that I have to spend my money this way; I'm not used to spending it unless it's on something that benefits me.

FUL: One cannot always make a profit, Crisobolo; however, if by investing a small sum of money one can avoid considerable injury and, besides this, disgrace and public shame, it can be called more than a small gain. If my master, the captain, finds out that your Erofilo has ruined and misused a poor foreigner by such deceit, where will you find yourself? Will you be able to bear having your son undergo an inquiry, having him called to the dock, and having a ban pronounced against him? Besides this, you have the reputation of being the richest man in Sibaris; and, while others might get away with paying a small amount in compensation, you wouldn't get by without paying a great many scudi. You're a prudent man; you understand what I mean.

CRIS: What do you advise me to do?

FUL: The procurer is poor and, like others in his trade, he's timid and cowardly. If the girl were paid for, he would keep his mouth shut. Our Caridoro has already given him to understand that taking you to court would do him more harm than good, for you have enough money ...

CRIS: Good Lord, I have much less than everyone thinks.

FUL: ... to keep the lawsuit going for the rest of his life; and that you're not without good friends and relatives who would make him regret having troubled you.

CRIS: Do you know how much he wants for the girl or what he could have gotten for her?

FUL: I heard that a merchant from Thessaly had offered him a hundred and forty ducats; but that he wouldn't let her go for under two hundred.

CRIS: That's too much. One could buy fifty cows for less. I won't have anything to do with it. Let him complain and do the worst he can.

FUL: I'm surprised that you value such a small amount ...

CRIS: Does it seem small to you?

FUL: ... more than your own son, more than yourself, more than your honor. I'll report to my master, then, that you don't intend to do anything.

CRIS: Couldn't we keep him quiet for less?

FUL: One could slit his throat with a knife; that would cost less, and it would keep him quiet.

CRIS: I don't mean that; yet, two hundred scudi or two hundred ducats seems such a large sum.

FUL: I agree. Maybe you could appease him with less. I believe that if he received the same amount that he was offered before, he would remain quiet.

CRIS: And no less?

FUL: I wish, for your sake, that I could keep him quiet without any expense. Pardon me, if I give you some advice. I'll tell you anyway. Why don't you send Erofilo with me right now with the amount you think would suffice. Caridoro will see to it that the procurer comes to an agreement with him and that he spends as little as possible. He won't be able to refuse; all of us will get on him and make him give in.

CRIS: Wouldn't it be much better if I went myself?

FUL: Not in my judgment. If the procurer sees that you're so interested in this matter he'll think that Erofilo cheated him with your consent; and he'll hesitate and be as stubborn as a mule, hoping to get you to pay more. On the contrary, I think it best for Erofilo to go alone and pretend that he's seeking this accord without your knowledge and that he managed to borrow the money from some friends or, better still, that he borrowed it with great difficulty.

CRIS: Have him go alone? Naturally, by God, for he's such a cautious youth! He would immediately be taken in and led by the nose like a buffalo.

FIL: Don't you have any among your servants who are experienced enough to be able to deal with him? Vulpino seems capable and quick-witted; he would be perfect for the job. You couldn't find anyone better.

CRIS: That little thief? He was the chief cause; he was the director and the instigator of this trouble and of all this scandal. I have him in irons and, by God, I'm determined to punish him as he deserves.

FUL: Come now, Crisobolo, don't let your anger get the better of you and cloud your reason. Send him with your son; you couldn't do any better, believe me.

CRIS: He's the worst villain . . .

FUL: The greater the villain he is, the more useful he'll be in this matter. So send him anyway; you couldn't choose someone more able from among a thousand men. Send him with your son, and have them go right away.

CRIS: I suppose I'm forced to have recourse to him, even though he
is what he is and I'd like to punish him. I know of no one else
among all my servants who can put two words together. God
only knows how much this bothers me!

FUL: Forget it; you'll be able to punish him some other time when
you find it more convenient.

CRIS: The fact is, it pains me, and it's rather a tough bone to chew.
But don't go away; wait for them here. I'll have both of them go
with you.

FUL: Go ahead; I'll wait.——Now comes the triumph that I really
deserve; now it's fitting that this head of mine, so full of wisdom,
be crowned with a laurel, for I've routed my enemies and defeated
them. I've destroyed and razed their strongholds and have
invaded them in force. I've captured their fortresses and burned
them. I've sacked [their territories], I've levied taxes on them,
and I've made them tributaries of my treasury for greater sums
than I had hoped for at the beginning, and all this without any
injury to me or my forces.

Now, Fortune, if you'll continue to provide me with successes,
as you have been doing, then nothing remains to be done except
to fulfill the vow that I made to stay drunk in your honor for
three full days, and on wine more putrid than Moschino[22] and
his friends ever tasted. Ah, there, the door's opening; perhaps
it's Erofilo and Vulpino. It doesn't look like them. Who's that
fellow? Now I recognize him: he's our merchant whose tongue
was loosed and whose speechlessness was cured by the miracle of
the sacred rope.

SCENE FIVE
TRAPPOLA; FULCIO

TRAP: Never again will I do someone a favor at the risk of injury to
myself. It's my fault, and it's also due to Vulpino's carelessness
that I was almost tied up like a thief and sent to the captain of
justice. If he got hold of me, he wouldn't have failed to have
me hanged right off. He would have given me two lashes even
before he knew anything about me; then he would have questioned me about this and that, all the time having me singing in
midair like a lark. . . .

FUL: (He guessed correctly.)

TRAP: I ran the risk of never seeing Naples again, although they
might have raised me high enough above the ground that the
trees wouldn't prevent me from seeing it from afar.

FUL: (He was lucky that Crisobolo decided to let him go without doing anything else to him.)

TRAP: Now that I escaped this time, like a virtuous woman, I won't let them catch me again. If I'm to swindle anyone else and do wicked things, I'm going to do them for my own and not for someone else's benefit.

FUL: (He's not repenting for being a villain, but only for doing villainous things without profit.)

TRAP: I wasn't even able to get a supper out of it; and this because I had planned to enjoy myself and to continue in my bliss until dawn.

FUL: (One's plans don't always succeed.)

TRAP: I especially regret it because I'm very hungry tonight. If I return to the inn I'll provide that fool of a peasant with something to laugh at; yet I'm forced to return there, for I have no other place where I can get food. If it weren't for my hunger pangs, I'd forego eating so as not to let him perceive that which, if he does know, would give him great pleasure. But I would sooner suffer his mockery than have this hunger gnaw at my stomach all night and eat it away.

FUL: (I think that would be better, for hunger surpasses all other ailments; being mocked and laughed at isn't nearly so hazardous. But there, I hear the door being opened, and I see my soldiers returning to their captain laden with rich booty.)

Scene Six
VULPINO; EROFILO; FULCIO

VULP: Don't worry, I'll try to keep him quiet with as little expense as possible; and I hope to do better than if you yourself went there. Leave it to me; I know that you'll be pleased with my work. Oh, I see Fulcio.

ERO: Where is he?

VULP: Over there.

ERO: I see him. Oh, Fulcio, how will we ever thank you in a way that would be commensurate and appropriate for the favors you've done for us? If I placed all my worldly goods at your disposal they would seem insufficient to discharge my enormous obligation to you.

FUL: It would be enough for me, Erofilo, to have you regard me kindly.

VULP: Oh, my unfailing hope, oh, my refuge, oh, my only real salvation! Fulcio, you've delivered me from immense tribulation; you've freed this poor life of mine from the cruelest of torments, and I place it forever entirely at your command.

FUL: These are favors, these are services, that we owe one another.

Don't mention it, Vulpino. Erofilo, do you think that I was able to find enough funds, to raise plenty of money as I promised you?

ERO: More than was necessary.

VULP: If you have more than you need, then return the surplus to your father.

ERO: No, I wouldn't do that.

FUL: Nor does Fulcio advise you to.

ERO: I'm not going to take it myself either.

FUL: What's left over will be enough for you to have a good time with Eulalia for a few days.

ERO: How much should we give Lucramo?

FUL: As little as possible. Caridoro has to contribute his half.

ERO: Take it and do what you want with it.

FUL: No, you take it instead and, as soon as I've brought the girl to Caridoro, I'll meet you at Galante's house.——

Now, you in the audience may as well go home, for the girl whom I'm going to take with me doesn't want to be seen, perhaps because she's not as well prepared as she would like to be. I mean well adorned, for in every other respect she's no less prepared than any other woman is at any time. And, as the procurer has to flee, he wouldn't want, nor would it be desirable for him, to be seen by such a large crowd.

Exactly why Ariosto rewrote the *Coffer* is not certain. In the new prologue he complains that the play had been printed by literary pirates and the text distorted; in fact, the very first edition was leaked to the printers by the players and not given by the author. Yet the fact that the second *Coffer* was a complete renovation rather than a correction or a recasting of the original points to other motives. It may be that once Ariosto had turned to verse he wanted to redo all his plays in the *sdrucciolo* form (the *Pretenders* had been rewritten in verse some years before) or merely that a more mature poet saw the possibilities of improving his play, incorporating additional criticisms of Ferrarese society. The final version of the *Coffer* received its initial performance in Ferrara at the carnival of 1531.

1. A Greek colony in Magna Graecia situated on the Gulf of Taranto near the northern limits of Calabria (at approximately the site of the modern town of Sibari). During the sixth century B.C., when Sibaris was at the height of its power, it gained a reputation, perhaps unfounded, for luxury and immorality. The city was destroyed by its rival Croton in 510 B.C.

2. See preliminary note.

3. An island west of the Gulf of Naples.

4. *Picciolo.* See the *Necromancer,* n. 5.

5. See the *Necromancer,* n. 4.

6. See the *Necromancer,* n. 8.

7. Drepano or Trapani: a city situated on the extreme western end of Sicily.

8. See first version, n. 7.

9. See first version, n. 9.

10. Francolino: that is, where lodging is free (*franco*). See the *Necromancer,* n. 16.

11. The text has . . . *che i partiti entrar fan gli uomini/ in galea* (literally: ". . . that profits get men aboard a galley"). This can mean either that the pursuit of profits leads men to illegal practices and eventually to the galleys or that the desire for gain can move men to board a boat. In the latter case Lucramo could be referring to his own plans.

12. See first version, n. 4.

13. Furbo's line and the first part of Lucramo's speech are in jargon. See first version, n. 11.

14. See the *Pretenders,* n. 18.

15. . . . *che non suonano due ore.* For the method of determining modern time equivalents see the *Lena,* n. 6.

16. See first version, n. 10.

17. Taroc or tarok or tarock: a popular European card game played with a pack consisting of twenty-two tarots or pictorial cards serving as trumps plus the equivalent of a modern deck of playing cards.

18. See first version, n. 14.

19. See the *Necromancer,* n. 5.

20. The *soldo* was a small Italian coin, theoretically worth a twentieth of a Carolingian *lira,* or twelve *denarii.* It came into popularity in the fifteenth century when the high cost of silver resulted in a silver *denarius* that was too small for practical usage.

21. The text has *beccio:* that is, *bezzo,* a Venetian coin worth six *denarii* ~ half-*soldo,* first minted in 1497.

22. Antonio Magnanino, known as Messer Moschino, was a person of some importance at the court of Hercules I. He had the reputation of being the outstanding Ferrarese toper of his day. See M. Catalano, "Messer Moschino (Beoni e buffoni ai tempi di L. Ariosto," in *Giornale Storico della Letteratura Italiana* 88 (1926): 30–31. See Ariosto, *Satire* 2, ll. 64–65 and *Orlando Furioso*, canto 14, stanza 124.

THE STUDENTS
I Studenti

A Comedy Originally in Verse

THE SCHOLASTICS
La Scolastica

Continuation by Gabriele Ariosto

CHARACTERS

BONIFAZIO	*An old man*
MASTER CLAUDIO	*A scholar*
MASTER EURIALO	*A scholar, Bartolo's son*
ACCURSIO	*Eurialo's servant*
PISTONE	*Bartolo's servant*
VERONESE	*An old woman*
IPPOLITA	*Eurialo's sweetheart*
STANNA	*Bartolo's maid*
RICCIO	*A messenger*
FRIAR	
MASTER BARTOLO	*Eurialo's father*
MASTER LAZARO	*Doctor of Law, Flamminia's father*
FLAMMINIA (silent)	*Lazaro's daughter*
LUCREZIA (*silent*)	*Lazaro's wife*
GIANNELLO (*silent*)	*Bartolo's servant*

The action takes place in Ferrara

PROLOGUE BY GABRIELE ARIOSTO[1]

I HAVE BEEN SENT HERE TO RECITE THE PROLOGUE OF A PLAY CALLED the *Scholastics*. After preparing the play for public performance, the author decided to give it this title because it is about two scholars. These scholars are not so engrossed in their studies that they don't have time to chase after girls, as is the custom.

I have been sent to do the prologue by someone who has taken pains to please you. In doing this, there's no need to follow the style of these new comics, who don't use their prologues to present the plots of their plays or to answer the slanders of their competitors, as did Plautus and Terence.[2] Rather, they have begun to torment women, whether rightly or wrongly, touching as much as possible on the places that hurt most—especially on those places that are not very nice to write about. They don't realize how little glory there is in this, for everyone knows how easily women are overcome: all it takes is a small shove and they fall over backward. This is not without danger, for, while they don't break a shoulder or an elbow, nevertheless, as a result of the fall they often become so swollen that it seems a miracle. So, instead of presenting the plot, replying to slander, or offending women, our prologue will have another purpose.

I would like you to know that shortly before your playwright gave up his body to the earth and his soul to the Eternal Mover, he had begun a play and was getting ready to finish it, just as he had done his others. It was always his intention to gain the favor of his Prince, of foreigners, townsmen, and noblemen who had enjoyed his stories many times in public and in private, so much so that they still praise them. When he departed, the story was left unfinished; but the interest of those who had seen the beginning remained. And so, a number of intimate friends of the deceased poet turned to one of his three surviving brothers and begged and pleaded with him to finish the story. These friends all followed the same line of argument: both brothers had had the same teacher;[3] they had pursued the same course of study; and time had been no less propitious to the one than to the other, for there was not much difference in their ages.

Their pleadings, however, fell on deaf ears. The brother knew that his talents and his energies were quite insufficient for such an enterprise. Much more is needed than to have seen a grammar book, to have mastered the accents and the syllables, to have studied Horace's *Poetics*, and to have devoured as many books as are printed. Whoever intends to write fine verses and adorn the stage with beautiful subjects must have help from above. Besides,

he realized how difficult it was—almost impossible—to figure out
how the original author had proposed to conclude the story he had
begun; and he was convinced that it would have been easier to
write an entirely new play.

There were still other reasons for him to shy away from the ranks
of the poets, for nowadays they seem to be a laughingstock. It isn't
enough that their toil and long vigils go unrewarded; but a thousand infamies are ascribed to them: they say that poets don't
believe in things divine because they sometimes speak of Jupiter,
sometimes of Venus. Yet, these slanders hardly penetrate the
surface. I don't want to go deeper into this matter now, nor will I
philosophize when I'm barely capable of reciting a prologue. It is
said that if you don't have an ox then plow with a donkey. I don't
understand this proverb too well, but I do know that there's no
harm in using every available means when necessary. They also
unjustly condemn the poets for hanging on like leeches and drawing out the lifeblood of those who listen to their verses. But who is
there who doesn't lose himself in his own work when it is a question
of glory? Other accusations have been made against them—
wrongly as well—but I won't dwell upon these. In any case, the
minds of those previously mentioned, who wanted him to finish the
play, were put at ease. Then, a few days afterward, he received
word that even his Prince wanted him to complete the work, and
this certainly was not because he knew how to do it, for a good
critic could see, as I have told you, that he has no aptitude for this
sort of thing.

The person of whom I speak did everything possible to please His
Excellency; and, knowing of no one better to turn to, he decided,
with humble prayers and tears, to try to bring his brother's spirit
back from celestial regions so that it could let him know how the
story should end. So he called upon his dead brother. He begged
him and informed him of the wishes of the Prince, while reminding
him of the long and hospitable stay that he had enjoyed at his court
and of the innumerable favors that the Prince had granted him.
After he had called upon him three or four times in prayer, his
brother appeared in a dream in the same form and in the same
clothes in which he had appeared on this stage several times in the
past when he recited prologues, took part in the plays, and even
directed them. And he said to him: "Brother, your many pleas,
and, even more, the respect that I have for my Prince, have induced
me to tell you the ending of the play. You must commit it to
memory so well that your mind will be an ample receptacle for the
large part that remains to be finished." It was well before dawn
when he began exactly where he had left off and, in the clearest

words, he brought the play to a conclusion, to the point where one says, "Now, audience, go in peace." And, having finished, he went to rest in peace. The listener arose at once and, seeing that it was now light enough to write by, and not trusting his memory, he took up his pen and didn't put it down until he had recorded the ending of the story just as the saintly spirit had dictated it to him.

Listen, then to the *Scholastics*, which was written entirely by your poet; but don't be surprised if the style of the last part seems somewhat different, for the dead are not like the living. As is usually the case, the plot will be revealed by the first characters to appear on the stage. Those of you who like comedies, pay attention; those who don't can leave, or, on seeing the shining faces of so many beautiful women, can stay and be quiet.

ACT ONE
SCENE ONE

BONIFAZIO, *an old man;* MASTER CLAUDIO, *a scholar*

BON: I'm sorry that you decided to leave, Master Claudio. It's not that I lack other students to whom I can rent my rooms, for there have been many inquiries about them; but in these few days I have taken such a liking to you that it seems as if you are my own son.

CLAUD: I thank you for your kindness and I will always be greatly obliged to you wherever I may be. Really, I feel as sorry as you do about leaving; and you can be sure that your sweet and loving nature has tied me to you with such a strong bond of friendship that I don't think it will be dissolved as long as I live.

BON: Why must you leave so suddenly?

CLAUD: Because of the bad luck that usually follows me wherever I go. And so that you won't think that my leaving is due to flightiness and that I go willingly, I'll tell you something that I wouldn't reveal to many people; I mustn't hide it from you, for I consider you almost like a father. Now, listen.

BON: I'm listening.

CLAUD: When my father first sent me to university from Verona, my native city, I went to Pavia and lodged with a certain Master Lazaro, who taught civil law[4] there in the evening. At about the same time Master Eurialo, the son of Bartolo, your neighbor, came to live there and he, also, enrolled at the university. Here began that friendship, that brotherhood between us that I have often told you about.

BON: Was this, perhaps, the main reason why you came here?

CLAUD: I admit it was a reason, but not the main one. But listen, I'll tell you the whole story. This Doctor Lazaro has a very beautiful

daughter whose name is Flamminia, and the first time I laid eyes
on her I fell ardently in love with her and she with me. However,
we did not fulfill our love because her father and mother watched
over her day and night with great care. The help that I got from
her nurse and from Eurialo—his was more unpretentious and
discreet—was of little avail. He helped me partly out of friendship and partly because I was doing him the same sort of favor.
It was through my efforts that he was enjoying a pretty and very
sweet girl, although of humble origins, who was there in the
service of a countess with whom I was quite friendly and on
familiar terms. In the same household there was also a woman
from my native city whom I knew I could count on. She served
me in such a way that within a few days Eurialo succeeded in
his designs.

Now, coming back to my case, my pleasure was short-lived,
for we couldn't keep the affair secret. Her mother began to
suspect it, and then Master Lazaro did as well. Prudent man that
he is, showing no anger, he found a good reason—a different
one—to throw me out of the house with an appropriate good-
bye. Despite this, I continued to court Flamminia by appearing
on her street all too frequently, by often stopping at her corner,
and by performing acts and making gestures that could reflect
upon the entire family. My behavior was such that the doctor
resolved to have me remain in Pavia no longer; he succeeded.
One night, shortly thereafter, one of the friends of the rector
was murdered. I happened to be nearby that evening and ran
to see the commotion. The doctor immediately had me accused,
and proceedings were begun against me. All of a sudden I found
myself condemned for contempt of court and I was forced to
flee and leave the company of my gentlemen friends and fellow
students; but my greatest sorrow was to lose sight of my Flamminia. And if it were not for the fact that Eurialo often sent me
news about her in his letters, I don't know how I could have re-
sisted for so long the desire that gnaws at me, afflicts me, and
mortifies me day and night.

BON: If you loved her so much you should have asked for her as
your wife. Perhaps the doctor would have given her to you; I
wonder why you didn't do so then.

CLAUD: I wouldn't have dared to ask for her or take her as a wife
without the consent of my father, who was alive at the time;
and there is no doubt that he would never have consented to
it. I knew what his intentions were: to have me first complete my
studies and get a degree and then to select for me a very rich wife
from my own city.

BON: Now that your father is gone and you're free to act, why don't you and your friends try to convince him to give her to you?

CLAUD: I wrote to Eurialo a few days ago asking him to begin negotiations, and his reply made me leave Padua immediately and come here. He informed me that Master Lazaro had tried to obtain a teaching position here through his father, Bartolo. He was not able to continue teaching at Pavia, for they had stopped the salaries of all doctors and had suspended studies because the wars were expanding every day.[5] Eurialo said that he actually had obtained a position and was getting ready to move, with his entire family, to this city, where he was to live in their house. He advised me to be here also, for things are better accomplished in person than by letters. And, for this reason, I came and took lodging in your house so that I could . . .

BON: I understand.

CLAUD: . . . enjoy the sight of my Flamminia all the more.

BON: You couldn't have found a more convenient place.

CLAUD: Now that I'm here, it seems that it will no longer be possible for me to continue studies in this city. As you know, Eurialo arrived the day before yesterday with news that Master Lazaro has obtained a chair at Padua and would be heading there via the Po road that leads to Venice without coming here at all.

BON: Oh! So this is the reason why Bartolo, who has been waiting for him for some time, left with his household this morning saying that he was going as far as Naples.

CLAUD: You can now understand, without my saying it, what induces me, what forces me, what makes it necessary for me to leave Ferrara and go to Padua. In order not to lose any time, I'll go to where the teamsters gather to find out whether a boat will be leaving Francolino[6] for Venice either today or tomorrow. If I can, I want to be in Padua before Master Lazaro.

BON: I had better go inside and have dinner cooked so that we can dine when he returns. Here's Bartolo's son coming this way. I'll find out whether Bartolo has left. Good day, Master Eurialo.

SCENE TWO
EURIALO; BONIFAZIO

EUR: May God give you a thousand of them, Bonifazio.

BON: Has he left?

EUR: Just now. He probably hasn't reached the bridge yet.

BON: Why did he wait so long? I should think that he would have been at San Prospero[7] by now.

EUR: That ass, Giannuolo, had promised to lend him a horse that, to hear him last night, was a Pegasus; but then all he let him

273

have was a mule that stood on three legs like a trestle and is worse tempered than the devil.

BON: How did he manage?

EUR: We went to a livery stable on the way to the bridge—I think it's the last one—and there he obtained an old nag with the finest gait in the world, but in such a sorry state that it took us more than an hour to fit it out with a harness, stirrups, a collar, and reins. Finally, I got him on the horse and away he went. May God guide him.

BON: Will he be traveling alone?

EUR: A servant is waiting for him at Bologna—one who has been in our employ on other occasions—and he has two draft horses ready for him, according to what he writes, perfectly suited for the trip. Once he arrives in Bologna he intends to stay there three or four days until he comes across some party that's going to Naples.

BON: What business takes him there?

EUR: He made a vow to do so many years ago. Is Master Claudio at home?

BON: No.

EUR: When he returns tell him that I'd like him to have an informal lunch with me today.

BON: I'll tell him. Is there anything else you want of me?

EUR: No, nothing else.

BON: (Since he's going to give him lunch, I'd better not cook those partridges. I'll give orders not to put them on the fire.)

EUR: That fellow over there looks like Accursio. Is it he or isn't it? There's no doubt, it's my servant, Accursio, whom I had left behind in Pavia to see to it that my books and cases were loaded on a boat. He must have brought me a letter from my Ippolita. Oh, my life, how sad and painful it is for me not to be able to see you! It would be impossible for me to live without your presence.

SCENE THREE
EURIALO; ACCURSIO

EUR: When did you arrive?

ACC: Just now.

EUR: Do you have any letters?

ACC: I have so few that I can scarcely read, even though I've been at the university with you.

EUR: Don't joke with me. Did you bring me any letters from my love?

ACC: No, sir.

EUR: You would have me curse, growl, and lose my patience. Why are you laughing? Give them to me. Don't torment me, for I don't believe that you would be such an ass as to come here without speaking to her; nor would she have ever let you go without writing to me.

ACC: The fact is, I did speak to her; and still I've come without letters.

EUR: Alas! How is it possible? I mean ... But you're laughing ...

ACC: Can I not laugh and still not have any letters? What if I have something from her that's better than letters?

EUR: What?

ACC: I'll tell you; but, first, tell me, when is the old man leaving for Naples?

EUR: He's just left and he couldn't have gone more than a mile.

ACC: Tell me the truth.

EUR: That's the truth; he's left.

ACC: God speed his journey. Now, Master Eurialo, you can consider yourself very lucky that he's gone.

EUR: How come?

ACC: Had he not left today there was the chance that instead of bringing you joy I would have brought you trouble and sorrow.

EUR: What did you bring?

ACC: I can say to you that had I brought it my shoulders would have been too heavily burdened.

EUR: Come on, out with it.

ACC: If I tell you that Ippolita has come to Ferrara, would you consider it a miracle?

EUR: How is it that she's come?

ACC: By boat.

EUR: My Ippolita is in Ferrara?

ACC: Yes, she's in Ferrara?

EUR: Where?

ACC: I left her at Saint Paul's Gate, and she's waiting for me to bring her your response.

EUR: I cannot believe you unless I see her.

ACC: Come and you'll see her.

EUR: How is it that she came?

ACC: I told you, by boat.

EUR: I don't mean that; I'm asking you through what means and how it was that she left her mistress's house.

ACC: The usual way, the way everybody does; she must have come out the door.

EUR: You're torturing me and mocking me, you rascal!

ACC: On the contrary, I'm telling you the truth, and you won't

275

believe me.

EUR: Are you sure that she has come?

ACC: I'm certain of it.

EUR: Oh, my precious soul, oh my life! I'm consumed; I feel my heart melting with joy. But tell me exactly what happened.

ACC: I will, if you'll listen to me.

EUR: I'm listening.

ACC: I met the Veronese woman and told her that I was going to leave the following Tuesday—it was on a Friday—and I said that if Ippolita wanted to write, she could [send a letter along with me]. With tears in her eyes and excited with anger, she apologized for not being able to tell her this because that very day the countess had thrown her out of the house to her disgrace. Some evil-minded person had revealed to her the love affair that Ippolita had carried on with you through the woman's connivance. [She also said] that the girl had received a great deal of abuse and beatings, and there was more to come. But she assured me that some way or other she would let Ippolita know what I told her.

Then, that same evening she came to see me bringing two small chests and a sack full of odds and ends, and she asked me to put them on the boat along with your things. I took them without giving it a thought. The next day—that is, Saturday—I heard it said in town that Ippolita and the Veronese woman had run away from the countess, and nobody knew where to. To tell you the truth, I was worried, although I thought that they had headed in this direction; I was afraid of the dangers that they might have encountered along the way.

EUR: They were certainly very brave.

ACC: Rather bold and audacious.

EUR: On the contrary, pleasant, gentle, and lovable.

ACC: I had our belongings loaded on the boat and I started on my way; and, when we stopped for customs at Piacenza, I found the women waiting for me.

EUR: This isn't the first or the second sign, but the clearest indication, of her love for me. Continue.

ACC: I then had her come aboard the boat and brought her here. But my heart was continually pounding for fear either that her mistress would send one of her servants after me, or that she would be abducted during the voyage, or that, if we found your father here when we arrived, you would not be able to receive her; so that instead of giving you joy, her coming would only make trouble for you.

EUR: Her coming at any time, whether or not my father is here, could only be a joy to me; and I'll always be grateful to her.

ACC: I had better go back and bring them here.

EUR: Where?

ACC: Here to the house.

EUR: Here to the house? Good Lord, no! Don't you know how disagreeable Pistone is? He would say that I'm starting off too soon.

ACC: What the devil! I'm really surprised at you! Are you going to submit to a rascal? You're no longer a child. Show him that you're going to be the master, and if he tries to lord it over you, make him look like an ass.

EUR: If my old man were so far away that there would be no possibility of his returning if Pistone wrote to him, then I would follow your advice; but you can be certain that the very hour, the very minute, the instant they enter the house he would send someone after the old man and make such a fuss that he would return. It would be better if we found them lodging today with a good woman.

ACC: Where can one find a good one?

EUR: How do I know? I meant to say one who isn't too bad.

ACC: In the meantime do you want them to remain hungry in the church, or do you expect them to be reduced to eating with the friars in the refectory? But let's do this another way.

EUR: How?

ACC: Let it be known in the house that they're the wife and daughter of Master Lazaro who were supposed to come but who wrote saying that they weren't coming. We'll say that they've changed their minds again and that they want to see Ferrara before going on to Padua.

EUR: That's a good idea; but how can this appear very likely if they've come without Master Lazaro and if they don't even have a maid with them?

ACC: We'll say that Master Lazaro has gone on to Venice with his household and belongings along the other branch of the Po; and that, being a respectful and considerate man, he didn't want us to incur too many expenses. Let me take care of it.

EUR: Do whatever you think is best.

ACC: You can begin by finding Pistone and telling him that Master Lazaro's wife and daughter have reached Saint Paul's Gate and that they're coming here; tell him that I ran ahead to inform you about it and have returned to meet them. Then wait for me in the house; and, in the meantime, have the room swept, and have the beds made and the shoulder boards put in place. Show how concerned you are, as if indeed persons of quality were coming to your house; and, above all, see to it that you set a good table.

EUR: What are you going to do?

ACC: What else should I do except go back to where I left them and tell them to come along?

EUR: Go, then, but advise them of the situation and instruct them before they come.

ACC: I'll advise them; but it will be your job to instruct them.

EUR: Stop joking. Instruct them about how to behave.

ACC: I'll make them so learned you would think they had been brought up at the university. But wait a moment. I almost forgot something. By chance I let the Veronese woman know that Master Claudio was here, and she begged me to ask you please not to tell him that either she or Ippolita are in the city.

EUR: Why?

ACC: I think I know why. It was Master Claudio who placed her with the countess, and she's ashamed and thinks that the fact that she ran away from her and led Ippolita astray may reflect on him. Furthermore, she told me that, since the countess was going to send someone after her, she was sure that she'll send him to Ferrara; and, since Master Claudio is here, the messenger will go to him as he's a very good friend and close associate of the countess.

EUR: Don't the Veronese woman and Ippolita know that if Master Claudio is a friend of the countess he is a closer friend of mine? Nothing harmful to me would ever escape his lips.

ACC: But don't you realize that it would be easier for Master Claudio to say that they are not here, believing that he was telling the truth, than to say something that he knows is a lie? Words that proceed from the heart flow better than those that are merely mouthed and are contrary to one's true feelings.

EUR: You reason well. Now, tell her not to worry, for if she doesn't think I should, I won't say anything to him.

ACT TWO
Scene One
BONIFAZIO; PISTONE, *a servant*

BON: I had better go to the piazza and arrange with the beadle to find me a nice young man to rent the rooms; I don't want them to be vacant now that Master Claudio said he's leaving.

PIST: (I'm going to leave the house and I won't be found there today until Vespers have rung.)

BON: Here comes the dregs of all the world's negligent, arrogant, and gossiping servants. I don't know how Bartolo has been able to put up with him so long.

PIST: (They should have sent a messenger ahead or have written and have given at least a half-day's notice. For the past month I have heard nothing but "They're coming," "They're not coming." The final word was "They're coming" and that arrived at a most inconvenient time for us. Now let them eat whatever is in the house and fend for themselves, for I cannot see how I can provide for them on such short notice. Even if I could, I don't have the time. The tasks that my master has given me are more important for me to do than stocking the pantry and preparing the table.)

BON: What are you talking about preparing?

PIST: Guests are coming.

BON: And who are they?

PIST: I can't tell you.

BON: Why not?

PIST: Because Eurialo has ordered those in the house not to say anything to outsiders.

BON: Come here and whisper it in my ear; he wasn't referring to me.

PIST: I don't know. He particularly specified that nothing be said to the young man who boards in your house.

BON: And why is this?

PIST: To tell you the truth, he also said not to tell you.

BON: Is that possible?

PIST: It's exactly as I told you. Nevertheless, I'm going to tell you anyway for I consider you one of us; also, the matter doesn't seem so important that I have to keep it secret. Let him crow as much as he wants. They're the same guests whom we have been expecting and who then wrote that they weren't coming. Now they have arrived unexpectedly when Bartolo is gone.

BON: And who are they? Is it Master Lazaro, the doctor from Pavia?

PIST: It's not Master Lazaro himself, but his wife and daughter. They'd like to see Ferrara. They took one of the cargo boats at Fellonica[8] and just two of them are coming. Our Accursio is the only other person with them.

BON: And where is Master Lazaro staying?

PIST: He's continuing down the other branch of the Po. It was said that he didn't want us to go to too much expense.

BON: He must really be a miser if he worries about such little things!

PIST: You mean big things, for they're already rather annoying to me.

BON: Will they stay long?

PIST: For five or six days. They'll wait for an old servant of theirs who should arrive soon and who will then accompany them to Padua.

BON: Why doesn't Eurialo want anyone to know?

PIST: In my opinion the women are embarrassed, for they're coming here without maids or servants. Well, I have to be going.

BON: The road is clear and free.

PIST: Now, for God's sake, Bonifazio, keep this a secret.

BON: Don't worry. You won't find a confidant more close-mouthed than me.——If a hundred people asked him he would tell all of them what he told me; but always on condition that they don't repeat it to anyone else. And I think he's lying when he claims that Eurialo ordered that nothing be said, especially to Master Claudio and me. That's just his usual way of relating stories, of sowing discord, and of starting quarrels and dissension. May God give him the plague.

Ah, those must be the women whom they're expecting, for I see Accursio coming with them. I want to see whether this Flamminia is as beautiful as Claudio claims she is and see if his judgment in love has been sound.

Scene Two

VERONESE, *an old woman*; IPPOLITA; ACCURSIO; BONIFAZIO

VER: Our actions and our words must be in keeping with the scheme that we decided upon, Ippolita. We mustn't let the other servants or the housemaids find out that we're not the persons who our mutual self-interest requires us to pretend to be.

IP: I'm sure I can do my part.

VER: Yes, if Eurialo wasn't around.

ACC: On the contrary, she'll do it better with him here.

VER: I wasn't talking about that. I meant that with him here it will be difficult for her not to make some gesture, not to stare at him more than she should, not to signal to him and smile at him, or flirt with him so that it would be very obvious to others that they're in love.

IP: If there is anyone here about whom I have to be careful I'll be reserved and modest, with my eyes lowered as if I were a nun.

ACC: There's our Eurialo's house.

IP: Oh, my dear sweetheart; oh, my life! It will be difficult to restrain myself from running and embracing him.

VER: You see, Accursio, how well she listens!

IP: Hurry up, old woman. Quicken your tortoise pace a little. Is it going to take you a hundred years to reach the house?

ACC: I guess it's impossible to lay down the law to lovers. Here we are at the house. Go inside.

IP: Go in, Mother.

VER: Go ahead, Daughter; I'll follow you.

ACC: This isn't a bad beginning.

SCENE THREE
BONIFAZIO, *alone*

BON: She's very beautiful and, good Lord, what a figure she has. But what am I waiting for? I'd better go find Claudio before someone else sees him and gives him the news ahead of me. Where should I look for him? He's going to leave tomorrow or perhaps even today. Maybe he went to say good-bye to his professors and his friends; or else he's gone to declare his goods at the customs house. It would be easier to find him and I would be more certain of doing so if I stayed here, and then I wouldn't waste my energy. It won't be ... But here he is, here he is, by God. It's him. He'd better buy me a drink, for I deserve it.

SCENE FOUR
MASTER CLAUDIO; BONIFAZIO

CLAUD: I don't know if he's telling the truth, but it doesn't seem possible that they would be coming without Master Lazaro. But if they really are coming, why has Eurialo ordered everyone in the house not to say anything to me? Even if he doesn't want outsiders to know about it—why he doesn't I don't know, nor can I imagine—at least he shouldn't hide the fact from me. Ah, here's where I can clarify the matter.

BON: What would you give me, Master Claudio, for some news that will make you very happy?

CLAUD: I know what it is, for I met Bartolo's servant at the corner, and he told me about it.

BON: Did Pistone tell it to you?

CLAUD: Yes, Pistone told it to me.

BON: What an idiot! First he begs me not to tell you and then he goes and tells you himself.

CLAUD: He asked me also to keep it a secret and not to say a word to anyone. But I don't believe him.

BON: On my word, believe him, for it's true. If you had arrived just a little earlier you would have seen them going inside.

CLAUD: You saw them?

BON: With my own eyes.

CLAUD: If you say that you saw them then I believe it. Who is with them?

BON: I saw no one other than the mother and daughter.

CLAUD: How is it possible that they don't even have a maid with

281

them? Well, Master Lazaro certainly has changed his ways. The flies about his house used to make him suspicious and he never would leave the house unless he first locked Flamminia in her room.[9] He would take the key with him, for he didn't trust his wife and he hardly trusted himself. So it seems to me a miracle to learn that now he let her come here without his protection— to a place where the young and old are generally given over to idleness, where they have nothing else in mind and no other occupation than to solicit women, and where women are more free to say and do what they wish than in any other city. Foreigners get so accustomed to the way of life here that even if it were Lucrezia and Virginia[10] who came here they would not be able to preserve their purity.

BON: Ah! You shouldn't say that, for you're greatly mistaken. Even though our women have their freedom, you must not think that they're better or worse than women elsewhere; and if, perhaps, there's some truth in what you say, why not put the blame on the men who allow it? But it seems to me that you're speaking out of anger rather than with reason. And whereas I thought that I would be bringing you joyful news, I see that the news I brought is sad and you're not pleased to learn that they're here.

CLAUD: To tell you the truth, Bonifazio, the fact that Eurialo has tried to hide this from me turns my stomach.

BON: Don't listen to that poltroon. I doubt whether Eurialo has given such an order; and even if he has, I wouldn't construe it as having bad intent. Perhaps he wanted to be the first to tell you the news or he wished to show her to you as a surprise.

CLAUD: That "perhaps" is a weak excuse. One can be certain about the things that one can see; the events of the future, though, are always in doubt, for they may or may not occur.

BON: Do you want me to remove your doubts and find out whether he had good or bad intentions in keeping their arrival secret?

CLAUD: I wish you would.

BON: I'll plant a spy in his house so that he won't be able to say or do the least little thing without our knowing it at once.

CLAUD: Please do that, and I'll pay whatever it costs.

BON: I don't want you to spend too much, but I'm sure that in the end you'll find that it's just a story. He wants to play a joke on you by having you show both surprise and joy on seeing her. But I just remembered that a short while ago Eurialo asked me to invite you to have an informal lunch with him; so, by God, you can see that what I said was correct. Here is his housemaid. I think she's coming to ask you in. If your stomach was upset before, you can settle it by eating.

Scene Five

STANNA, *a housemaid;* BONIFAZIO; MASTER CLAUDIO

STAN: I'll look for them, but it's always difficult to find any pigeons during the last days of the carnival, for the gentlemen who prepare feasts and banquets buy them a week or two earlier.

BON: Stanna would be just perfect if she would act as a spy.

CLAUD: It would be excellent if she were willing.

BON: She will; you'll see.

STAN: If I cannot find pigeons, I'll get a piece of veal, a duck, or something like it instead. But first I'll tell Master Claudio what I'm supposed to tell him.

BON: There, she mentioned your name. You'll see, in the end, that it's exactly as I thought.

STAN: Ah, there I see him just in time.——Master Claudio, my master, who had asked Bonifazio to invite you to dinner, sent me to let you know that he cannot have you over. He received some important news that necessitated his going out of town. He'll discharge his obligation another time.

CLAUD: As he pleases.

STAN: He begs your forgiveness.

CLAUD: There's nothing to forgive. Where is he?

STAN: He left a little while ago: he's going out of town.

BON: Am I correct in imagining that he's so indiscreet as to leave the ladies who came to his house by themselves?

STAN: What ladies?

BON: We saw them—don't deny it—and we're positive that Eurialo didn't go out of town. In fact, if he had started to leave, upon learning of their arrival, he would have flown back immediately —running wouldn't be fast enough for him—and with very good reason, by God, for she's a gorgeous girl and she comes from a good family.

STAN: Did you really see them?

BON: I saw two of them, mother and daughter, when they arrived. Treat them well and with honor, both because they deserve it and out of respect for Master Lazaro to whom, I hear, Eurialo is eternally obligated.

STAN: We're trying to do everything possible for them. It's true that everybody was unprepared for them when they came, as Bartolo is away.

BON: Don't say "everybody" for I know that even if the others weren't ready, you would always be.

STAN: You're trying to make fun of me.

BON: One always makes fun of older people who cannot turn the tables. But let's stop this nonsense. Come here. Would you do me a great favor, Stanna? We'll promise to keep it a secret; and we'll give you a tunic with silk sleeves. You have never dressed so well in your life.

STAN: I could use one; yet, whenever I can, I'm ready to serve you without any payment.

BON: My dear Stanna, for my sake and for your own benefit, I would like you, while being discreet, to find out whether Eurialo is in love with this girl. You can easily do that.

STAN: Why do you want to know?

BON: I'll tell you. We know that her father would like him to marry the girl and that Bartolo is so inclined. Bur Eurialo doesn't seem very pleased with her, if one is to believe what he says; and, to tell you the truth, we don't believe him. Try to find out what's what.

STAN: I know without looking any further that he's not telling the truth, and I'm positive that what you think is correct. They're in love with each other, and there's more than idle talk between them.

CLAUD: (Ah, pity me! It seems that I've put my finger in a hornet's nest.)

STAN: And, furthermore, her mother herself knows about their love. But, for God's sake, Bonifazio, don't say anything about it; don't let Eurialo know that I told you, for he ordered me specifically to keep quiet and to behave in such a way that neither you nor this young man would suspect that they're here.

BON: Wasn't I here in the street when they arrived? Don't worry that he knows about it. But what proof do you have that what you say is correct?

CLAUD: (Woe is me! I've looked for something that will prove to be unpleasant and annoying when I find it.)

STAN: I'll tell you. When the women arrived at the house a little while ago, I was ashamed to be seen, for I was all full of dust and black with smoke and soot, as I had just swept the fireplace and the room in which they would stay. I was unable to withdraw so I ran and hid in the room under a writing-desk with boards across the front; by peeking through the opening between the boards one could see and hear everything that went on in the room. From where I was I saw Eurialo come in, followed by the women and then Accursio. I didn't make a sound, and I saw Eurialo turn his head this way and that way two or three times and then run with open arms toward the girl and they embraced. Then they put their lips together, so that they seemed like a swallow feeding its young.

CLAUD: Did her mother see them?

STAN: In the same way that you see me. But that's nothing.

CLAUD: We've had enough; we don't care to hear any more.

BON: Keep your eyes open and report what you see.

STAN: Do you want anything else?

CLAUD: Is Eurialo at home?

STAN: What better place can he be?

BON: You said that he had left the city.

STAN: Maybe he's reached Ficarolo, or has gone beyond Garofalo to Pelosella.... [11]

CLAUD: For God's sake, send her away; she's killing me!

BON: Go ahead, don't waste any time, go. We'll pay you what's due you.

STAN: Debts always have to be paid.

BON: Well, Master Claudio, since Eurialo's invitation to dinner is like the one that young monks dream about when they're fasting in their dormitory, then we have to do what snails do when it's hot: live on the moisture in our own house. So I'll go home and have the partridges put back on the spit.

CLAUD: Go ahead and do whatever you want. As for me, my stomach is upset, and I don't think that I'll ever be able to recover.

BON: Now, why are you worrying about this? Do you expect to die from it? As if there weren't enough girls in the world! You're young, rich, and handsome. You'll have so many that you'll be sick and tired of them.

CLAUD: Alas! I want to die.

BON: Take heart.

CLAUD: Would you do me a favor? Let me alone.

BON: This would be shirking my duty, considering my love for you.

CLAUD: Since the only person in the world I love doesn't love me, since the only one I trusted betrayed me, I don't care for the love or friendship of anyone else. Everyone hates me; everyone cheats me and betrays me. Why shouldn't I hate everyone also and never be faithful to anyone? I'm going to treat all men and women alike, whoever they may be.

BON: These are not the words of one who has a masculine soul.

CLAUD: I don't know whether my soul is masculine or feminine. I do know that it's unhappy and that it regrets being part of me; and it's getting ready to leave me soon, for the person who could turn it as she wished has abandoned me.

BON: Such talk is not becoming to you—you who are so well versed in letters and in the writings of the philosophers and who should show wisdom to others.

CLAUD: Alas! Many things are written and read in books that are not borne out in practice.

BON: At least come in the house and give vent to your feelings as you wish, and don't stay out here in public shedding tears like a child who's been beaten. If you decide that you don't want any comfort or advice from me, at least I can keep you company in your crying and tears.

CLAUD: I don't want to remain in your house or in Ferrara, Bonifazio, any longer than it takes to pack my belongings so that they can be taken to Mantua for shipment to Verona. I'll go immediately to the port to see about this and then I'll find a horse to carry me away. I'll never be seen here again, nor in Padua, Bologna, or any other university town. I'll never again pore over textbooks or glosses, and I'll tear up and burn the books of Baldus, Cinus, Bartolus,[12] and others. May the day and the hour that I came into the world be cursed as well as that whore of a nurse who didn't drown me in the baby bath.

BON: Oh, he really is desperate! The poor fellow and all the other wretches who allow their intellect—the most precious thing that men have—to be taken over by that assassin whom they call Love! But here is Stanna returning.——Well, did you find any?

STAN: I found some without having to look too far; and they're lovely, upon my faith. Feel them.

BON: Oh, they're nice and firm!

STAN: I don't mean these; they're not to be cooked.

BON: No, not to be cooked, but to be enjoyed alive and intact.

STAN: They would be food for young men, not for you. They would harm you rather than help you.

BON: Listen, Stanna.

STAN: Let me go. I have enough to do without wasting time with idle talk.

BON: What if there were deeds?

STAN: I'd get up in the middle of the night to be there.

ACT THREE
SCENE ONE
EURIALO; ACCURSIO

EUR: Anyone who lets himself be governed by the mind of a woman or by those who try to please[13] women can never produce any good. I let myself be persuaded by her pleadings and by your urging that I conceal their arrival from Master Claudio. Now he knows they're here. Bonifazio, who saw them come, told him so, and even more; and he actually has led him to believe—what he and all my household believe—that Ippolita and the other woman are really Flamminia and her mother. Now that Master Claudio also believes this and also realizes that I've kept it secret from him, he undoubtedly suspects that I'm in love with her and that I have taken his place during his absence. He must really bear me ill will. If he continues in his erroneous belief, our long friendship will soon turn to hatred on his part. It would have been better had I informed him of the situation at the beginning.

ACC: We cannot undo what has already been done. Let's see if we can administer some emollient before the injury gets any worse. It would be best to call upon him and tell him the whole story.

EUR: And bring him to the house and let him see her. Let's remove his ignorance. Here is Pistone returning. I'll wait for him and bawl him out as he deserves. That ass always leaves the house when he sees that men are needed to do work.

Scene Two
PISTONE; EURIALO

PIST: Even if I had consulted an astrologer's horoscope I couldn't have set foot out of the house at a better time so that I would arrive at the right moment. I would like to think that it was God who inspired me to take that road today against my own inclinations, for I hadn't been on it in the last six months.

EUR: (From what I hear he's happy about the news he has.)

PIST: It was my good fortune to have met him when my need was greatest and there was little hope.

EUR: (He must have found some money or a ring or something like that. I'll find out.) What did you find, Pistone? I want to share it.

PIST: Your father, who . . .

EUR: God help me!

PIST: . . . has returned.

EUR: How is that?

PIST: He told me that hardly had he reached the bridge when his horse lost a shoe and he had to take the animal to the blacksmith to have it replaced—you know, he's the last one that you come to a short distance down the road from the Church of the Angels.

EYR: Will my father then be leaving?

PIST: No. I told him that these ladies had come to the house.

EUR: Ah, you ignorant, indiscreet blockhead! Didn't I specifically order and threaten you not to say a word about it?

PIST: You forbade me to say anything to strangers; but I don't consider your father a stranger.

EUR: Well, then, didn't I forbid you to tell Brusco or Biagiuolo de l'Abaco? But when did I say anything to you, you ugly ass, about strangers and servants?

PIST: I thought that I was doing a good deed in getting him to stay and that you would be greatly obliged to me.

EUR: Idiot! May you get a hundred plagues! Has he then postponed his departure?

PIST: Yes.

EUR: He's not leaving today?

PIST: I don't believe that he'll leave tomorrow either, not until they return to Padua. He has decided to entertain them and treat them well regardless of the expense.

EUR: Where is he now?

PIST: We went back to return the horse, and I helped him off with his boots and put on his shoes. Then, as he was going off to the piazza to buy some provisions, he said to me: "Go back to the house and bring me a canister and the big market basket and meet me at the castle;[14] I'll be among the delicatessen vendors."

EUR: Then do as he told you, may you break your neck!

PIST: I broke it the very day I came to stay with you.

EUR: If I could only lay my hands on an oak rod two yards long I'd...

PIST: What the devil! Can I not leave without you chasing me out with a stick as if I were a dog?

EUR: My how arrogant that lazy lout is. By God, by God! Now what will I do? Alas, poor me, the old man is coming to ruin my pleasure to such an extent that it's being transformed into pain and grief! It will be difficult to convince him, as we have convinced Pistone, that they're the wife and daughter of Master Lazaro. As soon as he becomes aware of this fraud he'll throw the women and me out of the house in disgrace. I don't matter much, for I care little about myself; but I'm so concerned about the women that I'm distressed at the very thought of it. Now here comes my adviser who persuaded me against my better judgment to bring them into the house and who has got me into this fix.

SCENE THREE
EURIALO; ACCURSIO; PISTONE

EUR: Did you hear what Pistone said?

ACC: If only he were a mute today and hadn't spoken to you or to the others!

EUR: See what a mess we're in, and it's all your fault.

ACC: Make me a prophet and I'll make you rich. Would you have guessed it?

EUR: My old man is here.

ACC: Let him be *in nomine Domini*. What can happen? Why trouble yourself because of this?

EUR: When should I trouble myself? When the [dangers] mount?

ACC: Those who live at the foot of mountains mount; so do the falcon and the eagle. In another sense the rooster mounts, as does the monk when he goes into the pulpit. And there are many who mount elsewhere whenever they have the opportunity.

EUR: What's all this mounting you're talking about! Your chatter doesn't amount to so much as a donkey's hair. My father is still on our soil.

ACC: (I wish he was underneath it, like his own father and grand-father!) What do you mean by this ?

EUR: I mean to say that you mustn't think that you can make him believe what you got Pistone to believe.

ACC: If he's not a believer we'll go to Saint Dominic's.

EUR: What will we do there?

ACC: We'll have the Father Inquisitor proceed against him as a non-believer or heretic.

EUR: Go away, you're annoying me with your nonsense. For God's sake, forget about it and attend to the matter at hand.

ACC: For heaven's sake, enjoy yourself and leave all the worry and trouble to me. Let me take the risk and bear the cost of any mishap that occurs. I'll make your father believe me better than a devotee ever believed a monk. This very evening we'll have an old man come here on horseback, so that it will seem as if he had just then arrived from Pavia; and we'll say that he's the fellow who is supposed to accompany them to Padua. We've already let it be known in the house that they're waiting for someone.

EUR: Who can we get to do this without his being recognized?

ACC: By God! Is there a scarcity of cheats in this city? Do you want foreigners or local citizens? Well, then, at dawn tomorrow a wagon will be ready to pick them up and take them a short dis-tance from here, thus making it seem that they're on their way. But they won't go beyond the gate. Today, at our leisure, we'll find them a room where they can hide for four or five days until the old man has gone.

EUR: Here is Pistone coming outside.

ACC: I wish he were being carried out feet first! Why don't you send me along with him, and I'll impress this story so deeply on the old man's mind that he couldn't possibly fail to believe it? You can go back to the house and warn the women and instruct them about what to say and do; point out to them the danger they'll be in if they don't behave correctly.

EUR: I'll do that.——Pistone, I want Accursio to go with you. Aren't you listening? Make sure that you don't tell my father that

I was angry; tell him that I immediately was pleased and happy. Otherwise I promise you that I'll make you regret your mistake.

PIST: I didn't realize until now that anyone who seeks to serve others when he doesn't have to deserves this and even worse.

ACC: For God's sake, let him say what he wants. Don't argue with him. He's the master, he's young and he'll [learn with] time.

EUR: (Before I go back to the house I'd like to speak to Master Claudio.)

ACC: He became somewhat angry with his father and a short while ago he said this to me about him: "What do you think, Accursio? As if I didn't know how to entertain two women without his being there! This is all the credit he gives me! Everyone will say, when they learn of the reason why he returned, that he regards me as rather a clod without any ability...

EUR: (It would be better to call him to dine with us...)

ACC: ... for he didn't trust me enough to give me discretion in such a small matter."

EUR: (... so that by seeing them his mistaken notion will be corrected.)

ACC: He wanted the glory all to himself so that the women would afterward report to Master Lazaro how, with his father being away, on the spur of the moment, he... you know what I mean. Such thoughts do enter the minds of young men.

PIST: And what did I do that he turned against me so viciously?

ACC: Forget about it. (Who is that coming this way? Lord help us! It seems to be a servant.)

PIST: What's the matter? Your face has suddenly grown pale.

ACC: (It's Riccio.) Go on without me, Pistone. I have to go back to the house for a moment.

PIST: Good-bye.

ACC: It's him. The countess must have sent him out after the women.——Hey there, Master, turn around. Do you see that fellow? Do you know who he is?

EUR: Yes, by God! It's Riccio! Alas, alas, poor me! It's him. Now the affair has become entangled in more danger and complications than before.

Scene Four

RICCIO, *messenger;* ACCURSIO; EURIALO

RIC: (I know I'm not mistaken. This is undoubtedly the street. But I don't know in which house it is that he lives....)

ACC: He's looking for us. Listen.

EUR: I'm listening, and I don't want to hear.

RIC: (Maybe these young men will point it out to me. But they seem to be the ones I'm looking for. It's them, all right.) Hello, my good men; may God protect you.

ACC: May he protect you from good and defend us from evil.

RIC: You put the wrong intrepretation on my words. Tell me something, Accursio, I'll ask you first . . .

ACC: Don't ask me. Ask those humanists who collect medals and who delight in contrarieties.

RIC: Put aside this nonsense. Do you think that it was a commendable thing to abuse my mistress?

ACC: How did I abuse her?

RIC: Don't you know? Don't you consider it an abuse to remove a young lady from her house like this, a girl whom she had raised from childhood? It was you who made her run away; you brought her here with you.

ACC: Me?

RIC: Yes, you. Don't pretend to be so astonished, for I know exactly what the situation is. I know that your master, Eurialo—and I want him to hear me . . .

EUR: Don't involve me in this, Riccio.

RIC: . . . left you behind in Pavia when he departed.

EUR: Someone else may be at fault. As for me, I'm completely innocent, and I believe that Accursio is just as guiltless.

RIC: I'll reply to that when I have more time. Right now I'm speaking to him. As I told you, I know that this young man left you in Pavia so that as a good servant you would carry out his scheme. Ippolita and the Veronese pimp left ahead of you and went to Piacenza to wait for you. Then you picked them up and brought them to Ferrara.

EUR: If you could recite the rest of the story as well as you did the epilogue you'd be a magnificent orator.

ACC: One will never find . . .

RIC: You cannot deny it. I made inquiries aboard the boat that carried you here, and the helmsman told me everything.

ACC: It's true that two women, one old and the other young, boarded the boat at Piacenza and came with me as far as this place. They said that they were looking for a boat that went to Ancona, for they intended to go on to Rome. I can assure you that these aren't the women whom you want.

EUR: Don't you see, the helmsman told you about these two! You must have mistaken them for the others.

ACC: That must be what happened.

RIC: You can pretend and distort things as you please. I still believe what I want. But, Master Eurialo, I warn you that I brought letters with me to the duke and to a number of other noblemen, so that if these women are in Ferrara you won't be able to conceal them.

ACC: They're not the ones you think they are. These two were coming from Turin, and, if what they said was true, they are mother and daughter. I believe that they've already left, for they seemed to be in a hurry to get to Rome where they heard it said that the blood of the Apostles and Martyrs is very sweet, and where one can live in luxury at their expense.

RIC: Don't try to change the subject with your nonsense. The ones whom I'm looking for are here, and they're here as result of your malevolence and infamy. And if it weren't for the fact that Master Lazaro asked me not to present these letters until he arrives here...

EUR: Is Master Lazaro coming here?

RIC: ...by God, you would be beyond repentance by this time!

EUR: Answer me. Is Master Lazaro coming?

RIC: It won't be long before he arrives.

EUR: (We're in some trouble!) Where did you last see him?

RIC: At Sermide.[15]

ACC: When I saw him last—and we both left Pavia the same day—he didn't intend to come to Ferrara.

RIC: People easily change their minds.

EUR: (See how Fortune persecutes me!)

RIC: He was going to travel by the other branch of the Po; but when I told him the reason for my coming he changed his mind, and he and his wife immediately got on a boat along with his daughter and, I believe, a maid....

EUR: (Ah, woe is me, I'm destined for disaster!)

RIC: He sent the others on a barge loaded with his things to Francolino where they'll wait for him.

ACC: Then is Master Lazaro coming here?

RIC: Do you want me to repeat it? I told you that he's coming, and he would have arrived an hour ago had he not encountered unfavorable winds all day long. He said that he wanted to come here so that the differences between you and me can be compromised without a great fuss.[16]

ACC: They'll easily be compromised as you'll see that we're not guilty.

RIC: Don't count on it, and don't think that it will do you much good to be deceitful and pretend with me. I won't say anything until Master Lazaro arrives and I see what course he wants to pursue. I wasn't going to say a word to you about this; but when I left him in order to get here sooner he asked me to inform you on his behalf that he would like to see you this evening. That will give you all day to think about it. Good-bye.

ACC: Go in peace. May God convince you of the truth and make you see how unjustly you slander us.[17]

SCENE FIVE
EURIALO; ACCURSIO

EUR: Now we're out of danger.

ACC: Out of danger? How come?

EUR: There's no longer any danger. Danger exists when one's mind is suspended between hope and fear; but what we have here is a manifest evil, an unmistakable disaster. This is inevitable ruin. Alas, I'm dead.

ACC: The dead don't speak . . .

EUR: Help me, for God's sake.

ACC: . . . nor can one suggest a remedy or give help to the dead.

EUR: Well, then, prepare a grave for me and put me under before my father and Master Lazaro arrive, before I see Ippolita thrown out of the house like a wicked and notorious hussy with a barrage of accusations against me to my never-ending humiliation and shame.

ACC: If you're going to lose yourself like a coward, you'll certainly lose Ippolita also. But, if you put your hands, your feet, and your mind to work to defend yourself, both of you will be saved.

EUR: What should I do? Tell me what to do, for I, myself, am so bewildered that I don't know where I am.

ACC: I would suggest that we immediately tell Claudio and Boni-fazio the whole story and then beg them to let the women stay at their house. Once they're gone, all the danger will have been removed. Let Master Lazaro come when he will; let the old man return whenever he pleases. There will be no more risk. We'll let Stanna in on it. Leave it to me to speak to her and instruct her as to what to say. If Pistone has told him something different, if he has said that they already have arrived, we'll make him sound like a liar. I know he hasn't seen them. We can say that we made him think that they were coming so that he would be speedier and more diligent than he usually is.

EUR: I like your advice. Now, to make it work quickly. You go back to the house and inform the women. I'll speak to the others.

ACC: Here he comes now!

EUR: My father? Alas, it's him. We've been building castles in the air! We can no longer protect ourselves; with his appearance all our defenses crumble. Accursio, I'm really dead now.

ACC: It's better to be really dead than half-alive. Now get hold of yourself. We'll find a way to get out of this predicament as well. Go back home and warn the women. Come to think of it, it would be better for them to remain quietly in their room and close the door and windows. You can say that they're asleep because they had been awake during the night. What harm is there in having time to think before the old man sees them? I'll go to see Master Claudio. I want to speak to him about something that I have in mind. Go ahead, and rely on me—as they say, sleep calmly and securely with my eyes.

SCENE SIX
FRIAR; BARTOLO

FRIAR: You can read my credentials and see what authority I have and you'll find that it's quite ample. You'll see, Bartolo, that I can absolve you of your vows or commute them without your having to undertake this pilgrimage. I'm surprised that, being such a close friend as I am, you didn't ask me about it before. If you give me only the amount that you and your servant would have to spend on the journey, I could absolve you. You could thus avoid a considerable inconvenience that would be unbearable at your age as well as an infinite variety of dangers, which travelers may encounter.

BART: Reverend Father, although I have told the others that I go to fulfill a vow, I want to tell you the truth, *nihilominus*.[18] The trust that I put in your charity, your exemplary life, and the very odor that comes from the cloth, seem to demand that I reveal all my secrets to you; all the more so since you could perhaps give me some useful advice and even remove this obligation that I labor under, if it can be done. But what I have to say I'll say in confession.

FRIAR: And I'll hear it in confession.

BART: There's no one else who knows about this except for our parish priest who confesses me during Lent. Although he knows a little about canon law, he's not a theologian like you and he's not able to resolve this matter.

FRIAR: I'm ready, insofar as my knowledge goes, to give you the same advice that I myself would take. Tell me your problem.

BART: I'll tell you. Twenty years ago I was in Milan in the employ of the duke. At that time there was another young man at court, a Ferraran, with whom I struck up such a close friendship that it seemed as if our two bodies were united in one will, one heart, and one soul. The young man kept a mistress from whom he had a daughter—this was around the time of the disturbances in Milan in which Lodovico [the Moor] fled from his city and went to Germany.[19] Now, Gentile and I—the young man's name was Gentile—we were among those who followed him. When he arrived in Germany, Gentile fell gravely ill and died. Since he could not find a friend or relative as benevolent as I was, he named me as sole beneficiary in his last will; but he made me promise that when I returned to a liberated Milan I would marry the woman with a suitable dowry and marriage arrangement and that I would take care of his little girl just as I do my Eurialo. I was to feed her, raise her, and, at the appropriate time, marry her off to someone of her own rank. He relied entirely upon me to fulfill this promise, without calling any witnesses, without any public or private documents.

FRIAR: The simple promise of a faithful friend, nevertheless, is valid without the necessity of oaths, testimonies, or legal documents.

BART: As you know, the duke returned to Milan, but he remained there only a short time, for the very ones who brought him back betrayed him and took him prisoner. I returned to Milan with him and found my family safe; but Gentile's woman was gone. Upon learning of his death she had changed her address, for a lord had taken a liking to her—a Neapolitan, they said.

FRIAR: He probably was a lord since he was from Naples. From what I hear, there is an abundance of them there just as there is an abundance of counts in Ferrara. And I believe that the Neapolitan lords have as many dominions as the Ferrarese counts have counties.

BART: This Neapolitan, whatever he was, lord or commoner, had taken her and the little girl with him. They sold part of their household goods, took the rest with them, and left me with an empty house. After finding this I delayed looking for her until a more convenient time. Instead, I immediately returned to Ferrara where, by producing Gentile's legal will, I obtained his entire estate without any difficulty; and, whereas I had been a poor man, I now became rich. Nevertheless, I continued to have pangs of conscience for not having found these women right away or at least having undertaken a thorough search; and I'm still troubled by guilty thoughts of this. It's true that I have always had intentions of looking for them, but I've put it off from year to year until finally I've come to this state. Now, my priest will no longer give me absolution unless I go to Naples to look for the nobleman who took away the women and find out whether they're with him or with someone else. When I find them I must discharge the debt that I have owed for many years.

FRIAR: Would you be willing to avoid this trouble if you could?

BART: Who wouldn't?

FRIAR: It could easily be commuted into some pious act. There isn't any obligation in the world so binding that it cannot be undone by an act of charity.

BART: Let's go inside and talk about it at our leisure.

ACT FOUR
Scene One
BONIFAZIO; EURIALO

BON: Go, hurry, get there before they arrive and before they find another guide. And, remember, bring them here without passing by your door. I'll call Eurialo out here and let him know about the plan that you and I have devised to help him. ——I'm going to help Eurialo any way I can and, if I have to, I'll tell ten lies to prevent him from getting involved in a fight with his father and in a scandal; and I'll assist this other young man of mine as well, who has been driven to desperation by his mistaken belief and by his jealousy, which incites him unreasonably. I won't be ashamed to think up lies and weave plots and do all the things cunning servants usually do in ancient comedies. In truth, helping a poor lover doesn't seem to me to be a servile task, but one that requires a gentle soul. I don't know why the Church doesn't include it as the eighth work of mercy. Ah, here is Eurialo, right on time.

EUR: Bonifazio, did Accursio speak to you?

BON: Yes.

EUR: Did he tell you what a predicament I'm in as a result of listening to his advice?

BON: He told me everything as it happened.

EUR: What do you think?

BON: His advice was rather bold in any case. However, we'll find an appropriate solution for this quandary, and I hope it will succeed.

EUR: I, too, would have some hope if I could get my father out of the house *solummodo*[20] fifteen minutes so that the women could move over to your house. But the friar who preaches at the cathedral is there with him and has been talking to him for quite some time. They're seated at a table opposite the room in which the women have locked themselves and are pretending to sleep.

BON: If you aren't able to hide them, forget about it.

EUR: I don't know where to turn other than to you. I wish that I had come to you at the start; then I wouldn't find myself in a situation fraught with such danger, for I expect to see Master Lazaro with his wife and daughter at any moment now. I place myself in your hands.

BON: Are you afraid that we'll abandon you, Master Eurialo?

EUR: Please help me out of your goodness and kindness. I find myself with more trouble, with more worry and greater anxiety, than any wretch ever found himself.

BON: I won't fail you; take heart.

EUR: Then get my father out of the house for a little while; tell him that you need his help in the piazza.

BON: What do I need his help for?

EUR: Make up some excuse. Say that you want him to present a lawsuit of yours to one of the secretaries or to the *podestà*.

BON: I have no lawsuits.

EUR: Pretend that it's some business of a friend of yours.

BON: This is an inconvenient time to get someone like your father out of the house. All the offices are probably closed, and only the dogs remain in charge of the piazza. But we'll find a comfortable place where these others can stay without getting your father out of the house, without the two women moving here, and without any commotion.

EUR: How? Are you going to let Master Lazaro and his family come here and find the women in the house?

BON: That's not what I have in mind. Listen to me a moment. I have already sent Accursio to the port to meet them when they arrive. He'll give them a hearty welcome and bring them to my house where both of us will receive them. We'll tell them that I'm Bartolo.

EUR: That you're my father?

BON: That's right. We're about the same age so it will be very plausible. I know that your father and Master Lazaro have never seen one another and that they know each other only through letters and your reports. It will be easy to make him believe that he's staying with Bartolo when he's actually lodging with me. What do you think of this?

EUR: *Est generis promiscui.*[21] It can be good or bad.

BON: There's no risk. You'll act as if I were your father. Accursio will help you keep up the pretense. We'll honor him no less here than if he were in your house.

EUR: The doctor won't be pleased to see Master Claudio.

BON: For the time being we'll keep Master Claudio out of sight. Then, as things progress, it will be up to us to adopt a new scheme or to put it aside. We have a comfortable and respectable house, and the rooms are nicely furnished. I have enough courage to manage this affair in such a way that afterward, without any danger, I can let Master Lazaro find out about it and he'll be sympathetic to us. I understand that he's kind and agreeable. I hope to arrange things so between Claudio and him that before he leaves my house they'll be father-in-law and son-in-law.

EUR: I don't know what to say. A number of things could arise to interfere with our plans.

BON: What do you expect to happen? Let's make sure that disaster doesn't overtake you. Don't you see how close it approaches?

EUR: Unfortunately, I see it; and, as there is no other recourse, I had better stick to your plan whatever its merits, strong or weak.

BON: You can rest assured that it's stronger than steel.[22] I think, though, that it would be best if you also went to the Po to welcome them and escort them to the house.

EUR: I'm still worried that, if these other women remain in my house without me, they may say or do something that will give them away.

BON: What could they say or do that you haven't already warned them about? Oh, look, Accursio is returning.

EUR: Oh, my goodness! It's Master Lazaro, his wife, and the whole brigade! Lord, help me, I'm shaking!

BON: Ah, you coward! Have you become so pale? Come, let's go meet them; but put on a different expression. The one that you have now would be more appropriate to say good-bye to them than to welcome them.

EUR: Oh, God, if my father happens to look outside now!

BON: How the devil would he know who they are if he has never seen them before?

EUR: Let's get them into the house.[23]

Scene Two
MASTER LAZARO; BONIFAZIO

LAZ: (I see Master Eurialo coming toward us. The person in front of him must be his father.)

BON: Welcome, Master Lazaro, and welcome to you, ladies.

LAZ: And you must be Master Bartolo....

BON: I'm Bartolo, at your service.

LAZ: I'm happy to see you. I'd be happy to see you a hundred times, a hundred-thousand times. Oh, my disciple! Master Bartolo, you look as young as your son. One might think that he was your brother.

BON: I keep fit by not worrying too much and avoiding all inconveniences. Let's go inside the house; the ladies must be cold. How this wind does penetrate![24] They must have really suffered from it on the boat this morning! Accursio, run upstairs and get a good fire going. Come inside, Master Lazaro, and make yourself at home, for your fine qualities make you welcome to our house as well as to our possessions, our servants, all that we have, and all that we ever will have.

LAZ: Your kindness, Master Bartolo . . .

BON: Please, let's not stand on ceremony. Either forget about it, or postpone the ceremonies until we're inside sitting by the fire.

SCENE THREE
ACCURSIO, *alone*

ACC: We're just like birds caught in the net; the more they struggle to escape, the more entangled they become. We seek a remedy for one misfortune, and, in the process, we bring on three of them that are worse and more difficult to cure without getting rid of the first one. If our scheme succeeds—a scheme that we came upon more out of necessity than good judgment—we can attribute it to a miracle rather than to our prudence. But what else could we do with misfortune assaulting us on all sides? The bowstring is drawn as far as possible; it will stretch no more and is about to snap rather than propel the arrow to its mark. I simulate hope and courage and try to bolster my young master; but I feel my heart beat within me no less faintly than his does. I don't see how a plan so feebly executed can well succeed. But since we have trapped ourselves in this labyrinth, and it was because of me that we're in it, it's mainly my duty not to be dismayed or to lose heart, even if all the others do. I must keep my eyes open, I must watch out for possible difficulties and prepare the remedies for them before they do. First of all, I must find Master Claudio and warn him about the danger we're in. I must let him know that circumstances forced us to lodge Master Lazaro in this house, for he might come here and make things worse than they already are. Perhaps I'd better wait here until he decides to return home; if I go looking for him without knowing where he is, I could easily miss him. Oh, there's my old master coming out of the house along with that hypocritical rascal who has kept him gabbing all day long, much to our inconvenience.

SCENE FOUR
FRIAR; BARTOLO; ACCURSIO

FRIAR: I'll bring it to you and let you read it. You can be certain that the bull is plenary and that by coming to an arrangement with me I can fully absolve you no less than the pope himself.

BART: I believe you. Still, to ease my conscience I'd like to read it, and I would also like my parish priest to see it.

FRIAR: *Sit in nomine Domini.*[25] I'll bring it, and you can show it to whomever you please. Until then may the Lord be with you.

BART: And with you also, Father. Oh, here is Accursio.

[*Continuation by Gabriele Ariosto*]
ACT FOUR
SCENE FOUR
BARTOLO; ACCURSIO

BART: Where is Eurialo?

ACC: Eurialo, Master? I was just looking for him. I never came across any young man who was on more familiar terms with women than he is. Does he think that these two women are serpents, Master? When he was in their house he was treated so lovingly by both mother and daughter that, God, I cannot begin to tell you; and now he's so unsociable toward them that it would seem as if he had never met them before today. It was his duty to entertain them and to give them a hearty welcome, just as people do who return a favor to someone.

BART: Truly, in being discourteous, Eurialo is not at all like me, his father; for there wasn't a young man more affable toward women than Bartolo. With beautiful women I was no less pleasant than Cicero or even Tullius.[26] But what is there to say? Eurialo is constantly busy with his studies. This is his main interest, and he pursues it more than others pursue food and drink. Apart from his studies what else does he care for? I was very different when I was his age. But let's change the subject. It seems strange to me, Accursio, that this Master Lazaro should be a person of so little common sense. Yet I've heard him praised for his learning. But to send his wife and daughter so casually to a place such as Ferrara, where you can find even the barbers trying to appear as gentlemen! They didn't have even a single servant accompanying them. Truly, he must either be poor or a miser.

ACC: You guessed it; it's the latter. He chants the *Miserere.*[27] These people would give their souls to the devil to make money; I mean those, Master, whose job it is to review lawsuits and assign debts. They would endure hunger, thirst, cold, and heat, and make others endure them as well in order to avoid spending fifty soldi[28] extra. When you see the two women you'll know that what I say is right.

BART: Now that I think of it, aren't they awake yet? When are we going to eat? At Vespers? I was up early this morning, before Matins. What's keeping Eurialo? If he were here the meal would be over with. Now who is that fellow walking with Bonifazio and wearing a long robe? Is it some new judge?

ACC: Lets go, Master. We have no time to waste. After all, it's highly possible that an old man such as you could run the risk of starvation, and a grave risk at that.

BART: How happy I am, Accursio, that your experience among the scholars at the university has taught you—so I see—some principles of medicine.

ACC: (God, how annoying this is; how their very presence turns me off. Oh no, they're heading toward us!) Let's go, Master.

BART: Come on. Hold it; wait a moment. I'd like to meet that man if possible; he must be an important person.

ACC: (That's exactly what I hoped to avoid. Oh, what bad luck!)

Scene Five

BONIFAZIO; MASTER LAZARO; BARTOLO; ACCURSIO

BON: I could almost say that you have offended me by refusing to eat a couple of eggs and by going out as soon as you had changed your clothes.

LAZ: Forgive me, Bartolo; I was made this way in my mother's womb. I'm more concerned about my friend's affairs than my own.

BART: What's this Bartolo? Our Bonifazio has been newly rebaptized Bartolo by that wise man. Accursio, didn't he call him Bartolo?

ACC: I don't think he said Bartolo, but Bonifazio. It's hard to distinguish between the two names. They almost sound alike.

LAZ: *Ulterius,*[29] don't I consider our Eurialo more a part of me than if we were one and the same person? I actually like him more than I used to now that he has agreed so readily to do the decent thing and hence avoid some misfortune that might have occurred.

BART: Accursio, Accursio, didn't he say Eurialo?

ACC: No, Master, no. He did mention a queer name. Oh, it escapes me now! It's true, it did resemble that of Eurialo.

LAZ: Anyhow, I want to settle my debts with you; but I'm afraid that my messenger may have gone to present his letters to the secretariat and hasn't arrived here yet. He also could be delayed in doing me a favor; but to assure that no other scandal arises through my negligence, I won't waste a moment in settling the matter without any fuss. So, then, if I inform the countess, as I will do immediately by writing to her, that Eurialo has married this girl...

ACC: (God! Why doesn't he become a mute?)

LAZ: ... with the consent of his father, and that the disgrace of having induced her to run away with the other woman...

ACC: (Oh, may your tongue fall out, Lazaro!)

LAZ: ... of having abducted her—has turned into honor, she'll be extremely satisfied.

BART: Let's not go any further [in this direction]. Let's turn down this street. There's construction ahead, and if we continue we would only be stopped.

SCENE SIX
BARTOLO; ACCURSIO; PISTONE; STANNA

BART: Did you hear what that gentleman said, Accursio? What does it mean when he says that Eurialo has married the young lady? Who is this Eurialo and who is the girl? Didn't you hear the story? Why don't you answer? May you get the plague!

ACC: I'm not answering because I don't know what to say, for I didn't hear what they were talking about. If I don't hear I cannot understand.

BART: You don't understand? Were they speaking Hebrew? You know the whole story from beginning to end better than those who were discussing it. Tell me, who is this Eurialo and who is the young lady?

ACC: Don't beat me, Master, I'll tell you.

BART: Then say it: who is this Eurialo and who is the girl?

ACC: Enough, enough, Master, enough; I'll tell you.

BART: Come on, speak up.

ACC: It's your son. He fell in love with a girl in Pavia and made her flee here in the company of another poor woman.

BART: You'll have to clarify this enigma for me, you glutton! Is this the study that Eurialo pursued away from home at so much expense? You must have rendered good and faithful service, didn't you, Accursio? You must have shown him a fine way to spend money! And through your cleverness, you glutton, the money that I had saved with difficulty to pay for his board, his clothes, and to buy him books has ended up in a fine place. Shouldn't you have been at his side constantly to remind him about his studies—as we can see, you've done exactly the opposite? What do you deserve for this?

ACC: Was it up to me to teach him Cato or the rules?[30]

BART: I understand. You find another task more to your liking. You would prefer to do something like arranging an affair with a

young woman, and weaving it in fine manner; like finding a
way for him to spend money in dressing her well and seeing to it
that she lives comfortably; and like feeding yourself at Bartolo's
granary. That's precisely it.——Pistone, come here right away
with Stanna; but first undo the rope on the valises and bring it
downstairs. Also, call the porter and hurry and cut up some
wood.——Are you thinking of running away? You'll not escape,
by God.

ACC: Master, listen to me! Why are you having me tied up?

BART: Because you deserve it.——What are you waiting for? May
you break your neck coming down the stairs!

ACC: I beg you to forgive me, Master; and if everything I told you
isn't true, you can have me hanged by the neck.

BART: I may do just that, but not because I question the truth about
your wickedness.——Tie him securely.

PIST: Accursio, let me tie you up; keep your feet still. May you get
the plague! Oh, you got me where it hurts. You could have hit
me anywhere else and it would have hurt less.——Tie him up,
Giannello. And you, Stanna, what are you doing?

STAN: Damn it, don't you see that he almost made me show
my...? Now, stop it, Accursio.

BART: There are so many of you, and yet you find it so difficult to
hold this idiot still. I can see that it will take you all day.——
That's the way to do it; now he's fine. Take him upstairs. If I
manage to survive today, Accursio, I hope to make you realize
how far your tricks have gotten you. May God be my witness,
you'll be an example to others who have disdain for their
masters. What did he say just now? "I never knew any young
man who was on such familiar terms with women!"——Oh, you
wicked and evil-minded sons who reward your fathers this way,
who sell your souls to the devil to get money or to become
gentlemen. I, myself, did just that. I broke every tie with
humanity and my close friendship with my companion, Gentile.
I kept his possessions and didn't keep any of my promises to him.
Why did I do this shameful thing? For you, for you Eurialo.——
Are you back already, Stanna?

STAN: May the devil slit his throat! He grabbed hold of my...do
you know what I mean? Oh, God, I'm afraid it's going to bleed
if I don't take care of it. He made me see fireflies in the day-
time. Punish him, punish him severely. Did you hear about his
fine deeds? What did he say, that these women are the wife and
daughter of that Master Lazaro? Whom does he think he's
dealing with, some fool?

BART: Who are they, then? So this is another story.

STAN: Oh, wretch that I am; I wish I was never born. This time Eurialo will really cripple me, and I'll deserve it, for I unintentionally revealed his secret.

BART: Go on, Stanna, I want to know the whole story.

STAN: I don't want to continue any further. I've said more than enough. I know that I'm going to get into trouble.

BART: Go on, don't make me angrier than I am. I may do the same thing to you that I did to Accursio. You can no longer hide what you know.

STAN: I'll tell you, then. Forgive me, Eurialo, I'm forced to reveal it.

BART: Say whatever you please. This is the usual excuse of women in disgrace; they say that they've been forced. You, too, can use it. Tell me, what did you mean? Aren't they the wife and daughter of Master Lazaro? Where did you get this idea?

STAN: I'll tell you. Maurizia, the maid of our neighbor, Bonifazio, just now told me in secret that the guests whom we were expecting are staying at their house. I wasn't to say a word about it. And she did mention this Master Lazaro by name.

BART: Is it possible?

STAN: I've seen them all. It's him for certain along with his wife, his daughter, and a maid. Weren't you out here standing in front of the door when they came out, that is, Master Lazaro and Bonifazio?

BART: Yes, I saw them. Then who in heaven's name can those two women be whom you said are asleep upstairs? Ah, why am I searching for something that's obvious? How stupid of me! It must be the woman and her friend whom the two men were talking about. Accursio admitted that it was them after being beaten and kicked. I'm astonished at myself for allowing these hens to be fed at my expense.

STAN: Master, dinner is ready whenever you wish to have it served.

BART: Dinner is ready, eh? A fine dinner Eurialo served me. I'm so full that I'm ready to burst. Go in and eat without me, Stanna. I want to follow the two men, for they intend to settle a certain account without dealing with the innkeeper. Perhaps things won't work out as they expect. I'll find out from my lawyer whether the law allows children to get married without their fathers' consent and whether contracts made this way are valid. Ah, here's the one who gives me such pleasant thoughts; here comes my Eurialo. I don't know how he has the nerve to face me. But what am I saying? He doesn't realize that I know all about this business.

Scene Seven

EURIALO; BARTOLO; PISTONE; STANNA

EUR: So many troubles surround me at the same time and suddenly close in on me that I don't know where to turn for help. Oh, the unhappy and miserable condition of lovers, against whom misfortune always works and sets snares! I had been enjoying greater bliss and happiness than any other lover. Now see how a small mishap has brought me to this sorry state! A little while ago when my sweet Ippolita held me in her arms, my heart and my soul seemed to rise higher than an eagle when it flies to heaven to bring lightning to Jupiter, as the legend goes; and now I find myself like someone hit by lightning in the depths of a cruel hell. What has caused this is the unexpected return of my father and the bold advice that I got from my stupid servant. I'm more distressed about having gotten my Ippolita into this fix than about the possible harm to myself, for I deserve it. Were there no other places where I could bring her without putting her into a jail such as this, from which I see no way of getting her out? But I'm acting like a timid bird trying to protect its young from a snake. Even though there's no possibility of saving them, it doesn't budge from the nest. I don't see how I can get my shining star out from behind these thick clouds; yet I, myself, cannot leave this place.

BART: I couldn't hear a thing that he was saying; but I could see that his mind is greatly troubled.

EUR: (Woe is me. I see my father over there. My limbs are shaking one by one with fear and my mind is numb. I have no ideas. I feel my whole expression changing. Come on, what would I do if I were going to fight?)

BART: Eurialo?

EUR: I'm coming, Father.

BART: (He comes like a snake attracted by a charmer.)

EUR: Did you meet our guests, Father?

BART: No, but I heard a thing or two about them.

EUR: Do you know who they are?

BART: I know, and it won't do you much good.

EUR: They're the wife and daughter of our Master Lazaro.

BART: The ones whom that glutton Bonifazio has in his house are the women of our Master Lazaro.

EUR: (Nothing can be done now; the cat is out of the bag.)

BART: What are you muttering?

EUR: Nothing.

BART: Nothing, eh? Oh what inestimable nerve! Oh what a good-for-nothing! Wouldn't you expect him to reconsider what he has done or be ashamed of it? Are these the deeds of an innocent son? Do you bring women of this sort into your father's house, you foolish idiot?

EUR: Alas, poor me.

BART: Now do you realize the error of your ways? You should have thought about it before, Eurialo, when you and Accursio conceived of such schemes. Now what? Shall we settle this by saying that you'll marry her? Oh, what fine advice! Did your doctor teach you that? That would be to his interest and, besides this, it would be to his honor.

EUR: It's not like that, Father. Listen to me.

BART: What a wonderful arrangement! The moment he saw me leave the house my son made a good start at taking care of matters. He had begun to do his good deeds so that, on returning from Naples, I would find my things tidy and in order, and the whole house turned upside down.

EUR: Believe me, Father, I wouldn't have married her without first getting your permission.

BART: You wouldn't have married her? Yet you promised this Master Lazaro that you would, and that liar, that wicked rogue of a Bonifazio, gave you permission. Ah, upon my soul, I'll have him punished before this day is over!

EUR: Father, I did it only to avoid difficulties and because they say that she comes from a noble family.

BART: To avoid difficulties and because they say that she comes from a noble family? Eurialo, go inside and wait for me. Oh, Pistone?

PIST: Yes, Sir.

BART: You and Stanna make sure that he doesn't get close to the poor girl. I'll be back right away, for I want to deal with her as she deserves.

STAN: Don't worry, we'll watch him and we'll fit him with fetters like those they put on rams to prevent them from mounting the sheep.

SCENE EIGHT
BARTOLO, *alone*

BART: Now, see how I've come to the trap and how, as the proverb has it, I hold the wolf by the ear. If I don't consent to this wedding, I know that this woman will take legal action and do all the harm she can. But, let come what may, should I take on a wife for him without a dowry? Oh, how profitable, oh what joy it is to have such birds in one's cage if they haven't brought some food with them! I'd like to see what will happen.

ACT FIVE
Scene One
veronese, *alone*

VER: It had been quite some time since Ippolita and I were taken to one of the bedrooms and told to pretend to sleep. But our pretense turned out to be real, for we fell asleep so easily that if I had not been awakened by a great uproar in the house I would yet be asleep, as Ippolita is. Although still drowsy, I immediately ran to see what was going on, and I found two men—members of the household—and a maid holding our Accursio, who was tied up and in bad shape. I saw him being placed in a certain room—I couldn't determine whether it was a storeroom or a toilet—and then locked up securely. From what I could gather, this was done at the order of Master Bartolo—that's what they call the old man of the house—who must have found out who we really are, we poor creatures. There's never a shortage of people who care more about someone else's business than their own and who cannot keep their mouths shut about anything they know.

I became very frightened at this; still, I wanted to wait for Master Eurialo so that he could tell us what to do. He came a short time later, but his face was as pale as ashes. I immediately went up to him and asked him what he wanted us to do, and I told him what I had seen happen to poor Accursio. He answered me as if he were almost dumb, and he looked more lost than the dead themselves. So I figured that we were not very safe under his protection. I thus decided to look out for my own interests, leaving the ill-advised Ippolita in the hands of God and to Him alone I entrusted her; not to her lover, who is less capable of providing help and advice than we women are. I think that I did the best thing, for I was able to get out of the house and I doubt very much that I would have been able to defend myself if the old man returned in a rage. He would have insulted me with horrible language and would have called me a pimp and even worse. If it had only been a matter of words I would have stayed, but the risk of getting a beating and being laughed at everywhere in the city induced me to escape.

But who will give me a place to stay, for I don't know a soul in this city? I see someone over there who seems to have my share of happiness and who's as gay as someone who has found a pile of money. He must be well fed and he must have raised his glass more frequently than I did, for I haven't touched a drop since yesterday. I think I know him. Is it Master Claudio, or am I going mad? It's him all right, but I cannot be sure how he'll treat me. If I let him see me he'll direct a shower of abuse at me for having left my lady's house without permission. But the times dictate one's action, and one must compromise with necessity. Whereas a short while ago I thought it best to hide from him, I now am forced to appeal to him to save me from that Bartolo. However, I don't think he's so harsh as to be hostile to me for such a small thing. I also take comfort from the fact that he seems so happy. I think I'll go to him.

Scene Two
CLAUDIO; VERONESE

CLAUD: I occasionally meet some of my friends on this street. Why is it that I don't see any of them now even though I keep looking all around me? No one is wrestling or tilting at the quintain[31] in the piazza; there's no carousing, and there's no procession of the *Corpus Domini.* Oh, my priceless joy and bliss! Is there no one whom I can share it with? I have come from the arms of my Flamminia. Oh, kind and pleasant Fortune!

VER: I'm glad that he's so very happy.

CLAUD: It's not Good Friday, so there are no sermons; nor are they hearing cases at the Palace of Justice. Why are the streets so empty? Why don't I meet my dear Eurialo so that I can confess the enmity that I had toward him and tell him about my joy? But whom do I see coming toward me? It looks like Veronese.

VER: Oh, dear Master Claudio, may God grant you every happiness! I've found you.

CLAUD: Veronese, are you here?

VER: At your service, as I have always been.

CLAUD: You're welcome. Do you know what happened to me?

VER: No, but I hope that it wasn't anything bad.

CLAUD: I've been changed from the unhappiest of men, which I was a little while ago, into the happiest.

VER: Exactly the opposite happened to me. But let's go to your house where we can talk about it more conveniently.

CLAUD: No, no, listen to me. Because I had heard the very worst news about my Flamminia, I was determined to give up all human companionship.

VER: Had she, by any chance, passed away?

CLAUD: Worse than that. And I was going to the port to find a boat or a punt to take me out of this world if it were possible. But as soon as I got there, I saw Master Lazaro and his wife with

Flamminia and a maid disembarking. I shielded myself with my cape as well as I could so that the doctor wouldn't recognize me—I don't know whether you know it, he dislikes me. Now, all of a sudden, Veronese, think of what I became. Jealousy had so taken hold of my heart that I began to feel pangs. I didn't have to wait long before they set out for Saint Paul's Gate; and as they entered the city they turned in this direction. I followed them at a distance with my eyes, and soon I saw them go into Bonifazio's house. They couldn't have gone to a better place, for they took lodging at the same house where I have room and board. That's the house. Do you see it?

VER: I see it. Oh, God, I'm consumed with fear! I beg of you, let's go inside.

CLAUD: Eurialo and Bonifazio were in front of the door; but, without anyone seeing me, I suddenly darted into the lane here on the right that leads to my study and quickly opened the door. I went in and proceeded to my bedroom where, through a hole, one can see everything that goes on in the entranceway of the house. While I was around the house they came upstairs and soon after that they all descended and left the house together. I'm speaking only about the men.

VER: (What do I care about this story?)

CLAUD: But even then I didn't know what I was to do, for if Flamminia was in the house her mother was also there to watch her. Then Lady Lucrezia and the maid appeared with veils on their heads, and Flamminia was with them. Her mother turned to her and said: "I'm afraid that the cold air here may give you a chill. Go upstairs and wait until I return. I'm going with our host's maid to hear Holy Mass in honor of that most devout Saint Agatha, whose feast day is today." Having said that, they went out and my sweetest Flamminia was now alone. This seemed like a convenient time to reveal myself. I opened the door and leaped clean out of my den. She was frightened by my sudden appearance and tried to run away; but I didn't give her the opportunity. I held her so long that her fears turned into tears. She recognized me and let her head rest on my chest; and she seemed ready to give in to my desires. Oh, what unheard-of rapture! I took her in my arms at once. Oh, I feel like jumping up and down right here, even if the townspeople and the duke were present! So there.

VER: (Now see in what a fine situation I find myself with him!)

CLAUD: And so immediately, without losing any time, I went back to my room and closed the latch on the door. The rest can be told by others who have found themselves in a similar situation.

Alas, if only I didn't have to leave so soon afterward! Oh, God, when will I have more of that snow-white body, of that sweetly scented breath?

VER: I knew it. I knew that you would delay too long to rescue me. Oh, pity me. Look, there are two old men; if I'm not mistaken, one of them must be that wicked man, our host.

CLAUD: What host?

VER: Do you know that Bartolo?

CLAUD: I've never seen him, but I believe he's quite a devil. What were you doing in his house? Oh, I know. Who else was there? (Oh, my sweet Flamminia, when will I be with you again?)

VER: Ippolita was there and she still is. For her own good I wish she wasn't!

CLAUD: Oh, that's how my suspicions arose! (Oh, my dear Flamminia!)

VER: I beg you to help me. Isn't Bartolo one of the two men I see down there?

CLAUD: Let me see. It's Master Lazaro with Bonifazio. Come with me to my study. You can remain there quietly until I see what's going on. I want to find out what's the meaning of this and why this fellow is staying with Bonifazio and not with Bartolo as they had agreed. Take this key, Veronese; run down this lane on the right, then turn to the right again, and you'll immediately come to a small door. That's the door to my study. Go ahead and wait for me there quietly. I can listen and find out what they're saying from here without being seen.

SCENE THREE
BONIFAZIO; MASTER LAZARO; CLAUDIO

BON: I realized, after we had walked a little, that those men almost certainly would not be at the Chancery, for today is a holiday; these masquerades seem to be an invitation for everyone to have a good time, and all the important people willingly participate.

LAZ: There's nothing better to do. This Riccio is very late in coming. He was supposed to attend to a rather important matter for me, but I doubt whether he's doing it; in fact, this makes me firmly believe that he's not in the city, as I was led to believe last night in Sermide. I'm sure that he's done his work diligently and that if that fellow had been there. he would have found him and reported it to me. But I see now that I've wasted my time.

BON: I don't know who that fellow is. If I did know, believe me, Master Lazaro, I would do for you what you seem to be ready to do for us.

LAZ: Even though our friendship is a recent one—I mean our personal friendship, for our friendship through letters and good intentions started many months ago—it certainly entitles you to know some of my innermost thoughts; and especially this one that disturbs me more than any other I have, that I have had or ever will have.

BON: I thank you, and furthermore I want to say that I would be very happy if I can be of any help to you; I'm ready to do anything you wish, provided I can.

LAZ: Then, listen to me. I had promised my only daughter to a young man from Alexandria. This just seemed to suit my purpose, which was to have my daughter married in my native city; perhaps you know that I'm Alexandrian. . .

BON: I certainly know it.

LAZ: And I hope to return there, for I've come to the conclusion that I'm really tired of teaching; besides, jobs are very scarce. But it was pointed out to me at that time that a certain Master Claudio had fallen in love with her, and Flamminia—that's my daughter's name—was no less in love with him. To prevent my plans from being upset, I forced him to leave the house; and because he didn't stop coming around. . .

CLAUD: (I'm beginning to comprehend this story very well.)

LAZ: . . . I acted in such an unfair manner that he was forced to leave the city. Then, in order to complete the arrangements with the young man from Alexandria, I had Lucrezia tell my plans to Flamminia, who had already begun to look pale, no doubt because of Claudio's absence.

CLAUD: (How happy I am! This is undoubtedly an indication of her love.)

LAZ: One by one, Lucrezia extolled the virtues of the youth I had chosen, trying all the while to persuade Flamminia to abide by her parents' decision. But, instead of responding, she behaved as if we had proposed life imprisonment and appeared ready to drown herself in tears.

CLAUD: (Oh, blessed tears!)

LAZ: I then decided to convince her myself. But what good did it do! The only thing I got out of her was her usual silence and incessant crying. To tell the truth, Bartolo, it was difficult for me also to hold back my tears.

CLAUD: (A true father!)

LAZ: The poor thing was looking worse every day. We became very worried about her health, and we asked her nurse to find out what was bothering her. It was exactly as we thought; she didn't want to live without Master Claudio. I then came to regret that I had ever started this business. I came to regard the status, the wealth, and everything else about the young Alexandrian as a fabrication, and I tried my best to get out of my promise.

CLAUD: (This could only benefit me.)

LAZ: Now I have to go to a great deal of trouble to find the very one whom I let slip through my fingers when I had him in my grasp and whom I myself forced to flee.

CLAUD: (Don't worry, Lazaro, he's closer than you think.)

LAZ: Riccio, the fellow whom I said had brought those letters, promised to find him...

BON: Continue, I understand you very well.

LAZ: ... but he surely must have gone on to Padua, as I thought.

BON: Don't worry about it; he's here in the city.

LAZ: Then do you know him?

BON: What do you mean, do I know him? I know him as well as I know Eurialo.

LAZ: If I care about my Flamminia's life, I'm compelled to accept Claudio as my son-in-law...

CLAUD: (God be praised! I can understand how you feel.)

LAZ: ... but I'm not sure that he'll agree because of the grave injury I caused him.

CLAUD: (It would take a greater injury than that to make me reject Flamminia.)

LAZ: Since he's in this city, you would be doing me a tremendous favor...

BON: He's here, and I can fully appreciate your desire, which is no less honest than necessary; and, if you succeed in it, you'll benefit considerably, for he's been left very wealthy.

LAZ: Has his father died?

BON: He died two months ago. Now I'm going to look for Claudio and I hope to do something...

CLAUD: (What am I waiting for?)

BON: ... that will please you considerably.

LAZ: I would be eternally grateful to you!

BON: But here he is, Master Lazaro, look.——Master Claudio, you almost led me to think that you had left. (Be careful not to call me Bonifazio.)

CLAUD: (I'll be careful; but why not mention your name?) Oh, Bonifazio, I would like to pay my respects to Master Lazaro there with you...

BON: (Oh, damn it! He really put me in a fix.)

CLAUD: ... but I'm afraid that I would offend him. (Oops, I forgot.)

LAZ: Master Claudio, I'm happy to see you; and, if I have ever done you an injustice, I'm extremely sorry and I apologize. Come on, give me your hand and let bygones be bygones. Let me embrace you.

CLAUD: And I ask your forgiveness for being so bold in your house.

LAZ: You're forgiven.

BON: Excuse us, please, Doctor, I have to speak to Master Claudio. We'll be but a moment.

LAZ: Go ahead, then, and take your time. I'm not about to butt into your affairs. (I'll draw back so that they can talk privately and won't suspect that I'm listening. . . .)

CLAUD: (I heard my landlord being called by an assumed name. Something pleasant must be behind all this.)

LAZ: (But I won't go so far away as to lose sight of them, for I'll be able to tell by their appearance what the outcome of this will be.)

CLAUD: What do you want, Master Bartolo? Are you pleased with that name?

BON: That depends upon what follows. I'll tell you at a more convenient time how I acquired this name. Right now there's something else I must take care of.

CLAUD: I know that you have to take care of something else.

BON: Really? How do you know?

CLAUD: I know because I heard you talking about it from beginning to end, and very clearly, as I was nearby where you couldn't see me.

LAZ: (He must be telling him the story from the beginning—how, when I realized what was going on, I threw him out of the house.)

BON: Then I don't have to tell you that he wants you for a son-in-law.

CLAUD: I heard the whole story; and you know whether I like it or not.

LAZ: (Now he must be telling him about how I had him exiled. It really was a terrible thing that I did, and it could cause him to refuse my wishes. If I thought that no one would notice, I would take off my glasses to see them better.)

BON: We had better chatter like monkeys and manipulate our fingers like those who play mora.[32] Pretend that we're having difficulty coming to an agreement when in fact we're in perfect accord. But why should we waste any more time? I see that the old man is worn out with waiting.

LAZ: (Fine. They're laughing as they come. . .)

BON: Happily you were able to get a hold of yourself, Master Claudio; you were in quite a state.

CLAUD: Yes, happily, indeed; I'll tell you something that will make you laugh.

LAZ: (. . . toward me.)

BON: Shake hands again and embrace him warmly, Master Lazaro; here is your son-in-law, your son.

CLAUD: That's what I want to be.

LAZ: What more can I desire than to have you as a son? And you, Master Bartolo, take this little gift and enjoy it as a token of your Lazaro's gratitude. I owe you much more than this for the benefits you have brought me.

BON: This would place me under too great an obligation. Oh, no, Sir, I cannot accept it! It's worth more than thirty scudi! Take it back, I say, Master Lazaro.

CLAUD: (Yet he holds it clenched in his fist.)

BON: I won't argue with you, but what you're doing is certainly wrong.

LAZ: As I told you, you deserve much more.

CLAUD: Then accept it, since he gives it to you so willingly.

BON: I'll never stop thanking you for it, Master Lazaro. I'll remember this present as long as I live and I'll always be obliged to you.

Scene Four

BARTOLO; BONIFAZIO; CLAUDIO; MASTER LAZARO; RICCIO

BART: I see Bonifazio and Master Lazaro. I'd like to get near them, if possible, without their seeing me. Between you and me, there's going to be . . .

BON: (Oh, the devil's ass! Bartolo is here.)

BART: . . . a strange and involved contest with the devil. My lawyer tells me that if Eurialo has married this girl, even without my consent, the marriage is valid. These laws are certainly peculiar; yet those who made them must have been wise men! So they say. But just like everything else, the laws change from time to time, and I believe they only become worse. They are like the fava bean, which is nice and large when you plant it, but then grows small. Indeed, those who comment on the law interpret it as they please.——Hold it, my good man; now you won't be able to turn the other way. I want to talk to you about why you tried to harm me.

BON: (For God's sake, how did he sneak up so quietly? He seems angry.)

BART: But first tell me your name.

CLAUD: (We have the makings here of quite a brawl.)

BART: I'm speaking to you; what's your name?

BON: He doesn't seem to recognize me! And yet it's a clear day.

BART: I didn't say that I don't recognize you; but I did ask you to tell me your name.

BON: If you, yourself, admit that you know me, then you must know my name. When you know something, why do you ask about it?

CLAUD: (That's a clever answer; it seems logical.)

BART: Well, since you won't answer me and tell me your name, then tell me this: Are you Bartolo or am I Bartolo?

BON: Why couldn't both of us be Bartolo? How many Giovannis, Filippis, and Antonios are there in the same house? Knowing this, how come it seems a miracle to you that we are both Bartolo and live on the same street?

CLAUD: (Oh, how clever he is! Oh, gallant Bonifazio! Doesn't he hold his own well without getting confused? I'll find out why he changed his name yet.)

BART: Oh, the wonderful trust of a rascal! Can I ever expect to find another like him?

BON: If you please, don't insult me, for I'm not offending you. Even if I have used your name for a whole day there's no need to complain. Even if I borrowed it for a month it's still in one piece. My basket, my washtub, my funnel, that your servants so often use, wear out. You're making a great fuss because I called myself Bartolo for two hours. You would lend me twenty-five scudi for two or three months if I needed them, as good friends should.

CLAUD: (Oh, Bonifazio, I want you to be my friend more than ever.)

LAZ: (What's this new controversy? Has the wedding that I have been arranging been called off? Eurialo will be in trouble with the countess.)

BART: Maybe you didn't use my name for my benefit.

LAZ: (I wash my hands of this; let them do what they please.)

BART: You wanted to be Bartolo in order to do me harm and cause me trouble, cheat that you are. You pretended to be Eurialo's father to complete the marriage agreement—perhaps you have already done it so honorably with that runaway girl. And as for you, Master Lazaro, I'd like to speak to you for a moment....

BON: (So far, so good; but here's another tough beard to shave.)

BART: Does Eurialo's respect for you and the friendship you showed in your letters deserve such treatment? Even though I've never seen you before, I know very well that you're Master Lazaro. God only knows whether you were trying to conceal your name! What is one to think of you when you honor one of your disciples with such a wedding? With such advantages?

LAZ: Hold it, Bartolo. Now that I know you're Bartolo, tell me why should I be blamed for these stories? Should you complain about me, or should I complain about Eurialo for leading me to believe that I was staying with you? And let him tell you to whose house he brought me with my wife and daughter, for I couldn't tell you.

BON: (I'd better withdraw from this discussion; I've been in this company too long.)

LAZ: And if you think I did the wrong thing in persuading Eurialo to rectify the blunder he committed and the serious injury he caused the countess, you're mistaken, and I tell it to you plainly. She's a woman of considerable influence.

BART: Just because she's a countess, is she so feared? She must be better off than those of her status here. Some of our countesses here often don't have enough to eat.

LAZ: Exceptions don't make the rule. Perhaps their husbands are scoundrels or stingy. This countess is truly wealthy and of aristocratic stock. She is genuinely respected and has powerful friends everywhere.

BART: I believe you. But am I to break my son's neck because of this? Should he take a serving-maid as a wife?

LAZ: What? Do you think that I would go to this trouble for a serving-maid? She's a free citizen of Ferrara.

BART: That's a fine thing, our citizens going about so informally. I'll admit that she's a citizen; yet even if she were from Rome, am I to accept her without a dowry? Only those who have a good dowry are called citizens. If Eurialo is such a fool as to marry this woman, all he'll get from me is exactly that which I cannot take away from him. But I think these stories that she's the protégé of a countess or a noblewoman from this city are fictions. They were all invented to gratify that scoundrel. You'll pay for it, Bonifazio; in any case I'll have you ride the donkey.[33]

CLAUD: You would be doing him an injustice, Master Bartolo; he did it out of affection for your son and not to offend you.

LAZ: And didn't I act for the same reason? I'm willing to bet anything that she's a citizen of Ferrara; and I'll say even more. If the poor thing hadn't made this mistake, the countess was going to send a reliable agent to this city to help recover her patrimony. I advised her to do so *in scriptis*, for she knows the name of her father who died in the service of the duke of Milan.

BART: Did she tell you his name?

LAZ: She did, and I believe I can recall it if I think about it a while.

BART: (I'm almost tempted to guess.)

LAZ: Polito... No, I'm not telling you the truth. He wasn't called Polito. Nor was it Galante. His name was Gentile, yes, Gentile. I had almost forgotten it.

BART: (I guessed right!) After Gentile died, did the girl immediately enter the countess's household?

LAZ: For her sake I wish she had, for her affairs would be in a much better state! Only after the countess met her in Naples did she first take her into her service. Her mother had brought her there when she was a small child, but I'm not acquainted very well with this part of the story. Someone should be arriving shortly who knows the whole thing from beginning to end. He's the same person who followed these women with letters of reference. His name is Riccio.

BART: (All the pieces fit together. Wasn't he the errand-boy of my comrade, Gentile? It's all clear to me now.) Do you remember the girl's name?

LAZ: I remember it. It was Ippolita.

BART: It's perfectly clear.

LAZ: Here comes Riccio. What took you so long, Riccio?

BART: (I don't know whether I would have recognized him right away. The last time I saw him he was only a small boy. Oh, how time passes!)

RIC: Master Lazaro, I didn't find our friend.

LAZ: No? Look around. See if I'm not a better bloodhound than you.

RIC: Oh, Master Claudio, I'm so glad to see you looking so well!

CLAUD: Then were you looking for me, Riccio? I, too, am happy to see you looking well.

BART: Look at me, Riccio. Do you know me?

RIC: Do I know you? I think I do. Yes, I do recognize you. You're Master Bartolo, the friend of Gentile, who was the father of the girl I followed here. I'm very happy to have found you and recognized you. I hope that for the sake of your dear Gentile you'll do everything possible to find her and bring her back to her mistress. A certain Accursio...

BART: Enough, Riccio, enough. I know all about the matter. Master Lazaro, and you too, Master Claudio, listen to me. You listen as well, Riccio. My son Eurialo has wronged the countess. I want to make amends, and it seems to me the most decent thing to do is to let the marriage arranged by Master Lazaro and my neighbor Bonifazio proceed. Do you understand, Riccio? They were giving the girl to Eurialo as his wife.

RIC: Continue. I understand you very well.

BART: And so we'll remove the guilt from the girl, and the countess will lay aside her ill will. Riccio, do you think that the countess will be satisfied after that?

FIC: Very much so. I can confirm it by her letters.

BART: I won't fail in my obligation to Gentile, for, if nothing else, I'll be content that things turned out this way. Master Lazaro, I'm very sorry for not having shown you the respect that my duty requires of me and your merits deserve. Now, to show that you're ready to forgive my mistake, I want you, along with your family, to come over to my house, as we already agreed, where we'll celebrate the nuptials.

LAZ: We'll have a double celebration in your house, Master Bartolo, for Claudio has consented to be my son-in-law.

CLAUD: On the contrary, you agreed to be my father-in-law, my father.

BART: Oh how pleasing this news is to me! So you've given your daughter to him?

LAZ: When you arrived we had just come to an agreement.

RIC: Are you a bridegroom, Master Claudio? Congratulations.

CLAUD: I thank you, Riccio.

BART: We'll almost have a double comedy. Now, Master Lazaro, be sure that your women accompany you.

CLAUD: Master Bartolo, for my sake, I wish you would send for Bonifazio and become reconciled with him.

BART: With pleasure.

LAZ: Let's go, Master Claudio. We'll let Master Bartolo alone so that he can continue with his plans and meanwhile we'll tell our women to get ready.

BART: Go then.——Riccio, you come along with me, for I'll need you. I know that you have attended banquets such as these and are familiar with the arrangements.

RIC: Go ahead. I'll follow right away.

BART: It didn't seem necessary for everyone to know—and I wouldn't have been very pleased if they did know—the real reason why I let Eurialo marry the girl. I'll go and have Accursio untied right away, for he offered to do the work of ten men.

Scene Five
RICCIO; VERONESE

RIC: I see Veronese over there. Where the devil did she come from? She didn't come out of Bartolo's house. The old ass is as red as a ruby.

VER: I could have waited forever for Master Claudio. I think I would have died of a whorish thirst had I not found a cabinet that contained a small jug, which I tasted. It was full of delicious Malmsey. I also needed the two cans and the pot as well. When I left the house I was depressed; now I feel altogether different.

I'll go back and see what happened to Ippolita.

RIC: Are you here, Veronese? Don't try to hide; I saw you. Don't worry, I won't harm you; everything is peaceful. Go to the house; go find Ippolita, for we have found her fortune. (She can hardly stand up straight; see how she gropes to find the door!)——

Oh, noblemen and commoners, don't wait around expecting the ladies to come out in public. One of them already took to her room, and the other thinks nothing about making herself up for an hour or more as brides are wont to do. Therefore, I suggest that you go home now; but, before you do, I ask you to give us an indication that you have been pleased with our story, for he who has worked so hard to make it pleasing to you so wishes.

Ariosto began writing the *Students* as early as 1518 or 1519; but he managed to finish only three acts and three scenes despite many subsequent years of activity in the theater. After the poet's death, his son, Virginio, sought to have his cousin, Giulio Guarini of Modena, complete the play, but he was unsuccessful; thereupon he put his own pen to the task, producing a prose ending that has never been found and one in verse of which, until recently, only the prologue was available. The version translated here is that finished in verse by Ariosto's brother, Gabriele, which he retitled the *Scholastics*. Gabriele completed it sometime between 1543 and 1547 at the request of Duke Hercules II, and for centuries it was the only version published. Until the discovery by Abdelkader Salza of the entire manuscript of Virginio's *Imperfect* in 1915, it was impossible to determine exactly where Ludovico Ariosto had ended his work on the play; by comparing the two versions Salza was able to determine that Ludovico had reached the fourteenth line of Act Four, Scene Four.

1. Cf. the prologue to the *Imperfect* by Virginio Ariosto:

"I come before you simply to let you know the name of the author of this story, which is rightly called the *Imperfect*. It was begun by the same author who gave us the *Coffer*, the *Lena*, the *Necromancer*, and the *Pretenders*, comedies that must be well-known to you. Now, the author left this unfinished play, along with other personal property, to his son, who accepted it as he would a dearest sister; and he tried to have it completed in such a way that the end would be in harmony with the beginning. This didn't succeed as he had hoped, so that he had to take up the pen himself and become a playwright. Thus, while he tried to be a devoted son, and this was his intention, he most certainly will appear bold and arrogant for having dared to put his hand to the play of Ariosto, a unique figure in our time. Oh, how difficult it is to defend oneself from slander!

"Now, I'd like to speak for him and say that I realize he's lacking in erudition, particularly when compared with such a writer, with such a mind. Yet, even though we sometimes see a man with a wooden leg or an iron hand that may look rather odd, it seems to me that these limbs do not bring censure to those who made them. Rather, they bring praise and glory for being the means by which the body is rendered capable of doing many things, things that it could not do without them. So this is the reasoning that induced him to finish the play.

"Now it seems to me that many of you would like to know at what point the work of the first author is joined with that of the second. I would willingly tell you; but the new author insisted that I remain silent, for there are present men of considerable judgment and understanding whom I would only make laugh if I were to tell them that which is so clearly evident. Besides, they would be able to say: 'See what an ignoramus and a blockhead he must be, for he thinks that we are incapable of distinguishing black from white!' And, as they would be telling the truth, he asks you, he begs you, to please excuse him. He promises that you will derive much pleasure from this story, a tale never before told, and quite unlike the old ones of Plautus and Terence. So, be thankful and well-disposed to him by listening to the whole story in silence."

2. Plautus used his prologues to provide the argument of the play; Terence to answer his critics.

3. Gabriele is probably referring to Domenico de Argente, a young student of law who was hired by Niccolò Ariosto as a tutor for his two eldest sons when Ludovico was eleven years old. On Ariosto's early education see M. Catalano, *Vita di Ludovico Ariosto* 1:88–103.

4. *Ordinaria*: a part of the Roman civil law.

5. Evidently a reference to the famous battle of Marignano (13–14 September 1515), fought some fifteen miles from Pavia.

6. See the *Necromancer*, n. 16.

7. A village located about halfway between Ferrara and Bologna.

8. A town upriver on the Po, approximately fifteen miles from Ferrara.

9. On the whole we have followed the modern texts of the play edited by Catalano and Borlenghi. There are, however, some minor differences between these and Gabriele's published edition of 1547, one of which occurs here: "CLAUD: . . . unless he first bolted her in her room. BON: Bolted her? CLAUD: I'm speaking seriously now; so listen seriously. And he kept the key in his belt, for he didn't trust his wife. . . ."

10. Lucrezia and Virginia were names commonly associated with strict morality, the latter for obvious reasons. Lucrezia could be a reference to Lucrezia Borgia, whose piety in her later life as duchess of Ferrara had made a deep impression on her subjects and whom Ariosto had previously praised in his *Epithalamium* (1502) as *pulcherrima Virgo*.

11. Stanna recites the names of the towns in an obscene double-sense, which Claudio immediately discerns. Since Ficarolo is in the opposite direction (N.W. of Ferrara) from Garofalo and Pelosella (N.E.), the towns forming a triangle with Ferrara, the names can refer to nothing else than the female anatomy and the amorous progress of Eurialo with Ippolita.

12. The so-called Post-Glossators, fourteenth-century commentators on Roman law whose texts had by this time become standard reading in Italian law schools.

13. . . . *ch'a lor piacere attendono* in the 1547 edition; . . . *ch'a lor pareri attendono* in the Catalano and Borlenghi texts.

14. See the *Lena*, n. 14.

15. A town on the Po about twenty-five miles northwest of Ferrara.

16. The 1547 edition adds: "He also wanted me to do something else."

17. The following is added in the 1547 edition: "RIC: Tell me, is Master Claudio here in the city? EUR: He was here this morning and should still be."

18. "Nothing less."

19. In August 1499 Louis XII of France, after asserting his dynastic claims to the dukedom of Milan, led a French army in the second invasion of Italy. When the French forces advanced toward the city, the Milanese defenses collapsed, and the duke of Milan, Lodovico ("The Moor") Sforza, escaped capture only by hurriedly crossing the Alps into Germany. Then, taking advantage of a temporary withdrawal by the French king, Lodovico gathered a force of Swiss mercenaries and in a surprise move expelled the small French garrison and recaptured the city in February 1500. Sforza deceived himself into thinking that he had regained his duchy; but when the French forces returned his unpaid mercenaries deserted him and Lodovico was captured. He died in a French prison in 1508.

20. "For only."

21. "It's a mixed bag."

22. "Marble" in the Catalano and Borlenghi texts.

23. The 1547 edition has: "EUR: Let's get them into the house quickly.

BON: You should have had two prods handy to push them in if they hesitate too long; or, if you want to, you can tie them together in a bundle and carry them in on your back."

24. *E come penetra quest'aria il capo!* Literally: "How this wind does penetrate one's head!"

25. "So be it, in the name of the Lord."

26. Bartolo shows his lack of erudition, for Cicero and Tullius are one and the same: Marcus Tullius Cicero.

27. Psalm 50 in the Vulgate, Psalm 51 in the King James Bible, in which David confesses his spiritual poverty and asks for mercy. By importing a secular connotation to this confession of poverty the author is able to play on the words *misero* (miser) and *miserere* (mercy).

28. See the *Coffer, second version,* n. 20.

29. "Besides."

30. Cato the Elder, "the Censor" (234–149 B.C.), renowned for his moral uprightness and his defense of traditional Roman simplicity and discipline.

31. A form of jousting whereby a knight tilts with his lance at a target on a pivot (the quintain) and seeks to avoid being struck by a counterbalance as the pivot turns.

32. An Italian game in which players try to guess the number of fingers that have been held up by the participants.

33. A means of heaping disgrace on those condemned as pimps was to require them to ride through town on a donkey.